THE RIGHT TO BE OUT

THE RIGHT TO BE OUT

Sexual Orientation and Gender Identity in America's Public Schools

Second Edition

Stuart Biegel

University of Minnesota Press

Minneapolis | London

Published by the University of Minnesota Press
111 Third Avenue South, Suite 290
Minneapolis, MN 55401-2520
http://www.upress.umn.edu

ISBN 978-1-5179-0573-6 (hc)
ISBN 978-1-5179-0572-9 (pb)
A Cataloging-in-Publication record for this book is available at the Library of Congress.

Printed in the United States of America on acid-free paper

The University of Minnesota is an equal-opportunity educator and employer.

25 24 23 22 21 20 19 18   10 9 8 7 6 5 4 3 2 1

CONTENTS

PREFACE TO THE SECOND EDITION

As an openly gay man who has written and taught about lesbian, gay, bisexual, and transgender (LGBT) issues in an education law context for more than fifteen years, I have marveled continually at the progress we have made but found myself deeply saddened all too often after experiencing the setbacks that we have faced. And in the decade since the first edition of *The Right to Be Out* was published, events seem to have been moving at warp speed, two steps forward and one step back, or sometimes even three steps forward and four steps back. But in the end, reflecting back on the larger picture, it has been a remarkable journey, with developments and progress that few would have predicted as recently as eight or ten years ago.

Thus, when I was asked if I would consider a second edition of *The Right to Be Out,* I agreed without hesitation, given the importance of documenting what has transpired and seeking to ascertain where these volatile developments might lead, especially in the fragile environment of America's public schools.

It is particularly valuable at the outset to reflect on the parallels between the LGBT rights movement and other rights movements over time. These movements include, but are not limited to, the women's rights movement, the disability rights movement, the civil rights movement for African Americans, the Chicano–Latino rights movement, the movement for greater equality for Asians and Pacific Islanders, and the veterans rights movement. The movements all have their similarities and their differences, but we can learn a great deal from the parallels. As Richard Socarides, former advisor on LGBT issues for President Bill Clinton, wrote in *The New Yorker* magazine in 2015:

Will nationwide marriage equality lead in time to full nationwide acceptance, or will [marriage equality activists] discover, like many civil-rights
activists before them, that there is a big gap between legal rights and true
equality? This is a big moment for the [LGBT]-rights movement, and an
important one in which to remember that there is likely more struggle
ahead.

Indeed, conflicting results in national polls exemplify the complexity
of attitudes toward gay and transgender persons during these unsettled
times. For example, although a majority of Americans generally support
legal recognition of same-sex relationships, approximately 30 percent of
the respondents in a 2015 poll who did not identify themselves as LGBT
said that it would unsettle them to learn that their physician or child's
teacher did. In addition, close to 45 percent said that they would be uneasy about bringing a child to a same-sex wedding.

Focusing on the positive LGBT-related developments in this country, however, it is not possible to ignore just how remarkable the recent
progress has been. The most prominent development, of course, has been
the legalization of marriage equality in all fifty states. Accompanying the
road to legalization, as the brand-new chapter on marriage equality in
this second edition demonstrates, there has been an undeniable trend
toward the strengthening of federal and state equal protection laws for
LGBTs. Courts are increasingly recognizing a heightened level of judicial
review in cases where discrimination on the basis of sexual orientation
has been shown, and this trend in equal protection jurisprudence has the
potential to substantially benefit LGBT students, teachers, and parents in
K–12 public school settings.

Other broad, general developments have had an undeniably positive
impact on the lives of LGBTs, particularly in the area of education. The
repeal of "Don't Ask, Don't Tell" in the U.S. military, for example, has provided major limitations on discrimination against LGBTs in an institution
that employs more teenagers than any other entity in the United States.
As this edition explains, the military embodies a strong educative function, and the values that are taught in the armed services inevitably impact the values that are disseminated in middle schools and high schools.
In a like manner, the NCAA's updated policy documents regarding equal
treatment for LGBT student athletes at the college and university level
have had a positive impact on the experiences of gay and transgender
athletes at the K–12 level.

Moreover, the landmark Seventh Circuit Court of Appeals decision in *Hively v. Ivy Tech Community College*—which found by a vote of 8–3 in 2017 that the Civil Rights Act prohibited anti-gay workplace discrimination—could very well mark a turning point in LGBT employment discrimination law throughout education communities at all levels. And as the expanded chapter on transgender issues in this second edition demonstrates, a growing cultural acceptance of transgender persons, along with a broad recognition of the challenges that they face, has begun to influence the strengthening of gender-expansive student rights under the law and as a matter of policy, with K–12 faculty and staff in many local school districts demonstrating a willingness to learn more about this area and understand the extent of the complexities that remain.

This second edition also documents several specific, K–12-related developments that have not received a great deal of attention at the national level but have made a significant difference at local school sites: a major case decision in counseling law, the banning of conversion therapy for minors in ten states, and the mandating of LGBT-positive content in California's social studies curriculum. With regard to counseling law, for example, the Eleventh Circuit Court of Appeals ruled in the 2011 case of *Keeton v. Anderson-Wiley* that a student could be prevented from obtaining a master's degree in school counseling after she indicated to her supervisors at Augusta State that because of her religious beliefs she would insist on counseling any LGBT student who consulted her to enroll in a conversion therapy program and seek to become straight. In the years that followed, ten states plus the District of Columbia banned conversion therapy for minors by mental health professionals and school psychologists after learning of the overwhelming consensus by experts in the field that such programs are highly detrimental and potentially very dangerous. And California became a trendsetter in the area of high school social studies when it adopted the FAIR Education Act in 2011 and, in so doing, mandated LGBT-positive content and prohibited negative portrayals of LGBTs in its public school curriculum. As explained in this edition, LGBTs were added to a list of other identity groups that were already receiving such protection under the state's Education Code.

Conversely, all too often, these positive developments have been accompanied by negative incidents and trends that were not always specific to education but have had a deleterious effect on LGBTs in America's public schools. In recent years, as this second edition explains, LGBTs have been confronted by hundreds of bills in state legislatures that would ban antidiscrimination laws designed to provide equal treatment. LGBTs have also experienced the tragic mass killing of gay Latinos in an Orlando nightclub, a marriage equality backlash that has been fueled by the politics of fear, a disturbing lack of empathy and civility in the public square, a move to reinstate the ban on transgender soldiers in the military, and efforts to roll back transgender rights generally. As a result of these negative developments and other long-standing practices documented in this book, LGBT youth in too many places continue to face troubling ordeals characterized by homelessness, attempted suicides, victimization through the misuse of the special education system, and disproportionate incarceration.

This book has been updated from beginning to end to take all of the aforementioned developments into account. A major new chapter on marriage equality provides extensive coverage of positive trends in equal protection law and an exploration of the parameters of a backlash that has included increased bullying and "gay bashing" along with a divisive "religious liberty" movement that seeks to characterize LGBTs as a threat to organized religion, ignoring the fact that many branches and denominations welcome LGBTs into their communities and that many gay and gender-expansive people are devoutly religious and/or highly spiritual. Along with chapter 1, the new chapter 2 provides central foundational material for the legal and policy analysis that follows.

This second edition also includes an expanded chapter on transgender developments and their implications, including but not limited to discerning categories of gender-expansive youth, coming out as transgender in a K–12 setting, realities faced by transgender youth and their allies, school climate strategies, professional-development content and related curricular reforms, legal and public policy mandates that are available to address day-to-day transgender issues, noteworthy legislation and litigation, and model policies generally.

In the end, as this edition emphasizes, the growing number of strategies that may be available for LGBT students, teachers, and parents would not have surfaced had it not been for the emergence and strengthening of the right to be out. With U.S. population estimates revealing that more LGBTs than ever are coming out, and with more people discovering that a substantial percentage of those with whom they interact on a regular basis are gay and/or transgender, a growing number of Americans have been willing to openly and actively support developments that point in the direction of greater equality down the road. This edition explores the many reasons for optimism, even as it identifies the challenges that remain and the barriers that must still be overcome.

Ultimately, the book is designed to be a resource for a wide-ranging audience that includes but is not limited to members of the legal, educational, and public policy communities. It does not presume for one moment that the task of effecting further positive change in K–12 education around these matters is easy. But the book concludes that an optimistic best-case scenario is essential if such change is to occur. We may not get to a best-case scenario anytime soon, but it is imperative that we continue working in that direction.

Los Angeles, California
Summer 2018

ACKNOWLEDGMENTS

It has been my great fortune to be in contact with a remarkable array of people who provided encouragement and support for this work. At UCLA, my colleagues contributed valuable perspectives and ongoing optimism over time. In particular, I thank Tina Christie, former dean Aimee Dorr, Megan Franke, Amy Gershon, Kris Gutierrez, Patricia McDonough, Jeannie Oakes, John Rogers, Linda Rose, Assistant Vice Chancellor Suzanne Seplow, and Danny Solorzano, with whom I have worked at the UCLA Graduate School of Education and Information Studies, and Devon Carbado, Elizabeth Cheadle, Joel Handler, Vice Chancellor Jerry Kang, Rob Schwartz, and Richard Steinberg, with whom I have worked at the UCLA School of Law.

Within the larger legal and education communities, I have benefited greatly from the insights and advice of David Campos, Maureen Carroll, Alex Ferrando, Ryan Fox-Lee, Jonathan Grady, Scott Graham, Allan Keown, Sheila James Kuehl, Catherine Lhamon, Rigoberto Marquez, Timna Naim, the late Eric Rofes, Zach Shepard, Diane Steinberg, Zak Szymanski, Ryan Tacorda, Dylan Vade, Luis Vasquez, Felipe Velez, Kevin Welner, Desmund Wu, and Jason Wu.

The feedback I received from many Williams Institute faculty and staff has had a major impact on this work: I thank Lee Badgett, David Cruz, Gary Gates, Nan Hunter, Holning Lau, Christy Mallory, Doug NeJaime, Adam Romero, Bill Rubenstein, Brad Sears, and Dean Spade for their invaluable contributions to the project.

I was blessed with amazing research assistants. Not only did Ryan Dunn and Kevin Minnick bring a wealth of personal knowledge to the project but their day-to-day work reflected a level of professionalism and sophistication that went far beyond anything I might have expected.

Finally, special thanks should go to Bob Kim, Shannon Minter, Rick Mintrop, and my editor at the University of Minnesota Press, Pieter Martin. From their patient feedback and their depth of knowledge to their commitment to a better future for all people, they were instrumental in enabling me to complete this work.

INTRODUCTION

At its most basic level, "being out" can be characterized as a condition or state of genuine openness. The term is most typically associated with lesbian, gay, bisexual, and transgender (LGBT) persons, but it is appropriately viewed as applicable to everyone.[1]

Indeed, a principled reading of current legal doctrine reveals that, in our pluralistic society, all persons have a right to be open regarding fundamental aspects of identity, personhood, and group affiliation. Contextualizing this right to be out and reviewing its development in the public sector today, it is clear that it reflects a classic combination of First Amendment and Fourteenth Amendment principles. It is both a right to express an identity and a right to be treated equally as a result of expressing this identity. Emerging under court decisions and a range of relevant federal and state statutes, the right to be out encompasses—but is not limited to—disclosure of one's race, ethnicity, religion, sexual orientation, gender identity, political views, medical conditions, past experiences, present involvement, and future plans.[2]

Within LGBT communities today, nothing is more central than the right to be out. Not only is there still so much pressure, in so many settings, not to come out, but as recently as thirty-five to forty-five years ago, the U.S. legal system set forth such imposing hurdles to living openly that being out was typically not an option. Public school teachers, for example, could lose their jobs if they were openly gay. Bars were actually prohibited from serving drinks to persons who were known to be gay. Dancing with same-sex partners in public was restricted. And propositioning another person of the same gender was not only a crime but an act that could lead to "sex offender" status and the accompanying loss of employment, legal rights, and social standing in the community.[3]

William Eskridge has written that as recently as the early 1960s, gays and lesbians were "smothered by law." He explains that people during that era risked "arrest and possible police brutalization" even for such things as possessing a publication that addressed gay issues or writing about homosexuality without disapproval.[4] LGBT persons of color often faced additional challenges above and beyond all these daunting hurdles.[5]

Despite all the challenges and legal hurdles, however, the percentage of LGBT persons who are out today may be higher than it has been at any time in this nation's history. Particularly in major urban centers, the lonely and incomplete life of the "closet" that gays and lesbians and transgender persons used to face as a matter of course is rapidly becoming a relic of an anachronistic and discredited era. Increasingly, LGBTs do not have to feel stigmatized because of who they are or to live in constant fear, as many once did, of being found out. And legal protections have begun to reflect these watershed events.[6]

What It Means to Be Out

When people come out, they begin by recognizing their own LGBT status and typically follow up at some point by sharing this recognition and this status with others. The process of coming out and the long-term commitment to being out are both invariably communicative in nature, with LGBT persons sharing through word and deed the nature and extent of their identity. The day-to-day purpose of this communication, however, may vary significantly from person to person and from circumstance to circumstance. For example, coming out and being out can have a developmental component, a social-responsibility component, a political component, and even a religious component.

The American Psychological Association has emphasized the developmental nature of the act, stating on its website that "coming out is often an important psychological step for lesbian, gay, and bisexual people. Research has shown that feeling positively about one's sexual orientation and integrating it into one's life fosters greater well-being and mental health." Commentator Bruce Bawer has focused on social responsibility, arguing that "being honest about one's homosexuality . . . helps eliminate prejudice." Legal scholar Edward Stein has emphasized the political nature of the expression, explaining that "when lesbians and gay men speak as open lesbians and gay men . . . their speech is political and thus deserving of strong protection." And Chris Glaser, a religious leader in LGBT communities nationwide, has written that "coming out is a recurring if not central theme of the Bible . . . [that] links our own experience with that of our spiritual ancestors . . . [and] opens us up to the universality of the life-giving and life-changing coming out process for every human being."[7]

Being out can mean different things to different people, and of course, no two situations are ever the same. For some, it can mean participating in LGBT-related activism, along with a willingness to identify as LGBT whenever the conversation or the circumstances appear to warrant it. For others, it can mean proclaiming an identity through clothing, accessories, hairstyles, buttons, bumper stickers, decals, pride parades, community groups, and the like. For those who might be partnered or even married, it may mean nothing more than living together openly as a couple. Finally, for those who may present as gay or lesbian without even trying, it can mean being comfortable enough with their identity to stop trying to act straight.[8]

Needless to say, situations vary considerably in this context. Some who suspect that they might be LGBT cannot ever imagine being out, and they may remain "closeted from themselves" for their entire lives. Such denial happens much more than many might realize, even in major urban areas. Some come out to themselves but not to anyone else, while some come out to others but lead lives that may be indistinguishable from those of their straight counterparts. Of course, as can be imagined, being out is itself quite relative. Some may think of themselves as being completely out while others view them as pretty much closeted. Even those whom everyone considers openly LGBT are always faced with the question of whether and to what extent to come out to people in new situations that may arise.

The question of how out someone can or should be in a given circumstance is part and parcel of a larger inquiry: what are gays and lesbians and transgender persons supposed to do? Assuming that there are, always have been, and always will be LGBT persons—and the overwhelming majority of experts in all the applicable fields have found this to be true—how should LGBTs be living their lives?[9] A growing percentage of Americans agree that gays and lesbians and transgender persons should be embracing their identities and caring for those they love, yet there are still those who, for a variety of reasons, not only would deny that such an identity exists but would like to see gay and gender-expansive people live their lives in a completely closeted fashion, as far away from children and from mainstream society as is humanly possible.

The Emergence of the Right, and Its Value

Assuming that the experts are correct, and given that, as opinion polls have shown, a solid majority of Americans support the right of LGBT persons to live their lives fully and openly, it is understandable that during this era, a right to be out has emerged and is becoming stronger as the months and years go by.[10] The right to be out is clearly central, and it matters greatly. Without such a right, an LGBT identity retains a secretive and shameful veneer, and LGBT persons continue to be viewed as second-class citizens, with an integral aspect of their personhood relegated to the isolation of the closet and all that this isolation portends. Many more gay and gender-expansive people will find themselves in unfulfilled relationships, withdrawn and unable to love.[11] Otherwise appropriate career options will be deemed unattainable, lives will be played out at the margins, and suicide will continue to rear its ugly head in disproportionate numbers.

With the strengthening of the right to be out, however, the prospects exist for an improved quality of life that will benefit everyone. In an optimistic, best-case scenario, not only will the openness that comes with that right help further understanding and an appreciation of differences but it also will help decrease tension, reduce loneliness, save lives, minimize the pressure on so many to be something they are not, lower the number of bad marriages, increase the amount of caring for other human beings, enable a greater degree of love between and among persons, and help maximize human potential.[12]

Institutional Restrictions and the K–12 Education Community

Although great progress is evident across a wide variety of fronts, LGBT persons continue to face complex circumstances and significant impediments, particularly in the legal and public policy arenas.[13] Nowhere is the situation more complex and more challenging than in the military, organized religion, professional sports, and schools. Although many within these institutions are unequivocal in their support of LGBTs, and a notable percentage of people there are themselves gay or transgender, the stigma that was once associated with homosexuality and gender non-conformity throughout the country may still be widely prevalent in these settings. Indeed, disclosure of a person's sexual orientation or gender identity in many of these communities can lead to dismissal from institutions and the discrediting of one's professional and personal standing in the same way that it did for most people in the 1950s and 1960s. The impact of the shadow that is cast on our society by these institutions and the pressure they often exert on LGBTs not to come out should not be underestimated.

The tension regarding the right of gay and transgender persons to live their lives openly is perhaps most evident in our nation's educational institutions. Especially at the K–12 level, LGBT students, teachers, and school-site administrators have found themselves at the eye of the proverbial storm as school communities confront the rapidly changing realities in this area.[14] The intensive and ongoing level of personal contact in a setting where certain values are expected to be instilled can and often does lead to high emotions and volatile confrontations.

The 2008 killing of fifteen-year-old Lawrence King in a Southern California public school only a few days after he came out as gay is a notorious and tragic example of this volatility. King, a gender-nonconforming student of color, was shot by a fellow student while working on a computer during his eighth-grade English class. His friends described how the victim had been bullied by others over time, and they told of the highly negative reaction that many of his male classmates had to his recent coming out. Especially negative, apparently, was the reaction of the fourteen-year-old who shot King twice in the head in front of everyone.[15]

In a like manner, anti-gay aggression directed toward fellow students based on nothing more than the *perception* that they might be LGBT reportedly led to the widely publicized suicides of two eleven-year-old boys in 2009. News reports documenting the parallel circumstances of these horrific events included extensive interviews attesting to the trauma experienced by African American student Carl Walker-Hoover and Latino student Jaheem Herrera as a result of constant bullying at their respective public school sites that was accompanied by relentless name-calling and the mocking of their perceived gay identities.[16] Although neither child identified as gay, there was evidence in the news reports of a gender nonconformity to which their classmates responded in an all-too-common, callous way.[17]

Unfortunately, these catastrophic events reflect the persistence of the challenges faced by LGBT persons in K–12 education settings. Studies continue to show that LGBTs feel disproportionately unsafe in school and that the mistreatment they face interferes with their ability to succeed. Gay and gender-expansive students often stop attending classes regularly, and many drop out, run away from home, or attempt suicide. LGBT educators face more covert pressures, and they are often confronted with the message that they had better remain as closeted as possible. If they do not heed this message, they can be made to feel so uncomfortable by administrators, parents, and/or other members of the school community that they choose to leave K–12 education.

Data on LGBT educators are sorely lacking; indeed, it is an area ripe for further research. But extensive data have been compiled on contemporary gay and gender-expansive youth. The National Mental Health Association (NMHA), for example, has classified LGBT students as an at-risk population. "Gay and lesbian teens are at high risk," the NMHA reports, "because 'their distress is a direct result of the hatred and prejudice that surround them,' not because of their inherently gay or lesbian identity orientation."[18] A recent study has shown that K–12 students who are gay or thought to be gay are bullied more than twice as much as any other identifiable group. Given that such circumstances can be compounded by a lack of acceptance at home or in their communities, it is not surprising that LGBT runaways may compose up to 40 percent of the entire teen homeless population in certain places and that the suicide rate for LGBT students continues to be three to four times higher than the rate for their straight counterparts.[19]

It is no longer a mystery why such mistreatment persists. Dr. Karen Franklin's groundbreaking research, for example, sampled the attitudes and experiences of approximately five hundred young adults in the late 1990s and identified four distinct motivations for anti-LGBT aggression: perceived self-defense, enforcement of gender norms/ideology, peer dynamics, and thrill seeking.[20] Franklin's findings are reinforced and expanded on by other studies, including the work of C. J. Pascoe at the University of California, Berkeley. Focusing especially on the mind-set of males in their teens and twenties, who together compose by far the largest percentage of those engaged in LGBT mistreatment, Pascoe identified a widespread perception among younger men that they must constantly prove that they are not gay.[21]

This research goes a long way toward illuminating the complexity of anti-LGBT animus and identifying reasons why it persists in so many places. A key conclusion of the Franklin study is that anti-gay aggression—whether in the form of physical attacks, verbal assaults, failure to intervene when in a position of power, or even silent complicity—"can be seen primarily as an extreme manifestation of pervasive cultural norms rather than as a manifestation of individual hatred. . . . People who have assaulted homosexuals typically do not recognize themselves in the stereotyped image of the hate-filled extremist."[22] And although the focus of the research is primarily on the behavior of teens and young adults, the categories of perceived self-defense and enforcing gender norms clearly implicate the activity of older persons as well. Franklin provides numerous insights into why many adults in K–12 school settings not only continue to look the other way but even participate actively in the mistreatment of LGBT students and educators.[23]

This book explores the intricacies of recent developments within the legal, educational, and public policy communities, and—through an analysis of relevant findings—it seeks to discern the contours of a research-based road map for tackling the LGBT-related problems that remain. Consistent with the realities documented in this introduction, it relies on the premise that "the right to be out" is appropriately viewed as situated at the very heart of this process.

The inquiry set forth in these pages is designed as a series of building blocks, with each chapter expanding on what has come before. Part I addresses the legal terrain, and Part II examines the educational policy considerations that flow from the legal analysis. At the same time, the book can also be employed as a reference manual. Each of the parts can be viewed as an independent inquiry, comprising a foundational chapter followed by several case studies. In Part I, for example, chapter 1 sets forth the legal principles underlying the right to be out, and chapters 2, 3, 4, and 5 then apply those principles to an analysis of legal developments regarding marriage equality and its aftermath; LGBT students; LGBT educators; and the area of curriculum, religion, morality, and values, respectively. In Part II, chapter 6 sets forth the research-based principles that inform a proactive focus on school climate, and chapters 7, 8, and 9 then apply those principles to curriculum and pedagogy practices in the classroom, school sports, and transgender youth, respectively.

However, each of the nine chapters is also designed to stand alone. Thus persons seeking information to help inform particular areas of their work or to help address issues they are currently confronting will find that the section of the book that may be most relevant for them will be accessible even without having looked at what has come before. Nevertheless, such persons are likely to find, through this approach, that additional portions of the book may also become relevant for their purposes.

Pursuant to this structure and these purposes, Part I examines the emergence of a multifaceted right to be out under the law and locates the foundation of that right at the intersection of the First and Fourteenth Amendments. It concludes that the right exists everywhere, in all fifty states. At the same time, it emphasizes how different things still are from place to place, how much stronger the right can be in places that have explicitly mandated equal treatment, and how much work still needs to be done within the legal system before the access and the opportunities that accompany this right can be realized across the board.

Part II explores what K–12 schools might do—and indeed in many cases have already done—to implement the right to be out and to provide the best possible learning environment for all students. Through changes in the law and accompanying societal shifts, a significant number of schools are very different places with regard to LGBTs than they were even ten to fifteen years ago. Studies accompanying these changes help illuminate what can be done to further limit the incidence of mistreatment and abusive behavior. K–12 schools remain highly unwelcome and dangerously unsafe places for LGBTs in many locations, but they have become dynamic, welcoming, and collaborative places in many other settings.

Although the focus throughout the book continues to be on public education, the private school experience is also relevant here. Even though private schools do not typically operate under the same legal mandates, and even though many private schools continue to discriminate openly against LGBTs, many other private schools have implemented programs that serve as some of the best examples of what can be done to maintain a positive and inclusive campus climate. Thus the public policy findings that can be identified in these pages are equally applicable in both the public and the private sectors.

I

The Law

The Emergence of the
Right to Be Out

1

THE LEGAL FOUNDATIONS OF THE RIGHT TO BE OUT

The right to be out has emerged today as a strong and multifaceted legal imperative. Derived from a number of interrelated sources, it is indeed the sum total of all its parts. Such a pattern is not unusual in U.S. law, where it is often possible to discern rights that have developed from more than one source simultaneously over time. These rights can be among the most powerful, grounded as they are in several different legal doctrines and a significant number of court decisions.

The Intersection of the First and Fourteenth Amendments

At its heart, the right to be out is a combination of First Amendment and Fourteenth Amendment principles. Among the most powerful and certainly among the most popular of all our constitutional provisions, these amendments have often been the basis of our most noteworthy court decisions. Not only have legal scholars consistently placed the wide-ranging mandates on the highest possible pedestal but they also have repeatedly identified links between the two. Ronald Dworkin, for example, has labeled the First Amendment free speech clause and the Fourteenth Amendment equal protection clause the "great abstract clauses" of the Constitution, describing them as the "textual embodiments of fundamental moral principles."[1]

Kenneth Karst has pinpointed the power and potential of these clauses for LGBT persons, demonstrating that either can provide a "doctrinal

basis for protecting the expression of a gay identity." He notes in particular that the Fourteenth Amendment "resonates . . . strongly against the
stigmatic harm and group subordination that are the main targets of the
equal citizenship principle,"[2] an observation consistent with Dworkin's
assertion that the "fundamental moral principle embodied by the Equal
Protection Clause is the equal intrinsic worth of all humans."[3]

In the end, Karst concludes that although an equality emphasis by itself is valid, an analysis of gay identity issues appropriately involves *both*
"freedom and equality: the freedom to express an individual gay identity without suffering the harms inflicted on members of subordinated
groups."[4] It is at this intersection of free speech and equal protection,
where both the freedom principle and the equality principle can operate
simultaneously, that the right to be out can be located for lesbian, gay,
bisexual, and transgender persons in U.S. public education.

Examining the history and development of American constitutional
jurisprudence, it is possible to identify a broad, multidimensional relationship between the First Amendment free speech clause and the
Fourteenth Amendment equal protection clause. At times, the two clauses may appear to be in conflict, with commentators and jurists raising
questions regarding which mandate should take precedence.[5] More often
than not, however, the relationship between the clauses has been harmonious, with federal judges finding that basic requisite principles of each
amendment can be reinforced through the other. Notable examples of
such harmonious interplay between free speech principles and equality-
based principles can be found in First Amendment cases addressing the
"public forum doctrine" and in Fourteenth Amendment cases addressing
the scope of the "right to an education" under federal and state law.

The Public Forum Cases

The public forum doctrine recognizes that certain settings traditionally
associated with a more open level of interaction—such as street corners
and public parks—may attain the legal status of "public forums" and require public officials to provide a greater level of free speech protection
for those who choose to speak there.[6] The doctrine emerged in several key
court decisions over time, fueled by constitutional challenges brought by
plaintiffs who demonstrated that their expression in these settings was
restricted while the similar expression of others was allowed.

In the 1951 case of *Niemotko v. Maryland,* for example, a group of

Jehovah's Witnesses argued successfully that their free speech rights had been compromised because they were prohibited from presenting "Bible talks" in a public park, while other groups were permitted to put the same park to substantially similar uses. Although *Niemotko* presented itself as a First Amendment dispute, Chief Justice Vinson's opinion demonstrates that the Fourteenth Amendment ultimately played a key role in the decision:

> The conclusion is inescapable that the use of the park was denied because of the City Council's dislike for or disagreement with the [Jehovah's] Witnesses or their views. The right to equal protection of the laws, in the exercise of those freedoms of speech and religion protected by the First and Fourteenth Amendments, has a firmer foundation than the whims or personal opinions of a local governing body.[7]

Niemotko thus became an early example of how rights under both amendments could interact in a harmonious fashion, with the equal protection guarantee providing an important additional dimension to the plaintiff's freedom of expression.

Twenty years later, the U.S. Supreme Court faced a similar dispute when it considered a challenge involving a Chicago ordinance that prohibited picketing adjacent to public school grounds but included an explicit exception for labor-related activity. Writing for what was essentially a unanimous court in *Police Department of the City of Chicago v. Mosley,* Justice Thurgood Marshall centered his analysis on the interplay between the Free Speech Clause and the Equal Protection Clause. Declaring that the "equal protection claim in this case is closely intertwined with First Amendment interests," Marshall took a free speech clause fact pattern—one that had in fact been decided by the lower court under First Amendment principles—and bolstered the plaintiff's position by adding in a Fourteenth Amendment enhancement. "Because Chicago treats some picketing differently from others," Marshall wrote, "we analyze this ordinance in terms of the Equal Protection Clause."[8]

The *Mosley* decision continues to serve as a prototypical example today of how principles of free speech and equal protection can work together to enhance a litigant's position.[9] In both *Mosley* and *Niemotko,* a plaintiff's free speech rights were in fact strengthened by principles of equal treatment inherent in the Fourteenth Amendment.

The Right-to-an-Education Cases

Commentators and jurists have identified a broad-based right to an education under both federal and state equal protection guarantees, and a significant number of court decisions have sought to discern the parameters of this right by building on a combination of First Amendment and Fourteenth Amendment principles. In the pivotal Fourteenth Amendment cases of *San Antonio v. Rodriguez and Plyler v. Doe,* such an interplay is evident in several of the published opinions. Justice Powell, for example, considered the envisioned Fourteenth Amendment right in *Rodriguez* as flowing from the Free Speech Clause and from constitutional provisions that reflected a goal of individual political participation.[10] Expanding on this notion, Justice Brennan wrote that "there can be no doubt that education is inextricably linked to the [Fourteenth Amendment] right to participate in the electoral process and to the rights of free speech and association guaranteed by the First Amendment."[11] And in the *Plyler* majority opinion, nine years later, Brennan described the "important interest in education" in a similar fashion:

> We have recognized "the public schools as a most vital civic institution for the preservation of a democratic system of government [reflecting Fourteenth Amendment values]. . . . Education is necessary to prepare citizens to participate effectively and intelligently in our open political system if we are to preserve freedom and independence" [reflecting First Amendment values].[12]

Noteworthy state court decisions have followed a similar line of thought, viewing the education right in state constitutions as embodying the familiar combination of free speech and equal protection guarantees. In the 1971 equal protection case of *Serrano v. Priest,* for example, the California Supreme Court described public education as a "unifying social force" that could help foster equal access and equal opportunity, and it then noted the inevitable connection between these equal protection principles and First Amendment principles.[13]

In 1989, the Kentucky Supreme Court addressed the parameters of the right to an education under the state's education articles and concluded that "a child's right to an adequate education is a fundamental one," that a system of education "must have as its goal to provide each and every child with . . . sufficient oral and written communication skills to enable students to function in a complex and rapidly changing civilization" (reflecting First Amendment values), and that "common schools shall provide equal educational opportunities to all Kentucky children, regardless of place of residence or economic circumstances" (reflecting Fourteenth Amendment values).[14]

At this point, "a huge volume of literature" exists regarding the interplay between the First Amendment and the Fourteenth Amendment.[15] Examining the public forum and right-to-an-education cases, one cannot help but be struck by just how powerful an impact can be made by combining the principles inherent in the respective constitutional provisions. Both a range of formulas and a variety of approaches have been effective in this context. In the public forum cases, for example, Fourteenth Amendment principles are incorporated into First Amendment disputes to bolster litigants' free speech rights. In the education cases, First Amendment principles are incorporated into Fourteenth Amendment disputes to add both power and depth to the equality-based right to an education. In the former, the interrelationship is precise and transparent, whereas in the latter, the interplay may sometimes be more subtle. Yet in all cases, the result is the same: a stronger and more effective right located at the intersection of the free speech and equal protection guarantees.

The Development of the Right to Be Out at This Intersection

The history of the right to be out over the past fifty to seventy-five years reflects a confluence of interrelated developments. Case decisions interpreting the Free Speech Clause and the Equal Protection Clause constitute the majority of the building blocks, but legislative activity has also played a key role. Indeed, the courts and the legislatures have consistently reinforced their respective mandates in this area over time.

In the years following World War II, legal activists sought equal treatment for gays and lesbians under the First Amendment, and a series of victories between 1945 and 1965 led to the recognition of "freedom of expression" rights that typically included an implicit antidiscrimination component. The early gay rights movement was thus very different from the early civil rights and women's rights movements. By relying extensively on the First Amendment to protect their ability to gather together and to openly discuss and write about gay issues, LGBTs could benefit from the interrelated freedoms of speech, press, and assembly. And it is noteworthy that these victories came at the beginning of an era that saw the strengthening of First Amendment protections throughout the public sector.[16]

Over the course of the 1960s and 1970s, statutory modifications led to the abrogation of many laws that had precluded even the most basic self-identifying acts on the part of gays and lesbians. Two key turning points provided the impetus for the ramping up of legal efforts across the board. In 1969, an uprising at the Stonewall Inn in New York City highlighted the persistent and inequitable harassment of LGBTs by law enforcement officials.[17] And in 1973, the American Psychiatric Association's vote to remove homosexuality from its *Diagnostic and Statistical Manual of Mental Disorders,* which codifies psychiatric conditions and is used as a key reference work across the globe, was viewed by many as having transformed the entire landscape.[18] LGBT-related free speech lawsuits that followed these events established the right to form gay and lesbian student clubs at the postsecondary level, the right to take a same-sex partner to the prom, the right to establish gay–straight alliances at the K–12 level, and the right to dress consistently with one's gender identity on public school campuses.

At the same time, antidiscrimination laws continued to be bolstered. The right to equal educational opportunity, recognized by the U.S. Supreme Court under the Equal Protection Clause in *Brown v. Board of Education* (1954), expanded greatly over time.[19] And after initial attempts to invoke the equal protection guarantee on behalf of LGBTs hit major stumbling blocks in the federal courts, gay plaintiffs won a significant Fourteenth Amendment victory in the 1996 U.S. Supreme Court case of *Romer v. Evans,* which invalidated a Colorado constitutional provision that would have *prevented* gays and lesbians from being able to obtain explicit protection against discrimination in that state.[20]

Legislative activity during the era that followed led to statutes prohibiting discrimination against gays and lesbians in at least twenty-one states by 2010. A range of benefits that had been available only to heterosexual couples were increasingly granted to same-sex couples in both the public and the private sectors nationwide.[21] And LGBT persons in K–12 settings, increasingly willing to contest the discrimination against them, began winning major victories as well.

Several developments in particular can be viewed as exemplifying the changing legal terrain for LGBT persons across these decades. The postsecondary student organization cases of the 1970s and 1980s opened the door to a broad expressive right in an education setting, and both the *Nabozny* decision, in 1996, and *Lawrence v. Texas*, in 2003, clarified a protection against discrimination that the courts had simply refused to recognize in the past.

The Student Organization Cases of the 1970s and 1980s

Post-Stonewall legal activity not only led to a much more open and aggressive push for equality but also fueled an increasing number of challenges based on the Free Speech Clause. A foundational goal in these cases was the "right to come out" in a public setting, the "right of gay people to express themselves through public speech without fear of criminal penalty."[22] Litigation proliferated during this era, and institutions of higher education were a major battleground.[23]

An early example of this litigation was *Gay Students Organization (GSO) of the University of New Hampshire v. Bonner*.[24] The organization was officially recognized by the university in May 1973, but a GSO-sponsored dance held six months later led to a great deal of media attention, political pressure, and criticism. As a result, the university's board of trustees suspended the GSO's "scheduling" privileges until the "legality and appropriateness of their functions and activities could be determined." A lawsuit was soon filed against the university, alleging violations under both the First and the Fourteenth Amendments.

Ruling unanimously in favor of the students, the U.S. Court of Appeals for the First Circuit concluded that both the founding of the GSO and the activities in which it engaged were "communicative opportunities" that merited the full protection of free speech law:

> The GSO was created . . . to promote the free exchange of ideas . . . and to educate the public. . . . Social events in which discussion and exchange of ideas can take place . . . can play an important part in this communication. . . . The basic "message" GSO seeks to convey [is] that homosexuals exist, that they feel repressed by existing laws and attitudes, that they wish to emerge from their isolation, and that public understanding of their attitudes and problems is desirable for society.[25]

Chief Judge Coffin determined, in light of these conclusions, that the university had restricted this expression because of "a distaste both for the ideas held and communicated by GSO members and for the larger message conveyed by the very holding of such public events." Such a restriction, the court found, was a clear violation of principles articulated by the Supreme Court in cases such as *Police Department of the City of Chicago v. Mosley*. In particularly noteworthy language, the court located the gay students' rights at the intersection of the First and Fourteenth Amendments, stating that the "equal protection questions" were "intertwined" with the First Amendment issues and that "the equal protection challenge to the university policy strikes us as substantial in its own right."[26]

Bonner was followed by a series of major victories for gay student groups at other colleges and universities. In 1976, for example, the U.S. Court of Appeals for the Fourth Circuit ruled in favor of Virginia Commonwealth University's Gay Student Alliance, which had been denied the ability to register as a student organization. A year later, the U.S. Court of Appeals for the Eighth Circuit ruled in favor of "Gay Lib" in a similar lawsuit against the University of Missouri. And in 1987, principles from these cases were extended even to the private sector by a D.C. District Court decision on behalf of the Gay Rights Coalition of the Georgetown University Law Center.[27]

The courts in these cases clearly recognized the communicative aspects of forming and participating in student organizations. Indeed, Nan Hunter, a legal scholar who herself litigated one of these lawsuits, has noted that the expression in dispute was nothing less than self-identifying speech. Hunter has therefore labeled these rulings "expressive identity" decisions, and she has written that they came to compose "the largest single body of coming out speech cases" in U.S. constitutional jurisprudence.[28]

For the students, active involvement in such groups was often a vehicle for them to come out. By seeking to prevent them from forming campus organizations—even as they typically allowed the entire range of other self-identifying groups to exist—the institutions were endorsing the message that there was something about gays that was shameful and should not be allowed to see the light of day. By ruling in favor of the students in one decision after another at the highest levels of the federal appellate court system, the nation's top jurists were making it clear that treating gays differently was no longer acceptable and that gays had the same right to express themselves in this manner as everyone else.

The *Nabozny* Litigation (1996)

For a long time, at the K–12 level, people who were threatened, harassed, discriminated against, or otherwise mistreated because of their LGBT status or perceived LGBT status tended to keep this mistreatment to themselves. Complaining or taking a case to court would be tantamount to coming out, and coming out was not typically an option for either students or educators. By the 1990s, however, gays and lesbians were stepping forward to openly contest the mistreatment, and *Nabozny v. Podlesny* (1996) was the breakthrough case. Indeed, before the *Nabozny* decision, no U.S. court had ever found a public school district liable for discriminating against an LGBT person under the Fourteenth Amendment.

Beginning at age twelve and continuing for almost five years, Jamie Nabozny experienced relentless verbal and physical harassment by his classmates in the Ashland, Wisconsin, public school district. Despite ongoing attempts by both Nabozny and his parents to seek relief from this mistreatment, school officials consistently looked the other way and through their inaction allowed the behavior to continue. The record indicates persistent and pervasive verbal abuse in classrooms, in hallways, and on school buses; demeaning physical contact ranging from books being knocked out of Nabozny's hands to his being touched inappropriately; a mock rape performed in science class while twenty students looked on and cheered; being intentionally urinated upon by a fellow student; and physical beatings that in one case led to severe internal bleeding and required surgery.[29]

In addition to reporting these occurrences to faculty and staff as soon as they happened, Nabozny and his parents met formally with school-site administrators on six or seven occasions over time. At these meetings, the officials always promised to do something, yet no discipline of any consequence appears to have been administered. Instead, the message from these educational leaders was that "boys will be boys" and that Nabozny should expect this sort of thing because he was gay. Not only did there appear to be no remorse on the part of school officials but the record indicates active complicity by faculty and administration in the pattern of mistreatment. Teachers themselves called Nabozny a fag, and on numerous instances over time—in both private and public settings—the administrators in charge blamed Nabozny for bringing all this on himself by being out.

As a result of these events (among other things), Nabozny suffered a nervous breakdown, attempted suicide on three occasions, was hospitalized more than once, and was diagnosed with posttraumatic stress disorder. He was not able to complete high school, instead being compelled to leave home and move to another state.[30] On some level, it is remarkable that he survived at all.

That it took something of this magnitude to get a federal court of appeals to rule against a school district in an LGBT-related discrimination case says a great deal not only about the state of the law as recently as the mid-1990s but also about how far we have finally come. Today, in fact, many wonder how the Ashland school district had the audacity to defend its actions in federal court. But defend them it did, through extensive legal activity and numerous court appearances. It contended that the legal theories raised by the plaintiff were inapplicable, and it insisted that it was doing the best it could under the circumstances. The school district's lawyer reportedly told *Education Week* that such conduct was "impossible to prevent." And in a brief filed with the court, the school district sought to disclaim responsibility for what happened. "Defendants did not create this attitude in society," attorneys for the school district wrote. "Defendants did not raise the alleged persecutors in their homes to believe that harassment and assault are appropriate responses to someone perceived to be different."[31] Yet, as the Seventh Circuit Court of Appeals found, not only were the actions by Nabozny's peers clearly beyond the pale but the actions by school district officials were inexcusable as well.[32]

It is ironic that during the entire time that these events were unfolding, Wisconsin was one of a small number of states that not only prohibited harassment on the basis of sexual orientation but also required school districts to formulate policies to that effect. Nabozny's district actually had an antiharassment policy in place, one that addressed all types of harassment. Yet the plaintiff presented evidence that the policy was being enforced in a highly discriminatory fashion. When young women reported peer harassment directed toward them by young men on campus, actions by school-site administrators were swift and direct, leading almost immediately to the discipline of perpetrators. When Nabozny reported peer harassment directed toward him by young men, however, he was told that he had brought it upon himself. The appellate court found this to be concrete evidence of discrimination against Nabozny on the part of the school district, both on the basis of his gender and on the basis of his sexual identity.[33] He was awarded a settlement of $900,000, almost three times as much as he had originally asked for when he filed the lawsuit.[34]

By not disciplining the student perpetrators, by attempting to justify the perpetrators' actions through the anachronistic insistence that "boys will be boys," by blaming the victim for bringing it on himself (even though he did absolutely nothing to provoke the abuse other than being out), and by disclaiming responsibility for the perpetrators' actions in a court of law, the school district sent a clear message as to where its leaders stood. By ruling in favor of Nabozny, the federal appeals court also sent a clear message: that all such treatment must end. Indeed, since 1996, LGBT students who have been mistreated in this manner have won consistent victories in court and have achieved landmark settlements. These victories often included both monetary awards and mandatory professional development for faculty and staff.[35]

Lawrence v. Texas (2003)

The U.S. Supreme Court's 6–3 decision on behalf of the petitioners in *Lawrence v. Texas* (2003) removed the presumption of criminality that still shadowed LGBT persons in 2003 and severely impacted their right to be out, both under the law and as a matter of public policy.[36] The importance of this issue cannot be overstated. It was impossible for many LGBTs to be open about their identities if basic expressions of same-sex love remained illegal.

At the time the *Lawrence* case was litigated, thirteen states still prohibited consensual relations between people of similar gender in the privacy of their own homes. This prohibition was reflected in the so-called antisodomy laws, which typically criminalized both oral sex and anal sex. Nine states prohibited these acts across the board, mandating criminal penalties for either gay or straight couples. Four states—including Texas—prohibited these acts for homosexual couples but allowed them for heterosexuals. It was the constitutionality of the Texas statute that was challenged by petitioners John Lawrence and Tyron Garner.[37]

Paul Smith, the D.C. attorney who argued on behalf of the petitioners in front of the Supreme Court, explained on that day in March 2003 why the issue went far beyond the particular sexual acts prohibited by the Texas statute. Gays were treated as "second-class citizens," he asserted, because these laws branded them as criminals. As a gay man, Smith noted that although this was not an issue for him personally, in D.C., just over the Potomac River it *was* a major issue, because Virginia was one of the thirteen states that still criminalized homosexual conduct.[38]

Oral arguments can be very revealing, and they often provide insights into major case decisions that the opinions themselves may not reflect. Apparently, at this oral argument, only then Chief Justice Rehnquist and Justice Scalia expressed support for the Texas prosecutor who defended the challenged laws. "Most of the justices looked uncomfortable," as Houston District Attorney Charles Rosenthal Jr. contended that his state had the power to enforce "moral disapproval" by arresting adults in their homes.

In America, Rosenthal argued, there is no "right to engage in extramarital sexual conduct. . . . Texas has a right to set moral standards for its people," and sex can be made a crime if it is "outside the marital bedroom." Justice Souter then asked Rosenthal when Texas first prohibited homosexual sodomy, and he responded that it had traditionally been illegal in Texas and that there had been prosecutions of gays from the beginning. However, when Souter asked when Texas actually passed the law at issue in this case, Rosenthal conceded that it was in 1973. "So this doesn't reflect a long-standing tradition after all," Souter commented.

Throughout these exchanges, Justice Scalia repeatedly interjected his view that "moral disapproval of homosexuality" is an American tradition, dating back at least two hundred years. For example, when Chief Justice Rehnquist raised the question of whether a state "could prefer heterosexuals over a homosexual to teach kindergarten," Justice Scalia asserted that disapproval of homosexuality would in fact justify such a decision by the state. Otherwise, he said, children "could be induced to follow the path of homosexuality."[39]

Six of the nine justices, however, including four Republicans appointed by conservative Republican presidents, rejected Scalia's argument and appeared to disagree strongly with it. In broad, sweeping language affirming the rights of all Americans under the Fourteenth Amendment's fundamental right to privacy and its venerable equal protection guarantee, the Court agreed with Attorney Smith that "when homosexual conduct is made criminal by the law of the State, that declaration in and of itself is an invitation to subject homosexual persons to discrimination both in the public and in the private spheres."[40]

The privacy right on which Justice Kennedy relied in the majority opinion is located at the intersection of the Due Process Clause (liberty interest) and the Equal Protection Clause (equality interest). Kennedy focused primarily on the liberty interest but also emphasized the relevance of the equality component: "Equality of treatment and the due process right to demand respect for conduct protected by the substantive guarantee of liberty are linked in important respects, and a decision on the latter point advances both interests."[41]

Building on privacy-related precedents in this area that date back to decisions on marriage, procreation, contraception, and abortion, the Court concluded that the government has no place interfering with the private consensual conduct of adults in the privacy of their own homes. "Petitioners," Justice Kennedy wrote, "are entitled to respect for their private lives. The State cannot demean their existence or control their destiny by making their private conduct a crime."

The Court addressed the morality question head-on. Kennedy stated directly that many people still have "profound and deep convictions" based on interpretations of certain "moral principles" that lead them to disapprove in some way of "homosexual conduct." But, Kennedy explained, "the issue is whether the majority may use the power of the State to enforce these views on the whole society through operation of the criminal law. Our obligation is to define the liberty of all, not to mandate our own moral code." Justice O'Connor, concurring in the decision, added even stronger language in this context. "Moral disapproval of this group," she wrote, "is . . . insufficient. . . . We have never held that moral disapproval, *without any other asserted state interest,* is a sufficient rationale to justify a law that discriminates among groups of persons."

Lawrence v. Texas included language reminiscent of an analogous discussion of stigma in *Brown v. Board of Education.* It noted the many ways that U.S. law has stigmatized gays and lesbians and concluded in no uncertain terms that this can no longer be the case. It also addressed the dignity of individuals within the context of equal treatment and "equal worth." The Court explained that when homosexual conduct is criminalized, it "demeans the lives of homosexual persons. . . . The stigma this statute imposes, moreover, is not trivial. . . . It remains a criminal offense with all that it imports for the dignity of the persons charged."[42]

In the years following *Lawrence,* commentators and jurists wrestled extensively with questions regarding its applicability to a variety of prospective fact patterns. Interpretations ranged from the narrow view that the decision stood for nothing more than a determination that anti-sodomy laws of this type are unconstitutional to the expansive view that *Lawrence* represented a sweeping recognition of equal rights and privacy guarantees for all LGBT persons in every possible context.[43]

Read together with the growing number of victories in courts across the country, however, and especially in the aftermath of *Obergefell v. Hodges,* which legalized marriage equality in every state,[44] the decision clearly bolstered the position of gay and lesbian persons. *Lawrence* was the second U.S. Supreme Court decision within an eight-year period to rule unequivocally on behalf of gay plaintiffs under the Fourteenth Amendment, and in so doing, it also expressly overruled a 1986 U.S. Supreme Court decision that had gone the other way.[45] The sweeping and deferential language of both Justice Kennedy's majority opinion and Justice O'Connor's concurrence regarding the importance of honoring the "dignity" of gay persons and "respect[ing]" their private lives explicitly situated LGBTs in a very different place within U.S. constitutional jurisprudence than they had occupied before. The words truly hark back to Ronald Dworkin's statement that "the fundamental moral principle embodied by the Equal Protection Clause is the equal intrinsic worth of all humans."[46]

The Religious Dimension of the Right to Be Out

The First Amendment to the U.S. Constitution also addresses religion, and it can be argued that the so-called Religion Clauses add yet another dimension to the foundational intersection of the First and Fourteenth Amendments and may further strengthen LGBT rights in this context. Such an argument is not typically put forth, but the territory is shifting, and there is an increasing focus within both the legal and the educational policy communities on the efficacy of employing religious freedom guarantees on behalf of LGBT persons rather than against them.

Many contend that the religion provisions are generally irrelevant in this context, asserting both that LGBT issues in an education setting have little or nothing to do with religion and that the separation of church and state requires us to keep anything related to religion out of the public sector. Yet while the aforementioned research of Karen Franklin and C. J. Pascoe demonstrates that motivations for anti-LGBT aggression are typically secular in nature, Franklin also found that some of the assaults documented in her study were linked to "enforcement of gender norms" and that assailants in this category viewed themselves as ideologically based "social norm enforcers who are punishing moral transgression." In addition, the literature in this area reveals that the separation between church and state was never intended to be absolute and that there is an ongoing dispute over boundaries.

A second perspective, perhaps even more common, is that religion is definitely relevant in this context but is necessarily the antithesis of LGBT. As the argument goes, morality is appropriately defined by religious doctrine and should be employed to justify opposition to equal treatment for gay and gender-expansive persons.[47] Conservative Republican legislators, for example, invoked religious morality in debates regarding same-sex marriage, as have those throughout the nation who are pushing for stronger and more wide-ranging religious exemptions to current antidiscrimination laws. In both instances, the argument is rooted in the assertion that anything gay or transgender offends religious principles and negatively impacts the practices and beliefs of organized religion.[48] Yet while it often appears that the entire area comes down to the proposition that one is either with the gays or with the religious and never the twain shall meet, and while this may be true for some in this country, it may not be true for most at this time.[49]

A third position, which arguably exemplifies a reasonable middle ground between those who argue that religion has nothing to do with LGBT issues and those who argue that it has everything to do with LGBT issues but only to the extent that it can be used to support anti-gay positions, is that religion is not only relevant here but can provide additional support for gay and transgender rights because its principles apply equally to everyone and protect everyone.[50]

No area addressed in this book is more volatile than the topic of religion and homosexuality. The issues can be exceedingly personal, and emotions can run high no matter what position a person takes on the range of debatable points. Many put their religious beliefs front and center, fighting strongly for a particular point of view. Many others keep their beliefs to themselves, even as they take positions that are no less committed.

Yet there are significant differences between and among the various faiths and denominations with regard to these issues. While some are actively and officially opposed to anything gay or lesbian, others are actively and officially welcoming and even ordain openly LGBT persons as members of their clergy. Still others may be engaged in the ongoing process of sorting out all these issues.

In fact, many LGBTs are themselves affiliated with organized religion, and this affiliation can range from the most liberal branches to the most conservative. A substantial number of other gay and gender-expansive persons may not be affiliated directly but may be actively involved in the pursuit of spirituality.[51] Extensive dialogue, especially within the various subgroups of organized religion, has led many to conclude that this area is highly nuanced and that it merits careful and multifaceted exploration over time. It has also led to the growing realization that a reasonable middle ground may be reachable for many, if not most, Americans on these matters.[52]

Assuming both the validity and the desirability of such a middle-ground position, a principled reading of current First Amendment jurisprudence reveals that in the K–12 public schools, the religious freedom guarantees can be employed on behalf of LGBTs in a variety of ways. First, these provisions add strength to the argument that public officials may no longer justify the marginalization of gay and transgender persons by invoking religious doctrine in a way that would impose a particular religious view on others. Similarly, they reinforce the contention that those officials who act pursuant to interpretations of scripture that are unfavorable to LGBTs may be found to be discriminating on the basis of religion against those who have adopted a more favorable interpretation. In addition, these guarantees may even be employed to bolster arguments that, to the extent that LGBTs see their identity as intertwined with religion, their right to be out regarding the nature and extent of this identity is explicitly strengthened.

The Contours of the Religion Clauses

The First Amendment begins with the Religion Clauses, which state, "Congress shall make no law respecting an establishment of religion [the Establishment Clause] or prohibiting the free exercise thereof [the Free Exercise Clause]." These guarantees have been deemed applicable throughout the public sector, and they directly impact the types of policy decisions education officials can make at public schools, colleges, and universities.[53] In fact, a very large percentage of all the establishment clause cases decided by the U.S. Supreme Court over the past fifty years have been education-related. Especially under the Establishment Clause, several important limitations regarding the actions of public officials have evolved. The broad, general framework for all establishment clause disputes continues to reflect a foundational inquiry into whether the *purpose* of a policy or practice is secular and whether its principal or primary *effect* either advances or inhibits religion. In recent decades, however, additional inquiries have emerged, focusing on endorsement, coercion, or neutrality alone.[54]

Establishment clause jurisprudence remains relatively unsettled, with lower courts, unsure of which frameworks and principles to apply, sometimes taking the time to conduct as many as three or four separate analytical inquiries in a single opinion. In light of these realities, decision makers in public education settings would be wise to follow the guidelines for each inquiry. Policies or practices should have a secular purpose, should neither advance nor inhibit religion, should not endorse or disapprove of religion, should not coerce anyone to support or participate in religion or its exercise, and should be neutral toward religion.[55]

A built-in tension can be discerned between the two religion clauses, with the Establishment Clause often appearing to require a more secular approach and the Free Exercise Clause often appearing to require a more religious approach. Although there is much subtlety to these clauses and what they ultimately mandate, it is clear that they are there for all of us, no matter what our religious beliefs, sexual orientation, or gender identity might be.

A basic principle that appears often in the religion clause cases over time is that the nature and extent of the religion that can be included by public officials in public sector activities is not dependent on what percentage of people may be members of a particular religion, practitioners of a particular sect or denomination, or affiliated with organized religion at all. Justice O'Connor described this principle in her analysis of the 2005 Kentucky Ten Commandments case:

> Together with the other First Amendment guarantees . . . the Religion Clauses . . . embody an idea that was once considered radical: Free people are entitled to free and diverse thoughts, which government ought neither to constrain nor to direct. . . . Reasonable minds can disagree about how to apply the Religion Clauses in a given case. But the goal of the Clauses is clear: to carry out the Founders' plan of preserving religious liberty to the fullest extent possible in a pluralistic society. By enforcing the Clauses, we have kept religion a matter for the individual conscience, not for the prosecutor or bureaucrat. . . .
>
> It is true that many Americans find the [Ten] Commandments in accord with their personal beliefs. But we do not count heads before enforcing the First Amendment. . . . Nor can we accept the theory that Americans who do not accept the Commandments' validity are outside the First Amendment's protections. There is no list of approved and disapproved beliefs appended to the First Amendment—and the Amendment's broad terms ("free exercise," "establishment," "religion") do not admit of such a

cramped reading. . . . The Religion Clauses, as a result, protect adherents of all religions, as well as those who believe in no religion at all.[56]

At a minimum, school officials seeking to justify disparate treatment of LGBT persons on religious grounds risk violating the Establishment Clause. This is a paradigmatic scenario that is evident in numerous disputes addressed in this and later chapters. But additional features of the First Amendment impact this area as well, reflected in the points of intersection that can be identified between the respective clauses of the First and Fourteenth Amendments.

Locating the Religion Clauses at the Intersection of the First and Fourteenth Amendments

As Justice O'Connor explained, the Religion Clauses and the Free Speech Clause were designed to work together. It follows that the doctrinal intersection of the free speech guarantee and the antidiscrimination protections discussed throughout this chapter has an added dimension that is reflected in the mandates of the Religion Clauses. Indeed, a multifaceted interrelationship between and among these provisions can be found both in court decisions and in the scholarly literature. Parties setting forth arguments under one clause find that these arguments can sometimes be strengthened by related arguments under another.[57]

POINTS OF INTERSECTION BETWEEN
FREEDOM OF EXPRESSION AND THE RELIGION CLAUSES

The Free Speech Clause and the Religion Clauses often strengthen each other in this manner. Among other things, the Establishment Clause protects the freedom of religious expression by prohibiting public officials from establishing policies that inhibit those who wish to follow nontraditional interpretations of the scriptures, affiliate with a minority religion, or abstain from religion altogether. And the Free Exercise Clause strengthens the ability of persons to express such choices and engage in such practices.[58]

Commentators and jurists have also identified a natural intersection between freedom of expression and the free exercise of religion, with religious practice often being viewed as a type of expression. Thus, for example, to the extent that LGBTs come to view their sexual identities as intertwined with their spirituality, they would have the right to be open about the dimensions of this identity under both the Free Speech Clause and the Religion Clauses. This would conceivably be the case even if the religious practice at issue were to include a celebration of LGBT identities and relationships in the same manner that so many religious institutions celebrate heterosexual identities and relationships.

Many gays and lesbians commit to religious practice consistent with the interpretation of certain branches and denominations of organized religion. Such practice may include affiliation with a Unitarian Universalist church, for example, or an Episcopalian or Presbyterian church welcoming to gay and lesbian persons. Alternatively, it may include membership in an LGBT synagogue that operates within and has the blessings of Judaism's Reform movement. Many other LGBTs follow a less traditional path, identifying as spiritual and participating in creative events and activities that also celebrate their identities. Such participation may include affiliation with the Metropolitan Community Church, which provides options for those who seek to enhance their spirituality while building and maintaining a gay-positive identity. Under any of these scenarios, the First Amendment Clauses can work together to provide a heightened protection for those who wish to practice their religion openly in this manner.

POINTS OF INTERSECTION BETWEEN
EQUAL PROTECTION AND THE RELIGION CLAUSES

In addition to the interface between the freedoms of expression and religion, there are also clear intersections between the equality guarantee and religion in this context. Both establishment clause lawsuits and free exercise clause lawsuits have been bolstered by invoking equal protection arguments.[59] In the 1994 *Kiryas Joel* case, for example, the U.S. Supreme Court relied expressly on an "equal treatment" analysis to determine whether the Establishment Clause had been violated when the state adopted legislation to carve out a separate district for a religious enclave. Both Justice O'Connor and Justice Kennedy reinforced Justice Souter's majority opinion by emphasizing in their own separate opinions the relevance of equal protection principles. O'Connor went so far as to declare that "the Religion Clauses . . . and the Equal Protection Clause as applied to religion—all speak with one voice on this point." And Kennedy stated that "in this respect, the Establishment Clause mirrors the Equal Protection Clause."[60]

Numerous other education-related Supreme Court decisions stand for the proposition that public officials may not discriminate against either those who practice religion in a particular way or those who choose not to practice religion at all. In *Pierce v. Society of Sisters* (1925), for example, the Court recognized the right of parents under the Fourteenth Amendment to send their children to private religious schools. In *West Virginia v. Barnette* (1943), the Court determined under the First Amendment that the Jehovah's Witnesses would not be required to pledge allegiance to the flag in the public schools. And in *Wisconsin v. Yoder* (1971), the Court ruled that under the Free Exercise Clause, the state could not force Amish students to remain in school beyond the age of fourteen.[61]

Consistent with these principles, not only do LGBTs have a right to be open regarding the extent to which their sexual identities may be intertwined with religion but they cannot be discriminated against or treated differently as a result of this openness. No one in the public sector can dictate how or in what form the entire universe of persons in our pluralistic society choose to affiliate with religion or seek to pursue their own level of spirituality in reference to religion. Neither can a public official dictate how or in what form a person chooses to abstain from organized religion. Such restrictions are likely to be found unconstitutional.

Support continues to grow both under the law and as a matter of policy for the applicability of the Religion Clauses to enhance the position of persons, such as LGBTs, who seek to lead their lives in a way that may run counter to majoritarian practices of religious organizations. The legal terrain is unsettled, the theoretical frameworks can be controversial, and the applicability of such an analysis will continue to be contested in the courts. But to the extent that this reasonable middle-ground position gains recognition, it can further strengthen the rights of LGBT students and educators.

Under certain circumstances, and particularly in an education setting, the Religion Clauses of the First Amendment provide surprisingly powerful additional support for the right to be out. Indeed, when viewed together as part of a larger pattern, the entire range of constitutional provisions, statutory frameworks, and case decisions documented in this chapter reflects Kenneth Karst's conclusion that the right to assert a gay identity appropriately encompasses the core interests of freedom and equality that are guaranteed to all Americans.

2

MARRIAGE EQUALITY AND ITS AFTERMATH

Although much has happened on the LGBT front since the publication of the first edition of this book in 2010, no single set of developments has had such a direct impact on relevant law and public policy as the activity in the courtroom, the voting booth, and state legislatures that ultimately resulted in the legalization of same-sex marriage in all fifty states in 2015. By the time this second edition went to press, the U.S. had joined twenty-seven other countries in adopting "marriage equality" as the law of the land.[1]

In chronological order, these countries now include the Netherlands (first to legalize marriage equality, in 2000), Belgium (2003), Canada and Spain (2005), South Africa (2006), Norway and Sweden (2009), Argentina, Iceland, and Portugal (2010), Denmark (2012), Brazil, France, New Zealand, and Uruguay (2013), the United Kingdom, Finland, and Luxembourg (2014), Ireland, Mexico,[2] and the United States (2015), Colombia and Greenland (2016), and Taiwan,[3] Germany, Austria, Malta, and Australia (2017). Every continent is represented now, with particularly expansive representation in the western hemisphere, from northernmost Canada to southernmost Argentina. At the same time, a good number of other countries provide some form of civil union for their gay and lesbian residents, and several of these countries will recognize same-sex marriages that had been performed in countries where such marriages are legal.[4]

It should be noted, however, that efforts to legalize same-sex relationships nationwide would not have reached the point we are at today had it not been for the confluence of pre-2015 developments that reflected a culmination of triumphs for LGBT equality at every level of our legal system. These developments include, but are not limited to, *Romer v. Evans* (the first Equal Protection Clause victory by LGBT plaintiffs in the U.S. Supreme Court; 1996),[5] the long list of favorable outcomes for K–12 LGBT students in discrimination lawsuits against their school districts (beginning with the *Nabozny* case in 1996),[6] the aforementioned *Lawrence v. Texas* (2003),[7] the Matthew Shepard and James Byrd, Jr., Hate Crimes Prevention Act (2009),[8] the legalization of marriage equality by the New York State legislature (2011), the repeal of "Don't Ask, Don't Tell" (2011),[9] the invalidation of California Proposition 8 in the federal courts pursuant to the *Perry* case (2013),[10] and the invalidation of key portions of the federal Defense of Marriage Act in *U.S. v. Windsor* (2013).[11]

In addition, marriage equality in the United States would certainly not have happened had it not been for the emergence and strengthening of the right to be out over time. With population estimates in the United States revealing that more LGBTs than ever were coming out, and with more and more people thus discovering that a substantial percentage of the Americans with whom they interacted on a regular basis were gay and/or transgender, a growing number of these LGBTs and their allies were willing to openly and actively support legal developments that not only enhanced the right to be out but also pointed in the direction of marriage equality. Moreover, the equal protection component of the right has been further strengthened by the U.S. Supreme Court's 2015 decision to legalize marriage equality in *Obergefell v. Hodges*,[12] which constitutes a major tipping point for even more progress in the area of LGBT law.

The Changing Nature of Sexual Orientation Law in the Aftermath of *Obergefell* (2015): An Emerging Trend toward Heightened Judicial Review

Obergefell v. Hodges addressed the claim of petitioner James Obergefell, who had fallen in love and had established a lasting, committed relationship in Ohio with John Arthur over a twenty-year period. In 2011, however, Arthur was diagnosed with a debilitating disease for which there was no known cure. In 2013, the couple decided to commit to one another, resolving to marry before Arthur passed away. They did so, exchanging vows in a medical transport plane on the tarmac in Baltimore, Maryland, where same-sex marriage had been legalized. However, back in Ohio, after Arthur's death, when Obergefell sought to be listed as the surviving spouse, he was prevented from doing so under Ohio law, given that same-sex marriage was not legal in that state. He then brought suit to be shown as the surviving spouse on Arthur's death certificate.

Obergefell's Ohio lawsuit was consolidated with other pending cases from Michigan, Kentucky, and Tennessee, all states that defined marriage as the union of a man and a woman. Each of the plaintiffs sought to have "their marriages deemed lawful on the same terms and conditions as marriages between persons of the opposite sex." By a vote of 5–4, per Justice Anthony Kennedy, the U.S. Supreme Court found that the plaintiffs' Fourteenth Amendment rights under the due process and equal protection clauses had been violated and, in so doing, legalized same-sex marriage in all fifty states.[13]

Over the past twenty years, and culminating in the *Obergefell* decision, it is possible to discern substantial changes in the application of federal and state equal protection law with regard to LGBT equality. In particular, one of the most important trends in this context is the growing recognition of a heightened level of judicial review under the Equal Protection Clause and the further strengthening of the right to be out that has accompanied this trend.

Federal equal protection law, mirrored by the equal protection jurisprudence in many states, is characterized by different levels of judicial review. On one end of the spectrum is strict scrutiny, which requires the defendant in a racial discrimination case to demonstrate that the policy or practice at issue is narrowly tailored to further a compelling governmental interest. On the other end of the spectrum is rational basis, which is the default level of review for most other equal protection lawsuits and requires only a showing of a rational basis to justify a policy or practice.[14] Plaintiffs stand a very good chance of winning if they can get a court to apply strict scrutiny, while defendants stand a very good chance of winning if a court applies the highly deferential rational basis review.

Courts have also recognized an intermediate (or "heightened") level of review, sometimes known as heightened scrutiny.[15] This level of judicial review can be more complex, with some cases reflecting an analysis at a precise point on the spectrum, perhaps halfway between strict scrutiny and rational basis. Other cases may reflect an analysis that contemplates a sliding scale, with the level of review sometimes much closer to strict scrutiny and other times landing much closer to rational basis, depending on the type of discrimination at issue. For example, an intermediate level of review is typically applied in gender discrimination cases, but the analysis by federal courts in recent decades has required defendants in such cases to demonstrate an "exceedingly persuasive justification" for their action (a review that appears to be much closer to strict scrutiny).[16] On the other hand, in the landmark undocumented student case of *Plyler v. Doe,* where the Court appeared to be applying an intermediate level of review to find that the Texas statute barring undocumented students from attending public schools violated the Fourteenth Amendment, defendants were required to demonstrate that the statute "further[ed] some substantial goal of the State" (a review that appeared to be somewhere in the middle of the judicial review spectrum or perhaps closer to rational basis).[17]

In the aforementioned LGBT rights case of *Romer v. Evans,* the plaintiffs prevailed under rational basis review. But subsequent cases suggest that the courts are beginning to apply a more heightened level of review on behalf of LGBT litigants, sometimes without saying so explicitly.

In the Fourteenth Amendment case of *Lawrence v. Texas,* for example, although Justice Kennedy's majority opinion focused primarily on the right to privacy under the Due Process Clause, Justice O'Connor's concurrence addressed the applicability of the Equal Protection Clause. In so doing, she built on Kennedy's assertion that "equality of treatment and the due process . . . substantive guarantee of liberty are linked in important respects, and a decision on the latter point advances both interests."[18] O'Connor then asserted that "laws such as economic or tax legislation that are scrutinized under rational basis review normally pass constitutional muster. . . . We have consistently held, however, that some objectives, such as 'a bare . . . desire to harm a politically unpopular group,' are not legitimate state interests [citing *Romer v. Evans,* among other cases]." She then stated that "when a law exhibits such a desire to harm a politically unpopular group, we have applied a more searching form of rational basis review to strike down such laws under the Equal Protection Clause."[19] This language has led both commentators and jurists to conclude that an application of the *Lawrence* decision to future equal protection cases impacting LGBTs would require a heightened form of rational basis, as opposed to the traditional deferential rational basis.[20]

In *Perry v. Schwarzenegger,*[21] the federal lawsuit challenging the constitutionality of California Proposition 8, Chief Judge Vaughn R. Walker held that the marriage equality ban violated the Fourteenth Amendment. In so doing, he determined that Proposition 8 *cannot withstand any level of scrutiny* under the Equal Protection Clause:

> The Equal Protection Clause renders Proposition 8 unconstitutional under any standard of review. Accordingly, the court need not address the question whether laws classifying on the basis of sexual orientation should be subject to a heightened standard of review.
>
> Although Proposition 8 fails to possess even a rational basis, the evidence presented at trial shows that gays and lesbians are the type of minority strict scrutiny was designed to protect. . . .
>
> Proposition 8 cannot withstand any level of scrutiny under the Equal Protection Clause, as excluding same-sex couples from marriage is simply not rationally related to a legitimate state interest.[22]

Three years later, after the U.S. Supreme Court ruled that plaintiffs did not have standing to appeal Judge Walker's ruling, the Ninth Circuit, per Judge Stephen Reinhardt, dismissed the appeal for lack of jurisdiction.[23] Pursuant to these developments, same-sex marriage began again in California, and the original opinion by Judge Walker—with its powerful language asserting that Proposition 8 could not survive any level of judicial scrutiny under the Fourteenth Amendment—effectively became the final statement of the decision in the case.[24]

At the state court level, operating on a parallel track, the California Supreme Court in May 2008 had become the first state court in the land to explicitly recognize strict scrutiny for discrimination against gays and lesbians.[25] A year later, while upholding the constitutionality of Proposition 8 under California state law, Chief Justice Ronald George reaffirmed that in California, "statutes according differential treatment on the basis of sexual orientation are subject to the strict scrutiny standard of review. . . . With respect to the . . . designation of the word 'marriage,' Proposition 8 does change the rule, [but it] . . . must be understood as creating a limited exception . . . [that] does not alter the general equal protection principles. . . . Those principles continue to apply in all other contexts."[26] These contexts would certainly include the K–12 public schools.

Other state courts have since moved in a similar direction. In *Kerrigan v. Comm'r of Pub. Health,* for example, the Connecticut Supreme Court held that discrimination on the basis of sexual orientation warranted a heightened level of judicial review.[27] The Iowa Supreme Court, in 2009, ruled accordingly.[28]

Moreover, although the Court in *Obergefell v. Hodges* did not explicitly address the standard of review it employed when deciding that the fundamental right to marry applied to same-sex couples with "equal force," it can be argued that Justice Kennedy's Fourteenth Amendment analysis, accompanied by language regarding the importance of treating gays and lesbians with "equal dignity," was tantamount to a heightened level of judicial review.[29] In the most central portion of his majority opinion, Justice Kennedy began by referencing how changing times can lead to a different conclusion regarding an exclusion that demeans or stigmatizes:

> The limitation of marriage to opposite-sex couples may long have seemed natural and just, but its inconsistency with the central meaning of the fundamental right to marry is now manifest. With that knowledge must come the recognition that laws excluding same-sex couples from the marriage right impose stigma and injury of the kind prohibited by our basic charter. . . . Many who deem same-sex marriage to be wrong reach that conclusion based on decent and honorable religious or philosophical premises, and neither they nor their beliefs are disparaged here. But when that sincere, personal opposition becomes enacted law and public policy, the necessary consequence is to put the imprimatur of the State itself on an exclusion that soon demeans or stigmatizes those whose own liberty is then denied. Under the Constitution, same-sex couples seek in marriage the same legal treatment as opposite-sex couples, and it would disparage their choices and diminish their personhood to deny them this right.

He then turned directly to the impact and relevance of the Equal Protection Clause and its relationship to the Due Process Clause:

> The right of same-sex couples to marry that is part of the liberty promised by the Fourteenth Amendment is derived, too, from that Amendment's guarantee of the equal protection of the laws. The Due Process Clause and the Equal Protection Clause are connected in a profound way. . . . Each concept—liberty and equal protection—leads to a stronger understanding of the other.[30]

Indeed, in interpreting the Equal Protection Clause, the Court has recognized that new insights and societal understandings can reveal unjustified inequality within our most fundamental institutions that once passed unnoticed and unchallenged. . . . [Our] precedents show the Equal Protection Clause can help to identify and correct inequalities in the institution of marriage, vindicating precepts of liberty and equality under the Constitution.

Finally, he closed by building directly on the *Lawrence* case:

In *Lawrence* the Court acknowledged the interlocking nature of these constitutional safeguards in the context of the legal treatment of gays and lesbians. Although *Lawrence* elaborated its holding under the Due Process Clause, it acknowledged, and sought to remedy, the continuing inequality that resulted from laws making intimacy in the lives of gays and lesbians a crime against the State. *Lawrence* therefore drew upon principles of liberty and equality to define and protect the rights of gays and lesbians, holding the State "cannot demean their existence or control their destiny by making their private sexual conduct a crime."

This dynamic also applies to same-sex marriage. It is now clear that the challenged laws burden the liberty of same-sex couples, and it must be further acknowledged that they abridge central precepts of equality. Here the marriage laws enforced by the respondents are in essence unequal: same-sex couples are denied all the benefits afforded to opposite-sex couples and are barred from exercising a fundamental right. Especially against a long history of disapproval of their relationships, this denial to same-sex couples of the right to marry works a grave and continuing harm. The imposition of this disability on gays and lesbians serves to disrespect and subordinate them. And the Equal Protection Clause, like the Due Process Clause, prohibits this unjustified infringement of the fundamental right to marry.[31]

All told, Justice Kennedy's opinion was filled with broad language affirming the rights of LGBTs under the equal protection clause guarantee: the mandate of "equal dignity," the recognition that "laws excluding same-sex couples from the marriage right impose stigma and injury of the kind prohibited by our basic charter," and the conclusion that "new insights and societal understandings can reveal *unjustified inequality* within our most fundamental institutions." In addition, the Court referenced *Lawrence v. Texas* very prominently, applying the principles of equal protection that had been set forth in that case both by the Court's majority opinion and by Justice O'Connor in her concurrence. Justice Kennedy may not have actually mentioned "heightened scrutiny" in his analysis, but the thrust of his conclusion mirrored the result that such scrutiny would attain. The prospects for the further protection of LGBT rights down the road under a heightened judicial review were arguably exemplified by the language of *Obergefell v. Hodges*.[32]

A New Day, and the Challenges That Lie Ahead

With the victory in the *Obergefell* case in June 2015, a major turning point had indeed been reached. But at the same time, the unprecedented speed with which the marriage equality movement had prevailed and the accompanying changes under the law that had occurred not only resulted in a level of uncertainty and indeed discomfort in many K–12 school settings but sometimes led to a dangerous backlash and increased challenges on a day-to-day level for LGBT youth, LGBT parents, LGBT educators, and LGBT people of color generally. As Richard Socarides, former advisor to President Bill Clinton on gay and lesbian issues, wrote in early 2015,

> it's not unreasonable to expect that the Supreme Court will make same-sex marriage legal in all fifty states. The question, for longtime marriage-equality activists, is what exactly will this achieve, and what will happen next? Will nationwide marriage equality lead in time to full nationwide acceptance, or will they discover, like many civil-rights activists before them, that there is a big gap between legal rights and true equality? This is a big moment for the gay-rights movement, and an important one in which to remember that there is likely more struggle ahead.[33]

In light of these thoughts, this section of the chapter documents the parameters of the backlash that has ensued and the "religious liberty" debates that have accompanied this unsettled time. It concludes with an overview of the positive developments that continue to occur and the reasons for optimism going forward.

The Parameters of the Marriage Equality Backlash

Although the precise moment when the backlash to the marriage equality movement began is the subject of some debate, a reasonable conclusion is that it began soon after the movement gathered force and gained momentum as marriage equality continued to spread and continued to be accepted. For purposes of this analysis, then, a logical starting point for the backlash would be 2010–11.

By the end of 2010, ten entire countries (including Canada and Argentina) plus Mexico City had legalized same-sex marriage, and by mid-2011, New York had joined five other states plus the District of Columbia in doing the same.[34] Most notably, in 2011, the Pew Research Center's longitudinal poll documenting public opinion on same-sex marriage showed more Americans favoring it than opposing it for the first time, with the number favoring it continuing to rise and the number opposing it continuing to drop in the years that followed.[35]

The parameters of the marriage equality backlash have ranged from increased bullying and "gay bashing" followed by increased LGBT homelessness to the "religious liberty" movement and the politics of fear. Contextually, looking back at what transpired between 2010 and 2016, commentator Peter Montgomery in *The American Prospect* characterized this backlash as "the latest manifestation of a longer-term struggle that well predates the high court's landmark [*Obergefell*] ruling." "For decades," he wrote, "social conservatives have resisted every step toward cultural visibility and legal equality for LGBT people. In a by-now familiar pattern, progress triggers resistance marked by shifting strategies and new clashes."[36]

In late 2010, a spate of suicides and attempted suicides by LGBT youth who were victimized by relentless bullying at their schools and in their neighborhoods caught the nation's attention. Commentators documented the growing problem in this area and its apparent relationship to the increased visibility of gay and transgender persons.[37] Researchers focused on studies such as the work of Karen Franklin, referenced in the introduction to this book, where she identifies four distinct motivations for anti-LGBT aggression: perceived self-defense, enforcement of gender norms/ideology, peer dynamics, and thrill seeking. According to Dr. Franklin, the largest number of assailants justified their behavior by characterizing it as self-defense. This justification, she found, "is employed by perpetrators who believe they are defending their neighborhoods or workplaces from minority encroachment." In this context, she explains, "negative stereotypes proliferate. These [stereotypes], in turn, foster both bias crimes in the wider community and most tragically a climate of pervasive harassment and violence against schoolchildren."[38]

In 2011, according to the FBI, the number of anti-gay hate crimes rose from previous years, even as the overall number of hate crimes against Americans was going down.[39] And in New York, at the same time that marriage equality was in the process of being legalized, the New York City Anti-Violence Project saw a 13 percent increase in LGBT hate crime reports; 2013 saw a continuation of this trend, with a 70 percent spike in anti-gay hate crimes reported in New York, according to the city's police commissioner, Ray Kelly.[40]

The following year, according to a Harris Poll commissioned by GLAAD, even while more Americans than ever were supporting the legal recognition of same-sex couples, about 30 percent of the respondents who did not identify themselves as LGBT said that it would unsettle them to learn that their physician or child's teacher did. In addition, close to 45 percent said that they would be uneasy about bringing a child to a same-sex wedding. Thirty-six percent felt uncomfortable when they saw a same-sex couple holding hands. Even among those respondents who formally approved of gay marriage or civil unions with full benefits, 20 percent said they would nonetheless feel uncomfortable attending a same-sex wedding.[41] And at about the same time that this poll was released (early 2015), *The Advocate* warned that "the marriage equality backlash [had] only just begun."[42]

In June 2015, the Williams Institute released a new study on LGBT homelessness. The study confirmed that homelessness continued to be one of the major problems facing gay and gender-expansive communities in K–12 education settings, and it highlighted the need to further understand the differences in experiences between "LGBTQ youth and non-LGBTQ youth experiencing homelessness, as well as between cisgender LGBQ and transgender youth."[43] Among the findings are the following data points:

- Sexual and gender minority youth are overrepresented among those experiencing homelessness, according to estimates of the percentage of LGBT youth accessing homeless services providers.
- LGBT youth accessing these services were reported to have been homeless longer than non-LGBT youth. Notably, providers were more likely to report that transgender youth experienced these disparities.
- LGBT youth accessing these services were reported to be in worse mental and physical health than non-LGBT youth. In particular, providers were more likely to report that transgender youth have worse mental and physical health than other youth.

- Most notably, providers indicated that the most prevalent reason for homelessness among LGBT youth was being forced out of home or running away from home because of their sexual orientation or gender identity/expression.[44]

It is important in this context to note the inevitable connection between homelessness and school dropout and between dropout and incarceration. Indeed, in July 2015, new data were released that demonstrated how the juvenile justice system was failing LGBT youth. In an article titled "Why Are There So Many LGBT Youth in Prison?," the author cites several interrelated studies. According to one study, LGBT and gender non-conforming youth make up 5–7 percent of young people in this country, but they are 15 percent of the young people in the juvenile justice system. Moreover, low-income and LGBT youth of color are particularly affected: 60 percent of the LGBT youth arrested or detained each year are Black or Latino. "Factors ranging from family rejection to school discipline to homelessness—each exacerbating the other—increase [these young people's risk] of being funneled into the juvenile justice system."[45]

In August 2015, further evidence was disseminated regarding anti-LGBT violence, particularly as it affected transgender persons. According to the *New York Times,* the brutal death of a thirty-six-year-old transgender woman in Kansas City, Missouri, was "the latest in what activists [were] calling an alarming rise in anti-transgender violence. Tamara Dominguez was hit by a vehicle . . . and run over several times, making her the 17th transgender person reported killed [that] year, according to data compiled by the National Coalition of Anti-Violence Programs."[46] In the same month, on the international front, horrific killings by the Islamic State (ISIS) of gay men suspected of having engaged in homosexual relations were documented by the International Gay and Lesbian Human Rights Commission.[47]

In early 2016, *The New Yorker* reported that since January of that year, "according to the A.C.L.U., . . . almost a hundred bills [were] introduced in state legislatures to chip away at [the previous] year's marriage-equality ruling. [And] the Human Rights Campaign [said] that forty-four anti-transgender bills [were] introduced in sixteen states over a similar period."[48]

Increasingly, in late 2015 and early 2016, additional respected sources were confirming the existence of a virulent marriage equality backlash. In December 2015, Kate Kendell, the executive director of the

National Center for Lesbian Rights, told *Time,* "We are just seeing the beginning on the backlash [against LGBT rights]. It will get worse before it gets better."[49] In February 2016, the *Washington Post* confirmed that "there's a political backlash after the Supreme Court's gay marriage ruling."[50] And a few months later, in May 2016, a *USA Today* headline for a lead story stated, "Gay Marriage Victory at Supreme Court Triggering Backlash."[51]

In the meantime, the country was involved in a volatile presidential campaign, and it appeared for a time that every candidate for the Republican nomination was trying to outdo the others by campaigning against "political correctness," a term that still was, for many people, just another expression that meant being courteous, civil, and empathetic toward one another. As Kareem Abdul-Jabbar explained in early 2016, "our country was founded on principles of inclusion, which means acting compassionately toward the many different people who make up our nation. . . . Our country needs more sensitivity, not less."[52]

By contrast, Abdul-Jabbar documented what the Republican candidates were saying about the term.[53] And he went on to analyze how the anti–political correctness "movement" reflected the times we live in, even as this movement's practices damage our sense of community and can lead to appalling results:

> The apocalyptic backlash against a benign combination of good old-fashioned manners and simple sensitivity toward others is easy to understand: Many Americans feel growing rage, fear and frustration as the country continues to evolve into something different than what they are used to. Plus, new technology accelerates cultural change, and the erosion of familiar and comforting traditions leaves us uncertain and uncomfortable. . . .
>
> Here's the problem with these attacks, though: Every political and social policy or tradition has examples of excess. We don't define the value of a policy based on its most extreme manifestations. . . . A fairer critique would ask whether political correctness had solved the problem it was devised to address: Has it scrubbed away American prejudices? Certainly not yet, and of course it's impossible to tell whether political correctness is even helping to diminish these, given how many other factors can influence behavior. But the task is worthy and vast: to erase centuries of bias in our country's collective unconscious—and one way to do that is with language. For the same reason we no longer use terms that came to seem

pejorative . . . , we should eschew phrases tinged with hate . . . from our vocabulary.[54]

However, in a devastating example of the worst possible hatred our country has seen, on June 13, 2016, almost a year after *Obergefell*, forty-nine mostly Latino people were victims of "the worst instance of anti-gay violence in American history" when Omar Mateen entered the popular gay nightclub Pulse in Orlando, Florida, at about 2:00 A.M., killed forty-nine people, and wounded at least another fifty-three before being shot and killed by the city's police.[55] Although Mateen had apparently pledged allegiance to ISIS by calling 911 during the attack, it was clear from facts that emerged after this horrific event that this was also an anti-gay event. Mateen's father, for example, told NBC that his son had recently become very angry when he saw two men in Miami "showing each other affection":

> "We were in downtown Miami, Bayside, people were playing music. And he saw two men kissing each other in front of his wife and kid and he got very angry," [the father] told NBC. "They were kissing each other and touching each other and he said, 'Look at that. In front of my son they are doing that.'"[56]

Despite the horrific events at Orlando, there was a sense that a turning point had been reached in summer 2016 and that perhaps the backlash was waning. Speaking in the aftermath of Orlando, Donald Trump, the presumptive Republican nominee, apparently agreed with Hillary Clinton, the presumptive Democratic nominee, who had said "to all the LGBT people grieving today in Florida and across our country, [y]ou have millions of allies who will always have your back. And I am one of them." Trump appeared equally supportive in the eyes of many when he declared, "This is a very dark moment in America's history[.] [Mateen] targeted the nightclub not only because he wanted to kill Americans, but in order to execute gay and lesbian citizens because of their sexual orientation." Trump went on to label the attack a "strike at the heart and soul of who we are as a nation" and an "assault" on people's ability to "love who they want and express their identity."[57]

In the weeks that followed, people hearkened back to Trump's April statement that trans woman Caitlyn Jenner could use "any bathroom she wants" in the Trump Tower[58] and noted that he had elicited what appeared to be warm support from the Republican National Convention audience in July when he spoke positively of supporting LGBT rights.[59] With both major candidates for the presidency appearing to be allies of the LGBT communities for the first time in American history, an argument could be made that the end of an era was at hand and that the marriage equality backlash would soon fade into the past.

However, numerous events that followed led commentators, policy makers, and members of the legal and educational communities to a very different conclusion. For example, in choosing Indiana governor Mike Pence as his vice presidential nominee and Alabama senator Jeff Sessions as his attorney general, President Trump had named two men to major national offices who were well known for their consistently anti-LGBT statements and actions.[60]

And in late July 2017, President Trump was responsible for three interrelated events on one day that together convinced many people that not only was this administration not a friend of the LGBT communities but that the marriage equality backlash was unfortunately alive and well. First, Trump tweeted unexpectedly that transgender soldiers would no longer be allowed to serve in the military in any capacity without explaining how or in what way this would be accomplished. Second, without being asked, the Justice Department intervened in a private employment lawsuit, "arguing that the ban on sex discrimination in the Civil Rights Act of 1964 does not protect workers on the basis of their sexual orientation." And finally, the president announced that Kansas governor Sam Brownback, "a vocal opponent of gay rights," would be nominated to serve as "the nation's ambassador at large for international religious freedom."[61]

Prominent commentator and Yale Law School professor Linda Greenhouse's analysis of the dissenting opinions in *Obergefell* are particularly relevant in reflecting back on the parameters of the marriage equality backlash that came to the forefront in the United States between 2010 and 2018. "Fomenting backlash is not a winning strategy," Greenhouse wrote. "Just as fire needs oxygen, stoking public anger against the Supreme Court can't succeed in a vacuum. Backlash needs to be fed and sustained by fear."[62]

She continued in this vein with the following observations:

Reading the opinions in the marriage case, *Obergefell v. Hodges,* I was struck by how determined the dissenters were to fan the flames of resentment. Be afraid, be very afraid, the dissenting justices warn those with religious objections to same-sex marriage. People who "cling to old beliefs" will be left having to "whisper their thoughts in the recesses of their homes," Justice Samuel A. Alito Jr. cautioned. "The majority graciously suggests that religious believers may continue to 'advocate' and 'teach' their views of marriage," Chief Justice Roberts wrote, adding: "The First Amendment guarantees, however, the freedom to 'exercise' religion. Ominously, however, that is not a word the majority uses." That is quite a word choice, "ominously."

Justice Alito's opinion, joined by Justices Antonin Scalia and Clarence Thomas, exudes a sense of anticipatory victimization. The decision "will be used to vilify Americans who are unwilling to assent to the new orthodoxy," he predicted.[63]

This analysis by Greenhouse appropriately serves as a prologue to the "religious liberty" debates that have accompanied the marriage equality backlash, debates that are addressed in more detail in the pages that follow.

The "Religious Liberty" Debates

In chapter 1 of this book, which focuses in part on the religious dimensions of the right to be out, the concept of a reasonable middle ground in this area is introduced. Moreover, the fact that the Religion Clauses are there for all Americans and belong to all Americans is set forth. Case law interpreting the Establishment Clause and the Free Exercise Clause makes it clear that these constitutional provisions do not belong to conservative religious Americans alone but that they belong to everyone equally. Yet an examination of the debates regarding "religious liberty," particularly as conceptualized by those who seek to employ the Religion Clauses to counter marriage equality, would lead many to believe that you are either with the gays or with the religious and never the twain shall meet. This book argues that although this may be true for some, it is certainly not true for all. Most notably, the book endorses a reasonable middle ground and stands for the proposition that a good faith compromise in this area is eminently attainable. Indeed, many people of goodwill are working toward such a compromise position, under the law and within the larger community on a day-to-day level.

Looking back at the developments at the early stages of the marriage equality backlash, it is evident that commentators and jurists were already wrestling with the prospective applicability of "religious liberty" under the law and that many were characterizing LGBTs and their allies as antireligion in this context. As far back as 2010, NPR was reporting a growing concern that "there may be a religious undercurrent to the harassment of teens who are seen as gay."[64] Yet those who were working to find a reasonable middle ground, more often than not, tended to be overlooked. For example, Mormon-backed legislation in Utah, which added sexual orientation and gender identity to the state's antidiscrimination laws for housing and employment, while clarifying exemptions for religious institutions and providing protections for religious expression, was hailed as a prospective model for other states wrestling with the same issues.[65] Yet although it was backed by gay rights advocates as well as the church, it received little attention outside of Utah, even as it was signed into law by the governor in March 2015. Moreover, in early June 2015, it was reported that "some evangelicals [were taking a] new look at [the] bible's stance on gays."[66] This, too, appeared to have received little attention across the country. And a month after the *Obergefell* decision was announced, Samuel G. Freedman in the *New York Times* reported that a "push within religions for gay marriage [was getting] little attention."[67]

"From the moment the Supreme Court ruled last month in favor of a constitutional right to same-sex marriage," Freedman wrote, "opponents placed the decision in a very specific analytical frame. Here, they contended, was an egregious example of secular culture triumphing over religious values and religious freedom." "Yet," he added, "the discussion of secularism versus religion is incomplete. It ignores or elides the growing number of theologians and religious scholars in a range of faiths who, over a half-century, have been assembling and espousing scriptural arguments in favor of gay rights and ultimately marriage equality. The debate about same-sex marriage that has gotten too little attention is the intrareligious one."[68]

In retrospect, it was an earlier U.S. Supreme Court decision, which had on its face virtually nothing to do with marriage equality, that helped fuel the growing backlash and the ongoing debates on "religious liberty." In *Burwell v. Hobby Lobby Stores, Inc.*, the owners of three closely held for-profit corporations[69] [who] have sincere beliefs "that it would violate their religion to facilitate access to contraceptive drugs or devices that operate after [conception]" brought separate actions against the Department of Health and Human Services (HHS) under the federal Religious Freedom Restoration Act (RFRA) and the Free Exercise Clause of the First Amendment.[70] Plaintiffs sought to put a stop to the Affordable

Care Act requirement that the companies, in providing health insurance to their employees, must facilitate access to four contraceptive methods that "may have the effect of preventing an already fertilized egg from developing any further by inhibiting its attachment to the uterus."[71] By a vote of 5–4 in 2014, per Justice Samuel Alito, the *Hobby Lobby* plaintiffs ultimately prevailed under the RFRA.[72]

Kevin Russell, an appellate attorney who teaches Supreme Court litigation at Harvard Law School, focused in on a key issue raised by Justice Ruth Bader Ginsburg in her scathing *Hobby Lobby* dissent—claims for religious exemptions from antidiscrimination laws:

> There are numerous state or federal laws that prohibit businesses from discriminating against employees (and potential employees) or their customers on various grounds, including race, sex, religion, disability, familial status, and, more recently, sexual orientation. Some business owners object to those laws on religious grounds. If the Religious Freedom Restoration Act (RFRA) requires giving Hobby Lobby a religious exemption from the contraceptive mandate of the Affordable Care Act, does it also provide other businesses with a defense against civil rights laws prohibiting discrimination?[73]

Legal scholars Douglas Nejaime and Reva Siegel questioned the efficacy of the *Hobby Lobby* decision in a widely read *Yale Law Journal* article that was published only a short time before the *Obergefell* decision was announced.[74] In so doing, they highlighted a central feature of the 2014 decision that opponents of marriage equality had embraced. "The claimants in *Hobby Lobby*," Professors Nejaime and Siegel wrote, "objected to providing their employees health insurance benefits under the ACA. They contended that providing insurance coverage would make them *complicit* with employees who might use the insurance to purchase forms of contraception that the employers viewed as sinful":

> Claims of this kind—religious objections to being made complicit in the assertedly sinful conduct of others—are often raised in response to contested sexual norms, and they now represent an important part of courts' religious liberties docket. Consider, for instance, claims arising in the same-sex marriage context. A growing number of business owners have begun to voice religious objections to providing goods and services for same-sex weddings. Baking a cake, it is claimed, makes a baker complicit

in a same-sex relationship to which he objects. [Indeed, in 2018, the U.S. Supreme Court issued a narrow ruling in favor of a plaintiff who apparently refused to bake a cake for this very reason. See *Masterpiece Cakeshop v. Colorado Civil Rights Commission*.[75]]

We term religious objections to being made complicit in the assertedly sinful conduct of others *complicity-based conscience claims*. . . . Complicity claims are faith claims about how to live in community with others who do not share the claimant's beliefs, and whose lawful conduct the person of faith believes to be sinful.[76]

The authors continue by referencing the growing number of cases seeking to build on an expansive interpretation of *Hobby Lobby*, cases that are at the heart of the "religious liberty" debates that have emerged:

The Court's decision in *Hobby Lobby* is now being cited to support accommodation of complicity-based conscience claims not merely in litigation involving insurance for contraception or claims under RFRA, but in a wide range of legal and institutional settings. In the LGBT context alone, *Hobby Lobby* has been used to bolster arguments for exemptions from state antidiscrimination laws requiring businesses to serve same-sex couples and from the federal executive order banning sexual orientation and gender identity employment discrimination by federal contractors.[77]

Professors Nejaime and Siegel then turn to the possible implications of these trends:

With growing acceptance of the contested conduct, appeals to religious liberty offer a more persuasive secular ground on which to base persisting objections to the conduct. The goal may be . . . to forestall or restrict an antidiscrimination regime that includes sexual orientation. In states with antidiscrimination laws that cover sexual orientation, religious objections to same-sex marriage have provided a basis on which to seek the expansion of already-existing exemptions in the laws. For instance, enacting an exemption that allows an institution or individual to refuse to "facilitate the perpetuation" or "treat as valid" a same-sex couple's marriage would significantly broaden existing exemptions to permit sexual orientation discrimination in situations that have nothing to do with weddings. In states without antidiscrimination laws covering sexual orientation, lawmakers have worked to restrict any future nondiscrimination obligations that may exist. While framed around marriage, the proposed legislation would allow businesses to refuse to serve same-sex couples more generally. . . . In this context, we can see how complicity-based claims for religious exemption are a part of society-wide conflict over LGBT equality.[78]

In March 2015, at about the same time that the Nejaime–Siegel article was being finalized, a measure described as "protecting religious freedom" in Indiana was signed into law by then Governor Mike Pence. Mirroring the concerns expressed in that article, advocates of equal rights for gays said the laws pose a threat of abetting discrimination, especially from business owners who object to participating in same-sex weddings. The measure was also assailed by political and business leaders because it could allow businesses to refuse service to gay couples. But Pence "defended the law as an overdue protection when 'many feel their religious liberty is under attack by government action.'"[79]

Other commentators argued in this context that the meaning of "religious freedom" was very different now than it was in 1993. For example, the *San Francisco Chronicle* reported that, pressed to defend the Indiana law, Pence "pointed out that the statute was modeled on the Religious Freedom Restoration Act of 1993, designed to protect believers of diverse faiths that was passed by a nearly unanimous Congress and signed by President Bill Clinton. But [according to interviews with prominent scholars in the area], there are at least two important differences between the federal law and its state successors: their motives, and the context":

> "A law that enables business owners to seek a faith-based exemption from civil rights laws in 2015 means something very different from a 1993 law that was focused primarily on protecting religious practices from government interference," said Suzanne Goldberg, a Columbia law professor and director of the school's Center for Gender and Sexuality Law.
>
> Neither Indiana nor any other state has described their recently enacted religious-rights laws as discriminatory, said Ira Lupu, a George Washington University law professor. "But with marriage equality roaring down on people, there's no mystery about why (these laws are) coming up," he said.[80]

By April, Governor Mike Pence and other state officials "insisted the measure was never intended to permit business owners to deny service to gays and lesbians." Over the previous weeks, "lawmakers had tweaked the law, adding language to 'clarify' that it cannot be used by businesses, landlords and others to turn away gay customers. After an outcry by major companies, sports organizations and entertainers—as well as gay activists—lawmakers in Arkansas, Georgia and North Carolina had amended similar measures or abandoned them."[81]

But supporters of the original measure apparently begged to differ with Pence. "For the socially conservative organizations that proposed the measure," the *Washington Post* reported, "protecting the right of Christians to opt out of any involvement in gay marriage ceremonies was a primary goal":

> Proponents of the religious-freedom measures do not deny that protecting business owners was one of their primary motivations. But they draw a distinction between turning away individual customers because they are gay and refusing to participate in a gay wedding—particularly for vendors whose services involve a level of creativity. . . .
>
> An Indiana pizzeria owner who was widely criticized this week for claiming a right not to serve at gay weddings made the same point in an interview on the Fox Business Network.
>
> Gays "are welcome in the store. Anyone is welcome in the store," said Crystal O'Connor, co-owner of Memories Pizza in Walkerton, Ind. "It is a sin, though, if we condone—if we cater their wedding. We feel we are participating. We're putting a stamp of approval on their wedding, and we cannot do that." . . .
>
> Daniel O. Conkle is a law professor at Indiana University who supports gay rights and same-sex marriage as well as Indiana's religious-liberties measure. During a hearing in March, Conkle testified that courts likely would not interpret the law to protect "a religious objector who refuses to serve African Americans, for example, or . . . gays or lesbians, simply because of who the people are."
>
> But "in narrow circumstances, the result conceivably could be different," he said, citing as a hypothetical example a Christian photographer. "For some religious people, this sort of participation in a same-sex wedding celebration would violate their deepest sense of religious conviction and conscience."[82]

After the *Obergefell* decision was handed down, the four dissenting justices were quick to bemoan a result that, in the words of Justice Thomas, would lead to "potentially ruinous consequences for religious liberty."[83] And Chief Justice Roberts's dissent led Seventh Circuit Judge Richard

A. Posner—a highly respected conservative jurist and scholar—to refer to the Roberts opinion as "heartless":

> The chief justice's dissent is heartless. There is of course a long history of persecution of gay people, a history punctuated by such names as Oscar Wilde, Pyotr Ilyich Tchaikovsky, and Alan Turing. Until quite recently, many American gays and lesbians took great pains to conceal their homosexuality in order to avoid discrimination. They value marriage just as straight people do. They want their adopted children to have the psychological and financial advantages of legitimacy. They are hurt by the discrimination that the dissenting justices condone.[84]

Ten months later, Mississippi governor Phil Bryant signed the Religious Objections Law (HB 1523), which commentators labeled "more sweeping than any other religious protection law we've seen before":

> It is the first law to prohibit state government from taking *any* discriminatory action against a person, religious organization, business or government employee for refusing services to LGBT people because of "sincerely held religious beliefs" or "moral conviction" against same-sex marriage, extra-marital sex and/or transgender people.
>
> Bryant and the law's supporters say the broad measure is necessary to protect people's freedom of religion in the wake of the Supreme Court ruling that legalized same-sex marriage.[85]

Later that month, the United Kingdom issued an unprecedented travel warning in which it advised LGBTs to avoid visiting Mississippi and North Carolina.[86]

A number of lawsuits were soon filed in federal court, seeking to block Mississippi's HB 1523. A decision on behalf of the plaintiffs in *Barber v. Bryant* was reversed by the Fifth Circuit Court of Appeals, and the U.S. Supreme Court declined to hear the case.[87]

By mid-2016, the *Washington Post* had reported on what it characterized as "The Dramatic Rise in State Efforts to Limit LGBT Rights":

> While the lesbian, gay, bisexual, and transgender community has become more visible and won more legal protections in recent years, state lawmakers have increased attempts to pass legislation that could restrict civil rights for LGBT people. Since 2013, legislatures have introduced 254 bills, 20 of which became law. According to data collected by the American

Civil Liberties Union and analyzed by The Washington Post, the number of bills introduced has increased steadily each year. In the first half of 2016 alone, 87 bills that could limit LGBT rights have been introduced, a steep increase from previous years. The latest wave of legislation comes at the heels of the Supreme Court decision to legalize same-sex marriage in June 2015. . . . Most of the bills are focused on protecting religious freedom.[88]

In the meantime, many people of goodwill were continuing their efforts to identify a reasonable middle ground in this regard. Noteworthy indications of such efforts could be found in recent law review articles on the topic of "religious liberty."

For example, in their 2013 *Virginia Law Review* article titled "Protecting Same-Sex Marriage and Religious Liberty," legal scholars Douglas Laycock and Thomas C. Berg contend that "the conflict between religious liberty and gay rights is bad for both sides and dangerous for the American tradition of individual liberty," and they assert that "the Court can protect the rights of both sides."[89] In the aforementioned piece by Professors Nejaime and Siegel, the authors identify "values to guide approaches to accommodation."[90] And in a more recent article published in the *Columbia Law Review,* Marie Killmond compares different types of religious exemptions, and she builds on this analysis to argue that the vaccination-exemption cases offer a road map that could help resolve the "religious liberty" debates.[91]

Reasons for Optimism Going Forward

Although evidence of a marriage equality backlash continues to appear in a variety of contexts nationwide and across the globe, and although "religious liberty" controversies continue to generate highly divisive litigation and legislation, there is continuing evidence on the LGBT front of reasons for optimism going forward. This section focuses on that evidence, and it concludes that even with all the challenges that remain, LGBTs and their growing number of allies should be highly optimistic regarding what lies ahead.

The road to acceptance of LGBTs in every corner of our country, and to complete equality under the law in every aspect of our society, has never been a smooth one. The history of the LGBT rights movements is filled with examples of events that can be characterized as two steps forward and one step back, and even, sometimes, three steps forward and four steps back. But the larger picture over the past fifty years is one of noteworthy achievement and great progress. Just as other rights movements can be viewed as highly successful in many ways but still at a point where much work is left to be done, the same can be said for the LGBT rights movements. Every chapter that follows in this book, from chapter 3 through chapter 9, reflects this pattern, highlighting the achievements even as the challenges that remain are set forth.[92]

With this larger picture as a guide, the pages that follow document examples of the progress that has continued for LGBTs even in the face of a volatile and often daunting backlash. In general, more people are coming out than ever before, and more allies than ever are willing to stand with LGBTs. There is more legal recognition of same-sex relationships, and stronger protection under federal and state equal protection case law, than ever before. There is also more recognition of the challenges that LGBTs face, and more Americans are willing to support efforts to confront these challenges.

Moreover, specific events with positive, wide-ranging implications for LGBTs over the past decade include, but are not limited to, the U.S. Supreme Court victory by UC Hastings Law School and the Hastings OUTLaw students in the *Christian Legal Society v. Martinez* case (2010); Augusta State's Eleventh Circuit victory in the counseling program dispute litigated by student Jennifer Keeton (2011); the passage of the FAIR Education Act in California, requiring the positive inclusion of LGBT content in the social studies curriculum (2012);[93] the banning of "gay conversion therapy" for minors by mental health professionals in a growing number of states (2012–18);[94] the banning of the gay and trans panic defenses in California (2014) and Illinois (2017); the Boy Scouts of America's reversal of anti-gay policies that had originally been upheld by the U.S. Supreme Court in 2000 (2015–17); the recent ongoing efforts by the NCAA to encourage and support equal educational opportunities for LGBT athletes in intercollegiate sports programs (2016–18);[95] the landmark 8–3 en banc opinion in the Seventh Circuit case of *Hively v. Ivy Tech Community College of Indiana*, which found that the Civil Rights Act prohibited anti-gay workplace discrimination (2017);[96] and the groundbreaking Seventh Circuit victory by transgender high school student Ash Whitaker under both Title IX and the Equal Protection Clause of the Fourteenth Amendment (2017).[97]

The following pages provide overviews for several of these developments. Others are discussed at greater length in subsequent chapters of this book.

CHRISTIAN LEGAL SOCIETY CHAPTER OF THE UNIVERSITY OF CALIFORNIA, HASTINGS COLLEGE OF THE LAW V. MARTINEZ (2010)

This high-profile lawsuit was filed by the Christian Legal Society (CLS), one of many student groups at Hastings Law School in San Francisco.[98] The local chapter, in existence for some time, chose to affiliate in 2004 with the national Christian Legal Society, which mandated that all chapters must adopt "bylaws that . . . *require members and officers* to sign a 'Statement of Faith' and to conduct their lives in accord with prescribed principles. Among those tenets is the belief that sexual activity should not occur outside of marriage between a man and a woman; CLS thus interprets its bylaws to exclude from affiliation anyone who engages in 'unrepentant homosexual conduct[,]' and also excludes students who hold religious convictions different from those in the Statement of Faith."[99] In addition to excluding gay and non-Christian students from membership in the organization, it appears that they also excluded students who advocate for gay rights.[100]

As a member of the Association of American Law Schools (AALS), as well as a public institution of higher education in California, Hastings was required to adopt a nondiscrimination policy, and it interpreted its policy as requiring its student groups to accept "all comers." Groups that did not comply could not receive official recognition from the law school.

At the time, there were approximately sixty recognized student groups at Hastings, including three other religious groups. CLS was the only group that "refused to comply" with the antidiscrimination/all-comers policy. As a result, while CLS students could still affiliate and meet on campus, they received no $250 stipend for travel and no official recognition (no use of the Hastings imprimatur, no listing on the law school website, and no priority in room scheduling).

CLS filed its lawsuit in federal court, arguing that its rights under the First Amendment were violated. Hastings OUTLaw (the law school's LGBT student organization) intervened on behalf of Hastings, and additional amicus briefs were filed in support of Hastings by the National School Boards Association, the National Association of Secondary School Principals, the California School Boards Association, the National Education Association, and the Association of American Law Schools, among others.

The Supreme Court's decision turned on an application of the viewpoint discrimination doctrine.[101] The CLS contended that First Amendment freedoms of speech, association, and religion had all been violated. In particular, it argued that viewpoint discrimination existed because of the inclusion of religion and sexual orientation in the antidiscrimination/all-comers policy. Hastings and Hastings OUTLaw contended that the policy was viewpoint neutral and enforced equally. Moreover, CLS students were free to organize, associate, profess their beliefs, and meet on campus, but Hastings would not put its imprimatur on an organization that did not allow all comers to become voting members.

A divided court, per Justice Ruth Bader Ginsburg, found (5–4) in favor of Hastings and against the CLS group:

> In the view of petitioner Christian Legal Society (CLS), an accept-all-comers policy impairs its First Amendment rights to free speech, expressive association, and free exercise of religion by prompting it, on pain of relinquishing the advantages of recognition, to accept members who do not share the organization's core beliefs about religion and sexual orientation. From the perspective of respondent Hastings College of the Law, CLS seeks special dispensation from an across-the-board open-access requirement designed to further the reasonable educational purposes underpinning the school's student-organization program.
>
> In accord with the District Court and the Court of Appeals, we reject CLS's First Amendment challenge. Compliance with Hastings' all-comers policy, we conclude, is a reasonable, viewpoint-neutral condition on access to the student-organization forum.[102]

The implications of this victory for LGBT law students and their law school are many and varied. In particular, parallels can be drawn between this victory and the passage of the FAIR Education Act in California, which requires the inclusion of LGBT-positive content in the K–12 social studies curriculum. In addition, there is an important implicit recognition here that pursuant to the religion clauses, students in this country—attending public educational institutions—have the right to identify as both LGBT and Christian should they wish to do so.

KEETON V. ANDERSON-WILEY (2011)

Jennifer Keeton, a graduate student at Augusta State University (ASU), brought this lawsuit under the First Amendment, arguing that the university's decision that she participate in a remediation plan if she wished to obtain a master's degree in school counseling violated both the Free Speech Clause and the Free Exercise Clause. The Eleventh Circuit Court of Appeals found in favor of ASU and against Keeton.[103]

At issue was Keeton's refusal to comply with several provisions of the American Counseling Association's (ACA) Code of Ethics, which ASU was required to adopt and teach to offer a counseling program accredited by the Council for Accreditation of Counseling and Related Educational Programs. Among the sections of the ACA Code of Ethics that Keeton's statements indicated she would violate was Section A.4.b:

> Counselors are aware of their own values, attitudes, beliefs, and behaviors and avoid imposing values that are inconsistent with counseling goals. Counselors respect the diversity of clients, trainees, and research participants.

In her brief, Keeton indicated that she holds several beliefs about homosexuality that she views as arising from her Christian faith. ASU's officials became aware that Keeton held these beliefs when she expressed to professors in class and to fellow classmates in and out of class that she believed that the "GLBTQ population" suffers from identity confusion and that she intended to attempt to convert students from being homosexual to heterosexual. She also said that it would be difficult for her to work with GLBTQ clients and to separate her views about homosexuality from her clients' views. Furthermore, in answering a hypothetical posed by a faculty member, Keeton responded that as a high school counselor confronted by a sophomore student in crisis, questioning his sexual orientation, she would tell the student that it was not OK to be gay. Similarly, Keeton told a fellow classmate that, if a client were to disclose that he was gay, it was her intention to tell the client that his behavior is morally wrong and then try to change the client's behavior, and if she were unable to help the client change his behavior, she would refer him to someone practicing conversion therapy.

In particular, the court found that ASU's decision was viewpoint neutral and that "Keeton remains free to express disagreement with ASU's curriculum and the ethical requirements of the ACA, but she cannot block the school's attempts to ensure that she abides by them if she wishes to participate in the clinical practicum, which involves one-on-one counseling, and graduate from the program."[104]

GAY CONVERSION THERAPY BANS IN MULTIPLE STATES

During the current decade, a growing number of states have banned "gay conversion therapy" by "mental health professionals" in K–12 settings. President Obama—responding to a petition on the White House website in 2015—also backed efforts to oppose seeking to convert minors from gay to straight. Senior White House advisor Valerie Jarrett wrote at the time that the "overwhelming scientific evidence demonstrates that conversion therapy, especially when it is practiced on young people, is neither medically nor ethically appropriate and can cause substantial harm. As part of our dedication to protecting America's youth, this administration supports efforts to ban the use of conversion therapy for minors."[105]

California, which became the first state to ban this activity, approved the following additions to its Business and Professions Code:

> 865.1. Under no circumstances shall a mental health provider engage in sexual orientation change efforts with a patient under 18 years of age.
>
> 865.2. Any sexual orientation change efforts attempted on a patient under 18 years of age by a mental health provider shall be considered unprofessional conduct and shall subject a mental health provider to discipline by the licensing entity for that mental health provider.

It should be noted that the legislation added the following definition for "mental health provider":

> 865 (a) "Mental health provider" means a physician and surgeon specializing in the practice of psychiatry, a psychologist, a psychological assistant, intern, or trainee, a licensed marriage and family therapist, a registered marriage and family therapist, intern, or trainee, *a licensed educational psychologist, a credentialed school psychologist* [emphasis added], a licensed clinical social worker, an associate clinical social worker, a licensed professional clinical counselor, a registered clinical counselor, intern, or trainee, or any other person designated as a mental health professional under California law or regulation.

It is clear from the language of section 865, and especially from the inclusion of "licensed educational psychologist" and "credentialed school psychologist," that this legislation was designed to have a direct impact on K–12 school communities.

Several of these statewide conversion therapy bans were challenged in federal court, but thus far none of the challenges have been successful. In 2015, the U.S. Supreme Court let stand a Third Circuit decision upholding the New Jersey ban.[106] In February 2017, defendants prevailed on a motion to dismiss the challenge to the Illinois ban.[107] And in May 2017, the U.S. Supreme Court let stand a Ninth Circuit decision that ruled against plaintiffs who were seeking to have the California ban overturned.[108]

BANNING THE GAY AND TRANS PANIC DEFENSES

The "gay panic" and "trans panic" defenses, which were arguably employed by defense attorneys in the volatile trials of the killers in the Lawrence King murder and the Gwen Araujo murder, respectively, have long been criticized as highly discriminatory vehicles for blaming the victims in tragic criminal cases.[109] Relying on anti-gay and/or anti-trans animus, defendants have used the defense "to persuade jurors that their . . . charges should be reduced to a less culpable form of homicide. To establish the defense, [they] argue that their victims had provoked them, driving them to react violently."[110]

In 2014, California became the first state to ban the gay and trans panic defenses.[111] It was followed by Illinois in 2017. The American Bar Association has called for such a ban to be enacted nationwide.[112]

THE BOY SCOUTS OF AMERICA WELCOMES GAY AND TRANS YOUTH

In several related and unexpected developments, the Boy Scouts of America reversed long-standing policy and announced that neither openly gay boys nor openly gay adults would be officially banned from the national organization. Ironically, almost two decades earlier, the organization had fought vehemently to keep this from happening, taking its case all the way to the U.S. Supreme Court and prevailing, 5–4.[113]

First, in spring 2013, the Boy Scouts voted to admit openly gay scouts to the organization. The proposal was voted upon by more than fourteen hundred voting members of the organization's national council at its annual meeting in Grapevine, Texas, near the Scouts' national headquarters in suburban Dallas. The policy became effective on January 1, 2014.[114]

Then, in July 2015, one month after the *Obergefell* decision, the Boy Scouts' National Executive Board "ratified a resolution removing the national restriction on openly gay leaders and employees," according to Boy Scouts president Robert Gates. "This change allows scouting members and parents to select local units, chartered to organizations with similar beliefs, that best meet the needs of their families. This change would also respect the right of religious chartered organizations to continue to choose adult leaders whose beliefs are consistent with their own," according to a July 13, 2015, statement by the Boy Scouts.[115]

Finally, in January 2017, the Boy Scouts announced that it would also allow transgender youth in its "boys-only" program.[116]

HIVELY V. IVY TECH COMMUNITY COLLEGE OF INDIANA (2017)

In a landmark 2017 decision that could open the door to a nationwide prohibition of employment discrimination against LGBTs, a bipartisan en banc panel of Seventh Circuit Court of Appeals judges determined by a vote of 8–3 that Title VII of the Civil Rights Act of 1964 prohibits anti-gay discrimination in the workplace.[117]

For decades, members of Congress—supported first by President Bill Clinton and then by President Barack Obama—had sought to enact such a nationwide prohibition, first under the Employment Non-discrimination Act[118] and more recently under the more expansive Equality Act.[119] President Obama had also sought to ban discrimination against LGBTs by federal contractors, only to have key aspects of his executive order blocked by a federal court in Texas. In short, an effort to win protection for LGBTs against workplace discrimination has been on the paradigmatic front burner in Washington, D.C., for close to fifty years. And *Hively v. Ivy Tech Community College of Indiana* could be the breakthrough that LGBTs were hoping and waiting for.[120]

In sum, this new chapter on marriage equality and its aftermath, combined with chapter 1, provides an updated overview of the legal foundations of the right to be out. Although the right is still emerging, and although it continues to be stronger in some parts of the country than others, the prospects for the continued strengthening of the right have never been better.

The chapters that follow focus on K–12 schools and document both the challenges that have arisen and the challenges that lie ahead for LGBT students, LGBT educators, and LGBT parents. But the consistent conclusion in all these chapters is that more people are rising to confront these challenges. In addition, more legal directions and more research-based road maps have become available for LGBTs and their allies, with the prospects for greater equality being more promising than ever.

3

EMERGING RIGHTS OF LGBT STUDENTS

The Impact of Litigation and Legislation

Building on the victories described in the preceding chapters, LGBT students have stepped forward to challenge the mistreatment they have experienced at K–12 school sites on a day-to-day level. Many of these challenges have been litigated, and a growing body of case law has emerged. The court decisions are bolstered by the legal obligations of school districts regarding campus safety and have been further strengthened in certain states by specific mandates requiring equal treatment for everyone on the basis of actual or perceived sexual or gender identity.

This chapter seeks to discern the current state of the law by analyzing two categories of cases impacting gays and lesbians: those brought on behalf of students primarily under the First Amendment and those brought on behalf of students primarily under the Fourteenth Amendment.[1] It then explores the extent to which related common-law frameworks and statutory developments inform these decisions and reinforce their holdings.

First Amendment Right-to-Be-Out Cases

Several noteworthy cases brought by K–12 LGBT students in a freedom-of-expression context have resulted in an increasingly broadening recognition of a right to be more open about one's sexual orientation or gender identity. Contextually, the central legal principles in this area are derived primarily from the 1969 U.S. Supreme Court decision in *Tinker v. Des Moines Independent Community School District*.

Legal Context: The *Tinker* Rule (1969)

The U.S. Supreme Court has long held that neither K–12 students nor their teachers shed their constitutional rights to freedom of expression at the schoolhouse gate. First Amendment rights are explicitly made available to public school students, subject to limitations that arise out of the "special characteristics of the school environment."[2]

In *Tinker*, students had been disciplined for wearing black armbands to a public high school as a protest against U.S. involvement in the Vietnam War, and they argued that this punishment violated their First Amendment rights. In the first U.S. Supreme Court decision to directly address K–12 student freedom of expression, the justices held that students do indeed have free speech rights. These rights may be limited, however, if the expression "materially and substantially" interferes with schoolwork, discipline, or the rights of others.[3]

Subsequent cases have clarified the parameters of the *Tinker* rule and how it might play out on a day-to-day level at individual school sites. A central principle is that educators do not have to wait for either "disruption" or the "interference with the rights of others" to happen before the expressive activity can be restricted, but at the same time, "undifferentiated fear" of disturbance is not sufficient.[4]

More recent federal court of appeals decisions have provided relevant guidelines for school officials. In a 2001 case addressing a dispute over a student poem that the school believed might constitute a threat in the highly charged aftermath of the tragic shootings at Columbine High School, the U.S. Court of Appeals for the Ninth Circuit synthesized the set of rules that govern the application of *Tinker*.[5] Judge Raymond C. Fisher explained that if the officials wish to "suppress speech" in anticipation of problems that have not yet occurred, they must "justify their decision by showing facts which might reasonably have led school authorities to forecast substantial disruption of or material interference with school activities." He noted that this standard "does not require certainty that disruption will occur" and that it contemplates an analysis based on the "totality of the facts."[6]

Moreover, in a 2001 decision addressing the constitutionality of student conduct code provisions in a Pennsylvania school district, the U.S. Court of Appeals for the Third Circuit noted that "the mere desire to avoid 'discomfort' or 'unpleasantness' is not enough to justify restricting student speech under *Tinker*." And the court determined that educators anticipating disruption under the *Tinker* rule must be able to "point to a well-founded expectation of disruption."[7]

In addition to *Tinker*, three other U.S. Supreme Court cases have confronted K–12 student freedom-of-expression issues directly. In the first, *Bethel v. Fraser* (1986), the Court ruled that *Tinker* did not protect a student from being disciplined after he gave a lewd and suggestive nominating speech at a mandatory student government assembly. In the second, *Hazelwood v. Kuhlmeier* (1988), the Court found the *Tinker* rule inapplicable to a dispute regarding the inclusion of articles on teen pregnancy and the effects of divorce in a school newspaper. In the third, *Morse v. Frederick* (2007), the Court determined that *Tinker* does not limit the ability of a principal to restrict the dissemination of pro-drug messages.[8] Not only were all three of these cases decided in favor of the school districts, but in each case, the Court also found *Tinker* inapplicable. Such a pattern led commentators to question whether *Tinker* has become an anachronistic ruling from another era.[9]

Yet an examination of court decisions applying *Fraser* and *Kuhlmeier* reveals that over time, they were increasingly being viewed as narrow exceptions to *Tinker* and not as holdings that diluted the *Tinker* rule.[10] And although the majority opinion in the 2007 *Morse* decision appeared somewhat ambiguous on the question of whether the case qualified as a third narrow exception to *Tinker* or whether the Court truly intended to cut back on the free speech protections for K–12 students, two of the five justices who joined in the opinion did so only "on the understanding that (a) it goes no further than to hold that a public school may restrict speech that a reasonable observer would interpret as advocating illegal drug use and (b) it provides no support for any restriction of speech that can plausibly be interpreted as commenting on any political or social issue."[11]

Thus a principled reading of *Tinker* and its progeny leads to the conclusion that the *Tinker* rule is still the basic starting point, and a court should first determine whether student expression can be restricted by inquiring as to whether there is or will be material and substantial disruption or interference with the rights of others. Yet even if there is no disruption, no interference with the rights of others, and no likelihood that either will occur, K–12 educators can still limit the expression of students if that expression is inappropriate (under the *Fraser* rule), if it is school-sponsored expressive activity (which may be broadly limited under the *Kuhlmeier* rule), or if it can reasonably be regarded as encouraging illegal drug use (under the *Morse* rule).[12]

Fricke v. Lynch (1980)

The *Fricke* litigation, focusing on a student's right to take a same-sex date to the prom in 1980, is perhaps the first example of a gay student attempting to apply the *Tinker* rule to the LGBT area.[13] Few coming-out statements are stronger or have a greater impact than attending a high school prom with a date of the same or similar gender, and increasing numbers of LGBT students seek to do so,[14] despite the difficulties that may ensue.[15]

The "prom" at issue in the case was a formal Friday evening dinner dance sponsored and run by the Cumberland (Rhode Island) High School Class of 1980 at the Pleasant Valley Country Club, across state lines in Sutton, Massachusetts. No senior was required to go, but all students who attended were required to bring an escort. Students were asked the names of their dates at the time the tickets were purchased.

The incident marked the second consecutive year that a dispute regarding same-sex couples had arisen at Cumberland High. A year earlier, in 1979, Paul Guilbert was denied permission to bring a male escort to the junior prom by Principal Richard Lynch, who feared "that student reaction could lead to a disruption at the dance and possibly to physical harm." The request and its denial were "widely publicized and led to widespread community and student reaction." Some students actually taunted Guilbert and spit at him, and one student slapped him. In response, the principal arranged for security to accompany Guilbert as he went from one class to the next.[16]

Likewise, when Aaron Fricke asked Principal Lynch for permission to bring a male escort to the senior prom, in 1980, the request was denied pending an appeal. A week later, Fricke asked Guilbert to accompany him (if it would be allowed), and Guilbert accepted. Fricke then met again with Lynch, appealed the decision, and during the discussion came out to him for the first time. In fact, for Fricke, this entire series of events constituted a very public and very complete coming out.[17]

Lynch denied Fricke's appeal, voicing as his primary concern "the fear that a disruption would occur" and that the boys "would be hurt."[18] The lawsuit was then filed in the U.S. District Court for Rhode Island, not only resulting in substantial additional publicity but also leading to an "unprovoked, surprise assault" against Fricke by one of his peers. The now openly gay student was "shoved" and "punched," and five stitches were required to close a wound under his right eye. As a result of these events, special parking and security were provided for Fricke, as they had been a year earlier to Guilbert, and no further incidents occurred.

After hearing the facts of the case and determining that the taking of a date of the same gender to the prom constituted a communicative act that implicated the Free Speech Clause of the First Amendment, the district court proceeded to analyze the dispute under *Tinker*. Judge Pettine found no evidence of bad faith or anti-gay animus on the part of the principal, who seemed motivated by a sincere concern for the safety of the gay students. However, the court concluded that although there was a possibility of some disruption, the *Tinker* requirement that the school point to a "well-founded expectation" of "material and substantial disruption" at the prom was not met. In addition, the fact that the setting was an extracurricular event also weighed in the student's favor, given that the *Tinker* rule is geared primarily toward preventing interference with educational activities. A key component of the court's ruling was the determination that a decision against Fricke would have amounted to granting the anti-gay bullies a "heckler's veto" over Fricke's expressive activity: "To rule otherwise would completely subvert free speech in the schools by granting other students a 'heckler's veto,' allowing them to decide—through prohibited and violent methods—what speech will be heard. The first amendment does not tolerate mob rule by unruly school children. . . . In such a context, the school does have an obligation to take reasonable measures to protect and foster free speech, not to stand helpless before unauthorized student violence."[19]

The two young men were allowed to attend the prom together, and apparently everything went well. The school district did not appeal this lower court ruling, but even though the case is therefore not binding precedent on anyone, it stands today for a principle that is generally accepted nationwide. Absent additional facts, few public school districts—after consulting with their attorneys—would seriously consider attempting to bar similar-gender couples from attending extracurricular dances together.[20]

Although the *Fricke* case was litigated primarily under the First Amendment, the complaint also raised issues under the Equal Protection Clause of the Fourteenth Amendment. Because the court found the school district's actions to be violative of Fricke's free speech rights, it did not need to conduct a full-blown equal protection analysis, and it chose not to do so. However, it should be noted that the court did react positively to the plaintiff's equal protection argument, which it characterized as reflecting a "hybrid" claim that "he has been treated differently than others because of the content of his communication."

Indeed, Judge Pettine explicitly highlighted the interplay between the two amendments. "This case can also be profitably analyzed under the Equal Protection Clause," Pettine stated. "In preventing Aaron Fricke from attending the senior reception, the school has afforded disparate treatment to a certain class of students."[21] The court then cited *Chicago Police Department v. Mosley,* which stands as a paradigmatic example of a case decided at the intersection of the free speech and equal protection guarantees. *Fricke,* coming as it did only a few years after the first rulings in the gay and lesbian student organization cases, thus became a noteworthy landmark in the progression of LGBT student victories at the intersection of the First and Fourteenth Amendments.

The K–12 Gay–Straight Alliance Cases

The 1990s saw the emergence of a new phenomenon at the K–12 level: the gay–straight alliance. Fueled in great part by the growing ability of LGBTs to establish connections with each other online, and strengthened by ties to organizations such as Parents, Friends, and Families of Lesbians and Gays (PFLAG), the Gay, Lesbian, and Straight Education Network (GLSEN), and the Gay–Straight Alliance Network—all of which provided resources, encouragement, and opportunities for networking—the new student organizations proliferated on public school campuses in a manner that paralleled the growth of college and university student organizations in the 1970s and 1980s. A key difference between the K–12 groups and the higher education groups, however, was that these new organizations of younger students also explicitly included straight allies.

Just as had been the case with the earlier higher education organizations, many school districts sought to ban the gay–straight alliances. Emotions ran high as contentions specific to the K–12 level were put forth, with some opponents of the alliances insisting that the students were too young to know they were gay and others suggesting that the alliances were vehicles for turning straight students gay. In addition, much opposition was rooted in the position, often associated with religious conservatives, that anything gay-positive was inappropriate in a public school environment.

In the end, the LGBT students prevailed in just about every lawsuit challenging school district efforts to keep the gay–straight alliances off school campuses. In an interesting and perhaps ironic twist, the gay students and their straight allies built on the legal efforts of religious organizations to secure the right of religious students to have their own clubs, prayer groups, and Bible study groups on K–12 campuses.[22]

Not surprisingly, the gay–straight alliance cases were litigated primarily in the more conservative parts of the country, where the opposition to these clubs was particularly intense. Much of the early litigation focused on Utah, and subsequent noteworthy cases were filed in Orange County, California, and in Boyd County, Kentucky. All the victories in these cases reinforce the expressive component of the right to be out, because such organizations often serve a communicative function and, for many members, constitute the functional equivalent of coming-out speech. In addition, by basing their decisions on the provisions of federal law mandating "equal access" for K–12 student clubs, the courts have reinforced the equal-treatment component of the right to be out.

Colin v. Orange USD (2000)

The *Colin* litigation is typical of the cases filed during this era. When their application to form a new Gay–Straight Alliance Club (GSA) at their school was denied, students at El Modina High School, in Orange, California, brought a lawsuit in district court that relied primarily on the Equal Access Act.[23] Under the act, passed by Congress in 1984 and signed by then President Reagan, "[K–12] schools that allow student groups *whose purpose is not directly related to the curriculum* to meet on school grounds during lunch or after school cannot deny other student groups access to the school due to the content of the students' proposed discussions."[24]

Early in its analysis, the *Colin* court noted the strong connection between the Equal Access Act and the First Amendment: "Due to the First Amendment, Congress passed an 'Equal Access Act' when it wanted to permit religious speech on school campuses. It did not pass a 'Religious Speech Access Act' or an 'Access for All Students except Gay Students Act' because to do so would be unconstitutional."[25] Relying on Supreme

Court precedent interpreting the scope of the 1984 statute, the *Colin* court ruled in favor of the gay–straight alliance, confirming the principle that students seeking to form such a group merit the protection of the Equal Access Act if a school has allowed any "non-curriculum-related" club to be formed.[26] "Once a school recognizes any . . . [non-curriculum-related] group," Judge Carter wrote, "it has created a 'limited open forum' and the school is prohibited 'from denying equal access to *any* other student group on the basis of the content of that group's speech.'" Then, citing the *Tinker* rule, the Court noted, "The only meetings that schools subject to the Act can prohibit are those that would 'materially and substantially interfere with the orderly conduct of educational activities within the school.'" The Court noted in this context that "this club is actually being formed to avoid the disruptions to education that can take place when students are harassed based on sexual orientation."[27]

Boyd County High School Gay Straight Alliance v. Bd. of Ed. (2003)

In another successful federal lawsuit that paralleled the *Colin* litigation in many ways, Ashland, Kentucky, student plaintiffs in *Boyd* claimed that the school district violated their rights under both the Equal Access Act and the First Amendment "by denying the Gay Straight Alliance (GSA) the same access to school facilities given to other student groups." Much the same way as in *Colin* and other cases of this type, the stated purpose of the GSA was "to provide students with a safe haven to talk about anti-gay harassment and to work together to promote tolerance, understanding and acceptance of one another regardless of sexual orientation."[28]

There were, however, two key differences between *Boyd* and *Colin*. First, there was evidence that a certain level of disturbance was taking place around LGBT issues on the high school campus. Second, as a result of the concern over the disturbances, the court devoted a key portion of its opinion to an analysis under the *Tinker* rule. The court found that "anti-gay harassment, homophobia, and use of anti-gay epithets" continued to be "serious problems" at BCHS. In an October 2002 incident, for example, students in plaintiff Libby Fugett's English class stated "that they needed to take all the fucking faggots out in the back woods and kill them." In another, during a January 2003 basketball game, "students with megaphones chanted at Plaintiff [Lena] Reese: 'faggot-kisser,' 'GSA' and 'fag-lover.'" On a regular basis, students called out "homo," "fag," and "queer" behind plaintiff Tyler McClelland's back as he walked in the hallway between classes. During a lunch-hour observance of the National Day of Silence in April 2002, while twenty-five participants sat in a circle in the front lobby of BCHS, "protesters used anti-gay epithets and threw things at them." At least two students reportedly dropped out because of such "harassment based on sexual orientation."[29]

After recognizing the parallels between the *Boyd* case and other gay–straight alliance cases brought under the Equal Access Act, the court turned to the *Tinker* analysis, noting that the rule had been expressly incorporated into the act. A school district, the court declared, may still ban a gay–straight alliance if it can show that the club will "materially and substantially interfere with the orderly conduct of educational opportunities within the school" or will limit the school's ability "to maintain order and discipline on school premises, [and] to protect the well-being of students and faculty."[30] The court determined, however, that the only current and perhaps future disturbances in this context were caused by opponents of the GSA. In a conclusion similar to the one in *Fricke,* the court found that ruling against the plaintiffs in this case would be the equivalent of granting their opponents a "heckler's veto" over the plaintiffs' First Amendment rights. The Equal Access Act permits the prohibition of a student group, Judge Bunning stated, "only upon a showing that *Plaintiffs' own disruptive activities* have interfered with Defendants' ability to maintain order and discipline. . . . Defendants have made no such showing in this case."[31]

Other First Amendment Right-to-Be-Out Cases

Henkle v. Gregory (2001)

Derek Henkle, a fifteen-year-old student in Reno, Nevada, filed his lawsuit in district court under both the First and the Fourteenth Amendments after experiencing a pattern of peer harassment and mistreatment. In one notorious incident, Henkle was approached on school grounds by several other students, who called him "fag," "butt pirate," "fairy," and "homo"; lassoed him around the neck; and suggested dragging him behind a truck. The events were exacerbated by both a failure to intervene on the part of school-site educators and the fact that Henkle was expressly blamed for bringing the mistreatment on himself by being openly gay. Most notably, he was told by one administrator to "stop acting like a fag." Not only were his educational opportunities severely impacted by these events but he also experienced a breakdown as a result of all that had occurred.[32]

Henkle's litigation resulted in both a favorable court decision on the First Amendment issues and a favorable settlement agreement addressing the Fourteenth Amendment issues. In the decision, the federal court considered Henkle's claim that the school district "violated his First Amendment rights by censoring, chilling, and deterring him from exercising his right to freedom of speech and by retaliating against him when he did exercise his rights." Henkle alleged several "actions and/or inactions by Defendants that warrant the inference that the actions and/or inactions were retaliatory in nature."

For example, he alleged that the harassment began after he participated in a discussion on a local cable station about gay high school students and their experiences, and it ultimately resulted in his transfer to an alternative high school. He also alleged that, rather than disciplining the harassers, the school district "treated him as the problem and told him numerous times to keep his sexuality to himself." Among other things, he alleged that his transfer to the alternative school was "conditioned on the fact that he keep his sexuality to himself." In addition, Henkle presented evidence that the alternative school severely limited the educational options available to students, including those who, like him, had been identified as gifted and talented. When he sought to transfer out of the alternative high school because of lack of educational opportunities, "Defendant [and former principal Robert] Floyd told him the transfer was not possible because he was openly gay and a traditional high school was not appropriate." Instead, he was transferred to an adult education program where he could not even receive a high school diploma because he was no longer enrolled in a public high school.[33]

Ultimately, the decision turned on an analysis of whether Henkle's expression was protected under *Tinker*. The court concluded that Henkle had made "sufficient allegations that his constitutionally protected speech was a substantial motivating factor in adverse action directed at him": "In *Tinker*, the Supreme Court clearly established that students in public schools have the right to freedom of speech and expression. This is a broad right that would encompass the right of a high school student to express his sexuality."[34] In ruling that under *Tinker*, K–12 students have a right "to express their sexuality," *Henkle* became perhaps the first federal court decision to explicitly determine that a student has the right to be out.

Nguon v. Wolf (2007)

Charlene Nguon's lawsuit not only explored the limits of the right to be out but also asked a U.S. district court to consider the parameters of the right *not* to be out. Nguon, an openly lesbian student at Santiago High School in Garden Grove, California, challenged what she alleged to be discriminatory disciplinary practices on the part of school officials, who had suspended her for her persistent and open displays of affection with her girlfriend, Trang Nguyen, on campus and then had outed her to her parents.[35] Represented by the ACLU, Nguon argued that her rights had been violated under the First Amendment, the Fourteenth Amendment, and both federal and state privacy laws. The 2007 decision ultimately found in favor of the school district, but it contained a number of determinations that could possibly augur to the benefit of LGBTs in future cases.

Addressing the freedom of expression claim, for example, the court reaffirmed a right to be out under the First Amendment: "The parties agree that the First Amendment also protects 'expressive conduct' . . . [and] the case law recognizes one's right to express his or her sexuality [citing *Boyd County, Henkle,* and *Fricke*]."[36] Central to this decision, however, was the court's finding that Nguon and her girlfriend were not engaged in run-of-the-mill hugging or kissing but that they participated in extensive and persistent making out on campus over a period of time, defying the school-site administrators' directives in the process. The court affirmed a right to be out but concluded that it did not extend to over-the-top conduct that was clearly inappropriate in a school setting.

As to the equal protection claim, the court found "that the School Defendants neither disciplined on a discriminatory basis nor did they engage in deliberate indifference with regard to inappropriate public displays of affection engaged in by heterosexual couples. When Charlene and Trang were initially disciplined with Saturday school, a heterosexual couple also received the same discipline."[37] Thus, although the judge appeared to be going out of his way to reaffirm the right of LGBTs to express their identity and to be treated equally as a result of their expression, he did not appear able to rule in the plaintiff's favor as a result of the nature and extent of the girls' defiant conduct, which he determined to be much more intensive than what typically took place between the heterosexual students on campus.

On the privacy question, however, many had hoped that on appeal, the Ninth Circuit would examine the "right not to be out" question in greater detail. Nguon argued that even though she had been out on campus, her privacy rights precluded the school officials from telling her parents that she was a lesbian. The principal contended that he was obligated to tell the parents why she had been disciplined, but Nguon apparently asserted that he could have provided a more general statement of the violation without outing her before she was ready to come out to her family. This was perhaps the first time a privacy issue of this sort had ever come before a federal court as a key issue in the proceedings. In 2008, however, the plaintiff apparently chose not to proceed with the appeal, stipulating to a voluntary dismissal of the Ninth Circuit proceedings.[38] Left unresolved, therefore, were the parameters of the right not to be out. Judge Selna had recognized that Nguon "had a Constitutionally protected privacy right with respect to disclosure of her sexual orientation," even though she was already out at school. However, he determined that the California Education Code's statutory requirement that parents be told why a child has been suspended outweighed Nguon's rights. Yet the court did not address the key question of whether it would be possible to comply with the Education Code without actually disclosing the gender of Nguon's friend.[39]

Analyzing the *Nguon* privacy issues in considerable detail, legal scholar Holning Lau has pointed out that although "an adult who has disclosed her sexual orientation to as many people as Nguon had would likely have no valid privacy claim . . . , children should not be—and have not been—subject to the same general rules developed for adult contexts." "To maintain fidelity to the notion of privacy rights," Lau asserts, "courts should extend special rights of privacy to children when it is necessary to protect their identity development." He concludes that, "because children are uniquely vulnerable to the harms of being outed, there should be a categorical rule unique to children: the government should not out gay and lesbian youth unless the government shows that doing so prevents cognizable harms."[40]

Gillman v. School Board for Holmes County, Florida (2008)

In a 2008 case applying *Tinker* to LGBT-related expression at Ponce de Leon, a rural Florida Panhandle school serving grades 6–12, Heather Gillman and her friends came to the defense of a fellow student who was badly mistreated when she complained of harassment on the basis of her sexual orientation. The mistreated student, identified only as Jane Doe, was not a party to the lawsuit, apparently deciding not to bring an action under her own First Amendment rights. But Gillman, a straight ally whose open expressions of support on behalf of Doe were met with resistance and punishment from school officials, took her case to the federal court and prevailed.[41]

The reaction of Principal David Davis to Jane Doe's predicament mirrored that of school-site administrators in other cases described in this chapter. Instead of providing the level of support required under the law for any student who has been harassed, Davis blamed her for bringing the harassment on herself, and in so doing, he dramatically exacerbated the situation.

Doe, a twelfth grader, reported that "she had been taunted by a group of approximately five middle school students because of her sexual orientation." After hearing about the incident, Principal Davis called Doe into his office and asked if she was a lesbian. When she said that she was, he admonished her, declaring that "it was not 'right' to be a homosexual." Ascertaining that her parents did not know she was out, he asked for the parents' telephone number so that he could tell them of her sexual orientation. He also instructed Doe "to 'stay away' from the middle school students or . . . he would suspend her." Doe left Davis's office in tears. Upon learning of these events, "numerous students expressed their support for Doe by writing 'GP' or 'Gay Pride' on their bodies, wearing t-shirts with messages supportive of gay rights, yelling 'Gay Pride' in the hallways, circulating petitions to demonstrate support for gay rights, and creating signs with messages supporting homosexuals."[42]

Davis subsequently interviewed approximately thirty students, interrogated them about their own sexual orientations, and questioned them about their involvement in what had come to be known as "the gay pride movement" at the school. During these meetings, he instructed students who identified as gay or lesbian "not to discuss their sexual orientations. He also prohibited students from wearing rainbow belts or writing 'Gay Pride' or 'GP' on their arms and notebooks. He required students to wash 'GP' or 'Gay Pride' from their arms and hands and lifted the shirts of female students to verify that no such writings were present on their bodies." Eleven of the students were suspended for five days each. "Davis told the mother of a student whom he had suspended that he could secretly 'send her [daughter] off to a private Christian school down in Tallahassee' or to the juvenile detention center and that 'if there was a man in your house, [and] your children were in church, you wouldn't be having any of these gay issues.'"[43]

Analyzing the facts under well-settled First Amendment principles and under right-to-be-out cases such as *Fricke* and *Henkle*, the court found in favor of the students, concluding that any disruption had been caused by Principal Davis and not by the students themselves. The court was particularly critical of Davis, who was subsequently demoted after the decision was released:

> The facts in this case are extraordinary. The Holmes County School Board has imposed an outright ban on speech by students that is not vulgar, lewd, obscene, plainly offensive, or violent, but which is pure, political, and expresses tolerance, acceptance, fairness, and support for not only a marginalized group, but more importantly, for a fellow student at Ponce de Leon. The student, Jane Doe, had been victimized by the school principal solely because of her sexual orientation. Principal David Davis responded to Jane Doe's complaints of harassment by other students, not by consoling her, but by shaming her. . . . Davis's conduct, in the capacity of a role model and authority figure, is particularly deplorable in light of studies which confirm the vulnerability of gay and lesbian students.[44]

Although this was not a case directly about the right to be out, given that it was brought not by the student herself but by a straight ally whose expression had also been restricted, issues relating to the right to be out and to gay-positive expression on a public school campus were at the heart of the dispute. In no uncertain terms, the Florida court ruled in favor of the LGBT students and their allies in this setting and, in so doing, further strengthened the rights of all gay and gender-expansive students under the First Amendment.

Fourteenth Amendment Right-to-Be-Out Cases

Just as the First Amendment lawsuits bolstered the right of gays and transgender persons to be more open about their identity on public school campuses, the Fourteenth Amendment victories that followed the *Nabozny* decision bolstered their right to be treated equally as a result of expressing their identity.[45] Courtney Joslin, formerly an attorney at the National Center for Lesbian Rights and now a law professor, has documented the steady stream of safety-related victories by LGBT plaintiffs in the decade following *Nabozny*. These cases followed a familiar, unfortunate pattern: students mistreated by their peers for no reason other than the fact that they were either openly gay or perceived to be gay, and the adults on site not only failing to intervene but often exacerbating situations by blaming the gay students for bringing it on themselves.[46] The 2003 *Flores* decision against the Morgan Hill Unified School District in the San Jose area and the 2005 *Ramirez* settlement on behalf of student plaintiffs in the Los Angeles Unified School District exemplify this pattern.

Flores v. Morgan Hill Unified School District (2003)

Plaintiffs in *Flores* explicitly relied on the *Nabozny* decision in setting forth their arguments under the Fourteenth Amendment. Alana Flores, Freddie Fuentes, Jeanette Dousharm, and three other former students documented a highly troubling set of facts that included both intensive mistreatment on the part of their peers and inexcusable conduct on the part of faculty and staff at these public middle schools and high schools.[47]

On numerous occasions over time, harassment took place in classrooms and in front of teachers, who either did nothing to end it or blamed the victims. For example, when Fuentes was called "faggot" and "queer" by other students in history class and told them to stop, the teacher took Fuentes out into the hallway, told him that *he* had disrupted class, and shoved him against a wall. Another student was subjected to daily harassment in math class as fellow students threatened him and called him "faggot" in front of the teacher, who did nothing to stop them. And in drafting class, Fuentes was harassed daily in front of the teacher, who did nothing. One student told him, "I want to beat you up after class but I need a baseball bat to hit you because I don't want to get AIDS."[48]

Harassment and mistreatment were also highly prevalent in the school cafeteria and in the hallways. One day, Flores and Fuentes were eating lunch when a student approached them, handed them a pornographic magazine opened to a page showing men and women having sex, and said, "It's women, faggot. This is the way you guys should be doing it." Although a campus monitor was nearby, nothing was done to stop what was going on. When the students reported the incident, the assistant principal refused to take their complaint and told them they were making "too much of a fuss."

Another time, students shouting anti-gay epithets pelted Jeanette Dousharm with food at lunch, and several of them placed penis-shaped balloons on the table in front of her, saying, "If you knew what this was, maybe you wouldn't be a lesbian." This took place in front of a campus monitor, who did nothing. When Dousharm was harassed in the halls, administrators told her to go to class early to avoid the students who were tormenting her. She was also told to change clothes for PE in an area away from the rest of her class because the other girls said her presence made them uncomfortable.

The Ninth Circuit decision highlighted two sets of events that it viewed as exemplifying the realities in the Morgan Hill district. The first concerned Flores's ongoing mistreatment with regard to her locker. Throughout her years in high school, students had placed pages torn from pornographic magazines in Flores's locker and had scratched anti-gay obscenities into the paint on her locker door. Although she reported the defacement, the school left the words on her locker for months before painting them over. Another time, Alana found a picture of a naked woman, bound and gagged, with her legs spread and her throat slashed, taped to her locker. On the picture, someone had written, "Die, die dyke bitch, fuck off. We'll kill you." Flores, frightened and crying, took the photo to the assistant principal's office. The assistant principal brushed her off and told her to go back to class, saying, "Don't bring me this trash anymore, this is disgusting." The assistant principal then asked Flores if she was gay and said, "If you're not gay, why are you crying?"[49]

The second set of events took place at a school bus stop when Freddie Fuentes was only in the seventh grade. A group of students surrounded him at the stop one morning and brutally beat and kicked him, calling him "faggot" and saying, "You don't belong here." The bus driver not only ignored the scene when he drove up but let the attackers board the bus and left Fuentes lying on the ground as he drove away. Fuentes had to be treated at a hospital, and he was ultimately forced to transfer to another school after officials said that they could not ensure his safety if he stayed.

In describing the pattern of on-site behavior by the adults, the plaintiffs stated that school officials usually did nothing about the incidents and that, on the rare occasions when they did respond, those responses were so halfhearted and ineffectual that they only emboldened the attackers. Indeed, other students were known to brag about how school officials let them get away with harassment or punished them very lightly. Ultimately, Jeanette Dousharm felt she had no choice but to drop out of school because of the pervasive harassment. Another student entered independent study to escape the daily taunting and attacks.

After years of litigation and several appeals, the plaintiffs won a clear victory in the Ninth Circuit in 2003. The court found, under the Equal Protection Clause of the Fourteenth Amendment, that there was "sufficient evidence for a jury to infer that defendants acted with deliberate indifference." It also held that "the evidence would support a finding that the administrators' actions were unreasonable." Furthermore, as in *Nabozny,* the court found that there were appropriate policies in place but that they were enforced in a discriminatory fashion. Chief Judge Schroeder emphasized that "the constitutional violation lies in the discriminatory enforcement of the policies, not in the violation of the school policies themselves": "The defendants do not advance any reason to justify the alleged differential enforcement of District policies." Here, as in *Nabozny,* the court concluded that "we are unable to garner any rational basis for permitting one student to assault another based on the victim's sexual orientation, and the defendants do not offer us one."[50] Consistent with the pattern that has emerged since *Nabozny,* a landmark settlement was reached in this case in early 2004. The plaintiffs won a record $1.1 million in damages, and the settlement also included mandatory professional development on LGBT issues for school district educators.[51]

Ramirez v. Los Angeles Unified School District (2004)

The *Ramirez* lawsuit, filed against the Los Angeles Unified School District (LAUSD) in late 2004, reflected the same level of horrific peer mistreatment evident in *Nabozny, Henkle,* and *Flores.* In addition, however, the *Ramirez* brief included documentation of faculty and staff complicity in mistreatment at Washington Prep High School that went significantly beyond refusing to intervene or blaming the victim.[52] Indeed, according to Catherine Lhamon, the ACLU attorney who represented the plaintiffs, "what makes this case particularly troubling is that the harassment came from school administrators, teachers, and security guards. . . . Students have no recourse when the school bully wears a security guard's uniform or happens to be the home room teacher."[53]

Following are examples of the many instances of mistreatment documented in the complaint:

Administrators, teachers, and staff called students names such as "faggot" and "sinner" and told the students they were "wrong," "unholy," "hate[d]," and "not supposed to be like this" because the students were, or were perceived to be, lesbian, gay, or bisexual.

Teachers threatened to, and did, out students to their families as punishment for being openly gay on campus.

A teacher stood idly by while one student physically assaulted another student during class based on the student's sexual identity, because the teacher thought the assaulted student "needed to toughen up."

Administrators and deans suspended and otherwise disciplined students for complaining about harassment and for choosing same-sex partners.

An assistant principal refused to speak the word "gay" over the school public address system to announce a meeting of the Gay–Straight Alliance club.[54]

Perhaps the most egregious mistreatment occurred when school officials, who routinely ignored expressions of affection on campus between different-sex couples, blatantly mistreated and humiliated plaintiff David Ramirez and a male friend for kissing during lunchtime. After videotaping the kissing via a campus surveillance camera,

> a security guard escorted both students to the security office/camera room, where security personnel, including Defendant Vince Samuels, and administrative staff, including the dean, Defendant Frank R. Devereaux, and campus police officers watched the videotape over and over again in front of the Plaintiffs. Mr. Devereaux taunted the two students by asking, in front of the group, "who is the guy, who is the girl in the relationship?" A security guard also told the two students that they were "not supposed to be like this."
>
> The gathered group of security personnel and administrative staff repeatedly laughed at the two male students and one of the security guards raised his voice and told the two students what the two boys were doing was "wrong." David and the other student were humiliated and became distraught.[55]

The students were not allowed to return to class and had to spend more than two and a half hours with Devereaux, after which they were both suspended for two days.

A coalition of attorneys from the ACLU and the National Center for Lesbian Rights set forth sixteen claims for "relief" under a variety of federal and state statutes and constitutional provisions, including both the First and Fourteenth Amendments. Allegations of discrimination were central, with the most prominent claims based on the Fourteenth Amendment Equal Protection Clause.[56]

The plaintiffs' case was a powerful one, and it was further strengthened by the fact that many attempts to resolve the hostile environment administratively—both at the local school site and at school district offices—apparently engendered little enthusiasm. As summarized in the plaintiffs' brief, "Defendants' intentional and deliberate failure to take reasonable remedial steps in response to the harassment caused Plaintiffs to suffer extreme emotional distress and psychological damage, including but not limited to an inability to concentrate on studies, serious depression, debilitating fear, despair, anger, humiliation, and anxiety, all of which are ongoing hardships."[57]

The LAUSD chose to settle this case rather than proceed to trial and risk not only substantial legal costs but the possibility of a financial award for plaintiffs similar in size to *Nabozny* ($900,000) or *Flores* ($1.1 million). The settlement included a mandatory day-long faculty training on diversity, discrimination, and harassment and focused primarily on issues pertaining to actual or perceived sexual orientation and gender identity. It also included classroom training sessions and ongoing assemblies for Washington Prep students that encourage diversity and aim to eliminate discrimination and harassment.

State v. Limon (2005)

The *Limon* litigation represents a different type of Fourteenth Amendment case. Unlike *Nabozny*, *Flores*, and *Ramirez*, the student in this case filed a constitutional challenge because he was subjected to highly disparate punishment in a court of law. In this manner, he was contesting mistreatment not by his peers or by school officials but by the legal system itself.

Matthew Limon was convicted for violating Kansas criminal law after engaging in voluntary sexual activity with another male student at a school for the developmentally disabled. Limon had just turned eighteen, and the fellow student was approximately three years younger. Had the two been of different genders, Limon would have been eligible for a significantly lower penalty under the Kansas "Romeo and Juliet" statute, but the statute applied only if "the victim and offender are members of the opposite sex."[58]

Limon's challenge went all the way to the U.S. Supreme Court, which then directed the Kansas state court system to reconsider its ruling against the defendant in light of the recent *Lawrence v. Texas* decision. The Kansas Supreme Court subsequently found, in 2005, that *Lawrence* indeed controlled the analysis and that a state statutory scheme requiring significantly higher penalties for voluntary sexual conduct between two teenagers of the same gender was unconstitutional under the Fourteenth Amendment.[59]

The state court found the differences in the punishments to be "harshly disparate" and not justifiable in the aftermath of *Lawrence*. In so doing, it clearly and directly found that *Lawrence,* a decision originally about adults, now also applied to young people. Indeed, the Kansas court noted that the stigma *Lawrence* sought to address was probably even greater for teenagers than for the adults in the Texas case.

The *Limon* decision was also noteworthy for its detailed rejection of numerous arguments that have often been employed in different guises to justify disparate treatment of LGBTs in a school setting. These rationales, relied on by the state court of appeals majority in its earlier ruling against the defendant, included "the protection and preservation of the traditional sexual mores of society," "preservation of the historical notions of appropriate sexual development of children," and "promotion of parental responsibility and procreation." Every one of the enumerated justifications for treating gays and lesbians differently than heterosexual teenagers was explicitly discredited in this context by the conservative Kansas Supreme Court.[60] Thus, even though *Limon* addressed a substantially different set of facts, when combined with the continued series of victories by aggrieved LGBT plaintiffs nationwide in cases reflecting patterns of peer mistreatment and educator complicity, the results of the Kansas litigation further strengthen the rights of gay and transgender students to be treated equally in the public sector.

Additional Laws Bolstering Students' Right to Be Out

Most of the disputes involving LGBT students in the public schools directly or indirectly implicate safety concerns. Thus students who are mistreated merely for the fact that they are open regarding their sexual and/or gender identity can also and often do rely on negligence law, threat law, harassment law, and a growing number of state statutes designed to maximize campus safety for everyone.

Negligence law is based on well-settled legal principles and is relatively consistent from jurisdiction to jurisdiction. K–12 educators typically have a duty to supervise and an obligation to act reasonably toward all students. If students are injured in a school setting and the injury can be linked to the acts or omissions of school district employees, both the employees and the district can be held liable.[61]

Threat law has become increasingly prominent in the years since the tragic shootings at Columbine High School and the September 11, 2001, attacks on the nation. Not only do school officials have the option of suspending or expelling students for threatening their peers[62] but also criminal statutes allow, and may in fact dictate, the arrest and prosecution of such perpetrators.[63] And if school officials do not intervene to put a halt to threatening behavior, or if they intervene to help some students but not others, they themselves may be found negligent for any subsequent injuries.

Harassment law has grown and developed over the past several decades, particularly with regard to the fine-tuning of frameworks governing hostile-environment sexual harassment in the workplace. These frameworks have been applied to peer-to-peer harassment in a school setting under Title IX, and school districts may be found liable for deliberate indifference to known acts of harassment.[64] Peer-to-peer sexual harassment generally differs from peer mistreatment of LGBT persons in that the former is typically sexually charged while the latter tends to be what is commonly viewed as "gay bashing," yet many LGBTs are victimized by sexual harassment, especially openly lesbian and transgender youth. The strengthening of laws in this area provides additional protection for them if they choose to be out.[65]

Moreover, the past decade has seen additional legal activity under Title IX, with commentators, jurists, and federal agencies beginning to find that this venerable federal statute directly protects LGBT students from discrimination.[66] In particular, there has been an extensive focus on the plight of gender-nonconforming students, who may or may not be gay but are disproportionately victimized by relentless bullying in school communities.

Two cases addressing the tragic suicides of young gay teenagers in this context reflect this legal activity. For example, in 2010, the U.S.

Department of Education Office for Civil Rights (OCR) and the Department of Justice responded to a complaint filed against the Tehachapi Unified School District in California by a parent following the September 2010 suicide of her thirteen-year-old son, Seth Walsh. The complainant alleged that, prior to his death, Walsh was subject to chronic sex-based harassment by his peers at a district middle school and that, despite having notice of the harassment, the district failed to respond to it appropriately. Walsh was in the eighth grade at the time that he hung himself.

On the basis of the evidence gathered, OCR and the Department of Justice concluded that the district violated Title IX as well as Title IV of the Civil Rights Act of 1964 after determining that the student suffered sexual and gender-based harassment by his peers, including harassment based on his nonconformity with gender stereotypes; that the harassment was sufficiently severe, pervasive, and persistent to interfere with his educational opportunities; and that despite having notice of the harassment, the district did not adequately investigate or otherwise respond to it.[67]

The resolution agreement between the U.S. government and the school district is instructive in its application of federal civil rights law to incidents of peer harassment of LGBT and gender-nonconforming students, whether LGBT or not. To settle the case, the school district agreed to be subjected to several years of monitoring on its antiharassment efforts and to train school staff on how properly to handle complaints.[68]

Superintendent Richard Swanson said in an interview that he looked forward to implementing the changes outlined in the district's agreement with the Department of Education's civil rights division, such as adopting lessons to combat bullying and conducting regular surveys on school environment. "The conclusions are devastating really," Swanson said. "Things get by us, there are things we need to do to respond and to change, and I think we have the chance to be exemplary. We can either be resistant or stick our head in the sand, or we can move forward."[69]

In a similar dispute that arose in the aftermath of thirteen-year-old Texas teenager Asher Brown's suicide, linked to alleged anti-gay bullying at his middle school, the district defended its case in court.[70] Although the court ruled in 2012 that the lawsuit could continue under Title IX, Brown's parents ultimately chose to drop the case in 2013 when their attorney concluded that the legal standard for prevailing under the federal statute could not be met. However, in a public statement accompanying the announcement that the case would be dropped, the family's attorney concluded that "the school system is better off because of the lawsuit. It prompted it to increase training and awareness."[71]

In addition to these basic categories of law that apply nationwide, individual states may adopt legislation that sets forth precise mandates relating to campus safety for LGBT students. In recent years, a growing number of states have moved in this direction. A March 2018 analysis of relevant state education laws reveals that fourteen states and Washington, D.C., have state-level antidiscrimination laws that protect students from discrimination based on their sexual orientation; thirteen of those states plus Washington, D.C., protect students from discrimination based on both their sexual orientation and their gender identity; and nineteen states plus Washington, D.C., prohibit bullying in schools on the basis of sexual orientation and gender identity.[72]

Moreover, the *Georgetown Journal of Gender and the Law*, in a 2017 analysis, identified relevant public accommodation laws that may provide additional protection for LGBT youth. According to the analysis, "six states' and Washington, D.C.'s public accommodation laws prohibit discrimination based on sexual orientation and apply explicitly to schools. Another twelve states' public accommodation laws prohibit discrimination based on sexual orientation and could be interpreted to apply to schools. The public accommodation laws of California, Maine, Minnesota, and Washington have already been interpreted to protect LGBT youth in schools; the remaining states' public accommodation laws remain untested."[73]

It should also be noted that, in addition to legislation specifically seeking to combat the mistreatment of gay and gender-expansive students, general prohibitions against employment discrimination on the basis of LGBT identity can further bolster these students' rights. As discussed in chapter 4 of this book, twenty states plus the District of Columbia have adopted such anti-discrimination legislation.

Finally, California Penal Code Section 422.6 merits attention as a noteworthy example of how existing laws can be strengthened by providing explicit protection for persons who have been mistreated on the basis of their sexual orientation. Subdivision (a) provides, in pertinent part, that "no person . . . shall by force or threat of force, willfully injure, intimidate, interfere with, oppress, or threaten any other person in the free exercise or enjoyment of any right or privilege secured to him or her by the Constitution or laws of this state or by the Constitution or laws of the United States in whole or in part because of one or more of the actual or perceived characteristics of the victim . . . [including sexual orientation]." Under California law, then, it may be the case that intentional egregious mistreatment of students on the basis of their actual or perceived sexual orientation by any person on campus may rise to the level of a crime and be punishable under this statute by arrest, prosecution, imprisonment and/or fine.[74]

It is clear that the law in this area today is very different than it may have been when even the youngest members of a school's faculty, staff, and administration were K–12 students themselves. Court decisions that are proving to be turning points have come down primarily over the past fifteen to twenty-five years, and long-standing doctrine addressing campus safety issues has been strengthened by relevant state statutes only over the past two decades.

The obligations of educators with regard to LGBT students in the K–12 public schools are affirmative and unequivocal, even in the states that have not adopted laws specifically addressing sexual orientation and/or gender identity. Under legal mandates that range from First and Fourteenth Amendment principles to negligence law, threat law, and harassment law, it is now undeniable that school district employees must be there for all students equally. States with more specific laws have only reinforced mandates that already apply everywhere.[75]

The laws impacting LGBT students in U.S. public education have undergone a clear and unequivocal transformation, but a recognition of this changing reality is only the beginning of the analysis in this book. If LGBT educators continue to be prevented from serving as valuable resources in this context because their own right to be out is compromised, and if issues relating to gay and gender-expansive youth cannot be discussed openly in school settings, then the rights won by young people thus far are necessarily limited and incomplete. Indeed, the 2008 Lawrence King tragedy appears to be a prototypical example of such a dynamic. School officials did recognize King's right to be out, but there is growing evidence that on-site educators (some of whom were themselves LGBT) failed to intervene in the sequence of events leading up to the killing. In addition, reports indicate that the topics of homosexuality and gender nonconformity were rarely discussed openly in formal settings, despite the fact that they were clearly on the minds of so many as the events continued to unfold. The next two chapters thus turn to the legal terrain and the day-to-day realities that implicate the rights of LGBT educators generally as well as the ability of school officials to address these issues openly in a collaborative and professional manner.

4

CHALLENGES FOR LGBT EDUCATORS

The Tension between Rights on Paper and the Realities of the Classroom

For LGBT teachers and school-site administrators, the realities are perhaps even more complex than those that exist for gay and gender-expansive youth. The history of public education in this country is filled with examples of K–12 educators who were excluded from employment initially or lost their jobs when it was discovered that they were lesbian, gay, bisexual, and/or transgender.[1] As recently as 1978, California Proposition 6 (the Briggs initiative) sought to completely bar "homosexuals" from teaching in the state's public schools.[2]

Indeed, the campaign for the Briggs initiative was not that far removed in time from the post–World War II era of pervasive government-sanctioned harassment, vilification, and brutalization of gays. In his extensive documentation of the cultural and historical forces that accompanied the anti-gay activity on the part of law enforcement officials, David Sklansky explains that related policies and practices "lasted well into the 1960s":

> Along with the Red Scare, the Lavender Scare quickly spread outward from investigations of government officials to embrace many other sectors of American life. Private businesses, particularly those hoping to sell goods or services to the government, began widespread screening and surveillance of their employees to ferret out homosexuals. School teachers, local government employees, and university professors came under scrutiny for their sexual practices and inclinations.[3]

Sklansky emphasizes that "gay men and lesbians remained objects of fear, ridicule, and contempt" throughout the decade that has come to be associated with an entire panoply of "rights" movements. He tells of a 1966 *Time* magazine essay titled "The Homosexual in America," for example, in which the editors concluded that homosexuality was "a pernicious sickness" and "a pathetic little second-rate substitute for reality" that deserved "no encouragement, no glamorization, no rationalization, [and] no fake status as minority martyrdom." The essay, Sklansky writes, "warned that mainstream values were under 'vengeful, derisive' attack from 'homosexual ethics and esthetics'; in some areas of the arts, 'deviates' were 'so widespread' they sometimes appeared 'to be running a kind of closed shop.'"[4]

Twelve years after the *Time* essay, many Americans still shared a similar mind-set, and the 1978 Briggs initiative was seen by large numbers of registered voters as a logical response to the emergence of the gay rights movement and the attendant coming out of gays and lesbians across the country. Yet, even twenty-five years after Briggs, Supreme Court justice Antonin Scalia, dissenting in *Lawrence v. Texas,* aligned himself unapologetically with the thinking behind the initiative when he insisted that "many Americans do not want persons who openly engage in homosexual conduct as partners in their business, as scoutmasters for their children, [or] as teachers in their children's schools." Two other members of the Court at the time, Chief Justice Rehnquist and Justice Thomas, joined in Scalia's opinion. And although the *Los Angeles Times* reported in 2004 that "almost seven in 10 Americans know someone who is gay or lesbian and say they would not be troubled if their elementary school-age child had a homosexual teacher," and although 61 percent in the same poll said that "a homosexual would make a good role model for a child,"[5] the Pew Research Center found in 2007 that 28 percent of Americans still agreed with the goals of the Briggs initiative and believed that school boards "should be able to fire" teachers who were known to be gay.[6]

The complex and highly nuanced nature of this area is reflected in additional noteworthy findings from the Pew survey. For example, in the twenty years that Pew had been tracking this issue, the percentage of people who would endorse the firing of gay and lesbian teachers merely because of their sexual orientation dropped from 51 percent in 1987 to less than 30 percent, for the first time, in 2007. And while such firing was backed in 2007 by 38 percent of those who did not have "close friends or family members who are gay," the percentage dropped to 15 percent for those who did have such a level of contact with LGBTs. In addition, geography was clearly a factor in this context. Pew found that "people living in the south (37%) were less likely to know gay people well than people living in the Northeast or West, and people living in rural areas (34%) were less likely to say so than those in urban or suburban areas."[7]

In sum, poll data and national survey results documented throughout this book continue to support the conclusion that there has been a significant positive change in the attitudes of Americans toward LGBT educators in recent decades. However, substantial percentages of people—particularly in certain regions and in rural areas—continue to oppose the idea that LGBT educators even be hired to teach their children. After all the progress that had been made, for example, a 2008 survey revealed that the number of people who opposed allowing gays and lesbians to teach even at the college and university level was as high as 20–25 percent in certain parts of the country.[8] And despite the positive correlation between knowing gay people well and support for them in this context, the Pew 2007 survey revealed that a full 15 percent of those "who have a close friend or family member who is gay" would still advocate firing them from teaching jobs for no reason other than their sexual orientation. With regard to transgender teachers, all evidence points toward the fact that opposition to their being teachers at any level continues to be even higher yet.

In light of these realities, K–12 educators are still confronted with a combination of subtle pressure and express admonition that together limit their ability to be open about who they are. Too often, such limitations continue to be reflected in job placement and promotion decisions that favor educators whose sexual orientations and gender identities appear to conform to mainstream norms. Public school educators may have an emerging right to be out under the law, but in day-to-day educational practice—and particularly in certain communities—that right may be severely curtailed.

A key distinction between K–12 educators and K–12 students in this regard is the difference in their respective roles. Teachers and school-site administrators are expected to build academic skills and impart knowledge, subject to relevant state standards and curricular frameworks. They may be delegated with the responsibility of imparting certain values that are contained in statutory or policy guidelines, but beyond these guidelines, they are generally prohibited from seeking to persuade students to adopt particular political, religious, or social points of view. Yet although public school educators cannot feel as free as their students might feel to speak about their own lives, identities, and personal perspectives, neither must they feel that they have to keep their identities to themselves. Within the parameters of their designated roles, they have the same right to be out regarding fundamental aspects of identity, personhood, and group affiliation as their straight counterparts.

Few people expect teachers to be automatons, but at the same time, it is generally agreed that under First Amendment principles, K–12 teachers should not be indoctrinating their students. While the courts have not provided a precise test for "indoctrination," the First Circuit Court of Appeals has set forth the contours of relevant guidelines in this area. The court concluded in 2008, under applicable precedent, that if it is assumed "that there is a continuum along which an intent to influence could become an attempt to indoctrinate," factors to consider include whether the alleged indoctrination is "systemic," whether students are "required . . . to agree with or affirm" a particular idea, and whether they are "subject to a constant stream" of similar content.[9]

It must be recognized that the growth of a K–12 teacher's right to be out in the public sector may have been slowed during this era by questionable lower court decisions that appear to have curtailed the First Amendment rights of public educators in certain parts of the country. Thus teachers and school-site administrators must be more careful about what they say now than they may have been in the recent past, and they should make certain that they know the nature and extent of the restrictions that might be in place in their districts.

Still, LGBT educators are not without protections in this context. Indeed, this chapter maps out the contours of their emerging right to be out, a right grounded in the equal protection guarantee of the Fourteenth Amendment and often buttressed by relevant state statutes, state case law, and collective bargaining agreements. Unlike the rights of gay and gender-expansive students, educator rights are not necessarily strengthened by freedom-of-expression law, but it may well be the case—especially in certain jurisdictions—that the First Amendment can still enhance this multifaceted legal imperative.

After examining the interrelated sources of the public educator's right to be out and the nuances of related public policy considerations, the chapter concludes with two real-life case studies. The studies high-light the current state of the law and demonstrate the potential effective-ness of the right, but they also reveal how much work still needs to be done before day-to-day realities unfold in a manner consistent with the overall thrust of the recent legal developments.

Fourteenth Amendment Rights of Educators

The Fourteenth Amendment Equal Protection Clause is the central guid-ing principle governing employment discrimination law in the public sector. Under this venerable constitutional provision, people similar-ly situated must be treated equally. When intentional discrimination is shown, the Fourteenth Amendment alone often serves as the primary basis for a plaintiff's victory. In addition, the mandate of the Equal Pro-tection Clause can be strengthened by specific federal and state laws pro-hibiting discrimination on the basis of categories such as race, gender, religion, age, and disability.[10] Gay and gender-nonconforming educators in a growing number of states can benefit from such specific laws, which grant explicit protection against discrimination on the basis of LGBT sta-tus. But the Fourteenth Amendment remains the primary vehicle that ag-grieved educators can employ in this context.

No education cases addressing alleged discrimination on the basis of LGBT status have yet reached the U.S. Supreme Court, but the Court did prohibit LGBT-related discrimination in *Romer v. Evans* and *Lawrence v. Texas*. Indeed, even in the years immediately preceding the 2003 decision in *Lawrence,* the tide had begun to turn in favor of out educators who were dismissed from their positions simply because of who they were. Under employment discrimination law, such dismissals are not holding up in court.

Glover v. Williamsburg Local School District (1998)

A noteworthy example of this trend is the 1998 federal court victory by Ohio teacher Bruce Glover. A forty-six-year-old openly gay white man in a relationship with an African American man, Glover left the insurance industry to pursue a career in education. After successfully completing student teaching and receiving an Ohio teaching certificate, he took a po-sition as an upper elementary teacher in Williamsburg, Ohio.[11]

Things started to deteriorate when a false rumor began circulating that Glover and his partner had been holding hands at the sixth-grade holiday party. In January, even after it had become clear that the rumor was false and that Glover had done nothing other than be out as a gay person, school district officials began warning him, lecturing him, monitoring his classroom excessively, and creating an increasingly hostile and humiliating environment. Administrators admonished him "to be careful not to do anything which might fuel rumors and upset the community" and warned him "that people in the community might be concerned if Glover had to stay after school alone with a male student." In addition, he was told "that he had better be careful because there was a small group of parents that was out to get him."[12] At the end of the school year, despite a solid overall record of teacher evaluations, Glover was not rehired.

Glover challenged the decision not to rehire him under the Equal Protection Clause of the Fourteenth Amendment. He alleged that the school board's decision was discriminatory "based on his sexual orientation, his gender, and the race of his partner." The court determined that "homosexuals . . . are entitled to at least the same protection as any other identifiable group which is subject to disparate treatment by the state." The court also explained that the principle would be the same if Glover had been arrested discriminatorily based on his hair color, his college bumper sticker, or his affiliation with a disfavored company. Furthermore, the court declared,

> a state action which discriminates against homosexuals and is motivated solely by animus towards that group necessarily violates the Equal Protection Clause, because a "desire to effectuate one's animus against homosexuals can never be a legitimate governmental purpose."[13]

The court found that the evidence, taken together, "demonstrates that the . . . purported reason for Glover's nonrenewal was pretextual, and in fact the Board discriminated against Glover on the basis of his sexual orientation."[14]

The court went on to find that the school board's "wrongful decision" had denied him the opportunity to teach at Williamsburg Elementary School in both 1996–97 and 1997–98 and that he had been unable to secure a permanent teaching job since the nonrenewal of his contract. Therefore the court ordered the board to reinstate him as a full-time teacher at Williamsburg Elementary School with a two-year contract, beginning with the 1998–99 school year. Glover was also awarded money for back pay as well as emotional distress. The court emphasized that, as a result of the board's wrongful actions, "he suffered considerable anguish as well as humiliation in the community. Glover's psychological injuries also had physical effects, including anxiety, sleeplessness, and digestive problems," for which Glover had been receiving treatment since fall 1996.

Weaver v. Nebo School District (1998)

The ruling in the *Weaver* case is consistent with the trend recognizing strong Fourteenth Amendment rights for openly LGBT educators in an employment discrimination context. In this 1999 lawsuit, a Utah federal court considered the case of nineteen-year veteran teacher and volleyball coach Wendy Weaver—a person with an "unblemished" record and a reputation as "an effective and capable teacher"—who answered affirmatively when asked by a senior team member if she was gay. She was subsequently admonished "not to make any comments, announcements or statements to students, staff members, or parents of students regarding... [her] homosexual orientation or lifestyle." In addition, she was removed from her position as volleyball coach.[15] Weaver brought a lawsuit challenging the school district's decisions under both the First Amendment and the Fourteenth Amendment.

The court found that, "to the extent [that the letters of admonishment] limit her speech in this area, they violate the First Amendment." Turning to the equal protection clause claim, the court also found in favor of the plaintiff. "The Fourteenth Amendment of the United States Constitution entitles all persons to equal protection under the law," the court explained. "It appears that the plain language of the Fourteenth Amendment's Equal Protection Clause prohibits a state government or agency from engaging in intentional discrimination—even on the basis of sexual orientation—absent some rational basis for so doing. [And] the Supreme Court has recognized that an 'irrational prejudice' cannot provide the rational basis to support a state action against an equal protection challenge."[16]

The court then found that the "negative reaction" some members of the community may have to gays and lesbians "is not a proper basis for discriminating against them":

> If the community's perception is based on nothing more than unsupported assumptions, outdated stereotypes, and animosity, it is necessarily

irrational and under *Romer* and other Supreme Court precedent, it provides no legitimate support for the School District's decisions.

Although the Constitution cannot control prejudices, neither this court nor any other court should, directly or indirectly, legitimize them.[17]

The school district was ordered to reinstate Weaver as the volleyball coach and to remove the offending letters of admonishment from her personnel file.[18]

The Dana Rivers Settlement

The former David Warfield had already built an impressive résumé when he was hired by a suburban Sacramento school district to teach history and journalism at Center High. He had been a navy electronics expert, a political consultant and school board member in Huntington Beach, California, a baseball coach, and a whitewater rafting instructor.

Warfield proved to be a highly successful teacher at Center High throughout the 1990s. Over a nine-year period, students often called him one of the best teachers they had ever had, and many remembered him as a major influence on their lives. According to the *New York Times,* he developed a program for unmotivated students that became the award-winning Media Communications Academy. He was the recipient of an $80,000 grant for the program, won the school's Stand and Deliver Award for the teacher who most inspired students, and received a standing ovation from the school district staff at its annual meeting in late 1998.[19]

Yet when Warfield revealed in a spring 1999 letter to his colleagues that he was transitioning from male to female, would be undergoing gender affirmation surgery, and planned to return to school as a transgender woman named Dana Rivers, it was not long before he was removed from his teaching position.[20] Although the exact parameters of what transpired during the intervening months may never come to light, it is well established that, upon learning the news of the teacher's transition, the school board sent a letter disclosing it to all fifteen hundred families in the district. Only a handful of parents protested the teacher's actions, but board members who were uncomfortable with Rivers's gender identity expressed their disapproval openly and triggered an increasingly rancorous debate.

Rumors abounded during that spring and summer, including allegations by a handful of parents that Rivers had shared inappropriate personal details regarding the decision with her students.[21] According to school board member Ray Bender, the majority of the board did not want a transgender teacher in the district, and the allegations enabled them to justify their 3–2 decision never to allow Rivers back. She was put on administrative leave in late summer and eventually dismissed.

Bender, who voted against dismissal, was quoted as saying that the Dana Rivers controversy had become "a cause for religious conservatives assisted by the Pacific Justice Institute, a local conservative legal organization that demanded that the school board fire the teacher or face a lawsuit." Indeed, one board member was heard telling a parent that this was "a holy issue."[22]

The parents' allegations were disputed by Rivers and several of her former colleagues. The colleagues stated that students learned the news of the transition when teachers read the original coming-out letter to their classes. Rivers reported that as rumors began circulating throughout the school and students began asking about them, she agreed to an interview with the school newspaper, which published a twenty-six-hundred-word profile during the final week of the semester. Teachers in the school district joined forces in a strong show of support for Rivers. On an annual district staff day in September 1999, two hundred district teachers—along with forty students—held a lunchtime rally for Rivers across the street from the district offices. But the school board majority ignored this show of support and voted for dismissal.[23]

Represented by private counsel but also in consultation with the ACLU, Rivers challenged her termination as discriminatory and as a violation of her First Amendment rights. Very quickly, she won a $150,000 settlement with the school district. Although she reportedly vowed that she would never teach again, she was offered a job eighteen months later in a suburban San Jose high school and returned to the classroom in fall 2001. In addition to her ongoing contributions as an educator, Rivers became a prominent public interest activist and continued working to achieve equal rights for transgender persons.[24]

Other Legal Developments Bolstering the Right to Be Out

Although the Equal Protection Clause of the Fourteenth Amendment remains the country's most basic prohibition against discrimination by the government and other public officials, a range of other legal developments provide additional protection in both the public and the private sectors. For LGBT educators, one of the most significant developments in this context was the California Supreme Court's 1969 decision in *Morrison v. State Board of Education.*

Most state education codes include the provision that a teacher may be dismissed for "immoral or unprofessional conduct." Yet these words are typically not defined, and it was not until *Morrison* that a major U.S. court interpreted their meaning and determined how they should be applied. Coincidentally, the dispute at issue in this case was LGBT related, arising over an attempt to revoke the credentials of a male teacher who had engaged in a brief, consensual affair with another male teacher in his school district.[25]

Marc Morrison was a fully credentialed educator employed by the Lowell Joint School District in the Whittier–La Habra area of Southern California during the early 1960s. His record was unblemished, with no one ever complaining about or criticizing his classroom performance or suggesting that even his "conduct outside the classroom . . . was other than beyond reproach."

By early 1963, Morrison had become friends with fellow teacher Fred Schneringer and apparently served as a trusted adviser for him and his wife. In spring of that year, a time when the Schneringers were "involved in grave marital and financial difficulties," Morrison spent much time with the two of them, frequently visiting their apartment and providing them with ongoing "counsel and advice." When Schneringer later obtained a separation from his wife, Morrison suggested a number of women whom Schneringer might consider dating.[26]

A year after these events, for reasons that remain unclear, Schneringer chose to reveal that during a one-week period in April 1963, he and Morrison "engaged in a limited, non-criminal physical relationship." At the time, most common homosexual acts were considered crimes in almost every state, so the fact that the conduct between the two was described as "non-criminal" indicates just how limited the physical contact must have been.[27] Yet, as a result of these events, Morrison was apparently pressured to resign from the district, and the state board of education followed by revoking his teaching credential, a revocation that Morrison chose to contest in court.[28]

Although Morrison acknowledged that the contact had been "of a homosexual nature," this was not a "gay rights" case in the traditional sense of the term. Morrison never claimed to be gay,[29] never asserted any rights under either the First or Fourteenth Amendment, and never argued that he was being discriminated against in any way. His entire argument, which ultimately carried the day, was that what he had done did not warrant revocation of his teaching credential because it had nothing to do with his fitness to teach.

Justice Matthew Tobriner, who later wrote on behalf of the California Supreme Court majority in the case, conducted a thorough review of other decisions addressing dismissal of employees, both within and outside of education, for alleged "immoral or unprofessional conduct" or "moral turpitude." Tobriner found that by using these terms in the Education Code, "the Legislature surely did not mean to endow the employing agency with the power to dismiss any employee whose personal, private conduct incurred its disapproval":

> In the instant case the terms denote . . . conduct . . . which indicates unfitness to teach. Without such a reasonable interpretation the terms would be susceptible to so broad an application as possibly to subject to discipline virtually every teacher in the state.[30] . . . We cannot believe that the Legislature intended to compel disciplinary measures against teachers . . . [for conduct that] did not affect students or fellow teachers. Surely incidents of extramarital heterosexual conduct against a background of years of satisfactory teaching would not constitute "immoral conduct" sufficient to justify revocation of a life diploma without any showing of an adverse effect on fitness to teach.[31]

The court examined the circumstances surrounding Morrison's brief affair and found "no evidence" whatsoever that his conduct "indicated his unfitness to teach."[32] In conclusion, Justice Tobriner emphasized that "the right to practice one's profession is sufficiently precious to surround it with a panoply of legal protection" and that "the power of the state to regulate professions and conditions of government employment must not arbitrarily impair the right of the individual to live his private life, apart from his job, as he deems fit."

The *Morrison* decision proved to have wide-ranging impact over the entire area of public employment law, and it soon took on the trappings of a national decision as one court after another followed its reasoning and adopted its conclusions.[33] For gays and lesbians, the decision was particularly important. The fact that private homosexual conduct between consenting adults would not result in the loss of employment, absent additional facts, was a giant step forward for LGBT educators. Only a decade earlier, it was gays who had suffered the most under the arbitrary dismissal policies of the McCarthy era, when President Eisenhower issued an executive order requiring that all "known homosexuals" be dismissed from government jobs.[34] More people lost their jobs under this edict than under any other category of alleged security threat during the McCarthy "witch hunts."[35]

In the decades that followed the *Morrison* decision, federal and state laws were adopted that seek to provide additional protection above and beyond the Equal Protection Clause. Some of these laws focus specifically on the workplace, whereas others are more general. Typically, the laws delineate exactly which groups are protected.

Title VII of the Civil Rights Act of 1964, for example, prohibits discrimination in the workplace on the basis of "race, color, religion, sex, or national origin." To the extent that LGBT educators alleging employment discrimination also fall into one or more of these categories, and should they be able to prove discriminatory conduct on the basis of such characteristics, their legal position might certainly be strengthened. But as a general rule, apart from the Equal Protection Clause and the *Morrison* decision, the most important guarantee of equal treatment for LGBT educators in this area is the passage of a federal or state law specifically prohibiting discrimination on the basis of sexual orientation or gender identity.

Although it should be noted that at the federal level, as of 2018, there was still no explicit statutory protection against discrimination on the basis of LGBT status,[36] there has been significant movement in this area at the state and local levels. By March 2018, for example, twenty states plus the District of Columbia had banned employment discrimination based on sexual orientation and gender identity, and two additional states had banned discrimination based on sexual orientation alone.[37]

Finally, an often overlooked area in this context is the opportunity to build protections against discrimination into collective bargaining agreements. Models exemplifying such an approach may be found nationwide, and indeed the prospects of forging alliances between LGBTs and labor movements should not be discounted.[38] All told, employment discrimination protection is an area that has seen much progress, and the right to be out for LGBT educators under our legal system continues to be strengthened as a result.

The Unsettled Role of the First Amendment
Free Speech Clause for LGBT Educators

The U.S. Supreme Court explicitly recognized the First Amendment rights of K–12 public school teachers in *Pickering v. Board of Education of Township High School District No. 205* (1968) and emphasized a year later in the *Tinker* case that neither students nor teachers shed their constitutional rights to freedom of expression at the schoolhouse gate. The Court went on to explain that First Amendment rights are explicitly made available to public school teachers and school-site administrators, subject to specific limitations that arise out of the "special characteristics of the school environment."[39] Yet much of what has transpired in the federal courts during the following decades appears to have cut back on both the guidelines of *Pickering* and the promising language of that era.

In *Pickering,* the Supreme Court directly addressed the free speech rights of public school educators. Illinois teacher Marvin Pickering brought a lawsuit challenging the school board's decision to dismiss him for sending a letter to a local newspaper expressing concern over a proposed tax increase and criticizing the way in which the board and the superintendent had addressed budget issues in the past. In its defense, the school board contended that the dismissal was justified because Pickering's letter was "sufficiently critical in tone" to result in interference with "orderly school administration" and because some of the statements in the letter were false.[40]

The Court ruled in favor of the teacher, finding that the statements were "in no way directed towards any person with whom [Pickering] would normally be in contact in the course of his daily work as a teacher" and that there were therefore no issues regarding either the maintaining of discipline or interfering with "harmony among coworkers." As to the apparent falsehood of some of the remarks, the Court found that, "absent proof of false statements knowingly or recklessly made," a teacher may not be dismissed for exercising his "right to speak on issues of public importance." Indeed, the Court concluded that, on matters of "legitimate public concern," "free and open debate is vital to informed decision-making by the electorate. . . . It is essential that [teachers] be able to speak out freely . . . without fear of retaliatory dismissal."[41]

Fifteen years later, in 1983, the Supreme Court revisited its decision in *Pickering,* discussing the case at length as it considered the scope of a public employee's free speech rights outside of an education setting. In the dispute *Connick v. Myers,* an assistant district attorney in New

Orleans was terminated from her position after distributing a question-naire soliciting the views of her fellow staff members on such matters as transfer policy, office morale, and level of confidence in supervisors. Rul-ing for the employer, the Court found this situation to be different from that in *Pickering,* because the distribution of the questionnaire was the equivalent of speaking "not as a citizen upon matters of public concern, but instead as an employee upon matters only of personal interest."[42]

Since 1983, the Supreme Court has not directly addressed K–12 teacher freedom of expression. Yet two subsequent cases ostensibly hav-ing nothing to do with teacher speech—*Hazelwood v. Kuhlmeier* (limiting student freedom of the press in 1988) and *Garcetti v. Ceballos* (uphold-ing the discipline of a deputy district attorney in 2006)—have been ap-plied by lower courts in a growing number of cases to rule against pub-lic school educators in First Amendment disputes. Decisions applying *Hazelwood* led to confusion among the federal courts and criticism in the legal literature regarding whether *Hazelwood* or *Pickering* or some combination of the two should guide the resolution of these disputes.[43] But the willingness of lower courts to apply *Garcetti* to teacher speech in the public schools in recent years has led to an even greater outcry from First Amendment advocates and scathing criticism from commentators generally.[44]

Garcetti was a 5–4 ruling against Deputy District Attorney Richard Ceballos, who alleged that he had been reassigned and denied promo-tion as a result of internal memos he had written to his supervisor.[45] In the memos, he complained that a search warrant central to a case he was prosecuting contained numerous inaccuracies and reflected shoddy work by law enforcement officials. "We hold," Justice Kennedy wrote, "that when public employees make statements pursuant to their official duties, the employees are not speaking as citizens for First Amendment purposes, and the Constitution does not insulate their communications from employer discipline."[46] The Court also identified a distinction be-tween educator speech and that of a deputy district attorney writing an internal memo, expressly mentioning teaching as an area where "some expressions related to [the] job" are in fact granted First Amendment protection.[47] In so doing, the Court recognized that there are different types of public employees and that employment circumstances can vary greatly in that regard.

Ignoring this distinction, however, a number of lower courts have applied *Garcetti* to rule that when public school teachers are "making statements pursuant to their official duties," they have virtually no First Amendment rights at all. A prime example of such a controversial ruling is *Mayer v. Monroe County Community School Corp.*[48] In *Mayer,* a non-tenured probationary teacher argued that her First Amendment rights had been violated when she was let go at the end of the 2002–3 school year because of comments she had made in response to a student question during a classroom lesson on current events. Apparently, the student asked Mayer whether she "participated in political demonstrations," and in response, she stated that when she passed a demonstration and saw a placard saying "Honk for Peace," she honked her car's horn to show support. Relying directly on *Garcetti,* the Seventh Circuit upheld the lower court ruling in favor of the Bloomington, Indiana, school district. Judge Easterbrook conceded that the court was not addressing statements teachers make "outside of class." "It is enough," he wrote, "to hold that the first amendment does not entitle primary and secondary teachers, when conducting the education of captive audiences, to cover topics, or advocate viewpoints, that depart from the curriculum adopted by the school system."[49]

Perhaps most troubling to critics of this decision was the Seventh Circuit's assertion that a district "hires" a teacher's speech. "Expression," Judge Easterbrook wrote, "is a teacher's stock in trade, the commodity she sells to her employer in exchange for a salary." Many see this as a demeaning characterization that views K–12 teachers as little more than functionaries charged with the figurative equivalent of playing back recorded messages to their students.

It can be argued that the basic principle underlying this decision—that teachers must keep to the curriculum in a formal classroom setting—is not a departure from a rule that has been in existence for some time now. But Mayer apparently was keeping to the curriculum. Students ask curriculum-related questions in virtually every lesson that is taught nationwide, and many of these questions—particularly in current events lessons—focus on whether and to what extent the teacher has been impacted by or is involved in these events. Especially given the realities of the K–12 public schools today and the intense level of conversation that occurs all the time between and among students and teachers, the dignifying of a student question by a teacher who is simply admitting that she honked her horn when she saw a sign that said "Honk for Peace" can hardly be characterized as egregious. Absent additional facts, it does not in any way rise to the level of indoctrination under the prospective guidelines described earlier in this chapter. It was not "systemic," students were not "required to agree with or affirm a particular idea," and they were not "subject to a constant stream" of similar content.

Yet, with a growing number of courts reading the U.S. Supreme Court cases as dictating similar results, especially after *Garcetti*, LGBT educators may have a very limited opportunity to employ First Amendment principles in support of their emerging right to be out. They still appear to have broad rights off campus and outside of work to speak as private citizens on matters of public concern, and thus, absent additional facts, teachers could write letters to newspapers, speak on television, or blog online about gay rights issues and, in so doing, identify as LGBT. Even on campus, the First Amendment may help enhance the right to be out in certain jurisdictions where courts have not explicitly delineated rigid allowable limitations for teacher freedom of expression.

In addition, it must be recognized that, as a general rule, individual states and local school districts may decide to adopt policies and programs that can enable more open dialogue in this regard. As discussed in chapters 5 and 7 of this book, California in 2011 became the first state to require the teaching of positive, age-appropriate LGBT content in the social studies curriculum.[50] And there are school districts (and private schools) across the country that mandate LGBT-related discussions and activities, sometimes at a particular time of year, that are generally linked to the teaching of tolerance and the celebration of differences. The Los Angeles Unified School District has done this by officially recognizing June as Gay and Lesbian Awareness Month. As reported in a 2000 Ninth Circuit opinion, an official school district memo designated the month as "a time to focus on gay and lesbian issues" and noted that the board of education's resolution setting this in motion was passed to support "educating for diversity."[51] The memo also informed schools that "posters and materials in support of Gay and Lesbian Awareness Month" would be provided to them and that these were designed to aid in "the elimination of hate and the creation of a safe school environment for all students."[52] In circumstances such as these, LGBT-related lessons consistent with district policy and delivered pursuant to a state's academic and curricular standards might appropriately include references by teachers to actual gay individuals and their work. Heterosexual teachers conducting such lessons might decide to mention gay friends or family members of their own. In a similar fashion, LGBT teachers might choose to reference their own identities in this context, especially if they are already out on campus and in the larger community.

In all jurisdictions, however, the key analysis starts with the Fourteenth Amendment, not the First Amendment. As explored in more detail in the case studies that follow, LGBTs must be treated the same as their straight counterparts in this context and must be allowed to say whatever those counterparts are allowed to say about fundamental aspects of their identity and personhood, should LGBTs choose to do so.

Case Studies of LGBT Educators
Who Asserted Their Right to Be Out

Building on the analysis in this chapter thus far, this section examines the stories of two LGBT educators who experienced difficulties in their respective school districts after they came out. In one case, the district backed away from its initial apparent attempt to discipline the teacher, and the matter was resolved quickly and quietly; in the other, the district consistently looked the other way while the teacher experienced devastatingly brutal harassment and mistreatment. After discussing the facts of the respective cases, the section analyzes the implications for gay and gender-expansive educators, both under the law and as a matter of public policy.

Case Study 1: The Fanelle Controversy and Its Implications

Teachers cannot plan for every possible interaction that may occur, and a classic example of unpredictability in the classroom is when a student asks the teacher a question of a personal nature. Indeed, it is rare for a school year to go by anywhere in the country without teachers being asked such questions as "Who did you vote for?" or "What's your opinion on this?" or "Are you married?" It was just this sort of unpredictability that led to a highly publicized controversy in 2004 regarding Ron Fanelle's coming out to his seventh- and eighth-grade students.

A popular social studies teacher at Monte Vista Middle School in Ventura County, California, Fanelle agreed to marry longtime partner Randy Serak when then San Francisco mayor Gavin Newsom opened City Hall ceremonies to same-sex couples in early 2004. Fanelle, who was out to his colleagues and his principal but not to his students, was congratulated on the marriage at a staff meeting, after which several teachers apparently spread the news.

According to reports in the *Los Angeles Times,* the *Ventura County Star,* and the *San Jose Mercury-News* and on CNN, Fanelle was asked by one of his students in front of his entire seventh- and eighth-grade class whether it was true that he had recently gotten married. He chose to answer yes. He was then asked whether it was true that he had married another man, and he answered yes to that as well. It is not clear from the news reports exactly what transpired, whether a formal lesson had already been under way, or precisely what interaction followed. It appears, however, that students gave him a standing ovation and that several follow-up questions were asked, such as how long the two had been together and why Fanelle did not wear a wedding ring or have a picture of Serak on his desk. It also appears that a boy in the class "began muttering negative comments under his breath" and that Fanelle then chose to conduct an unplanned discussion regarding suffrage, bigotry, harassment law, and the Magna Carta.

As a result of these events, one parent apparently requested that his child be removed from the class, and another—whose child was not enrolled in the class at all—chose to raise the issue publicly at the next school board meeting. The parent was quoted as saying that he came to the meeting "with a heavy heart. A seventh-grade history teacher announced to his students he's gay. I'm very upset and disappointed that this person was bringing his homosexual platform to the classroom." The story was picked up by the local media, a school district "investigator" showed up unannounced at Fanelle's home to ask him questions, and there were intimations that Fanelle might be disciplined or even fired. The California Teachers Association provided him with an attorney, and Fanelle also contacted the highly regarded legal director of the National Center for Lesbian Rights, Shannon Minter, who spoke on his behalf to the press.[53]

Several weeks later, after an outpouring of support for Fanelle among parents and students in the community, the school board announced that the "investigation" had ended and insisted that there was never any consideration of discipline or job-related action. Yet the emotional and very public nature of the controversy left Fanelle and many other LGBT educators concerned about the double standard that still apparently prevails in so many places.

The Fanelle matter was a widely reported incident that did not result in any legal action. But had proceedings gone forward, and had Fanelle chosen to contest any efforts by the school district to reprimand, censor, or discipline him in any way, Fourteenth Amendment principles and related legal doctrine outlined earlier in this book would have been central to his case. He would have been able to argue not only that he had the right to be out generally but that he had the right to be treated the same as any straight teacher who had revealed his or her different-sex marriage.

Absent additional facts, a married teacher, when asked if he or she is married, is entitled under U.S. law to answer the question honestly. Whether the marriage is a gay marriage or a straight marriage is irrelevant in these circumstances. Fanelle did not break any laws, and unless all teachers in the district are prohibited from responding to questions about their marital status, he must be allowed to respond as he did. Indeed, these assertions would be at the heart of his case under the Fourteenth Amendment and would likely result in a victory for him.

It is conceivable, however, that, had this case gone to trial, the school district would have acknowledged the preceding points but would have sought to focus on the discussion that ensued in Fanelle's class after his response to the questions, and perhaps also on the age appropriateness of his comments and actions. They might have argued that he was within his rights to answer the initial questions but that he should have then returned to the lesson of the day, consistent with the principle that in a formal classroom setting, a teacher is supposed to be delivering the curriculum.

Although it is unclear from the reports exactly what took place in the class following students' questions, the discussion apparently addressed the topic of marriage equality within the larger context of the history of our legal system. Fanelle appeared to have focused on highlights of the legal system's growth and development by acknowledging basic rights of human beings and addressing discriminatory practices of both monarchies and elected governments. Among these highlights were the Magna Carta and the right to vote.[54]

Building on the long-standing, research-based education principle that teachers cannot be expected to be automatons and that the direction a lesson takes is inevitably shaped by student questions and comments, there is no evidence from the reports that Fanelle engaged in a one-sided diatribe or exhibited any attempt to indoctrinate his students. Under the indoctrination analysis referenced earlier in this chapter, an attempt to indoctrinate arises only in circumstances when the alleged indoctrination is "systemic," when the students are "required . . . to agree with or affirm" a particular idea, and/or when they are "subject to a constant stream" of similar content. Nothing of this sort happened in Fanelle's class. In fact, there were no allegations of any efforts at indoctrination. The parent who complained to the school board did not have a student in Fanelle's class and focused not on the discussion that ensued but merely on the fact that Fanelle had acknowledged his homosexuality.[55]

Neither is there any evidence that the teacher even strayed from the content of his curriculum. This was a seventh- and eighth-grade social studies class. Seventh-grade curriculum in California includes world history, and eighth-grade curriculum includes U.S. history. Fanelle appeared to be conducting a focused discussion that brought together highlights from both.

As a matter of policy, Fanelle was also following two research-based guidelines that every K–12 teacher-preparation program recommends: seek to debrief highly unusual occurrences and take advantage of the "teachable moment." Something unusual had just happened in Fanelle's classroom. Students could not and should not be expected simply to return to the matters at hand without having a chance to process the event. This was also a classic example of a teachable moment, particularly in light of the fact that in spring 2004, the media was filled with pictures of gay and lesbian couples getting married in Massachusetts and San Francisco, Canada was in the process of legalizing same-sex marriage, and a debate over these matters was raging across the nation. The best social studies teachers are always expected to integrate current events into the curriculum, helping students see the relationship between present and past events as well as the larger scope of history across the board. What better opportunity to do this than to reveal that the students' own teacher had participated in the very events that were at the top of the news during that time?

As to the age-appropriateness question, there was no evidence that Fanelle's discussion was not age appropriate.[56] Traditionally, marriage has not been an off-limits topic in a K–12 classroom, and students at every age know that people form relationships, pair up, and often eventually get married. Middle school students in the earlier stages of adolescence are particularly cognizant of these facts as they begin to experiment with friendships and relationships of their own.

Yet, even though marriage as a topic has come up as a matter of course in K–12 classrooms throughout history—and indeed elementary school students in the United States have traditionally been taught a unit on "the family" in the primary grades—it must be acknowledged that the question of how to approach it in public schools today has emerged in the aftermath of unprecedented developments over the past two decades. Internationally during this time, as discussed in chapter 2, twenty-seven countries legalized same-sex marriage. In the United States, marriage equality was legalized in all fifty states plus Washington, D.C., in 2015.[57]

The tension regarding the dramatic developments that led to the legal recognition of same-sex relationships in so many contexts and on so many fronts since the year 2000 came to a head during and after the fall 2008 California Proposition 8 campaign. Advocates of Proposition 8, which sought to take away the newly won right of gays and lesbians to marry the persons they loved, had great success turning the debate away from marriage equality and directly toward the public schools. In the eyes of many, a widely distributed television campaign ad featuring Pepperdine University Law School professor Richard Peterson was seen as helping to turn the tide in favor of proponents of the proposition, which was approved by the voters by 52 percent to 48 percent.

The *Yes on 8* ad with Professor Peterson unfolded as follows:

GIRL: Mom, guess what I learned in school today?

MOTHER: What, sweetie?

GIRL: I learned how a prince married a prince, and I can marry a princess.

PETERSON, *voiceover*: Think it can't happen? It's already happened. When Massachusetts legalized gay marriage, schools began teaching second graders that boys can marry boys. The courts ruled parents had no right to object. [*Video shows the phrase "No Legal Right to Object" and then the name of the case cited, Parker v. Hurley (2008).*]

NARRATOR: Under California law, public schools instruct kids about marriage. [*Video shows California Education Code, Section 51933(7): "Instruction and materials shall teach respect for marriage."*] Teaching children about gay marriage will happen here unless *we* pass Proposition 8. Yes on 8.[58]

Although the ad clearly tapped into a fear of the unknown and a discomfort with change on the part of many voters, it must be noted that whether and to what extent the California public schools "taught" gay marriage was not dependent on the passage of Proposition 8. Many teachers were already addressing these issues within the context of the state curricular standards, and students were bringing in front-page newspaper articles reporting on developments in this context across the country and around the world. The Fanelle incident was just one of many examples. These practices did not stop when Proposition 8 was approved. Indeed, if anything, the volatile aftermath of the ballot-initiative campaign led to much more "teaching" of gay marriage in public school classrooms than ever before.[59]

The events surrounding Ron Fanelle's out speech reflect what can and does happen in some areas of this country when a K–12 educator reveals an identity that may vary from the expected norm. Such events can be particularly difficult during times when emotions are running high regarding gay and lesbian issues, as they were in March 2004, fall 2008, and summer 2015, both locally and nationally. The Fanelle controversy also reflects the continuing prevalence of "conspiracy theories," as indicated by the one parent's allegation at the school board meeting that the teacher was "bringing his homosexual platform to the classroom."[60] Even so, despite all that occurred and all the emotions that were stirred up within this community, no case was ever brought against the teacher. While we may never know precisely why the district decided against taking disciplinary measures, officials may have concluded that, both under the law and as a matter of policy, Fanelle had been well within his rights and had conducted himself both appropriately and professionally.

Case Study 2: Schroeder v. Hamilton School District (2002)

The *Schroeder* case is perhaps the most egregious example in recent memory of an educator who was abused and vilified for no reason other than his LGBT status. Not only was a twenty-year veteran of a suburban Milwaukee, Wisconsin, school district mistreated by school officials but he was also mercilessly harassed over an extended period of time by members of the school community, including colleagues, parents, and students. Despite the fact that the mistreatment led to both a nervous breakdown and the loss of employment, the *Schroeder* case was decided against the teacher.[61]

The facts of the case document at great length a pattern of indifference by school officials to the persistent and pervasive mistreatment of an openly gay teacher who had come out after being with the district for more than fifteen years. In the years immediately after he came out, Tommy Schroeder experienced harassment primarily from students at Templeton Middle School. This included "a student calling him a faggot and remarking 'How sad there are any gays in the world'; another student physically confront[ing] Schroeder after shouting obscenities at him; catcalls in the hallways that he was a 'queer' or a 'faggot'; obscenities shouted at him during bus duty; harassing phone calls with students chanting 'faggot, faggot, faggot' and other calls where he was asked whether he was a 'faggot'; and bathroom graffiti identifying Schroeder as a 'faggot,' and describing, in the most explicit and vulgar terms, the types of sexual acts they presumed he engaged in with other men." Schroeder reported this harassment on several occasions, and the defendants apparently "consequenced" students who could be identified. Yet much of the harassment was allegedly anonymous, and the school district made little or no apparent effort to discover who might have been behind it.

After repeatedly requesting a transfer, Schroeder was finally reassigned to Lannon Elementary School in fall 1996. At Lannon, the harassment came primarily from parents in the school community. An anonymous memo, for example, was circulated by a parent stating that "Mr. Schroeder openly admitted at a District meeting that he was homosexual. Is that a good role model for our 5-, 6- and 7-year-old children?" People began calling him a pedophile and suggesting that he was sexually abusing small boys. The tires on Schroeder's car were slashed, and he began receiving anonymous harassing phone calls at home, which included comments such as "Faggot, stay away from our kids" and "We just want you to know you . . . queer that when we pull out all our kids, you will have no job."

Not only did district colleagues consistently fail to intervene but they often made things worse through their own comments and messages they conveyed to others. Fellow teachers at both schools reportedly made numerous insulting and homophobic comments about Schroeder behind his back over time. The assistant principal refused to relieve Schroeder of bus duty, even after repeated requests and extensive evidence that some of the most egregious harassment occurred when students shouted antigay epithets at him from bus windows. Little or no apparent effort was expended on the part of either bus drivers or the administration to limit this student behavior. Instead, Schroeder was told that "you can't stop middle school kids from saying things. Guess you'll just have to ignore it."[62]

After repeated complaints by Schroeder over time, the administration at Templeton finally sent a memo to faculty and staff. However, the memo stated only "that students were continuing to use 'inappropriate and offensive racial and/or gender-related words or phrases,' and that 'if you observe or overhear students using inappropriate language or gestures, please consequence them as you feel appropriate.'" Indeed, perhaps the most egregious behavior on the part of school officials was the refusal by Templeton administrators even to mention the word "gay" or the words "sexual orientation" in their communication with the school community. People reading the memo could reasonably conclude that it had absolutely nothing at all to do with LGBT issues.

However, the comments of the Lannon principal a few years later may be even more egregious than the decision to treat terms such as "sexual orientation" as unmentionable in a school setting. At Lannon, as a result of completely unsupported allegations on the part of certain parents that Schroeder was a pedophile, the principal told Schroeder that they might need to implement "proximity supervision," meaning that Schroeder would not be allowed to be alone with male students.[63]

At trial and during the appeal, the school district asserted that its officials did "all that could be done." The Seventh Circuit's majority ultimately disagreed with the district and acknowledged that more could indeed have been done, yet the panel found no violation of the Equal Protection Clause, because it concluded that school officials had done "all that [was] required." The panel majority held that the evidence presented by Schroeder did not amount to proof that he had been "treated differently from his non-homosexual colleagues."

Yet the judges also held that even if there had been differential treatment in particular instances, that treatment was justified. Judge Manion, writing for the majority, focused extensively on the refusal of district administrators to use the word "gay" or the term "sexual orientation" in the memo to the school community. The court acknowledged the differential treatment between an earlier response to racial harassment and the response to the harassment of the openly gay teacher but found this differential treatment to be justified. Manion concluded that the school was right not to mention the words in a middle school environment. "Unfortunately," he stated, "there is no simple way of explaining to young students why it is wrong to mock homosexuals without discussing the underlying lifestyle or sexual behavior associated with such a designation."[64]

A principled reassessment of the *Schroeder* court's opinions leads to the conclusion not only that the *Schroeder* case was wrongly decided under the law and as a matter of public policy in 2002 but also that today such a case might very well be decided differently. First and perhaps foremost, the majority in *Schroeder* failed to acknowledge key facts. In the words of dissenting Judge Diane P. Wood:

> *never,* in the course of these events, did the administration ever attempt to dissuade either students, parents, or anyone else in the broader community of the school district, to refrain from discrimination or harassment based upon sexual orientation. Indeed, . . . school officials never even told the students that the words being used to describe Schroeder transgressed the general code of civility the majority is recommending to schools. Schroeder was just told to tough it out. . . .
>
> The only thing Schroeder wants is the *same* treatment that everyone else is receiving.[65]

Schroeder argued, essentially, that the school district violated his rights by treating him differently than others because of his openly gay identity. The district replied that, practically speaking, it could do only so much, and that in any case, its legal obligations did not extend to "protecting" its employees from the type of mistreatment Schroeder experienced, especially when at least some of the mistreatment took place outside of the work environment and when at least some of the perpetrators were persons outside of the district's control.

It must be acknowledged that society often asks more from school officials than they are reasonably able to do. Indeed, the duty to supervise on school grounds under tort law is generally viewed as a duty to protect students, not as a duty to protect teachers. Yet, as a matter of policy, it is unfathomable to imagine school district officials telling faculty that they should not expect their personal safety to be addressed on campus. Indeed, laws mandating safe environments for employees in the workplace generally are widespread and extensive at both the federal and the state levels.

Perhaps the strongest argument set forth by the defendants in the *Schroeder* case is that they should not be held accountable for the portion of the harassment that took place outside of school grounds. Even so, the law recognizes that the obligations of school officials do not stop at the boundaries of district property, whether online or offline. Relevant legislation and recent court decisions often include explicit obligations in this regard.[66] In addition, bonds between schools, families, and communities are recognized in both the scholarly literature and the policy mandates of school districts as an integral component of the work that takes place in K–12 public education. On a day-to-day level, such mandates are reflected in parental advisory groups, school-site councils, joint ventures with local businesses, and a wide range of school–family–community partnerships. Education leaders are not generally expected to limit their work to what takes place within schoolhouse gates; the most effective district officials always see their responsibilities as extending out into the larger school community, including but not limited to building bridges between people and maximizing communication. Such responsibilities are informed by the recognition that what takes place outside the schoolhouse gates often impacts what goes on within those gates, and vice versa. In the end, there is much that officials can and should be doing if a teacher is being mistreated off campus for reasons that relate directly to and flow from what is taking place on campus.

Schroeder demonstrated that he was in fact treated differently in this context than others were and still others might have been.[67] The panel majority did not acknowledge the differential treatment, even as it attempted, in almost the next breath, to justify the very differential treatment it would not acknowledge. In retrospect, the court was wrong on both counts: compelling evidence was presented of disparate and differential treatment by school officials of the openly gay veteran teacher, and Judge Manion's attempts to justify the school's treatment of LGBT harassment as different from other forms of harassment demonstrates a disappointing lack of familiarity with the scholarly research regarding age-appropriate methods of addressing peer mistreatment in the schools. Manion suggested that the only way to address anti-gay harassment among middle schoolers is to discuss homosexual activity in explicit detail, a suggestion that flies in the face of consistent findings by both scholars and practitioners today. Upper elementary and middle school students know what being gay means. They do not need to be given any details; they simply need to be taught that every person, gay or straight, deserves to be treated with equal dignity and equal respect. These are lessons that can and should be imparted at any age level.

Moreover, the court's attempt to negate the existence of any actual injury because the harassment was not physical but simply verbal is particularly disingenuous. In any harassment inquiry, the court is expected to look at the totality of circumstances, and in this fact pattern, it is undeniable that the aggregate result of the mistreatment led to devastating injuries: Schroeder's complete nervous breakdown and loss of employment. As Judge Wood described it, "there is no dispute that Schroeder was a very good teacher; he taught successfully for the District for 22 years. . . . [Yet] he left the school [on February 11, 1998,] . . . a ruined man."[68]

With so much discrimination still evident *within the law* in 2002, the *Schroeder* panel majority was not a complete outlier when it concluded that differential treatment could be justified under a principled reading of federal antidiscrimination law. The decision bucked the emerging trend, but cases such as *Glover* and *Weaver* were decided by the lower courts, and the LGBT student cases could conceivably be distinguished as inapplicable precedents because they also included ongoing physical abuse. Perhaps most important, a good number of states—both at the time that the events unfolded and even in 2002—still criminalized private consensual relations between gay adults.[69]

Given the 2003 decision in *Lawrence v. Texas,* however, an attempt to justify the type of differential treatment that was evident in *Schroeder* is likely to be more difficult in the future. Blanket assertions such as the one by Judge Manion that "a student cannot . . . be disciplined for expressing a home-taught religious belief that homosexual acts are immoral" would likely be deemed incorrect as a matter of law today. Students do indeed have the right to express home-taught religious beliefs, but a student's religious beliefs cannot be invoked to justify or explain away the brutal mistreatment of an openly gay employee when similar mistreatment of other employees would not be tolerated. Manion's reasoning not only runs counter to *Lawrence* but also ignores central principles identified by the courts under the Establishment Clause of the First Amendment.

Absent additional facts, a school district's persistent refusal to intervene on behalf of a beleaguered employee and a federal court's attempts to justify such actions in this context fly in the face of the broad liberty and equality principles articulated in *Lawrence.*[70] In addition, *Lawrence* is reinforced in a growing number of states by local laws explicitly prohibiting discrimination on the basis of LGBT status.[71]

Sixteen years after the decision by a divided appellate panel, and at least twenty years after most of the events took place, a reassessment of this case leads to the conclusion that, were the lawsuit to be filed today, Tommy Schroeder would likely emerge victorious. Indeed, such a principled reassessment serves as an example of just how significant the gains by LGBTs have been and just how strong the aggregate power of both case law and statutory law has become in this area.

Heightened Judicial Review of
Discrimination against LGBT Persons

During this difficult transition period, gay and gender-expansive teachers must make sure to know their community and be aware of rules and regulations adopted by their school districts. But under the legal and public policy principles identified in this chapter, and absent additional facts, public school educators do have an emerging right to identify openly as LGBT should they wish to do so. It is not an absolute right, and it still may be contested in many places, but it is increasingly being recognized in a growing number of districts across the country. Moreover, in circumstances where it may be viewed as appropriate for heterosexual colleagues to reference their relationships or even to introduce boyfriends, girlfriends, spouses, or children, it is equally appropriate under the law for gay persons to do the same.

LGBTs also have the same right as their colleagues to play supportive roles as advisers for students with similar interests and identities. For example, just as an openly Christian teacher can serve as a faculty adviser for an after-school student Bible club, so too can an openly gay or transgender teacher serve as a faculty adviser for a gay–straight alliance. Just as a teacher with a strong ethnic identity can serve as an adviser for students who seek a safe place to discuss their own identity-related issues, so too can an openly LGBT educator serve as an adviser for queer or questioning students pursuant to district-approved "safe zone" programs.

Both school districts and courts of law continue to acknowledge the implications of these changing realities in a wide variety of contexts. The movement toward a heightened level of judicial review for discrimination against LGBT persons, discussed in chapter 2 of this book, is a notable recent example of such acknowledgment. As referenced in the *Schroeder* analysis, under the Equal Protection Clause of the Fourteenth Amendment, discrimination on the basis of sexual orientation has traditionally merited the lowest level of judicial scrutiny, rational-basis review, with great deference given to lawmakers, policy makers, and practitioners on a day-to-day level. Although LGBT plaintiffs have begun to prevail even under rational-basis review, there has been significant movement on this front over the past ten years, with both federal and state courts considering whether a heightened level of judicial review is warranted for sexual orientation discrimination.[72]

The unanimous 2009 ruling by the Iowa Supreme Court is a noteworthy example of this trend. In holding that the state's prohibition of same-sex marriage violated the Iowa Constitution, the court found that discrimination on the basis of sexual orientation warranted a heightened level of judicial review under state equal protection principles.[73] The Iowa court analyzed whether heightened scrutiny was applicable by examining four factors that courts have considered in making such a determination: (1) the history of invidious discrimination against the class burdened by the legislation, (2) whether the characteristics that distinguish the class indicate a typical class member's ability to contribute to society, (3) whether the distinguishing characteristic is "immutable" or beyond the class members' control, and (4) the political power of the subject class. The court found that all four factors cut in favor of the gay and lesbian plaintiffs.[74]

Of particular interest within the larger context of this book is the Iowa court's analysis of "immutability" as a factor that would support a finding of heightened scrutiny. The court concluded that it "need not definitively resolve the nature-versus-nurture debate currently raging over the origin of sexual orientation in order to decide plaintiffs' equal protection claims. . . . We agree with those courts that have held the immutability prong of the . . . inquiry surely is satisfied when . . . the identifying trait is 'so central to a person's identity that it would be abhorrent for government to penalize a person for refusing to change [it].'"

Applying this principle, the court noted that even the defendants in the case acknowledged that "sexual orientation is highly resistant to change." Iowa Supreme Court justice Mark S. Cady, a Republican appointed by a conservative governor, went on to explain that, in the determination of all seven justices, "sexual orientation 'forms a significant part of a person's identity'":

Sexual orientation influences the formation of personal relationships between all people—heterosexual, gay, or lesbian—to fulfill each person's fundamental needs for love and attachment. Accordingly, because sexual orientation is central to personal identity and "may be altered [if at all] only at the expense of significant damage to the individual's sense of self," classifications based on sexual orientation "are no less entitled [to be reviewed under heightened scrutiny] . . . than any other group that has been deemed to exhibit an immutable characteristic."[75]

Not only is the Iowa court's analysis of the immutability factor under federal and state equal protection principles certain to inform decisions in future cases but also the explicit recognition that everyone has a sexual orientation—which "can be altered, if at all, only at the expense of significant damage to one's sense of self"—could be an important breakthrough in this area. Many lawmakers, for example, may be less willing to oppose the inclusion of the term "sexual orientation" in antidiscrimination legislation if they come to view it as not just about gays but about everyone. Similarly, many in both the education community and the legal community will be less willing to support differential treatment for LGBT educators, in the way that the key players in the *Schroeder* case did, if it is indeed acknowledged that everyone has a sexual orientation and that "it would be abhorrent for government to penalize a person for refusing to change [it]." Such a construct will inevitably provide additional support for the conclusion that discrimination against anyone on the basis of sexual orientation is as pernicious as any other discrimination on the basis of fundamental aspects of identity and personhood.

5

CURRICULUM, RELIGION, MORALITY, AND VALUES

As more and more gay and gender-nonconforming persons come out, issues relating to their lives are increasingly coming out into the open as well. Homosexual attraction, for example, was once referred to as "the love that dare not speak its name," because LGBT-related topics were rarely discussed in public places. But all that has begun to change. Along with a right to be out as a person has come a right to speak openly regarding the issues.

In a sense, at this time, it can be said that the subject matter itself has come out of the closet. Reviewing the progression of developments, it is evident that what was once limited to private conversations, secretive gatherings, and often-anonymous publications ultimately spread to courtrooms, bookstores, entertainment media, the arts, and increasingly society as a whole. The emergence of the internet as we know it today proved to be another major turning point. Encouraged by the apparent freedom of cyberspace, its seemingly protective nature, and the unparalleled ability to communicate with so many persons simultaneously, people became much more willing to speak openly about gay and transgender matters. Indeed, this dynamic was dramatically enhanced by the distributed and anarchic nature of the online world.[1]

Perhaps the most compelling breakthrough has come even more recently, as LGBT-related issues are discussed openly and increasingly at the dinner table and in public places. Many people no longer feel that they need to lower their voices at restaurants and in airports, for example, when they mention words such as "gay" or "lesbian." As a result of these societal shifts and the accompanying changes in the law, educational institutions in growing numbers are also addressing LGBT-related topics. Educators are talking about these issues openly in professional settings for the first time, and the topics are also finding their way into the K–12 curriculum.

There are many reasons why it is appropriate to include LGBT-related content in the curriculum. From an academic perspective, in the cognitive domain, such content fits within state curriculum frameworks and is aligned with state standards developed pursuant to the Every Student Succeeds Act.[2] Gay and transgender issues are often the subject of front-page stories in the mainstream media, and the public school classroom has always been seen as an appropriate venue for the discussion of current events. In addition, from a school climate perspective, in the affective domain, such content has been shown to aid in the personal growth and well-being of gay, bi, and gender-expansive students, while at the same time fostering collaboration and helping to create a safer campus environment for all students, gay or straight.[3]

Yet fierce opposition to LGBT-related content has persisted in the K–12 schools. Some oppose the inclusion of the subject matter unless it is accompanied by disapproval of LGBTs, and others oppose the inclusion of any such content at all. Some oppose the content on religious grounds, some oppose the content on secular grounds, and some set forth arguments based on both religious and secular perspectives. Still others focus on the right to put forth a "countermessage" to what they perceive to be the "promotion" of homosexuality when it is addressed in something other than a negative manner.

This chapter identifies additional aspects of the right to be out within the context of the ongoing "morality and values" debates, and it seeks to clarify the extent to which the right includes both an ability to talk openly about LGBT-related topics and an ability to teach about these issues in a formal K–12 setting. It then examines the difficult controversies that have reached the courts regarding whether those who oppose the acceptance of an LGBT identity on religious grounds should be able to put forth their anti-gay and anti-transgender messages on public school campuses. Finally, and perhaps most importantly, the chapter addresses the extent to which a reasonable middle ground might be possible here.

Legal Principles Governing the Inclusion of
LGBT Content in the Curriculum

Under the First Amendment, students have a right to receive information and ideas, a right recognized by the U.S. Supreme Court in the 1982 case of *Board of Education v. Pico*. The *Pico* Court addressed the removal of certain books from school libraries and found the school board's actions to be unconstitutional under the First Amendment. Central to the Court's decision was Justice William Brennan's recognition that inherent in the right to speak was a right to receive information and ideas. Although Brennan's opinion initially garnered only a plurality of votes, major internet-related free speech clause decisions have further strengthened this right. Key language in the 1997 *Reno v. ACLU* case regarding the online world as a "dramatic" and "unique" "marketplace of ideas" and the positive references to *Pico* in several internet filtering cases over the next five to ten years bolstered the viability of the right and extended its scope.[4]

More recently, in 2017, plaintiffs successfully challenged the constitutionality of an Arizona statute that did away with a Mexican American ethnic studies program adopted by the Tucson Unified School District. In its First Amendment analysis, the trial court relied to a great extent on the right to receive information and ideas, emphasizing that the right applied "in the context of school curriculum design."[5]

Although there is a concurrent right of families *not* to receive information and ideas, buttressed by the long-standing right of parents to direct the upbringing of their children, the right to receive information is much stronger and much less limited in its scope. Parents who seek to overturn curriculum-related decisions in a court of law are rarely successful, with courts implicitly relying on the principle that members of the community have delegated the responsibility of developing curricular requirements and identifying appropriate instructional materials to duly elected officials at the state and local levels. Should families become unhappy with these decisions, they are seen as able to replace the officials with new representatives who can then change the status quo.

The paradigmatic case addressing a parental challenge to K–12 curriculum and instructional materials is *Mozert v. Hawkins County Board of Education*, decided by the U.S. Court of Appeals for the Sixth Circuit in 1987.[6] *Mozert* involved a challenge by seven families to the Tennessee County Board's use of the popular Holt, Rinehart, and Winston basal reader series for its elementary school reading curriculum. The series was a traditional, mainstream collection of stories and poems used in public schools nationwide.

Plaintiff families, who did not belong to a single church or denomination but considered themselves born-again Christians, argued that their First Amendment "free exercise of religion" rights were being violated by requiring their children to read and discuss content that was contrary to their sincerely held religious beliefs. In support of their argument, they referenced seventeen categories of offending material, which "ranged from such familiar concerns of fundamentalist Christians as evolution and 'secular humanism' to less familiar themes such as 'futuristic supernaturalism,' pacifism, magic and false views of death."

In an opinion that has come to be viewed as the equivalent of a national decision on this issue, the court ruled against the plaintiff families. It found that mere exposure in the public schools to ideas that might offend a family's religious beliefs does not constitute a violation of that family's rights under the Free Exercise Clause of the First Amendment. The court concluded that the element of compulsion is critical and that it would in fact be unconstitutional to require students "to affirm or deny a religious belief or to engage or refrain from engaging in a practice forbidden or required in the exercise of . . . religion." But the court found that such compulsion was lacking in this case. There was "no proof that any plaintiff student was ever called upon to say or do anything that required the student to affirm or deny a religious belief." There was no evidence that any student "was *required* to participate beyond reading and discussing assigned materials, or was disciplined for disputing assigned materials."[7] In language that has withstood the test of time and is particularly relevant within an LGBT-related context, Chief Judge Lively wrote:

> The "tolerance of divergent . . . religious views" referred to by the Supreme Court is a civil tolerance, not a religious one. It does not require a person to accept any other religion as the equal of the one to which that person adheres. It merely requires a recognition that in a pluralistic society we must "live and let live."

Perhaps the most consistently prevalent argument set forth by those seeking to prevent LGBT-related content from being included in the public school curriculum is that either the mere inclusion of such content or its inclusion without simultaneously casting gays and gender-nonconforming persons in a negative light constitutes the promotion of homosexuality and thus the fulfillment of a key conspiratorial goal of the "homosexual agenda."[8]

In light of the well-settled principles governing curriculum and instructional materials in the public schools, however, objections to gay and transgender content based on the allegation that the mere inclusion of such content is the equivalent of promoting and normalizing "homosexuality" have no basis under First Amendment jurisprudence. Not only has the right to receive information in the U.S. public schools been strengthened in recent years but a central feature of the 1987 *Mozert* ruling is the determination that exposure is not the same thing as promotion. The court found in explicit and direct language that the mere inclusion of material in the curriculum that might offend certain families' sensibilities, absent additional facts, cannot be deemed the equivalent of promotion. "While it is true," the *Mozert* court stated, "that these textbooks *expose* the student to varying values and . . . backgrounds, neither the textbooks nor the teachers teach, indoctrinate, oppose or *promote* any particular value."[9]

In this context, it must be noted that, under sexual and health education statutes set forth in Arizona and six southern states, legislators have limited the manner in which LGBT-related content can be included in the curriculum.[10] Most notably, Alabama and Texas require sex education programs to present homosexuality in a negative light. In Alabama, sex education course materials must emphasize, "in a factual manner and from a public health perspective, that homosexuality is not a lifestyle acceptable to the general public"; similarly, in Texas, such programs must "state that homosexual conduct is not an acceptable lifestyle." Arizona, though not requiring a negative portrayal, prohibits a positive portrayal. The Arizona sex education statutes prohibit any course of study that "promotes a homosexual life-style" or "portrays homosexuality as a positive alternative life-style," and the Arizona K–12 schools may not suggest that homosexual relations can constitute "safe methods of sex."[11]

However, it must be emphasized that only a relatively small number of states have such laws and that they are generally limited to the sex education context. In addition, researchers at the Gay, Lesbian, and Straight Education Network have noted that "several of these stigmatizing laws . . . have been repealed in a number of states and school districts. . . . At the district level, [for example,] the Anoka-Hennepin school district in Minnesota revised their Sexual Orientation Curriculum Policy, a similar law that applied to all school curriculum, after being sued by several students who claimed the school did little to address rampant bullying and harassment based on sexual orientation, gender identity, and gender expression." Moreover, efforts to pass new laws of this nature, such as Tennessee's "Don't Say Gay" bill, have also been largely unsuccessful.[12]

Indeed, under current law in the great majority of states, school districts and educators have the right to include LGBT-related content should they choose to do so; not only do they have the right to do this without simultaneously casting negative aspersions on gay and transgender people but they have the right to include gay-positive content in a wide variety of contexts. As a general rule, schools can allow gay–straight alliances to be formed and to meet on campus, they can allow Day of Silence and National Coming Out Day demonstrations, and they can establish safe zones where faculty are trained and made available specifically for LGBT students who want to discuss issues relating to sexual orientation or gender identity.[13]

It has also been established that school districts can choose to recognize a gay and lesbian awareness month, can mandate gay-positive displays, and can concurrently prohibit anti-gay displays by dissenting faculty, should the district so choose. In *Downs v. LAUSD* (2000), a conservative religious high school teacher objected to the Los Angeles Unified School District's decision to establish June as Gay and Lesbian Awareness Month and objected as well to the accompanying materials that were distributed and displayed.[14] Across the hall from one such display, Robert Downs had put up a competing bulletin board, replete with anti-gay invective, quotes from Leviticus, and the like.[15] After being asked to take the material down, he filed a lawsuit in federal court, arguing that his freedom-of-expression rights under the First Amendment had been violated.

Upholding the lower court's ruling in favor of the school district, the U.S. Court of Appeals for the Ninth Circuit found the district's acts to be the equivalent of "government speech" and determined not only that, under the First Amendment, the district had the right to engage in such speech but also that district employees could not engage in speech on school grounds that ran counter to the district's memorandum setting forth the parameters of the awareness month.[16] In direct and unequivocal language, the court explained that, as "an arm of local government, [a] school board may decide not only to talk about gay and lesbian awareness and tolerance in general, but *also to advocate such tolerance if it so de-*

cides, and restrict the contrary speech of one of its representatives."[17] The Court went on to say that, "just as a school could prohibit a teacher from posting racist material on a bulletin board designated for Black History Month, [LAUSD] may prohibit [Downs] from posting intolerant materials during 'Gay and Lesbian Awareness Month.'"

In the years following *Downs,* courts have also recognized the appropriateness of orientation programs for students and professional development programs for educators that have as their goal the treatment of openly LGBT persons with equal dignity and equal respect. Such recognition can be found not only in the approval of settlement agreements and consent decrees that resulted from litigation in this area but also in decisions such as the 2006 court ruling in Kentucky addressing a challenge to such mandatory sessions.

In *Morrison v. Board of Education of Boyd County, Kentucky,* conservative religious families objected to the mandatory student "diversity training" that the school district was legally obligated to conduct as a result of an earlier lawsuit and the consent decree that followed.[18] According to the court, the purpose of the training was "to address the issue of harassment at school, including harassment based upon actual or perceived sexual orientation," with the goal of "maintain[ing] a safe environment." Separate sessions for students and staff were mandated by the decree, with the requirement that the student training be age appropriate. Both the middle school and the high school sessions consisted of a one-hour video and comments from an instructor. After the video, students were given comment cards as well as the opportunity to ask questions. As specified by the decree, all students were required to attend.

Plaintiffs were parents of students at these schools who notified the district that their children would not be attending the sessions. After their children received unexcused absences, they filed a lawsuit in federal court alleging that the required attendance violated "their constitutional rights of free speech, equal protection, and free exercise as well as their right to direct the ideological and religious upbringing of their children." The parents objected because the sessions not only included extensive LGBT content but also did not present homosexuality in a negative light. They alleged that they were "prohibited from conveying their views on homosexuality by virtue of the Board's policies and practices."[19]

The Kentucky court ruled in favor of the school district, finding that under legal principles governing curriculum and instructional materials, no constitutional rights had been violated.[20] The court held not only that the district could legally address LGBT subject matter in middle school and high school settings without getting parental permission but also that addressing such content in an objective and dispassionate manner without also including anti-LGBT perspectives did not constitute the sort of one-sided "indoctrination" that the families alleged had taken place.[21]

The rulings mentioned here are further bolstered by several major appellate court decisions upholding the right of officials to make curriculum-related decisions without acceding to the demands of individual families who might question such decisions. For example, in ruling against parents who filed a lawsuit objecting to the sexually explicit content of a high school assembly, the First Circuit stated in 1995 that "if all parents had a fundamental constitutional right to dictate individually what the schools teach their children, the schools would be forced to cater a curriculum for each student whose parents had genuine moral disagreements with the school's choice of subject matter. We cannot see that the Constitution imposes such a burden on state educational systems."[22] Similarly, in deciding against a father who objected to the content of a seventh-grade health education course and sought a right to opt out, the Second Circuit concluded in 2003 that requiring a public school to accede to such demands by individual parents "would make it difficult or impossible . . . to administer school curricula responsive to the overall educational needs of the community and its children."[23] The Ninth Circuit came to a similar conclusion in 2005 when it held that "parents have no due process or privacy right to override the determination of public schools as to the information to which their children will be exposed while enrolled as students."[24]

Finally, consistent with these decisions, the First Circuit determined in 2008 that religious parents were not entitled to "prior notice" and an "exemption from . . . instruction" when supplementary reading materials in the primary grades included publications that in their view "indoctrinate[d] young children into the concept that homosexuality and homosexual relationships or marriage are moral and acceptable behavior." One set of parents had objected to a picture book that their child had brought home that "depicted different families, including . . . a family with two dads and a family with two moms." Another set of parents had objected to the fact that a teacher had read aloud to the class from a book titled *King and King*, which "tells the story of a prince, ordered by his mother to get married, who first rejects several princesses only to fall in love with another prince." In ruling against the parents, the court found the 1987 *Mozert* decision to be on point and controlling.[25]

Moreover, in what may be seen as a culmination of the aforementioned legal developments, the California State Legislature adopted the FAIR Education Act. In so doing, California became the first state in the country not only to require the inclusion of LGBT content in its K–12 public school social studies curriculum but also to ban any content that cast negative aspersions on LGBTs in general. The legislation added LGBTs and people with disabilities to an existing law that already included the same mandate and the same ban for other identity groups.[26]

In addition, the right to be out has been bolstered by statutes adopted by ten states and the District of Columbia prohibiting *mental health providers* from engaging in *sexual orientation change efforts* (sometimes known as conversion therapy) with patients under eighteen years of age. California, which was the first state to adopt such a law, defines mental health providers broadly to include licensed educational psychologists, credentialed school psychologists, and licensed clinical social workers, all of whom may be working with young people in K–12 educational settings.[27]

Legal Controversies Addressing "Countermessages" with Religious Content

A different type of LGBT-related education case has emerged in the past two decades, with lawsuits filed by religious students who argue that under the First Amendment, they should have the right to make statements of an anti-gay nature. Plaintiffs appear to be conceding—explicitly or implicitly—that open discussion of gay and transgender content is not only a given but also generally legal on K–12 public school campuses. What they want, however, is a right to counter what they view as gay-positive expression with messages of their own, typically rooted in conservative religious doctrine. The following pages explore the nuances of these volatile and highly publicized disputes.

Chambers v. Babbitt (2001)

Of all the cases discussed in this section, the *Chambers v. Babbitt* lawsuit may be the least controversial. Yet in some ways it may be the most instructive, because the judge's balanced approach showed sensitivity to both sides. In fact, it can be argued that the manner in which the judge approached the dispute points toward the identification of a reasonable middle ground in this highly controversial area.

The litigation stemmed from a Minnesota high school principal's attempt to prevent student Elliot Chambers from wearing a sweatshirt that had the message "Straight Pride" on the front and a symbol of a man and woman holding hands on the back. The precipitating factor that led to the wearing of the sweatshirt was apparently a "heated discussion about Christianity and homosexuality" at a meeting of a student-initiated Christian group. Several students, including Chambers, "cited biblical passages for the proposition that homosexuality is a sin," while a student named Travis argued "that Jesus' teachings confirm otherwise." After Chambers wore the sweatshirt, it was Travis who complained to the assistant principal about the garment "on behalf of students who were upset by it."

In explaining his decision to ban the shirt, Principal Babbitt referenced the negative reactions of certain students as well as generalized safety concerns. He noted also that fourteen physical fights had already taken place on campus by January of that year. Yet the court found under the *Tinker* rule that Chambers had demonstrated a strong likelihood of success in establishing that Babbitt's decision was unreasonable. The physical fights were apparently related to disputes on the basis of race, not LGBT status, and although the "Straight Pride" shirt had caused some tension, the court found that, on balance, the public's "unequivocal interest in the protection of First Amendment freedoms for all its members" outweighed the principal's concerns in this case.

Although the decision came down ostensibly in favor of an anti-gay plaintiff, the court went out of its way to make it clear that the opinion should not be construed as anti-gay. In fact, Judge Frank's comments in the final portion of his opinion may be among the most supportive of LGBT students ever to be recorded in a federal court decision. The court first began by expressing great empathy for the challenges faced by LGBT youth.[28] It then expressly rejected the plaintiff's contention that the school was "promoting homosexuality" by including sexual orientation in its "tolerance of diversity" posters and by establishing safe zones for LGBT youth:

> By displaying posters and lists of staff members who are willing to talk about issues of sexuality and now race, disability, gender, and religion, the

school has made a conscious and commendable effort at creating an environment of tolerance and respect for diversity. . . .

All students benefit from the respectful and thoughtful exchange of ideas and sharing of beliefs and practices. Schools, in particular, are vital environments that can provide an education of both the substance of diversity and the responsible manner with which such diversity is approached and expressed.

Finally, Judge Frank concluded, in words that are conceivably applicable to every dispute in this chapter, that "it is incumbent upon the school, the parents, the students, and the community . . . to work together so that divergent viewpoints, whether they be political, religious, or social, may be expressed in a civilized and respectful manner." Indeed, "the Court's emphasis on the public's 'unequivocal interest in the protection of First Amendment freedoms *for all its members*,' together with Judge Frank's clear and unambiguous support for the open expression of LGBT identity and the efforts of the school to be inclusive of gay and transgender students—even as he decided for the plaintiff—clearly provides a valuable roadmap for those addressing future controversies down the road."[29]

Hansen v. Ann Arbor Public Schools (2003)

The *Hansen* case presents a very different picture. The district comes across as very patient and very diligent in its efforts to craft a reasonable middle ground, while the judge appears to be completely disinterested in any attempt at compromising. Judge Rosen derides the Ann Arbor School District in language that contrasts dramatically with the *Chambers* decision, labeling its efforts one-sided and intolerant of "politically incorrect viewpoints."[30]

The dispute in *Hansen* centered on the student council's annual Diversity Week and the efforts of twelfth grader Betsy Hansen to share with others her sincerely held religious belief not only that homosexuality is a sin but also that it is not possible to reconcile homosexuality and religion. In theory, under long-standing First Amendment principles, and absent additional facts, Hansen would have a right to disseminate such a message, as long as she did so in a respectful manner that did not cause a material and substantial disruption and did not interfere with the rights of others.

Diversity Week in Ann Arbor traditionally included a series of campus events and activities, along with separate panels on race, religion, and sexual orientation. Hansen, a highly religious and outspoken Christian student who was a member of both the student council and the school's Pioneers for Christ (PFC) club, objected to the fact that sexual identity was included along with racial identity and religious identity in the school's celebration of diversity.

During the planning for the week, the school's gay–straight alliance (GSA) volunteered to organize the sexual orientation panel. The GSA put together a program focusing on homosexuality and religion, with six adult clergy and religious leaders from the community scheduled to present their views on different ways that religion and homosexuality might be reconciled. Upon hearing of this, Hansen demanded that she be allowed either to sit on the panel or to designate an adult panelist of her choice in order that she might disseminate her views. However, the panel was not designed to be a debate on the topic of whether homosexuality and religion could be reconciled, and her request was therefore denied.

The controversy around both the composition and the focus of the panel persisted in the weeks leading up to Diversity Week, and the faculty adviser for PFC continued to lobby for changes. On the Friday before the week was to begin, the principal convened a meeting of relevant faculty and other school officials to discuss whether it would be best to cancel *all* the panels. In the end, a decision was made to go forward with the events as planned, but PFC was offered the opportunity to organize and present its own separate panel on the topic of homosexuality and religion. The organization declined, giving as its reason the short amount of time left before the activities were to begin.

In an additional attempt to be inclusive, the school invited Hansen to present her views at a general assembly taking place that week, during which she would be one of three students giving two-minute speeches on the topic "what diversity means to me." All speeches at this activity apparently had to be submitted in advance for review. Hansen accepted the invitation, but during the review process, the principal found certain portions of her draft objectionable and "suggested" that she change the text accordingly. Hansen complied and then gave her speech, but she subsequently filed a lawsuit arguing that her First Amendment rights had been violated by the actions of the school during the entire series of events.

School officials appear to have engaged in a respectful and ongoing dialogue with both Hansen and the PFC faculty adviser. They did not agree to Hansen's demands regarding the existing panel, yet they did offer to allow the organization to present its own panel addressing a slightly different topic. In addition, they offered Hansen the opportunity to state her position at a different event later in the week. Although they required her to submit her speech for review and subsequently asked her to soften the language, the vetting procedures were apparently the same for every student speaker. There is no evidence that the school district did anything other than attempt to identify a reasonable compromise whereby Hansen could disseminate her views. Ruling in favor of Hansen, however, the district court found that the school's decisions to allow the panel to go forward, to keep Hansen off the panel, and to suggest certain changes to her two-minute speech were unconstitutional under applicable freedom-of-expression principles.

As a matter of law, it is questionable whether the court identified the proper legal principles that should govern this case. Instead of deciding the case under the *Tinker* rule, for example, the court determined that the student council event constituted "school sponsored speech" and that the proper standard was whether the restrictions were "reasonably related to legitimate pedagogical concerns." Even if the court was correct and this standard applied, it flies in the face of precedent for a court of law to suggest that the Ann Arbor District's attempts to impose reasonable limits on Hansen's expression for the purpose of fostering an atmosphere in which everyone might work together in a spirit of reconciliation were not an action "reasonably related to the legitimate pedagogical concerns" of a K–12 educator.[31] This rule has traditionally been applied by the courts in a manner highly deferential to school officials, recognizing their responsibilities and obligations to the students and the community. Certainly it is in the best interests of everyone that school-sponsored events in large public high schools reflect a spirit of community and a respect for differences, and federal courts have consistently deferred to the judgment of educators in this context.[32]

The court was also arguably incorrect in concluding that the school violated the viewpoint discrimination doctrine by presenting what the judge called a "one-sided," "pro-homosexual" panel and asking Hansen to tone down her speech. The U.S. Supreme Court has explained the parameters of the viewpoint discrimination doctrine in clear and precise language. According to Justice Kennedy:

> the necessities of confining a forum to the limited and legitimate purposes for which it was created may justify the State in reserving it for certain groups or for the discussion of certain topics. Once it has opened a limited

forum, however, the State must respect the lawful boundaries it has itself set. The State may not exclude speech where its distinction is not "reasonable in light of the purpose served by the forum," nor may it discriminate against speech on the basis of its viewpoint.[33]

Clearly the school district had opened a limited public forum for a discussion of racial, religious, and ethnic diversity. Thus it certainly had the right, as the Supreme Court stated, to set the boundaries of this forum. Indeed, its boundaries can best be understood by examining the express purpose of Diversity Week. According to Principal Henry Caudle, all the events of Diversity Week were designed with "the overall objective" of "teach[ing] young people that there are differences that should be celebrated, [that] because we are different doesn't mean that there has to be strife or discor[d,] and that we can work together, [and] should work together." Caudle added that the district was "trying to help students to understand that they should feel fortunate to be in such an environment where they can learn from others who are different. . . . We look different, we think differently, and we're . . . trying to set a comfortable environment for that to take place."[34]

Thus, under the viewpoint discrimination doctrine, a range of views must be tolerated within the boundaries set for this school's "limited public forum," but the expression must necessarily be limited by these boundaries. Under these guidelines, there is no evidence of any viewpoint discrimination at Pioneer High School. Every member of the highly disputed panel on homosexuality and religion took the position that homosexuality and religion could be reconciled, but there are many different views on how that might occur. Some members of the clergy, for example, accept a person's gayness but forbid sexual relations. Others go so far as to officiate at same-sex commitment ceremonies and to celebrate LGBT partnerships. Still others situate themselves somewhere in between. Viewpoints vary. Just because no one on the panel took the view that homosexuality and religion could not be reconciled at all did not make this a one-sided or "politically correct" panel.[35] The purpose of the panel was not to debate the question of whether homosexuality and religion could be reconciled but to explore the nuances of how those who wished to reconcile the two might be able to do so. In addition, the structure of the panel must be viewed within the context of the larger purpose of Diversity Week: to celebrate differences and work together in a spirit of reconciliation.

As a matter of policy, perhaps the best that can be said for the *Hansen* decision is that it supports the concept of a strong First Amendment in the public schools and does not in any way suggest that LGBT youth do not have the right to be open. Nor does it suggest, either expressly or by implication, that a school district does not have the right to include gay-positive content in its events. However, by mocking the district's efforts to create a supportive climate where all students might work together, the court contributed little or nothing to these debates. Moreover, by strongly suggesting that a school cannot present a panel that explores different perspectives on how homosexuality and religion might be reconciled—even when the question is so central for so many people—without being required to include an anti-gay viewpoint in such a panel, the court limited rather than fostered the contours of expression.

Harper v. Poway Unified School District (2004)

In spring 2004, fifteen-year-old Tyler Chase Harper arrived at his San Diego–area school on the day of a scheduled Day of Silence demonstration wearing a T-shirt with the words "Homosexuality Is Shameful" written on the back, along with a citation to Romans 1:27. In addition, on the front of his shirt, there was an accusation that the school, in allowing a Day of Silence by gay students and their allies, had "accepted what God had condemned."[36] The demonstration was one of many taking place across the country, part of an annual coordinated national effort by student groups to call attention to ongoing harassment and safety-related concerns negatively impacting gays on public school campuses.

Apparently no one told Harper he could not wear his T-shirt on the first day, but when he returned on the second day wearing a shirt with a similar message, school officials told him that it was "too inflammatory" and would not be allowed. The lawsuit he filed as a result led to a highly publicized and ongoing debate over free speech rights, religion, and related values in K–12 public schools.[37]

In a case with many parallels to the *Chambers* and *Hansen* disputes—both of which had been decided in favor of the conservative religious students—Harper had some strong arguments in his favor. Students certainly have a right to express their sincerely held religious beliefs, as long as they do so in a manner that does not violate applicable policies and principles. There was no evidence in this case of any material and substantial disruption of schoolwork or discipline, evidence that has been central to an analysis under the *Tinker* rule for almost fifty years. Harper's only expression was the wearing of a T-shirt with crudely lettered slogans taped on the front and the back. He appeared to be acting alone, and although some words were apparently exchanged between him and others, there was little or no indication from the facts on the record that allowing him to wear the shirt would have led to any sort of major altercation.

In addition, under the viewpoint discrimination doctrine, it could conceivably be argued that once the school had opened a limited public forum by allowing the Day of Silence demonstration to go forward, students with different views on LGBT issues should be equally free to express them openly. Ninth Circuit judge Alex Kozinski stated as much in his 2006 dissent in the case. Indeed, for all of these reasons, and also because strong First Amendment rights have been so central to the progress of gay, bi, and gender-expansive persons in their efforts to gain equal treatment under the law, many LGBTs and their allies *favored* the conservative religious students' position as the multitrack litigation wended its way through the courts.[38]

APPLYING THE *TINKER* RULE

In November 2004, the U.S. District Court, Southern District of California, ruled in favor of the school district, and eighteen months later, the Ninth Circuit Court of Appeals upheld the lower court decision by a vote of 2–1.[39] Ninth Circuit judge Stephen Reinhardt considered whether, in light of the special characteristics of the public school environment, the school district had acted consistently with the requirements of the *Tinker* rule. *Tinker* stands for the proposition that public school officials can restrict K–12 student expression if it is disruptive or if it interferes with the rights of others. Analyzing the free speech issues under the "rights of others" prong, Reinhardt concluded that "Harper's wearing of his T-shirt 'collides with the rights of other students' in the most fundamental way":

> Public school students who may be injured by verbal assaults on the basis of a core identifying characteristic such as race, religion, or sexual orientation, have a right to be free from such attacks while on school campuses. As *Tinker* clearly states, students have the right to "be secure and to be let alone." Being secure involves not only freedom from physical assaults but from psychological attacks that cause young people to question their self-worth and their rightful place in society.[40]

The panel emphasized that the decision was a narrow one, limited to "instances of derogatory and injurious remarks directed at students' minority status such as race, religion, and sexual orientation." Judge Reinhardt also made it expressly clear that the ruling would not be applicable at the higher education level or in the outside world.[41]

In a related argument at the intersection of the Free Speech Clause and the Religion Clauses, Harper had also contended that his free exercise of religion rights had been violated. But the appeals court found that the restriction on the wearing of the T-shirt did not constitute a substantial burden on the exercise of Harper's religious beliefs: "No one has the right to proclaim his views at all times in all manners in all places, regardless of the circumstances, and Harper does not contend that his religion suggests otherwise. Harper remains free to express his views, whatever their merits, on other occasions and in other places."[42]

INVOKING THE VIEWPOINT DISCRIMINATION DOCTRINE

Consistent with the position Judge Rosen had set forth in the 2003 *Hansen* decision, dissenting judge Alex Kozinski contended that not allowing Harper to express his sincerely held religious beliefs about homosexuality once the school district had opened the door to expression regarding LGBT issues was a violation of the viewpoint discrimination doctrine.[43] But Rosen's lower-court decision in the Ann Arbor case has little, if any, precedential value. It does not reflect a pattern or trend in the federal courts, and courts of appeal in other parts of the country are certainly not required to follow it. In fact, the extent to which the viewpoint discrimination doctrine may be applicable at the K–12 level remains unsettled at this time. The clearest expression of the doctrine in an education setting is found in a postsecondary case, the 1995 *Rosenberger* decision. The doctrine was incorporated into the 1984 K–12 federal Equal Access Act, but that act applies only to an analysis of whether a school has opened the door to noncurriculum-related student clubs.

In the *Harper* majority opinion, Judge Reinhardt concluded that the viewpoint discrimination doctrine does not apply at all at the K–12 level in circumstances where there is either material or substantial disruption or interference with the rights of others under *Tinker*. Only when *Tinker* does not provide school officials with the legal authority to restrict student speech, the court stated, may aggrieved plaintiffs invoke the doctrine.[44]

Still, it is important to analyze how the debate might have played out if the court had found the viewpoint discrimination doctrine to be applicable to this set of facts. The doctrine requires an examination of whether a school has opened a limited public forum and, if so, what the contours of that forum are. Once the contours are defined, the school may not limit opposing viewpoints that stay within the borders of the forum. Thus a key question would certainly be whether the school in *Harper* had opened the door to a discussion of homosexuality itself, with students able to take pro or con positions, once it allowed LGBTs to highlight on-going issues of name-calling, bullying, and harassment in an organized fashion on a particular day.

It is not clear that the school opened the door this far. By allowing the LGBT students and their allies to conduct a demonstration highlighting issues of name-calling, bullying, and harassment, the school certainly opened the door to a forthright discussion of these matters by others. Messages and T-shirt slogans put forth by students questioning whether and to what extent such name-calling, bullying, and harassment were a problem would certainly be consistent with the parameters of such a forum. But just the fact that LGBT students were out and visible during their demonstration does not allow those opposing the activity to turn the spotlight on gays and lesbians themselves and speak disparagingly of their very identities. A parallel situation might be a demonstration regarding immigration issues by Asian American and Latino student organizations on a K–12 campus. If the school allowed the student-of-color groups to advocate for immigration reforms, would that mean that under the viewpoint discrimination doctrine, students opposed to immigration reforms would be allowed to turn the spotlight on the Asian and Latino students themselves and speak disparagingly of their identities and their cultures? It is highly doubtful that a court of law would rule in favor of the students making the disparaging remarks in such a situation.

REACTIONS TO THE NINTH CIRCUIT OPINION

Reinhardt's opinion was both highly praised and vehemently criticized. Those who lauded it found it to be potentially groundbreaking in that it was one of the few opinions to analyze the contours of Tinker's "rights of others" prong. It was acclaimed by many for expressly addressing the rights of traditionally disenfranchised groups, including racial/ethnic minorities, religious minorities, and gays. In particular, LGBT groups and their allies hailed it for its sensitivity to the realities that gay and gender-nonconforming students face, and educators praised its understanding of the nature of U.S. public high schools.

Those who were highly critical of the court's opinion feared that it would lead to a proverbial slippery slope, with public officials in a wide variety of settings now being able to justify limiting speech that some might consider offensive or inappropriate. Others argued that the court's language was vague and overbroad, that the decision constituted "judge-made law" that exceeded the scope of what jurists are expected to be doing, and that the court's analysis reflected an overreliance on psychological injury. In fact, the court's opinion was disparaged by members of the legal and public policy communities who still appear to hold to the view that psychological injury is less egregious than physical injury. Many quoted approvingly from Judge Kozinski's dissent, which referred dismissively to Reinhardt's extensive documentation of the psychological harm that can be caused to young and impressionable gay and gender-nonconforming students confronted with demeaning comments and ongoing mistreatment over time.[45]

The opinion attracted a great deal of attention, with commentary both in the traditional media and on online blogs bemoaning its alleged blow to First Amendment rights. Many critics emphasized the fact that, absent additional facts, there is no right not to be offended. If free speech rights are to remain strong in this area, everyone needs to tolerate expression that he or she may find disagreeable. In addition, the argument goes, bad speech can be countered by good speech.[46]

In response to these assertions, people have pointed out that, while it is certainly true that under the First Amendment, not every comment in the public square will be pleasant or palatable to everyone, these events did not take place in the public square. They took place on the campus of a public high school, where young and impressionable students are required to go to school and where they interact on an ongoing basis in very close quarters. One can envision, for example, a gay or lesbian student having to stare at the inflammatory message on the back of Harper's T-shirt for an entire class period if he or she were assigned to the seat behind Harper. Unlike disagreeable messages that may come in on a person's computer or cell phone, this type of input cannot be avoided by going to a different site, switching to a different mode, or turning off a device.[47]

In addition, a key distinguishing feature of Harper's expression was that it directly implicated fellow students. It did not expressly say that gays were shameful, but this was certainly the implication. School officials are responsible under the law to treat all students with equal dignity and equal respect. In California, they are expressly required under the Education Code to implement policies addressing peer harassment and mistreatment, including both sexual harassment and mistreatment on the basis of real or perceived gay or lesbian status. As Judge Reinhardt pointed out in the oral argument for this case, what kind of a high school would it be if students were allowed to walk around with T-shirts alleging that members of other student groups were shameful? What sort of a learning environment would be available to these young and impressionable people?[48]

POST-2006 ACTIVITY IN THE COURTS

Harper appealed his case to the U.S. Supreme Court, and he requested an expedited review. However, the Court found the controversy to be moot and vacated the decision, because Harper had since graduated. Yet, given the fact that the Supreme Court did not reverse the Ninth Circuit panel's reasoning on the merits,[49] it remains possible that Judge Reinhardt's opinion will inform the reasoning of future courts in this area.[50]

Harper's younger sister Kelsie was subsequently added as a plaintiff in the case, and she sought to carry on the fight to be able to wear a disparaging T-shirt in school. District Court judge John A. Houston, who had originally heard the case in November 2004, issued a new opinion in February 2008, ruling in favor of the school district once again.[51] On appeal in 2009, however, the Ninth Circuit panel not only found the case suitable for decision without oral argument but also chose to issue an unpublished opinion on behalf of the defendants.[52] Determining that Kelsie Harper had now also graduated, the judges stated that they "could not adjudicate the claims for . . . relief because they are moot," and they vacated the 2008 lower court decision on procedural grounds. However, the portion of the decision that found that the plaintiff was not entitled even to a modicum of financial relief was affirmed, also on procedural grounds. And the appellate panel "declined to reach the difficult substantive constitutional question."[53]

At last, the protracted *Harper v. Poway USD* litigation, which extended over a five-year period, appeared to have come to an end. Given the

complex procedural posture of the lawsuit, there is probably no one decision that can be said to represent what the case stands for. However, one
thing is clear. The Harpers lost in the federal district court in 2004, 2007,
and 2008. They lost at the Ninth Circuit in 2006. And their claims were
found to be moot in 2007 at the U.S. Supreme Court and again in 2009 at
the Ninth Circuit. At no point over a five-year period did a federal court
find in their favor.

A reasonable middle ground is often difficult to discern in the *Harper v.
Poway* litigation, but it can be argued that Judge Reinhardt's decision on
the merits points the way to a viable compromise position. Under the
rule adopted by the Ninth Circuit panel, conservative religious students
are certainly able to share their sincerely held religious beliefs on issues
relating to sexual orientation and gender identity, as long as they state
these beliefs in such a way that they do not rise to the level of "verbal
assaults on core identifying characteristics." One can envision, for
example, religious students making dignified and respectful statements
such as "We believe that homosexual relations are prohibited by both the
Old Testament and the New Testament" and then citing perhaps Leviticus
and/or Paul's letter to the Romans. Such a message would be much more
detached and factual in nature than the inflammatory declarations on
Harper's T-shirt.

Indeed, characterizing the T-shirt as inflammatory may be an understatement. Harper's words unquestionably constitute the most volatile of all the messages at issue in this section. The T-shirt was not only
more egregious by far than Chambers's celebration of straight pride but
also much more critical of LGBTs than either Hansen's admonition that
homosexuality is a sin or the *Nuxoll* "Be Happy, Not Gay" missive discussed in the next section. It is considerably easier for gays and lesbians
to ignore the innocuous nature of the "Straight Pride" message and perhaps even the play on words of the phrase "Be Happy, Not Gay" than it
is for them to ignore the characterization of their lives as shameful. Even
the admonition that homosexuality is a sin does not rise to the same level
of degradation as Harper's T-shirt, given that many people do not accept
the concept of sin.

While Harper may not have intended his T-shirt to be viewed as denigrating in any way, shape, or form—especially given the fact that so many

Christians in this context view themselves as in a position to help rather than hurt—it is impossible for LGBTs to ignore the hot-button nature of the word "shameful," because feelings of shame so often accompany a desire to remain in the closet. Indeed, in many instances, it is because gay persons feel ashamed that they choose to be closeted. Only by overcoming the often-prevailing view that gayness is shameful can LGBTs get to a place of comfort where they can lead full and complete lives. The word "shameful" on Harper's T-shirt thus cuts to the very heart of the matter. Even if unintended, it comes across as particularly nefarious, defamatory, and personal—especially in a setting where young and impressionable people interact.[54]

By contrast, a statement that simply communicates a person's belief that "homosexual relations are prohibited by the Bible" is almost the diametric opposite of an attack on individuals by referring to their core characteristics as shameful and condemned by God. This statement simply summarizes matter-of-factly what a substantial percentage of religious thinkers have determined to be the case. Other religious thinkers, of course, have put forth the view that the scriptures should not be read in this way and that the interpretations remain open to debate among reasonable people who may ultimately agree to disagree.[55] There is nothing wrong with students engaging in such a debate. The lesson of the Ninth Circuit standard, in short, is that disagreement in K–12 settings must necessarily be civil and that it is not civil for students to refer to other students as shameful and condemned by God.

Nuxoll v. Indian Prairie School District (2008)

The *Harper* litigation provides an important backdrop for the suburban Chicago *Nuxoll* case, and in many ways the lawsuits are mirror images of each other. Both involved conservative religious students who felt obligated to speak out against Day of Silence demonstrations at their schools, and both students showed up on the day after those demonstrations wearing anti-gay T-shirts that condemned homosexuality.[56]

There is another key point of intersection between the two lawsuits. Harper's actions on the day after the Day of Silence in 2004 morphed into a structured national event called the Day of Truth in 2005, coordinated by the Alliance Defense Fund (ADF), the legal organization that represented him.[57] Harper himself donned a mass-produced ADF T-shirt to help publicize the event and posed for a picture that appeared prominently on the Day of Truth website, accompanied by text lauding his actions.[58] Heidi Zamecnik, the original plaintiff in the *Nuxoll* case, subsequently chose to wear her own anti-gay T-shirt on the Day of Truth in 2006. The front of the shirt read *"My* Day of Silence, Straight Alliance." The back of the shirt had the slogan "Be Happy, Not Gay." (Although Heidi Zamecnik had since graduated, former fellow student Alexander Nuxoll was carrying the case forward in the same way that Kelsie Harper was prosecuting her family's case in San Diego.)

In response to Zamecnik's choice of T-shirt, the Neuqua Valley High School (NVHS) dean of students met with her at lunchtime. After advising her that some students were offended by the shirt, he phoned her mother and apparently reached a compromise. The words "Not Gay" would be crossed off Zamecnik's shirt, but she would be permitted to continue wearing it the rest of the day. In addition, she would not be disciplined in any way, and no record of the incident would be placed in her file.[59]

A year later, in 2007, Zamecnik and Nuxoll sought to wear the same T-shirt at NVHS on the Day of Truth. The school indicated that it would not permit the slogan or others "negatively referring to being gay," but in an apparent effort to find a reasonable middle ground, the school suggested several alternatives. The administration agreed, for example, to permit messages promoting a heterosexual identity. "Be Happy, Be Straight" would certainly be permitted. The mass-produced Day of Truth shirt would also be permitted, a shirt that had the ADF logo on the sleeve, the words "Day of Truth" in a speaking balloon, and the words "The Truth cannot be silenced. www.dayoftruth.org" on the back. (This was the same shirt that Harper had modeled on the website.) But the students refused to compromise, and they took their case to federal court. In April 2007, a U.S. district court ruled in favor of the school district, upholding the decision to ban the offending shirt. After an appeal that was dismissed as moot and a new motion by the plaintiff that was denied again by the lower court, the Seventh Circuit agreed to hear the case in time to reverse the lower court ruling and grant Nuxoll a preliminary injunction enabling him to wear the T-shirt on the April 28, 2008, Day of Truth.[60]

On its face, the slogan "Be Happy, Not Gay" would appear to fall somewhere between Chambers's relatively innocuous "Straight Pride" sweatshirt and Harper's highly cutting messages of shame and condemnation. In fact, as Judge Posner intimated in his Seventh Circuit majority opinion, given that "gay" was once employed as a synonym for "happy," many might find the play on words to be low key and even cute. Yet when one begins to hypothetically substitute the names of persons and other groups in place of "gay," a slogan of this nature can take on a darker meaning. For example, bloggers have wondered whether it would or should be allowable for other students to wear T-shirts that say "Be Happy, Not Heidi Zamecnik" or "Be Happy, Not Alexander Nuxoll." Might a school reasonably ban such slogans in the interest of school climate, or would those who support allowing Nuxoll to wear his T-shirt also support the rights of others to put forth these alternative slogans?

Circumstances can become even more volatile if one substitutes the name of a religious group for the word "gay." What if a student chose to wear a T-shirt with a slogan that said "Be Happy, Not Christian"? Would or should this be allowed? What if instead the slogan referred to a minority religion, such as "Be Happy, Not Jewish" or "Be Happy, Not Muslim." Would any school district in the country allow such slogans? Even if they would, is there any court in the nation that would then uphold that decision? And if no court would rule in favor of students' being able to put forth such messages about minority religious groups, should the *Nuxoll* case be decided any differently? Absent additional facts, could the Seventh Circuit rule in favor of allowing a student to wear the ostensibly anti-gay shirt but not allow her to wear the ostensibly anti-Jewish or anti-Muslim shirt?[61]

Hypotheticals in this context can become even more complex. What if students who sought to put forth such messages about minority religious groups did so pursuant to sincerely held religious beliefs and with the express purpose of "trying to help" the members of the minority religions by convincing them to convert to Christianity? In such circumstances, it can be argued that the messages would be no more hateful than the messages of students who are only "trying to help" gays and lesbians by seeking to turn them away from homosexuality. And, of course, not only are there groups that in fact embrace a mission that includes converting "nonbelievers" to Christianity but also many persons within those groups embrace a mission that includes attempting to turn gay persons straight. Should they not have the right to put forth what they view to be a message of love?

THE U.S. DISTRICT COURT'S ANALYSIS OF *ZAMECNIK*

To their credit, both the U.S. District Court and the Court of Appeals appeared to show similar sensitivity to the religious plaintiffs *and* the LGBT students in their respective opinions. Judge William T. Hart, for example, sitting in the U.S. District Court, Northern District of Illinois, acknowledged that the plaintiffs "profess sincere Christian religious beliefs which condemn homosexual behavior as immoral" and that "they also believe that homosexual behavior is damaging to homosexual individuals as well as society in general." At the same time, he acknowledged that "it is taken as true that derogatory and negative statements about homosexuality tend to harm homosexual high school students by lowering their self-esteem and creating related problems."[62]

In determining whether to issue an injunction, courts generally examine whether the plaintiff's arguments are likely to succeed and who might suffer greater harm if the requested relief is or is not granted. Judge Hart considered the "likelihood of success" inquiry under *Tinker* and its progeny, and he found Judge Reinhardt's *Harper* opinion to be directly on point.[63] After quoting extensively from relevant portions of that opinion, Hart identified an inherent consistency between the Ninth Circuit's treatment of a very similar dispute and the Seventh Circuit's First Amendment precedents over time. Applying principles from these precedents, the court concluded that K–12 school districts are justified in adopting policies "of tolerance toward and respect for differences among students" and that they have "a legitimate interest in protecting gay students at school from being harmed, both physically and psychologically." This interest, the court determined, permits a school "to restrict negative statements about being gay that would be protected speech if regulated by a government entity outside the context of a public high school." Judge Hart also rejected the plaintiff's contention that the school engaged in viewpoint discrimination, finding that the defendants "do not permit any student or group to use language that is negative or derogatory about another student. In this sense, defendants do not discriminate among viewpoints."

Hart concluded that, on one hand, a ruling against the religious students would cause little prospective harm, because they would "still be permitted to do their silent protest and to wear or display messages positively expressing support for heterosexuality. . . . There is also no apparent threat of accompanying discipline, only an intention to prohibit plaintiffs from wearing or displaying the one phrase in dispute." On the other hand, the court determined, there would be a "significant likelihood of public harm" to gay youth if the plaintiff's request were to be granted.[64]

THE SEVENTH CIRCUIT'S ANALYSIS OF *NUXOLL*

The Seventh Circuit Court of Appeals came to a different conclusion regarding the respective questions and reversed the decision of the lower court. Judge Richard Posner, delivering the opinion for the panel, examined the likelihood of the plaintiff's success by engaging in a wide-ranging examination of potentially applicable First Amendment law. In doing so, he noted that the religious students not only were seeking to be able to wear the "Be Happy, Not Gay" T-shirt to school on the Day of Truth but also were asking the court for an injunction to put the NVHS "derogatory comments" policy on hold. This policy, set forth in the *NVHS Student Handbook,* prohibits "derogatory comments that refer to race, ethnicity, religion, gender, sexual orientation, or disability."

Analyzing the policy, Judge Posner was impressed by the fact that it prohibited derogatory comments only "on unalterable or otherwise deeply rooted personal characteristics about which most people, including—perhaps especially including—adolescent schoolchildren, are highly sensitive." He acknowledged that "people are easily upset by comments about their race, sex, etc., including their sexual orientation, because for most people these are major components of their personal identity—none more so than a sexual orientation that deviates from the norm. Such comments can strike a person at the core of his being."[65]

The court found the school policy to be viable, appropriate, and consistent with principles set forth in *Bethel v. Fraser* and *Morse v. Frederick.* It suggested that the school was on strong ground "in arguing that the rule strikes a reasonable balance between the competing interests—free speech and ordered learning—at stake in the case." Construing *Morse* as potentially enabling educators to restrict speech that may have negative "psychological effects," Posner wrote that "if there is reason to think that a particular type of student speech will lead to a decline in students' test scores, an upsurge in truancy, or other [similar] symptoms . . . of substantial disruption[,] the school can forbid the speech":

> The rule challenged by the plaintiff appears to satisfy this test. It seeks to maintain a civilized school environment conducive to learning, and it does so in an even-handed way. . . . The list of protected characteristics in the rule appears to cover the full spectrum of highly sensitive personal-identity characteristics. And the ban on derogatory words is general.[66]

Declining to limit the policy, the court then turned to whether the T-shirt in question should be allowed on the Day of Truth. Analyzing both its content and its potential impact under Tinker's "substantial disruption" rule, Posner found that the school district had failed to justify the ban. "'Be Happy, Not Gay' is only tepidly negative," he concluded. "'Derogatory' or 'demeaning' seems too strong a characterization." Posner went on to acknowledge that there had been "incidents of harassment of homosexual students" at the large suburban high school. "But it is highly speculative," he declared, "that allowing the plaintiff to wear a T-shirt that says 'Be Happy, Not Gay' would have even a slight tendency to provoke such incidents, or for that matter to poison the educational atmosphere." Speculation of this sort, the court found, is "too thin a reed on which to hang a prohibition of the exercise of a student's free speech." But he did indicate that the results could be different as more evidence was presented and a fuller picture emerged.[67]

Ironically, even though the lower court and the appellate court came to different conclusions regarding whether the T-shirt should be allowed, Judge Posner's opinion in many ways is not inconsistent with Judge Hart's. Instead of considering the Ninth Circuit test put forth by Judge Reinhardt, for example, Posner embraced the centrality and efficacy of the high school's policy prohibiting derogatory speech. The Reinhardt test and the NVHS policy are not dissimilar. Indeed, given the fact that both the Ninth Circuit test and the Illinois school policy articulate comparable limits on K–12 student expression, the two can be viewed as standing for virtually the same thing.

In addition, both the lower court and the appeals court recognized the egregiousness of psychological harm, and the respective judges showed similar sensitivity to both the LGBT student position and the religious student position. Both also sought to highlight examples of T-shirt slogans that would or would not cross the line. Their opinions were not always consistent in this regard, and of course reasonable people will disagree here, with different persons drawing the line in different places. But by attempting to put forth concrete examples in this very difficult territory, the two courts have provided a valuable resource for the education community.

Finally, both Judge Hart and Judge Posner wrestled at great length with trying to find common ground. They each respected religion, but they also highlighted the negative impact of derogatory comments on vulnerable LGBT students. In addition, they each clarified important components of the circumstances that may have been overlooked. Hart acknowledged that "there is no evidence that the school has permitted

[any] messages derogatory of Christian beliefs or being of heterosexual orientation."

In the same vein, Posner commented that none of the slogans on T-shirts worn by LGBT students and their allies on the Day of Silence "advocate[d] homosexuality or criticize[d] heterosexuality." In the same spirit, Judge Posner urged the lower court, as the case went forward, to strike a balance between the two positions, as difficult as such a task might be: "The district judge will be required to strike a careful balance between the limited constitutional right of a high-school student to campaign inside the school against the sexual orientation of other students and the school's interest in maintaining an atmosphere in which students are not distracted from their studies by wrenching debates over issues of personal identity."[68]

Case decisions in this chapter consistently reflect the First Amendment mandate that religion must be respected in the public sector, but they also reflect the principle that religious viewpoints are not automatically deemed to take precedence over relevant secular viewpoints. Interpretations of scripture by conservative religious leaders and scholars can and should be articulated in these settings, and interpretations of the same scripture by other religious leaders and other scholars are necessarily granted equal status and equal stature.

It may be the case that in K–12 settings, a simple "Do unto others as you would have them do unto you" mind-set can go a long way. As a matter of policy, for example, if Christian students would not want others to wear "Christianity Is Shameful" T-shirts or "Be Happy, Not Christian" T-shirts, then they themselves should not wear shirts with slogans such as "Homosexuality Is Shameful" and "Be Happy, Not Gay." Related issues of policy and implementation in a school climate context are explored at length in part II. But it is important here to emphasize that a compromise position in this area could address the needs and sensibilities of both sides. It would also recognize that there are many persons in our pluralistic society who embrace the values of *both* the gays and the religious and live their lives accordingly.

In principle, the equality component of the right to be out—enhanced by the religion clauses, the safety-related components of free speech jurisprudence, and individual state statutes—includes the right not to be demeaned in schools. But there is an ongoing battle over boundaries under these provisions, and LGBTs will need to be relatively thick-skinned if they choose to be completely out in K–12 public education settings during this transitional era.

Yet it must also be emphasized that the LGBT-related disputes documented in this chapter would never have happened had not gay and gender-nonconforming persons become so out and so visible. Some courts may uphold the constitutionality of putting forth anti-gay messages in these settings, but with rare exception, judges implicitly recognize the right of LGBT persons to be out, their right to be treated equally as a result, and their right to the same level of tolerance as anyone else.

II

Public Policy

Implementing the Right
to Be Out

6

ADDRESSING SCHOOL CLIMATE
Goals and Best Practices

Especially in an education setting, victories in the legal arena do not necessarily translate into substantive and effective change. Indeed, a legal victory is often only the first of many steps that may be necessary before stated goals are actually accomplished.

The educational system in general is particularly resistant to change. Education-related laws may be "on the books," but there may be no viable mechanism in place for their dissemination and implementation. Even if strategies for change are put in place, ascertaining the extent to which the changes are occurring is often the greatest challenge of all. Education administrators often have so many other responsibilities that it may not be humanly possible to monitor all relevant activity and enforce compliance.

In addition, when it comes to LGBT issues, there is a whole host of additional real-life obstacles that must be overcome before the facts on the ground can be changed. These obstacles include a history of doing things in a certain way and a school and community culture that may still view LGBT persons as outside of the mainstream or even as nonexistent in that environment. Yet with collaborative efforts on the part of both faculty and administration at individual school sites, encouraged and supported by strong, committed leadership at every level of the educational system, change in this area is not only possible but has already taken place in many settings. This chapter explores research-based principles that can inform such change and can guide professional development for school-site administrators, creative initiatives to address school climate, and the establishment of LGBT-specific programs.[1]

At their best, U.S. public schools embody inclusiveness, as reflected in equal access, equal opportunity, the celebrating of similarities, and the respecting of differences. Such a dynamic inevitably includes a conscious focus on school climate, which has proved to be a key feature of successful efforts to address issues relating to marginalized persons and disenfranchised groups.

Definitions of "school climate" may vary depending on context, but the term is generally seen as encompassing such things as school culture, mood, degree to which people get along, respect for differences, motivation, pride, and vision.[2] The linchpin of a positive school climate is the existence of collaborative and optimistic working relationships between and among all members of the school community, from the youngest students to the most senior faculty and staff. Research invariably points toward the conclusion that the proliferation of such relationships will go a long way toward preventing the type of mistreatment and discriminatory conduct documented in earlier chapters of this book, while at the same time enabling LGBTs to be as open about their identities as the next person, should they so desire.[3]

Proactive Strategies for Improving School Climate

There is near-unanimity among both education researchers and successful practitioners regarding the importance of focusing on proactive and preventive strategies to the extent possible, rather than waiting and thinking about what to do only after problems arise. In addition, there is widespread agreement that these strategies should not be just one-time events but that they should be ongoing, accompanied by time for reflection, adjustment, and updating as needed. In this context, it is important to note the effectiveness of multiple strategies implemented simultaneously. For example, teachers who consciously work toward developing engaging lessons, building rapport with their students, and facilitating active involvement during the learning process are prime examples of how educators can work effectively on multiple fronts to both avoid and ameliorate potential problems.

The spirit of community that accompanies a positive school climate can be particularly important for students of color and LGBT students who may have self-image issues and may see themselves, incorrectly, as not capable or as less capable than others. Such students, vulnerable and at risk, are often among the first to be negatively impacted by a less-than-supportive school climate, which can lead them either to stop coming to school regularly or to simply drop out. The same students, situated in a positive and encouraging environment, can be among the greatest beneficiaries of these changes.[4]

Inclusive Policies and Commitment to Shared Values

The Collaborative for Academic, Social, and Emotional Learning (CASEL)—which partners with the University of Illinois, Chicago, and numerous school districts—is one of many groups and organizations within the broader education community to exemplify a commitment to shared values within a pluralistic society. Indeed, CASEL's mission statement and goals, reflecting dedication to a process that helps make evidence-based social and emotional learning an integral part of education from preschool through high school, can serve as a road map for educators and policy makers in this regard.

Such an approach points optimistically toward a world where all children will become self-aware, socially aware, and responsible decision makers. In addition, it promotes research and practice informed by the goal that "school leaders are establishing a welcoming climate of teamwork and collaboration and integrating social and emotional learning (SEL) into all aspects of the school day." CASEL is committed to establishing classrooms where "teachers are modeling respect and empowering students in every interaction" and to facilitating the development of homes where "family members are modeling and supporting the kinds of positive behaviors that help children [become] competent and caring adults."[5]

The Association for Supervision and Curriculum Development (ASCD), a large, mainstream, national organization of educational administrators and school district leaders, has adopted a "whole child approach" that is consistent with these principles:

> ASCD's whole child approach is an effort to transition from a focus on narrowly defined academic achievement to one that promotes the long-term development and success of all children.[6]

The "Whole Child Tenets" that inform this approach include the following:

> Each student learns in an environment that is physically and emotionally safe for students and adults.

Each student is actively engaged in learning and is connected to the
school and broader community.

Each student has access to personalized learning and is supported by
qualified, caring adults.

Each student is challenged academically and prepared for success in college or further study and for employment and participation in a global
environment.[7]

These "Whole Child Tenets" reflect the broad recognition within the education community that a holistic approach to schooling maximizes the
chances of achieving the best possible outcomes for young people. The
tenets also serve as an important response to the all-too-common practice, during the present era, of determining school-site-administrator
performance primarily, if not entirely, through an analysis of standardized test scores, with no provision made for assessing school climate.
CASEL executive director Mary Utne O'Brien has cited research showing
that children score 10 percent to 15 percent higher on achievement tests
when they have been taught social and emotional skills. The evidence is
so convincing, O'Brien says, that the state of Illinois has created social
and emotional learning standards that must be covered, just as there are
standards for math, science, and English.[8]

Research-Based Implications for Those Working with Young People

The implications of the research cited above for LGBT students and others who have often been viewed as outside the mainstream are particularly poignant. If, for example, educators disseminate the prototypical
message of disapproval—directly or indirectly—that the needs of gay and
gender-nonconforming students are unimportant, that an LGBT identity
does not really exist, and that queer students should keep their feelings
to themselves, then such a message, magnified and further disseminated
by other students who pick up on it, can have a devastating cumulative
impact on the lives of young people just beginning to come to terms with
who they are. But if the opposite is taking place, and educators are setting the tone by demonstrating sensitivity to the needs of all students,
including an open and explicit respect for LGBTs, then the possibilities
for growth, development, and achievement are invariably maximized. As
Daniel Goleman explains, "social intelligence means . . . being empathetic,
sensing what the other person is feeling, understanding their point of

view. . . . It's both knowing what the person is feeling and acting effectively based on that."[9]

The principles identified in these pages are reinforced by the ongoing and overwhelming evidence in the literature regarding the importance of sensitivity to the needs of diverse learners generally.[10] Related studies, focusing in particular on discriminatory discipline practices and the misuse of the special education system, have reached similar conclusions. Indeed, there is near-unanimity among experts in the field regarding the importance of paying close attention to the diverse backgrounds and unique personal perspectives that young people bring to the table—backgrounds and perspectives that can include, but of course are not limited to, LGBT status.[11]

Brenda Townsend, for example, building on the groundbreaking work of John Ogbu in the 1980s, addresses discriminatory discipline issues by stressing the importance of reducing the "cultural discontinuity" that students may experience in school settings. Such discontinuity, she notes, prevents the building of relationships between educators and those young people who may not have had "mainstream cultural experiences."[12] Russell Skiba and coauthors add, "In many secondary classrooms, cultural discontinuity or misunderstanding may create a cycle of miscommunication and confrontation. . . . [In addition,] teachers who are prone to accepting stereotypes of . . . [certain students] as threatening or dangerous may overreact to relatively minor threats to authority, especially if their anxiety is paired with a misunderstanding of cultural norms of social interaction."[13]

A particularly egregious manifestation of this dynamic is the inappropriate referral of certain students to special education and related programs. Such a referral occurred in the *Nabozny* case, reflecting at best a misdirected response to the pervasive mistreatment of an openly gay student in a rural Wisconsin district. Not only did the facts indicate no apparent disability but the referral actually increased the level of mistreatment, because the special education class already included two students who were among the most persistent perpetrators of the physical and emotional harassment that had occurred.[14]

Similarly, in the *Henkle* case, the Nevada school district blamed an openly LGBT victim for the mistreatment he suffered and, as a result, transferred him out of a traditional high school and ultimately to an adult school. District officials actually told the student that "because he was openly gay . . . a traditional high school was not appropriate." In the end, as a result of his placement in the adult education program, "he could not receive a high school diploma because he was no longer enrolled in a public high school."[15]

The scholarly literature is also filled with extensive documentation of the disproportionate and inappropriate referral of students of color to *separate* special education classes. Findings consistently demonstrate that such within-school segregation amounts to nothing less than a misuse of the entire special education system.[16] LGBT students of color can be particularly impacted by this dynamic, especially given the proven relationship between the peer exclusion and victimization of a child and that child's classroom engagement and achievement.[17] However, the literature is also filled with a range of strategies that educators can adopt to prevent such egregious and too-often-counterproductive practices.[18]

Researchers emphasize that the guidelines and tenets for improving school climate proactively should not be communicated just to educators. In an age-appropriate manner, they can also be taught directly to young people, particularly in the older grades. Indeed, many of the strategies highlighted here contemplate this type of education—working with young people to build social and emotional skills, informed by the research literature.[19]

In addition to the scholarship cited in this chapter, Howard Gardner's groundbreaking theory of multiple intelligences is relevant. As set forth in *Frames of Mind: The Theory of Multiple Intelligences* (1983), Gardner posits the existence of at least seven relatively autonomous avenues of intelligence that educators can assess and monitor in creative ways. His research-based conclusions remain controversial for some, because they attack the classical notion of what constitutes intelligence. Yet the theory has had great staying power for many in the education community, who view it as a much more appropriate characterization of the complexities of the human mind than the arguably anachronistic conceptualization of an intelligence quotient (IQ) measurable by a single test.[20]

Gardner contends that intelligence entails a set of mental skills that enable us to recognize and resolve problems. Of the seven types of intelligence that he says we each possess to some degree, the first two are widely accepted: "mathematical-logical" and "linguistic." The other five include "spatial," "bodily kinesthetic," "musical," "interpersonal," and "intrapersonal." For purposes of school climate, the fact that the last two are viewed as no less important than the other five is especially noteworthy. Interpersonal skills include the ability to notice and make distinctions among other individuals and to be attuned to their moods, temperaments, and intentions. Intrapersonal skills include the capacity for self-knowledge—to detect and discern one's own feelings—and the ability to use that knowledge for personal understanding.[21] Gardner's conclusions that interpersonal and intrapersonal skills are actually types of intelligence reinforce the argument that the best educators work to strengthen such skills across the board. Indeed, the sum total of all the research-based implications in this section is that a truly effective educational process cannot be limited to either basic skills or traditional curricular content but must also include goals and objectives that focus on the building of social intelligence and emotional acumen.

Structured School Climate Programs

In addition to the proactive strategies for improving school climate across the board, structured programs are available that can serve the needs of particular campuses and communities. Such programs range from those that focus on building a positive and welcoming environment generally to those that may address more narrowly defined goals. Broad, general programs that are being implemented in districts throughout the country include Promoting Alternative Thinking Strategies (PATHS), for grades K–6; Project ACHIEVE, for pre-K through grade 8; and the Tribes Learning Community, for all grade levels. These programs often provide, but are not limited to, opportunities for service learning, diversity education, and character education. Lessons and activities are designed to develop the panoply of interpersonal skills that can help foster a positive and welcoming campus environment.[22]

More specific programs have also been developed that target certain types of behaviors and are designed to provide additional support for particular students. Such programs can especially benefit LGBT students who may be facing severe challenges on a day-to-day level.

TARGETING BULLYING, PEER HARASSMENT, AND
HATE-MOTIVATED ACTIVITY

Bullying is generally defined as behavior that can range from name-calling, threats, and social exclusion to serious criminal acts of libel and repeated physical attacks. Pervasive bullying is perhaps best seen as a type of peer harassment and mistreatment, and it continues to negatively affect persons of every race, ethnicity, gender, and sexual identity. Indeed, there is evidence that bullying is more prevalent than it was in the past. Thus, during the past two decades, state education departments and the National Education Association (NEA) devoted considerable time and effort to developing materials and model policies in this area.[23] NEA efforts were exemplified by the work of Robert Kim, who organized a national summit on "GLBT" issues in 2008, which brought together leading researchers, community leaders, and NEA members. A year later, the organization released its first-ever national report on the status of LGBT people in education, the fifth in a series of NEA reports on "underserved groups" in education. Not surprisingly, bullying was one of the key issues addressed in the publication.[24]

Bullying is a significant issue for LGBTs. A paradigmatic National Mental Health Association survey, for example, found that more than 75 percent of all teenagers witnessed bullying of classmates who were gay or thought to be gay. The same survey also asked students from twelve to seventeen years old, "Who gets bullied all the time?" The groups ranking highest were students with disabilities (6 percent), overweight students (11 percent), students "who dress differently" (12 percent), and students "who are gay or are thought to be gay" (24 percent).[25]

Yet the relevant research clearly shows that bullying is a problem for everyone, gay and straight alike. Gloria Moskowitz-Sweet, for example, who has worked in this area extensively over time, explains that "any child who does not fit narrow definitions of masculine or feminine behavior—or is not part of the dominant race, religion, culture, or appears different from the majority—is an easy target. Approximately 85 percent of children are affected by it: as perpetrators, recipients, or witnesses." She adds, "With the advent of electronic communications, the incidence of bullying has escalated into cyberspace, as our young people taunt through texting, Twittering, Facebook, . . . and other modern modes of communication." And she reports that "mental health experts are now recognizing bullying's long-term effects." In 2009, for example, the American Academy of Pediatrics, for the first time, addressed the problem of childhood bullying when it published a policy statement on preventing school violence.[26]

One of the most volatile and relatively unexplored aspects of the bullying problem in K–12 schools is the potential for escalating violence. A single bullying event is often not an end point but the beginning of a series of events that may have truly tragic consequences for many people.[27] The bullying of Lawrence King over time, for example, culminated in his tragic murder and also had a devastating impact on others, including (but not limited to) the virtual destruction of the life of the fourteen-year-old who shot him and the potentially career-ending consequences for the English teacher who was supervising the class when the shooting happened.[28] The bullying of eleven-year-olds Carl Walker-Hoover, in Springfield, Massachusetts, and Jaheem Herrera, in DeKalb, Georgia, led not only to their highly publicized suicides but also to still-undetermined repercussions in the lives of those who came in contact with them.[29]

Moreover, the aspect of bullying that very few appear willing to confront is that victims of bullying in the present era may, as a result, turn on their tormentors and on many others around them, striking back in the most violent of ways. There is evidence, for example, not only that perpetrators of some of the worst school violence at the K–12 level over the past twenty-five years were victims of bullying themselves but also that they were targeted with anti-gay epithets meant to degrade and alienate them by suggesting a failure to meet gender- and sexuality-based expectations of masculinity. These include, among others, fourteen-year-old Michael Carneal, who killed three people in West Paducah, Kentucky, in 1997; high school seniors Eric Harris and Dylan Klebold, who killed fifteen, including themselves, at Columbine High School in Littleton, Colorado, in 1999; fifteen-year-old Charles Andrew Williams, who killed two people in Santee, California, in 2001; and sixteen-year-old Jeff Weise, who took his own life after killing seven people at the Red Lake Indian Reservation in Minnesota in 2005.[30]

Details emerging in subsequent news reports regarding these horrific events included reports that Carneal "endured years of anti-gay teasing after the school newspaper printed a rumor alleging he was gay and had a crush on another male student" and that classmates of Harris and Klebold "said that they were often called 'gay' by athletes and other students. 'They're a bunch of homos. . . . If you want to get rid of someone, usually you tease 'em. So the whole school would call them homos,' a Columbine football player told *Time* magazine." And Williams "was reportedly teased as 'gay' by students at his new high school, and was troubled by the homophobic bullying, according to an ex-girlfriend and her mother."[31] It should be noted that none of these students identified as LGBT, and no evidence indicated that they were anything other than straight. But they were victimized in this context nonetheless, as many are in K–12 schools across the country.

Summarizing the latest research in the area, Robert Kim explains that "bullying of [LGBT students and those perceived as LGBT] stems largely from discomfort with students who do not conform to traditional gender roles in their appearance or behavior, i.e., who are gender-nonconforming. A student's actual sexual orientation may be far less relevant to his or her social victimization than his or her gender identity or gender expression."[32]

Not only has bullying by fellow students in a school setting consistently been found to have a negative impact on everyone's ability to learn but recent research has also shown that bullying is more common and more potentially damaging to children than was previously thought. In fact, a definite link has been identified between bullying and later delinquent and criminal behavior.[33]

In "Safe at School: Addressing the School Environment and LGBT Safety through Policy and Legislation," this author, along with Sheila James Kuehl, released a legislative and policy brief that built on the first edition of this book, setting forth research-based policy recommendations to address the broad area of peer harassment and mistreatment in the U.S. public schools.[34] Our recommendations were based on certain key principles, which include the following:

> Organizational change should include teacher education and administrator training in credentialing programs, professional development within individual districts, school–family–community partnerships, and collaborative leadership by educators.
>
> LGBT students should not be viewed as separate and apart from other identifiable persons and groups, particularly since gay and gender-non-conforming youth often have multiple identities, and may also be people of color, English-language learners, students with disabilities, devoutly religious, dedicated athletes, etc.
>
> Strategies do not always have to be LGBT-specific to be successful. Indeed, broad, general approaches applicable to all students can help address many LGBT needs.
>
> It is not possible to address problems without being able to talk about them. To fully and effectively take on the [range of bullying] issues that persist in schools, all members of the school community must be able

to discuss the topic openly, in a courteous, respectful, and professional manner, and in all possible settings.[35]

PROGRAMS AND INITIATIVES FOR AT-RISK STUDENTS

Definitions of *at-risk students* may vary, depending on context, but it is generally agreed that the term refers to persons who are more likely than others to drop out of school and may also be in danger of experiencing severe physical and/or emotional harm in their lives. Children of poverty are typically overrepresented in this category.

As referenced earlier, LGBT students in general have been classified as an at-risk population. Depending on their individual circumstances, many of them can benefit from multifaceted initiatives designed to address the needs of at-risk students across the board. Indeed, both gay and transgender youth may fit appropriately into more than one category of students at risk.

Many programs and strategies have been developed to provide additional support for young people in general who may be at risk. The Capstone Institute at Howard University, for example, is "a multidisciplinary center that implements and supports school reform and school improvement initiatives that focus on 'educating the whole child,' and interlinks research, theory and practice in the areas of learning, curriculum and instruction, professional development, social work, policy, parent and community engagement, organizational change, assessment and evaluation, and psychosocial/ emotional development." Their academic interventions, community support services, and research activities "are conducted by an interdisciplinary team with a demonstrated track record of evidenced-based accomplishments in urban and ethnically diverse schools, districts and communities."[36]

Capstone Institute is an extension of the Center for Research on the Education of Students Placed at Risk (CRESPAR), which operated as a federally funded educational research and development center at Howard University in collaboration with Johns Hopkins University.[37] CRESPAR's mission was "to conduct research, development, evaluation, and dissemination of replicable strategies designed to transform schooling for students who are placed at risk due to inadequate institutional responses to such factors as poverty, ethnic minority status, and non-English-speaking home background."[38] CRESPAR programs have included Success for All and Roots and Wings at the early childhood and elementary levels;[39] Talent Development Schools at the secondary level;[40] and a range of school, family, and community partnerships.

Another example of a noteworthy initiative in this area is the highly acclaimed Upward Bound, a federally funded program that has helped prepare at-risk students for higher education.[41]

Addressing the Particular Needs of LGBTs through School Climate

A positive and welcoming school climate will help everyone and hurt no one. But K–12 educators invariably recognize that a generalized focus may not be sufficient to address the particular needs of certain students, including LGBTs. A first step toward meeting the needs of LGBTs is the dissemination of information regarding gay and gender-expansive persons.

At a minimum, administrators, faculty, and staff should be familiar with what has transpired in recent LGBT-related litigation and should be cognizant of the fact that the courts are increasingly intolerant of actions or inactions by school officials that contribute to the mistreatment of LGBT youth. In hearing about these events and discussing the implications of the decisions, people will inevitably develop a greater understanding of the issues and gain a better sense of their responsibilities under the law.

A recurring theme in Part II of this book, however, is that school districts and states can go much further than what some might consider the de minimis requirements of court decisions and relevant legislation. Treating every student with equal respect and equal dignity in a school-climate context contemplates learning more about the challenges that members of marginalized and disenfranchised subgroups face. Indeed, educators and other public officials can learn a great deal from the growing body of research addressing LGBT youth.

Many gay and transgender students are happy, well-adjusted, valued, and fully accepted members of their families, their schools, and the larger community.[42] Many others, however, face radically different circumstances and encounter horrific mistreatment on an ongoing basis. Still others are somewhere in the middle, experiencing a combination of support and denigration that can make day-to-day realities rocky and unpredictable.[43] It should be emphasized that students *perceived* to be LGBT may experience harassment and mistreatment equal in intensity to those who identify openly as gay or transgender. And those who are closeted or sorting things out can find themselves in still more difficult positions, with fewer people to turn to and a personal situation that may be much more unsettled. For the young people who are confronted with such a range of challenges, additional efforts on the part of school officials—informed by the wealth of research-based findings on this topic—can make a world of difference.

Although a detailed analysis of the literature in this field is beyond the scope of this book, it is important to recognize the extent to which the work of educators, social workers, and mental health professionals in this area today is informed by such research. Especially given the fact that some federal judges continue to write dismissively and perhaps even disparagingly of "psychological" evidence introduced on behalf of gay and gender-expansive persons, an overview of the findings that continue to accumulate is essential. These findings are of different types, ranging from highly structured empirical studies to detailed personal stories documented in memoirs, biographies, novels, poetry, art, film, and court decisions themselves. The evidence is growing, wide ranging, cumulative, and consistent. When read together with research findings on school climate in general, the picture is compelling and cannot be ignored.

Scholarly Research Documenting the Challenges Faced by LGBT Youth

The ongoing work of scholars in this interdisciplinary area over the past three decades is exemplified by the groundbreaking research of six people who have held academic positions while at the same time building connections with K–12 educational institutions and with LGBT communities nationwide. Benefiting from these multiple connections and perspectives, their work has helped guide the efforts of many practitioners on a day-to-day level, even as it continues to inform the research of other academics in this expanding field.

Caitlin Ryan, a mental health professional specializing in child development and adolescent issues, has focused on documenting the unmet needs of young LGBT persons. The 1998 book *Lesbian and Gay Youth: Care and Counseling,* which she coauthored, is recognized as a landmark in the field.[44] Ryan continues to work in this area today, providing research-based guidance for members of both the education community and the legal community. Her more recent projects have ranged from service as an expert witness in LGBT-related litigation to collaboration with other scholars and practitioners on family-related and early childhood issues that arise in K–12 settings. She is currently director of the Family Acceptance Project, which is "a research, intervention, education and policy initiative that works to prevent health and mental health risks for lesbian, gay, bisexual and transgender (LGBT) children and youth, including suicide, homelessness and HIV—in the context of their families, cultures and faith communities."[45]

James T. Sears began writing about gay and lesbian issues in the K–12 schools when most educators could not even imagine talking about these matters openly. In 1987, for example, he published "Peering into the Well of Loneliness: The Responsibility of Educators to Gay and Lesbian Youth," followed by many articles and books that helped build the case for including LGBT-related topics in the K–12 curriculum. Noteworthy examples include his 1991 piece "Helping Students Understand and Accept Sexual Diversity," his 1998 book *Curriculum, Religion, and Public Education: Conversations for an Enlarging Public Square,* and the 2005 volume *Gay, Lesbian, and Transgender Issues in Education: Programs, Policies, and Practices.*[46]

Kimberlé Crenshaw, a professor at Columbia Law School and the UCLA School of Law, is a pioneer in the area of critical race studies. She is most well known for coining the term *intersectionality,* which has emerged over the decades as an invaluable lens for examining the interplay between race, class, gender, and sexuality. As Crenshaw explains in a recent overview,

> intersectionality is an analytic sensibility, a way of thinking about identity and its relationship to power. Originally articulated on behalf of black women, the term brought to light the invisibility of many constituents within groups that claim them as members, but often fail to represent them. Intersectional erasures are not exclusive to black women. People of color within LGBTQ movements; girls of color in the fight against the school-to-prison pipeline; women within immigration movements; trans women within feminist movements; and people with disabilities fighting police abuse—all face vulnerabilities that reflect the intersections of racism, sexism, class oppression, transphobia, able-ism and more. Intersectionality has given many advocates a way to frame their circumstances and to fight for their visibility and inclusion.[47]

Kevin Kumashiro has worked extensively with the NEA and with academics nationwide, and his scholarship is most noteworthy for tackling issues impacting LGBT persons of color. In his 2001 edited work *Troubling Intersections of Race and Sexuality,* for example, Kumashiro brought together a collection of essays representing the wide range of perspectives within diverse racial and ethnic communities. Kumashiro frames the inquiry by clarifying issues of identity formation and cultural development against the background of the U.S. multicultural education movement, which in its first three decades failed to afford a prominent place to the multifaceted interplay between sexual orientation, gender identity, and race/ethnicity. Ultimately, Kumashiro presents an optimistic assessment of possibilities in this regard, highlighting key strategies for moving forward in the areas of curriculum and pedagogy.[48]

Stephen T. Russell is currently the Priscilla Pond Flawn Regents Professor in Child Development at the University of Texas at Austin. He is the author of innovative empirical studies clarifying the range of hurdles and barriers faced by gay and gender-expansive students. Often examining these issues in a campus safety context, he has identified precise links between a safe and supportive environment and equal educational opportunity. As a coauthor of the groundbreaking study *Safe Place to Learn,* for example, he played a key role in analyzing data from a 2001–2 California State survey of student health risk and resilience factors and a 2003 survey by the California Safe Schools Coalition that examined school climate and harassment. The result was an analysis of the responses of more than 230,000 students throughout the state and the largest-ever study of school-based harassment based on actual or perceived sexual orientation. For the first time, researchers and practitioners now had a comprehensive study of the severity of the problem in California.[49]

The late Eric Rofes led a particularly complex and multifaceted life, from the time he was fired for being an openly gay K–12 teacher in Massachusetts through his years as an LGBT activist, a community leader, a teacher educator, and—throughout all this—a prolific author. In addition to a whole host of articles dating back to such pioneering works as his 1989 piece titled "Opening Up the Classroom Closet: Responding to the Educational Needs of Gay and Lesbian Youth," Rofes published twelve books on topics that ranged from the AIDS crisis to broad issues impacting the larger community.[50] In the last years before his untimely passing, he turned again to the challenges faced by LGBT youth in the schools.

Examining at length many of the attempts to provide support for gay and gender-nonconforming students in education settings, Rofes concluded that top-down programs had the least potential for success in this area and urged collaborative efforts between and among all members of the school community, calling for a much larger voice for students themselves in the process.[51]

Taken together, the research of these six scholars have complemented each other's work, as they have analyzed different aspects of interrelated inquiries. Moreover, as a result of their achievements and those of many who followed in their footsteps, interdisciplinary publications now contain a growing body of scholarship addressing the challenges faced by LGBT youth today. These publications range from edited volumes, such as Anthony D'Augelli and Charlotte Patterson's *Lesbian, Gay, and Bisexual Identities and Youth: Psychological Perspectives,* to journals like Ohio State University's *Theory into Practice,* which devoted an entire special issue in 2004 to "Sexual Identities and Schooling." They also include poignant studies, such as Nila Marrone's "Advice to Latino Parents of LGBT Children," and eye-opening research, such as Corrine Munoz-Plaza's "Lesbian, Gay, Bisexual, and Transgender Students: Perceived Social Support in the High School Environment."[52]

Common findings and recurring themes appear throughout this scholarship, including the inescapable fact that significant percentages of LGBT youth enrolled in K–12 public schools are continuing to experience a negative self-image, stunted growth, and ongoing challenges above and beyond those of the prototypical adolescent. At a minimum, gay and transgender youth often encounter tremendous tension between themselves and members of their biological families as expectations are adjusted, disappointments are revealed, and accommodations are attempted. They must confront a lack of acceptance generally in many geographical locations and many communities. Major adjustments may be required between and among friends, and friendships may be terminated when the LGBTs begin to come out. Homophobic and transphobic comments, threats, and even physical assaults may be part of the daily experience for too many LGBTs, both within school and in society as a whole.[53]

In addition, across the globe, LGBTs are still among the most prominent scapegoats in our society, often blamed for just about every public event that has gone wrong or that has been perceived to have gone wrong.[54] Victims of reasoning that defies all logic, they have experienced the loss of employment, the destruction of property, physical confinement, banishment, and even death. Perhaps the most extreme example of such horrific scapegoating took place in Europe between 1933 and 1945, when the Nazis incarcerated, tortured, and brutally murdered gays for the mere fact that they were gay. Although things are infinitely better for a large percentage of the gays, lesbians, bisexuals, and transgender persons during the current era, with the blaming of LGBTs for illogical reasons increasingly confined to the margins, the already fragile sense of self-esteem experienced by many LGBT youth can be further damaged by negative statements that continue to be disseminated in this regard.[55]

Not only do so many levels of input continue to perpetuate the message that there is something wrong with being queer, but gay and gender-expansive students are often not able to experience the stages of development that unfold easily for so many of their straight counterparts. When heterosexual students reach adolescence, they can invariably benefit from road maps developed over many centuries and communicated to them by friends, family, books, the entertainment industry, and myriad other sources regarding how they can and should be acting and what the consequences of such actions might be. When LGBT students reach the same point, however, there is no comparable set of road maps available to them. If anything, they are typically confronted with messages that shout out to them that they are out of sync with generally accepted patterns and norms.[56]

Thus the social and emotional growth of LGBT adolescents is often stunted. While their straight counterparts participate in activities that enable them to experience the range of emotions that accompany the process of growing up, the gay and gender-nonconforming students often hit the proverbial wall. It is therefore the case that by the time LGBTs reach their late teens and early twenties, many are far behind emotionally and are only beginning to learn things that heterosexual persons have typically already mastered.[57]

In addition, the circumstances facing LGBT youth are compounded by the fact that they are often pigeonholed based on negative stereotypes and nefarious myths. These range from the fallacious perception that a gay identity is the equivalent of a hedonistic "lifestyle" that is only about sex to the highly defamatory negative stereotype that gays are hypersexualized predators who lack self-control and cannot be trusted.

This stereotype is still employed in courts of law by attorneys in most jurisdictions who invoke the "gay panic" and "trans panic" defenses, an attempt to blame LGBT victims for the violence committed against them. The strategy has been used in cases when the victim is either gay, as in the Matthew Shepard case, or transgender, as in the 2002 murder of Gwen Araujo, a transgender teenager.[58]

As a result of this combination of realities, LGBT youth often find themselves approaching the world around them as outsiders. From conversations at school to interactions in the workplace, from the content of K–12 curriculum to portrayals in the media, from dating rituals to religious rituals to family gatherings, gays and transgender persons can find themselves feeling alone, inadequate, and apart. The challenge of adjusting to outsider status and perhaps seeking to overcome it to the extent possible can remain a central feature of an LGBT person's life.[59]

In this context, Corrine Munoz-Plaza, Sandra Quinn, and Kathleen Rounds have highlighted the fear, the isolation, and the lack of social support that have been documented in the research addressing LGBT youth. The authors found, for example, that the major barrier preventing gay and lesbian students from disclosing their sexual orientation to friends, family, and teachers was fear: fear of losing support, fear of unfair treatment, and fear of being thought of as a sexual predator. Accompanying this fear was a cognitive, social, and emotional isolation. And a perceived lack of social support was a paramount feature of this study.[60]

Indeed, an LGBT identity often emerges quietly and secretly within a young person. It may be the case that the young person has no one to turn to—no friends to talk with about it, no family or community members to open up to. And as they are realizing this secret identity, they are also learning about the stigma that is still attached to being queer in so many places and in so many ways.

In a noteworthy contribution to the literature in this area, Stephen T. Russell and Stacey S. Horn gathered together twenty new essays in the 2016 book *Sexual Orientation, Gender Identity, and Schooling: The Nexus of Research, Practice, and Policy.*[61] Of particular relevance to the inquiry in this chapter are the following essays: Abbie E. Goldberg's "LGB Parent Families and the School Context," Shannon Snapp and Adela C. Licona's "The School to Prison Pipeline and the Pipeline Population: The Patterns and Practices of Its Production and Dismantling Possibilities," and Catherine A. Lugg and Jason P. Murphy's "The Shifting Political Winds[.]"

Especially pertinent, as well, is the reference to an intersectionality discussion between and among the authors:

> Intersectionality was a key theme that we repeatedly considered: how do
> race and ethnicity, social class, ability and disability, religion, immigration,
> gender identity and expression, and sexuality shape sexual orientation
> and gender identity (SOGI) issues in schools? . . . A related factor, not typ-
> ically considered in discussions of intersectionality, was developmental
> change, both in children and adults. For example, much of the focus of
> research and practice on SOGI issues in North America and other parts of
> the world [is] on secondary schools. [Yet] there is a dearth of research on
> SOGI issues in primary and middle level education.
>
> Similarly, there was much attention to geography—not only differ-
> ences among countries across the world, but within-country differences,
> both due to differences in provincial or state policies regarding SOGI is-
> sues . . . , but also to contextual differences in rural, suburban, and urban
> schools, for example.[62]

Consistent with the focus of this discussion, the 2009 NEA report found
that LGBT students "from poor and rural communities are acutely disadvantaged in obtaining resources, finding allies, and integrating into
school culture." It also documented the fact that "transgender students
are at elevated risk of severe harassment and physical harm as well as
dropping out of school" and that gay and gender-nonconforming youth
of color "are at elevated risk of harassment and social, familial, or community estrangement."[63]

Circumstances faced by LGBT youth of color continue to provide
an additional dimension to the challenges in this area.[64] A noteworthy
study by the National Gay and Lesbian Task Force, for example, found
that LGBT youth of color may confront a "tricultural" experience: they
can face homophobia from their respective racial or ethnic group, rac-
ism from LGBTs of other racial or ethnic communities, and a combination of the two from society at large.[65] Researchers have warned,
however, that educators must beware of generalizations in this regard,
especially since the topic is highly nuanced and only recently has become the subject of extensive scholarship. What appears to be constant
in such work, however, is that an LGBT person's racial or ethnic identity
may further compound the nature and extent of the complexities that
can arise.[66]

All told, taking every aspect of the documented realities into consideration and recognizing every nuance that may exist, it is difficult not to conclude from the growing body of scholarship in this area that additional efforts on the part of school officials are imperative if educational institutions are to fulfill their obligations to treat all students equally under the law.

Providing Support for LGBT Youth: Innovative Programs and Successful Approaches

Programs and activities with proven track records have been developed over the past several decades to assist school officials in providing needed support for LGBT youth at individual campuses. Most feature the active involvement of on-site faculty liaisons who agree to play prominent roles, and even those that have not involved faculty in the past may offer opportunities for such involvement in the future. Among the most successful approaches in this regard are safe zones, gay–straight alliances, suicide prevention programs, wellness programs geared toward students of particular races or ethnicities, and inclusive audiovisual materials developed by innovative media companies. In general, these initiatives focus on immediate issues of health and safety as well as on longer-term changes in both school culture and societal norms.

SAFE ZONES AND SAFE SPACES

Emerging over the past twenty-five years at both the K–12 and higher education levels, safe zones and safe space programs are very simple conceptually: identify spaces—typically a classroom at the K–12 level and an educator's office at the higher education level—where LGBT students can feel safe to be themselves and comfortable enough to talk about issues relating to their sexual and/or gender identities. Educators choosing to volunteer and participate in the training typically post pink triangles or some depiction of the rainbow flag on their doors, along with some language indicating that these are safe places for LGBT students. According to those who have planned and implemented such programs, "for many students, the presence of allies to whom they can turn for support—or even the simple knowledge that allies exist—can be a critical factor in developing a positive sense of self, building community, coping with bias, and working to improve school climate."[67]

GAY–STRAIGHT ALLIANCES

Scholarly literature has documented the benefits of gay–straight alliances for all students in a pluralistic society today. A 2009 study builds on these findings, exploring how youth define and experience empowerment in youth-led organizations characterized by social justice goals. The study offers insights into the ways that empowerment may be experienced differently among youth as compared to adults.[68] In addition, related scholarship has examined the importance of teacher mentoring in the lives of LGBT youth, focusing in particular on "how significant teacher-mentors are to the educational resilience of sexual minority women of color."[69] The faculty adviser in a gay–straight alliance is often able to serve as a mentor in this context, enhancing the positive impact of the student organization.

GLSEN, the Gay, Lesbian, and Straight Educational Network, has played a prominent role in the formation of these alliances from the beginning. The New York–based organization continues to provide a wealth of programmatic resources for K–12 educators, ranging from materials regarding safe zones and gay–straight alliances to national days of unification, such as National Coming Out Day and the Day of Silence. GLSEN also provides professional-development materials for in-class activities, lessons, and curriculum.[70]

The California-based Gay–Straight Alliance Network has also contributed extensively to the work in this area. The network has gathered together an extensive collection of resources, ranging from steps that can be taken to form and maintain gay–straight alliances to programs empowering LGBT youth and their allies to help counter discrimination in this context.[71]

SUICIDE PREVENTION PROGRAMS AND INITIATIVES

For some time now, research has found that the suicide rate for lesbian, gay, bisexual, and transgender youth is consistently higher than that of their straight counterparts. This takes into account both attempted suicides and completed suicides.[72] The problem is not limited to K–12 students. It is a major issue at the college and university level and among persons beyond this age as well. Indeed, the current data might very well be an underestimate, skewed by the fact that many suicides may never be contextualized as LGBT related, because the person attempting or committing suicide was highly closeted, perhaps even from himself or herself. In such instances, no one views the suicide as having anything to do with being gay, when in fact wrestling with sexual identity may have been a central factor.

Of course, suicide is not a problem in LGBT communities alone. Recent data, for example, have shown that young African American men and young Hispanic women are particularly at risk for suicide. For those African American men and Hispanic women who are also LGBT, the circumstances are only compounded.[73]

Suicide prevention programs are not generally school based, but they often involve express or implied partnerships with school officials, particularly those in the mental health field. Much work in this area is accomplished through telephone counseling, which persons contemplating suicide can tap via highly publicized hotlines. Schools across the country can and often do disseminate information regarding these hotlines.

In addition to suicide prevention programs designed for everyone, two noteworthy programs directly focus on LGBTs and their unique needs. The Trevor Project, which grew out of the success of the Academy Award–winning HBO film *Trevor,* is designed specifically to address suicide prevention among LGBT teenagers. It includes both a helpline and a Facebook page. The LGBT National Help Center includes both a national hotline and a national youth talkline.[74]

PROGRAMS ADDRESSING THE NEEDS OF LGBTS FROM A
RACIAL/ETHNIC PERSPECTIVE

A recent trend in LGBT communities has been the establishment of programs to assist people of color by addressing the unique combination of needs and challenges that many face. Color in Common, for example, is an HIV-related prevention program for young gay/bisexual men of color at the Los Angeles LGBT Center, "dedicated to forming lasting and rewarding friendships that support healthy lives."[75] The Asian and Pacific Islander (API) Wellness Center in San Francisco has been another trendsetter in this area. "API Wellness is an LGBTQ and people-of-color health organization that transforms lives by advancing health, wellness, and equality."[76]

AUDIOVISUAL RESOURCES

The proliferation of video and film projects addressing issues relating to LGBT youth has been yet another prominent development that can assist educators in developing and maintaining a positive school climate while also providing needed support for gay, bi, and gender-expansive persons. Many such films come with teacher's guides, lesson plans, and a range of additional resources.

Among the most noteworthy examples of such educational media are the films produced as part of Groundspark's Respect for All Project. These include *It's Elementary,* the first film of its kind to provide adults with practical examples of how to talk with children about gay people; *That's a Family,* a documentary that helps students in grades K–8 understand the different forms families take today; and *Let's Get Real,* featuring interviews with young people who have been victimized by bullying as well as those who have been bullies themselves.[77] Other films that can assist educators in this context include those produced by New Day Films, such as *Gay Youth,* which has been used by the Massachusetts Department of Education as part of its Safe Schools program.[78] In addition, films produced for a wider audience often have great educational value. Award-winning filmmaker Arthur Dong, for example, has directed several classic documentaries that can be employed to enrich humanities programs at the high school level.

The principles, approaches, and directions outlined in this chapter provide a foundation for school districts that seek to comply with the mandates of the emerging right to be out. At a minimum, a broad focus on school climate, accompanied by district-approved programs that selected members of the faculty and staff may choose to implement, can and will make a significant difference. And school officials can go much further in this area, should they so desire.

Curriculum and pedagogy, school sports, and transgender issues are among the most controversial arenas for educators in this context, not only because the relevant stakeholders are so resistant to change in general but also because modifications in the status quo may engender great opposition. Yet attempts to change these realities may constitute the proverbial final frontier in the push for equal treatment, and dedicated educators should not ignore the additional steps that can be taken here. The final three chapters in this book address these areas, outlining the parameters of the problems that remain, as well as the potential for moving forward boldly and confidently in a manner that will benefit everyone.

7

CREATING CHANGE IN THE CLASSROOM
Curriculum, Pedagogy, and LGBT Content

In contrast to the schoolwide and districtwide emphasis of the approaches identified in the preceding chapters, the focus in this chapter is on the level of the individual classroom and on what each K–12 teacher might do. Some level of professional development—locally determined and agreed upon by affected personnel—would necessarily inform teachers' actions in the classroom, but it can be followed by the option to go much further at the classroom level, whether or not such changes are mandated by the law.

At each stage of the process contemplated in this chapter, steps can be incremental in nature, and even minor movement forward can matter greatly. Pursuant to the research-based principles articulated here, for example, professional development can start off as simply and basically as an information sheet or an email; can expand to include guest speakers, film clips, and brainstorming regarding possible strategies; and can even go so far as to entail a dialogue regarding the efficacy of changes in classroom pedagogy and curricular content.

For those who commit to going even further and making district-approved adjustments in their classroom pedagogy or even including LGBT-related material in their curriculum, day-to-day changes can also be very basic and very minor, with the possibility of taking additional steps depending on the circumstances. But it is important to emphasize that although the first edition of this book contemplated only *voluntary* changes in pedagogy and curriculum, leaving details to the discretion of individual educators pursuant to the requirements of district program mandates and state content standards, this edition and in particular this chapter must take into account the fact that the largest state in the union now requires age-appropriate and LGBT-positive content in the public school social studies curriculum.[1]

When implementing professional development of this nature, school officials should be cognizant of the fact that such sessions inevitably touch on topics that, for some, are among the most controversial in our society. In addition to the volatility of issues relating to gay and transgender status generally, content addressing LGBT persons of color can raise emotional questions concerning race and ethnicity. Discussions relating to gender-expansive persons can raise a host of issues regarding gender, and of course all of these discussions can also implicate a person's religious beliefs.

Lessons can be learned from recent challenges to LGBT-related instruction in Maryland and Kentucky. These challenges were brought in federal court on behalf of students and not by faculty or staff, yet it is instructive to consider the applicability of the resulting decisions to teacher and administrator professional development.

In Kentucky, the court in *Morrison v. Bd. of Ed. of Boyd County* (introduced in chapter 5) upheld the constitutionality of the student "diversity training" that had been mandated by a settlement agreement.[2] But in Maryland, the court in *Citizens for a Responsible Curriculum v. Montgomery County Public Schools* held that a pilot eighth-grade and tenth-grade health curriculum violated students' First Amendment rights.[3] The distinguishing characteristic, according to Judge Bunning of the district court, was that the Maryland program "ventured . . . into the crossroads of controversy where religion, morality and homosexuality converge," whereas the Kentucky program "labors hard to dissociate itself from a particular view and leaves religion to the students and their families."[4]

Maryland's Montgomery County Public Schools had included in its program a "Myths and Facts" handout that appeared to characterize the statement "Homosexuality is a sin" as a myth, a depiction that is simply not correct. According to the tenets of the world's major religions, constituents and parishioners look to the religious leaders and scholars of the era for guidance in such matters, and it certainly cannot be characterized as a myth that homosexuality is a sin if some religious leaders and certain doctrinal writings say that it is.

By contrast, in Kentucky, at the end of videos shown to both the middle school and high school students, the compliance coordinator made the following statement: "We would never try to influence [your religious beliefs]. They are very sacred and they should only be influenced by you, your parents and your family. Please realize that with the video we showed today we are only trying to instill a sense of honor amongst our students to learn not to treat someone unfairly or harass someone because they are different."[5] The Kentucky court concluded that there had been no Free Exercise Clause violation. "There is no evidence," Judge Bunning wrote, "that the student-Plaintiff, or any other student, was compelled to disavow his or her religious beliefs. Nor is there evidence that the student-Plaintiff, or any other student, was called upon to endorse homosexuality, bisexuality or transgendered persons."[6]

Given the parallels between the apparent goals of the learning activities in these cases and the goals of the teacher professional development outlined in this chapter, the court's reasoning can be viewed as directly applicable. Professional development sessions on LGBT issues should not get into an analysis of religious doctrine, nor should they seek to make any statements regarding religion other than to recognize that there are differences of interpretation. And the sessions should be respectful of divergent perspectives, as the Kentucky sessions clearly were, in contrast to the Maryland sessions, which arguably were not.

Ideally, the efforts contemplated in this chapter would begin with administrative leadership and a core group of committed faculty. Professional development would be geared toward adjusting classroom pedagogy and designing additional curricular components. Depending on the school culture and the surrounding community, the level of professional development implemented and the actual change that would take place in individual classrooms might be very simple and very minor. Indeed, this entire area can be looked at as a continuum. But it should be emphasized that even very minor adjustments in curriculum and pedagogy can make a world of difference for individual students.

For example, literature in this area suggests that, if nothing else, faculty and staff should be informed that in any group of twenty to thirty students, it is appropriate to assume that there are gays and lesbians in the room. Intellectually, of course, few would disagree with such an assumption. Yet a very large percentage of educators do not have this mindset, and when they look at a group of students, they unconsciously assume that all of them are straight. According to consistent findings by researchers, the key implication is that when faculty make such unconscious assumptions, they often treat LGBT students as if they were invisible, and in so doing, they fail to show an equal level of caring and a sensitivity to what these students say and how they say it.

Thus, even if a professional development session does nothing more than address changing the way one looks at any group of people, and if faculty then begin doing that—each in his or her own way—this very minor and incremental change is likely, nevertheless, to have a positive impact on people's lives. Educators generally have a highly developed sense of empathy, and a slight change of mind-set in this context can lead many of them to view the realities of public education from the perspective of LGBT youth for the very first time.

This chapter begins by addressing professional development and identifying incremental steps such as these. Contemplating collaborative efforts on the part of the various stakeholders, it points toward a process that can turn ostensibly controversial proposals into logical next steps. In this spirit, the chapter then provides an overview of realistic strategies for change in curricular and pedagogical practices, taking into consideration the relevant laws, the comfort level of individual educators, and the culture of both the school and the community.

Professional Development around LGBT Issues: Strategies and Approaches

Ongoing professional development for both teachers and school-site administrators is one of the most important proactive steps that a school district can take to maintain a positive and supportive school climate for all students. It can be instrumental in combating peer harassment and discriminatory discipline practices and in fact has been an essential remedy in settings where such practices have been prevalent. It is particularly important with regard to gay and transgender issues, and indeed many court orders, consent decrees, and settlements addressing best practices in an LGBT context have relied to a great extent on professional development.[7]

Research has shown that professional development is best seen as a form of collaborative dialogue between educators and as a vehicle for keeping abreast of new developments in their respective fields. Mandatory "top-down" programs where so-called experts are brought in on a one-time basis to "lecture" faculty and staff are often found to be the least effective approach, whereas brainstorming regarding new strategies and follow-up meetings to share results are often viewed as the ideal. Indeed, an "unprecedented consensus" has emerged in the literature regarding what constitutes effective professional development. According to Willis Hawley and Linda Valli, the research suggests that high-quality teacher development is designed around collaborative problem solving, among other things. It is continuous and ongoing, providing follow-up support for further learning. Luz Maldonado, in a 2002 report for the College Entrance Examination Board, found that effective professional development activities embody inquiry-based learning, collaborative grouping, and the formation of ongoing learning communities.[8]

A Research-Based, Incremental Approach to Professional Development

ONLINE INQUIRY

Incremental LGBT-related professional development can start off as an email sent to faculty and staff that contains a news story or an op-ed piece about gay or transgender issues. A next step might be a Listserv or an online discussion forum where school personnel discuss recent events on an ongoing basis. In some communities, especially where LGBT issues are not discussed openly in a professional setting even today, online inquiry, at least initially, might be more palatable.

COMMUNITY RESOURCES

Another ostensibly preliminary but equally valuable approach might be to bring in people from both the school community and the surrounding neighborhood to engage in a dialogue about LGBT-related concerns and what might be done. This could include everyone from current and former students to out faculty and staff to members of community groups that work with LGBT youth. A key aspect of this approach is that it would be a dialogue rather than a lecture series.

In addition, such a structure is consistent with research findings that demonstrate the efficacy of treating students, out faculty and staff, and members of the larger community as valued resources. Eric Rofes, in particular, emphasized the need to understand youth culture and the importance of empowering students and enlisting their active involvement in both the establishment of policies and the responses to acts of peer harassment and mistreatment. It is clear from Rofes's findings that adults alone cannot change behaviors, especially when young people spend such a large percentage of their day apart from adults. In addition, with regard to community resources, research has shown that schools with a positive school climate are often ones that are also able to reach out to the larger community. Many models set forth approaches for "building capacity" by dialoguing with parents and members of the local community as a whole.[9]

MIND-SETS

At a certain point, incremental LGBT-related professional development might move into a more structured phase, informed by the dialogue that took place in the beginning. A set of facts and basic principles might be put forth, each with the potential to generate additional inquiry. At a minimum, an activity at this stage might seek to identify the best possible mind-set for addressing LGBT issues if faculty and staff are still not comfortable with the subject, for whatever reasons. Mind-sets that others have found useful in this context are the "legal compliance" approach, emphasizing the responsibility to comply with the law and treat all students the same; the "responsible for every student" approach, stressing that whether one agrees or disagrees with the law, teachers have a moral obligation to help everyone equally; and the "Golden Rule" approach, emphasizing kindness toward others and the dictum "do unto others as one would have them do unto you" in both faculty–student and student–student interactions.

THE CONCEPT OF HETERONORMATIVITY

Another topic that might be introduced at this point in professional development, should school officials wish to do so, is the concept of heteronormativity, which underlies the research-based conclusions regarding the inherent value of assuming that there are gays and lesbians in every room. One of the most overlooked realities in U.S. public schools, and indeed in U.S. society as a whole, is the widespread prevalence of heteronormativity and the way it can operate to marginalize gay people. Put simply, heteronormativity is the assumption or expectation that everyone is heterosexual, and the corollary to this assumption is that it is normal to be heterosexual and not necessarily normal to be anything else.[10]

In so many ways during day-to-day conversations and interactions, educators say and do things that perpetuate these social and cultural norms. Often without even realizing it, public schools are sending young LGBTs the message, at best, that something is wrong with them or, at worst, that they do not exist. The widespread prevalence of heteronormativity can play a major role in perpetuating the fact that gays, lesbians, and transgender persons are often looked down upon or seen, on some level—even by ostensible allies and even by LGBTs themselves—as lesser persons with major physical and/or psychological defects.[11] Yet few are aware of this dynamic, and awareness alone can lead to positive change.

An additional and interrelated agenda item that can dovetail with a discussion of heteronormativity, if so desired, is the issue of negative stereotypes. Many faculty and staff still view gay and gender-nonconforming students in a negative light, based on stereotypes and myths that have been instilled over time. For example, many educators have never even considered the idea that one can be both gay and religious, even though many LGBTs are deeply involved in religion and/or spirituality.

RELIGION AND HOMOSEXUALITY

School officials might choose at this point in professional development to share with participants some examples of how LGBT persons have sought to reconcile homosexuality and religion. Such examples should be presented not as conclusive evidence that such a reconciliation is possible, however (because the topic remains a debatable one for many), but simply as evidence that people have wrestled with this issue and continue to wrestle with it as time goes by.

A particularly significant volume in this regard is Brian Bouldrey's *Wrestling with the Angel: Faith and Religion in the Lives of Gay Men.* The book, a collection of twenty-one essays, reflects the diversity of viewpoints and perspectives on this topic within LGBT communities. Every author demonstrates a level of respect for religion, even if in the end some choose to live apart from its institutions.

In his essay for the book, "Coming Out and Born Again," Michael Nava discovers parallels between his gay identity and his uncle's evangelical Christianity: "Being 'born again' and 'coming out' are transcendent experiences that produce a profound change in perception. You never look at yourself, your life, or your culture in the same way again. Much of what you have been taught is true is revealed to be false. . . . You feel enormous relief when you surrender the baggage of shame and guilt produced by living a life that was not true to your experience of yourself. You look for a community that will support and reinforce your new direction, your new ideas, and your new identity."[12]

More recently, Rabbis Mychal Copeland and D'vorah Rose have assembled a groundbreaking book on the reconciliation issue, *Struggling in Good Faith*, which focuses on "LGBTQI Inclusion from 13 American Religious Perspectives." After a foreword by Bishop Gene Robinson and an introduction by the coeditors, the book presents essays on the following faith traditions by leaders and participants in the respective fields: the Black Church, Buddhism, the Church of Jesus Christ of Latter-Day Saints (Mormon), the Episcopal Church, First Nations (Native Americans), Hinduism, Islam, Judaism, the Lutheran Church, the Presbyterian Church, Protestant evangelical traditions, the Roman Catholic Church, and Unitarian Universalism.[13]

Sorting out the perspectives that are presented in the various essays, coeditors Copeland and Rose describe their optimistic vision of reconciliation as follows:

> The most powerful transformation will occur when people are able to bring their entire, authentic, spiritual selves to their communities. Rather than expanding the table to "include" a diversity of individuals within American religious life, we must look to see who is already there. . . . As Marvin M. Ellison and Sylvia Thorson Smith write in their chapter on the Presbyterian Church:
>
>> Non-heterosexual and transgender persons reside in every faith community, so the change agenda is not how to include "outsiders" and bring them inside, but rather how to create together the communal conditions of hospitality, safety, and respect so that people of diverse sexual orientations and gender identities alike can acknowledge and share what they have come to know, often at great risk, about resisting injustice, enhancing human dignity, and revitalizing community.[14]

Reverend Chris Glaser, a prominent Christian activist and spiritual leader, has written twelve books that reflect a similar attempt at synthesizing LGBT status and religion. "When I started a gay Christian support group at Yale Divinity School in 1974," he writes, "I had a respected scholar stop me on the campus quadrangle. He said he had finally connected me, a student in one of his classes, to the signs posted about the gay Christian group's formation. He said to me, as if I were not gay myself, 'What right do we have to tell these people they shouldn't be ashamed?' I was astounded, and replied, 'What right do we have to tell them they should be ashamed?—and we've been doing that for years!'"[15]

In a similar manner, Rabbi Steven Greenberg documents his "ten-year struggle to reconcile" his two identities in *Wrestling with God and Men*. An orthodox Jewish man who is also openly gay, Greenberg employs traditional rabbinic resources and methodologies to reexamine how same-sex love arises and is addressed in the Jewish canon as well as in Jewish poetry, prose, and traditional legal literature.[16]

Indeed, a growing number of gay activists have been speaking and writing about the viability of leading a life grounded in both an LGBT identity and a spiritual identity. Dr. Yvette Flunder, for example, founder and senior pastor of the City of Refuge United Church of Christ in San Francisco, urged attendees at the closing plenary session of the National Gay and Lesbian Task Force's 2005 annual meeting to stand up and "find their spirituality."[17] The Reverend Irene Monroe, an African American feminist theologian, has been a prolific author and speaker whose work uses an interdisciplinary approach "drawing on critical race theory, African American, queer and religious studies."[18] And Kevin VanWanseele, a founder of the Northeast Two-Spirit Society, continues to work toward reclaiming the honor and recognition for gender-nonconforming people that was a key part of the spirituality of certain Native American tribes in the past.[19]

Entire organizations have emerged, on both a local and a national level, that are built upon a dual foundation of spirituality and LGBT status. One of the most prominent of these organizations is Soulforce, an interfaith organization comprising mostly young and devout LGBTs who seek to build a positive recognition of gay identity within organized religion.[20]

Even if professional development programs go no further than taking these approaches, much will have been accomplished. Without even directly addressing possible changes in curriculum and pedagogy, many faculty members may think about these things in a different way. It is highly recommended, however, that the inquiry take the extra step of turning to questions of whether faculty are willing to adjust their classroom pedagogy and how faculty members might consider going forward with changes in the curriculum.

Adjusting Classroom Pedagogy and Curriculum

It is one thing to gain additional background that will help educators address LGBT issues that may arise in a professional setting or even in their personal lives, but it is certainly another for the same educators to commit to doing things differently in their own classrooms. Many people have made commitments of this nature, however, and it is appropriate to consider such additional steps if school officials choose to do so. Yet, because the area is still fraught with controversy for so many, it is also highly appropriate to engage in an open discussion regarding whether and to what extent to go forward in this manner, consistent, of course, with applicable law.

CLASSROOM PEDAGOGY

Changes in classroom pedagogy would include such things as a conscious sensitivity to school climate, working together, shared values, and a respect for differences. Many K–12 educators already have these things in mind as they interact with their students, although there are those who see themselves as delegated only with the tasks of imparting knowledge and building academic skills. Still others are cognizant of school climate and building a collaborative working environment but may not go so far as to acknowledge shared values or a respect for differences. Thus there is room for incremental change in this area. Some may wish to go only so far in their commitment to working in what is often known as the affective domain, while others may choose to go much further.

Beyond these key factors, an additional component of classroom pedagogy would focus on the extent to which K–12 educators choose to reference LGBT persons and topics as a matter of course. Some may not be comfortable even using terms such as *gay, lesbian,* and *transgender.* Some will be comfortable with the terms but not comfortable acknowledging the sexual orientation or gender identity of a student, should it come up. Some will be willing to go far beyond just using the terms and acknowledging the existence of a student's identity. It is useful for faculty and staff to explore these matters openly in a professional development setting, examining the pros and cons of committing to assumptions and approaches that may not have been part of a person's job description in the past.

LGBT-RELATED CONTENT IN THE CURRICULUM

An even more complex discussion is likely to ensue if faculty are given the opportunity to analyze how they might include LGBT-related content in the curriculum, whether or not the law mandates it. The prospective inclusion of such content is, of course, not the only hot-button topic in the area of curricular policy: the changing nature of U.S. society and the ongoing impact of globalization have led to many high-profile controversies regarding curriculum over the past several decades. At the higher education level, for example, disputes have focused on such interrelated issues as what courses should be required, whether and to what extent programs such as ethnic studies should be established, and whether traditional notions of what "the canon" comprises are still relevant.

At the K–12 level, disputes have ranged from debates regarding values education and the teaching of religious content to controversies regarding the efficacy and parameters of bilingual education and multicultural education. In this era of high-stakes, test-driven requirements built on assessments of basic skills, additional debates have focused on concerns over the depletion of coverage in social studies, humanities, and the arts—areas that have often not been included in legally mandated measures of academic achievement.[21]

Key arguments supporting the introduction of LGBT content into the curriculum include the benefits that can accrue from both a self-esteem and a school climate perspective, as well as the fact that LGBT issues arise in our society on a regular basis and are often front-page news. In addition, gay-related historical and literary developments often fit well within state-adopted curricular content standards, and the inclusion of such material is consistent with the principle that schooling is most effective when it addresses the world as it currently exists.

Opposition to such curricular changes is often rooted in a person's religious beliefs, and although school districts cannot generally seek to justify educational policy decisions by invoking religious doctrine, it may well be the case that individual faculty members might feel less comfortable going forward in this area because of their own individual religious values. However, for purposes of discussion in a professional development context, "secular" policy arguments would be the more appropriate focus. These include the assertions that LGBT-related curricular content will encourage dangerous experimentation, that the content is particularly inappropriate for younger students, and that what historical and literary figures did and do in the privacy of their bedrooms is irrelevant in a public school setting. Such arguments have been put forth by leaders across the political spectrum as well as by the mainstream media in arguing against mandatory inclusion of LGBT content.

With regard to curricular policy, at this point in time, this book stands for the proposition that the optimum scenario that would benefit everyone would be to go forward with such inclusion.

ADDRESSING THE ARGUMENT THAT LGBT CONTENT
WILL ENCOURAGE EXPERIMENTATION

The assertion that gay content will encourage dangerous experimentation is the functional equivalent of the allegation that the introduction of such content in the public schools will "turn people gay." Similar arguments have been put forth by those objecting to other types of content in the curriculum, in areas ranging from the study of war and the study of religion to drug education and sex education. In all of these areas, some have expressed the fear that after being exposed to such content, young and impressionable students will begin thinking about certain things for the first time—or in ways they had not thought about before—and will be more likely to engage in experimentation that could have serious negative consequences.

It is asserted, for example, that studying how wars are fought could lead to a desire to purchase and experiment with dangerous weapons; that learning about different religions could lead to experimenting with religious practices different from those of one's family or to abandoning religion altogether; that drug education programs could lead to the purchase of and experimentation with illicit substances; and that sex education could lead to thinking about sex in different ways and a desire to try out certain things for the first time.

Yet while there is always a possibility that *anything* covered in either a K–12 or a higher education setting will generate an interest in some sort of experimentation, that alone is rarely—if ever—a reason not to teach it. In addition, an analysis of the efficacy of a particular curriculum is incomplete if the focus is on content alone, given the importance of such variables as who is teaching the content and how it is being presented. It also should be noted that what is learned at home and within the larger community plays a key role here as well, and that students are never "at the mercy" of the curriculum, given the complex set of variables and circumstances that are always at play.[22]

ADDRESSING THE CONTENTION THAT LGBT CONTENT IS
INAPPROPRIATE FOR YOUNGER STUDENTS

As discussed earlier, and particularly in the analysis of the opinion by
Judge Manion in the *Schroeder* case, many still believe that references
to anything gay are inappropriate for younger students. To some extent,
such views are rooted in the misconception that "gay" is the equivalent of
"sex." In addition, however, there is still a prevalent view in many communities that young students are not ready to confront issues of sexual
orientation and gender identity.

LGBT activists in this area recognize that this is complex territory
and that instruction and content must be age appropriate. Yet such concerns do not justify refraining from *any* inclusion of LGBT content in the
younger grades. As noted in the discussion of the *Schroeder* case, young
people use the word "gay" all the time, and they are aware that people fall
in love with each other and pair up as a result. In addition, with the emergence of a right to be out, young people increasingly see same-sex couples in their communities. Their own parents and other family members
may be in same-sex relationships. Their friends may show up at back-
to-school nights or at other school events with same-sex parents. Thus
the inclusion of LGBT content in the younger grades does not constitute
"normalizing" gay and lesbian relationships at all but is instead consistent with the basic principle of curriculum policy that a public school education in a pluralistic society should address and reflect what is taking
place in our society rather than ignoring it or trying to wish it away.

ADDRESSING THE ASSERTION OF THE IRRELEVANCE OF
HISTORICAL AND LITERARY FIGURES' PRIVATE LIVES

A substantial number of people who are otherwise very supportive of
equal treatment for LGBT persons remain skeptical, in particular, of the
idea that curricular content should include information about the sexual orientation of historical and literary figures. They argue that what
should be documented are the achievements, not whom a person was attracted to or had fallen in love with. This argument gained the support of
the editorial boards at the *Los Angeles Times* and the *Sacramento Bee* in
summer 2006, when both newspapers came out against California Senate
Bill 1437, which would have required California public schools to include
LGBT content in the curriculum. The *Times* editorial relied on the "irrelevance" argument and stated that such a requirement would be a dis-
tortion of history education's true purpose, which is to report "important

contributions, and misdeeds, of people in history, regardless of their be-liefs and orientations." The *Sacramento Bee* claimed that requiring school districts to include contributions from LGBTs in curricula is "simply inap-propriate" and likened it to a mandate from the state to rewrite history.[23]

Yet such a position ignores the fact that textbooks do contain infor-mation about the spouses, different-sex partners, and children of many historical and literary figures. In the same manner that relationships and family environment might help explain the nuances of a heterosexual person's character, so too could such information help clarify the circum-stances surrounding a gay or lesbian person's life. Indeed, many historical and literary figures' sexual identity is reflected in their work and played a key role in the development of their lives. Not to include this identity would be to present a partial and often misleading picture.

In addition, LGBT-related controversies are themselves history. The gay and transgender rights movements of the past fifty years are part and parcel of a wide-ranging series of efforts by traditionally disenfranchised groups to obtain equal treatment under the law and in society as a whole. Not to teach about this is the functional equivalent of erasing aspects of recent history that have been central to the lives of many people, gay and straight alike.

An example of such a controversy that played out in a very public way was the apparent disagreement at the offices of the *Washington Post* in March 2008 over whether to include the sexual orientation of a U.S. war hero in his obituary. Major Alan G. Rogers was a highly decorated LGBT veteran of the army who was killed in Iraq earlier in the year. He was an African American and also a person of faith—apparently married to a woman at one time, but then divorced. He received a Purple Heart posthumously.

According to Deborah Howell, the *Post*'s public editor, the draft of the story about Rogers's burial at Arlington National Cemetery originally identified him as a gay man, given that friends interviewed for the story had disclosed that he was "well known in local gay veterans' circles." But the *Post*'s executive editor chose to delete that information from the final version: "For *The Post,* Rogers's death raised an unanswerable question: Would he have wanted to be identified as gay? Friends also struggled with that question but decided to tell *The Post* that he was because, they said, he wanted the military's 'Don't Ask, Don't Tell' rule repealed. Yet a cousin and a close friend felt that his sexual orientation was not important; his immediate family members are deceased."

Subsequently, the *Washington Blade,* a gay-oriented newspaper, did identify Rogers as LGBT in a story that was critical of the *Post.* The *Post's* public editor disclosed both the information and the controversy soon afterward. She told of his active membership in American Veterans for Equal Rights (AVER) and quoted several friends who spoke directly on the topic. Tony Smith, for example, an air force veteran who knew Rogers through AVER, said that Rogers "was very open about being gay. It was a major part of his life. It does a disservice to his memory" not to mention it. Austin Rooke, Rogers's friend and a former army captain, said, "He was among the most open active-duty military people I've ever met. I can't imagine him not wanting people to know." Tami Sadowski said that she and her husband traveled and socialized with Rogers regularly and that "being gay was a huge and very defining part of his life."[24] Howell concluded in her story that although *"The Post* was right to be cautious . . . there was enough evidence—particularly of Rogers's feelings about 'Don't Ask, Don't Tell'—to warrant quoting his friends and adding that dimension to the story of his life. The story would have been richer for it."[25]

Including LGBT-Related Content in the Curriculum

For those who are either required to include LGBT-related content in their classroom lessons and study units or choose to do so within the context of a collaborative curriculum development plan, an incremental approach similar to that described earlier can be employed. Some might choose to include only one discussion or even one portion of a discussion. Others might choose to go much further. The process offers great flexibility, even as it is important to keep in mind that individual educators in the public schools are not free to go beyond the relevant frameworks and standards. At the same time, K–12 educators considering changes in their curricula can learn much from the higher education experience and the voluntary inclusion of LGBT content that emerged there. And California's FAIR Education Act can serve as a relevant model for those stakeholders in other states who seek to update their own curricular requirements and prohibitions.

Curricular Lessons from the Higher Education Experience

In the area of curriculum, as in other areas relating to LGBT issues in public education, breakthroughs happened initially at the higher education level. Models were developed that could then be adapted in the K–12 public schools. According to John D'Emilio, there was not one openly gay or lesbian college professor in this country as recently as 1970. The first gay student group on a college campus was not formed until 1967, and the first organization of gay academics—the Gay Academic Union (GAU)—was not formed until 1973.[26] D'Emilio, one of the nation's premier gay historians and an academic who was at the forefront of the effort to include LGBT content in higher education, has chronicled the dramatic changes in this regard over the past fifty years.

In *Making Trouble: Essays on Gay History, Politics, and the University*, D'Emilio tells the story of the GAU, the issues and personal challenges faced by those who took part, and the overwhelming success of the organization's first formal event in late 1973, a two-day conference in New York City that drew more than three hundred people. Scholarly concerns were the focus of the first day, with "Scholarship and the Gay Experience" as the unifying theme. The second day addressed personal concerns, with "Coming Out at the University" as the central focus.[27]

Among the many other noteworthy highlights of D'Emilio's volume is his 1990 essay titled "Gay History: A New Field of Study," which documents the explosion of LGBT-related scholarship between 1973 (when virtually nothing existed) and 1983 (when landmark works had been completed and were being widely read), as well as an analysis of the central role such scholarship played in the ability to offer courses on gay and lesbian issues.[28] In addition, throughout the book, D'Emilio demonstrates what gay and lesbian content in courses and programs might look like. For example, in the area of U.S. history, he discusses two multifaceted developments in which knowledge of the gay and lesbian dynamic is integral to an understanding of what took place. In the first, he shows how the emergence of feminism and what transpired after suffrage had been achieved cannot be fully understood without acknowledging "the creation of a lesbian taboo" and its implications. In the second, he describes at length how the "preoccupation with a homosexual menace" was central to an understanding of the post–World War II Cold War era and the emergence of McCarthyism.[29]

At colleges and universities today, both within traditional departments and professional schools and through interdisciplinary LGBT studies programs, students can take courses that focus on similar gay and lesbian themes throughout history and on how sexual and gender identity is reflected in the work of noteworthy authors, poets, and artists. In law schools, both within traditional courses and in courses focusing on such topics as sexual orientation law, transgender rights, and the law of sexuality in general, students can study legal developments in this context. In education schools, future teachers and principals can address gay- and transgender-related issues that may arise in their work in public education. All of these courses and all of this content can and increasingly do provide a model for K–12 educators regarding what might be included in an age-appropriate manner in their own classrooms.

In addition, over the past thirty years, LGBT-related conferences and institutional projects have proliferated, reflecting the continued growth of scholarly literature in this area and helping to generate additional work across all academic disciplines. For example, the Williams Institute, established at the UCLA School of Law in 2001, supports legal scholarship, legal research, policy analysis, and education regarding sexual orientation and gender identity discrimination and other legal issues that affect LGBT people. The institute originated with the recognition that issues central to LGBT law have profound implications for the development of the law and public policy in general. It has provided a national center for the interdisciplinary exploration of these issues by scholars, judges, practitioners, advocates, and students.

THE FAIR EDUCATION ACT MODEL AND THE
K–12 SOCIAL STUDIES CURRICULUM

As mentioned earlier in this book, California became the first state to mandate the inclusion of LGBT-positive content in its public school social studies curriculum. The Fair, Accurate, Inclusive, and Respectful (FAIR) Education Act (Senate Bill 48) was signed into law by Governor Jerry Brown in 2011 and took effect in January 2012. The legislation made several additions to already existing Education Code sections dealing with the course of study, classroom instruction, and instructional materials. For example, the legislation added language to Education Code Section 51204.5, which prescribes the inclusion of the contributions of various groups in the history of California and the United States. This section already included men and women and numerous ethnic groups; the expanded language now includes LGBTs and persons with disabilities, as follows (new additions bolded):

> a study of the role and contributions of both men and women, Native Americans, African Americans, Mexican **Americans**, Asian **Americans**,

Pacific Islanders, **European Americans, lesbian, gay, bisexual, and transgender Americans, persons with disabilities**, and members of other ethnic **and cultural** groups, to the economic, political, and social development of California and the United States of America, with particular emphasis on portraying the role of these groups in contemporary society.[30]

In sum, the FAIR Education Act includes two key requirements and two key prohibitions:

Requires inclusion in social studies of the role and contributions of [specified categories of persons, including LGBTs] to the development of California and the U.S. *CA Ed Code Section 51204.5.*

Prohibits instruction or school sponsored activities that promote a discriminatory bias because of [certain recognized characteristics, including LGBT]. *CA Ed Code Section 51500.*

Prohibits adopting textbooks or instructional materials that contain any matter reflecting adversely on [members of particular groups, including LGBTs]. *CA Ed Code Sections 51501, 60044.*

Requires that adopted instructional materials shall include materials that accurately portray the role and contributions of [culturally and racially diverse groups, including LGBTs]. *CA Ed Code Section 60040.*

Four years later, in 2016, the state updated its History/Social Science Curriculum Framework, which is now consistent with the FAIR Act. And in November 2017, the State Board of Education voted to approve instructional materials for grades K–8 that align with the updated framework.[31]

Incremental Approaches to Curricular Reform at the K–12 Level

Although K–12 educators can choose from options for curricular reform across a broad continuum, it must be emphasized that even just mentioning LGBTs and acknowledging their existence, currently and throughout history, are important steps. Even if nothing else is done, such acts will be a significant contribution.

CURRENT EVENTS

Throughout the past fifty to seventy-five years, K–12 educational programs have placed great importance on an analysis of current events and have created opportunities for students to report on and discuss the major news stories of the day. Many of these stories document LGBT-related controversies and explore how they might be addressed by the legal and educational communities. Topics that arise focus on many of the key areas highlighted in this book, including campus safety; student activism; the right to be out; the right not to be out; school sports; the military; issues relating to family; the impact of the same-sex marriage debates; transgender persons and gender equity; the rights of LGBT educators, issues relating to curriculum, religion, morality, and values; and the unique challenges faced by LGBT students of color.

As is the case with other types of gay- and transgender-related content included in the higher education curriculum today, many, if not most, of these issues can be addressed at the K–12 level. For the most part, they are topics that K–12 students—especially ages twelve and older—are already very familiar with, and the overarching question "What can be done to make things better for everyone?" is as appropriate to address with younger students as it is with college-age students in a higher education classroom. Indeed, it is a question that people of all ages continue to wrestle with as time goes by.

The T-shirt controversies that have been litigated in the courts provide a particularly interesting example of how such issues can be relevant and compelling at the K–12 level. Students will be engaged instantly in such discussions, which will inevitably provide additional insights not only into LGBT-related matters and the concept of shared values in a pluralistic society but also into the parameters of First Amendment protections that currently exist in the public sector.

RIGHTS MOVEMENTS, NOTABLE LGBTS, AND
OTHER SOCIETAL CONNECTIONS

In addition to current events, some educators might also be willing to include the gay and transgender rights movements in study units that address other post–World War II rights movements. An additional step that would go even further would be to acknowledge the contributions of notable LGBTs in history, culture, and society.

Such steps would fit appropriately within the traditional construct of curriculum development, especially in an era of state content standards. In "Stonewall Jackson and the Stonewall Riots Together" (2003), for example, Scott Hirschfeld, former director of education for GLSEN, provides both the case for integrating LGBT content into the U.S. history curriculum and foundational resources for making it happen. Focusing in particular on the centrality of textbooks and other instructional materials, Hirschfeld not only discusses ways in which such content can be integrated naturally into existing history textbooks but also provides a list of places educators can go to find LGBT-related history resources.[32]

ALIGNING LGBT-RELATED CONTENT WITH
STATEWIDE CONTENT STANDARDS

Increasingly, it is not possible to include anything in a formal public school curriculum that is not linked to standards that have been adopted by individual states. To that end, school officials focusing on LGBT issues have begun to identify the many ways that gay and transgender content ties in with such standards. A brief examination of four standards for eleventh-grade U.S. history that are representative of social studies content standards adopted nationwide reveals that they offer numerous opportunities to consider the contributions and struggles of gays and lesbians in the American story:

A standard that mandates examining the roles of civil rights advocates. The story of Bayard Rustin, set forth in several recent highly acclaimed biographies and collected writings, has emerged in retrospect as a central feature of the civil rights movement.[33] A key organizer and intellectual force who worked closely with Martin Luther King Jr. and was in charge of putting together legendary nonviolent demonstrations such as the 1963 March on Washington, Rustin was also known to be a gay man during a time when tremendous stigma was attached to this identity. Enemies of the civil rights movement such as segregationist senator Strom Thurmond and FBI director J. Edgar Hoover attempted to use Rustin's sexual orientation to limit or discredit the movement. Rustin's achievements despite all the challenges cannot currently be found in any high school history text, but standards like this one provide an opportunity for teachers to include them.

A standard that requires educators to explain how government(s) have responded to demographic and social changes such as population shifts. Standards of this type provide an opportunity for teachers to reference the impact of LGBTs on urban planning, development, and renewal. Indeed, the extent to which areas of major U.S. cities, such as the Castro and West Hollywood, have been renovated, rebuilt, and in many instances transformed by gay residents and gay businesses is often pointed to as a model of what can be accomplished in other places.

A standard that requires teachers to discuss the response of the Roosevelt administration to Hitler's atrocities against the Jews and other groups. Too often, the extent to which Hitler's atrocities included the persecution, torture, and brutal murder of gay people is left out of the history books. A full treatment of the issues surrounding the U.S. response—or lack thereof—to ongoing reports from cities occupied by the Nazis and concentration camps run by the Nazis necessarily includes referencing what was nothing less than Hitler's effort to exterminate gays and lesbians.

A standard that mandates discussing forms of popular culture (e.g., jazz and other forms of popular music). Such a discussion, on any level, would be incomplete without including an analysis of the increasing prevalence of LGBT themes in television, film, and theater and without referencing the extent to which the work of composers and musicians like Cole Porter, Billy Strayhorn, and Elton John was informed by their gay identity.[34]

In light of the opportunities afforded by the development of statewide curriculum standards, educators across the country are beginning to address the many ways that LGBT content can enrich the curriculum across subject areas in an age-appropriate manner. Many individual teachers at local school sites across the nation, on their own initiative, have developed curriculum content that fits naturally within the prescribed courses of study.

Curriculum reform taken to this level can be central to implementing the emerging right to be out at local school sites. By helping to reinforce a basic message that under current law LGBT identity can no longer be equated with outsider status and that the ongoing story of our society and culture has always included the story of gays, lesbians, and transgender people, an enhanced curriculum builds understandings and helps foster an appreciation of commonalities. In this manner, such reform strengthens and enriches the curriculum, providing a higher-quality education for everyone.

8

THE CULTURE OF SCHOOL SPORTS
From Physical Education to Interscholastic Athletics

In addition to addressing curriculum and pedagogy at the individual classroom level, educators considering LGBT-related reforms at K–12 school sites can enact potentially transformative changes by working through the persistently challenging issues in the area of school sports. At the outset, it is important to emphasize just how substantial and just how direct the influence of organized sports can be on the lives of our young people. The numbers alone reveal the scope of the impact. A very large percentage of America's youth participate in organized sports, from the Little Leagues through high school, college, and beyond. In light of this level of participation, it is inevitable that a substantial number of young people will be influenced by the cultures, traditions, and mind-sets highly prevalent in these programs.[1]

Many who participate in sports vicariously are also affected in significant ways. An entire financial infrastructure is built on the interest and involvement of loyal fans, who provide ongoing support by attending events, purchasing products and services, and helping generate major advertising dollars as they dedicate significant amounts of time to tracking the exploits of their favorite athletes. Young people who immerse themselves in spectator sports in this way often adopt the traditions and live out the culture of sports even if they themselves never participate actively.

Moreover, at K–12 school sites, sports are an integral part of physical education (PE), and those involved in teaching PE are often the same persons who coach the sports teams. Thus the approaches and the values are generally the same, ensuring that just about everyone is affected by the culture of sports, and school climate is influenced accordingly.[2]

Perhaps even more significant, not only does sports cast a giant shadow on the day-to-day interactions and mind-sets of people in education settings but in many places it is the single most important factor in the school's climate and is located at the very center of a school's culture. At both the K–12 and higher education levels, numerous campuses are seen by many as "sports schools," proud of their successful, high-profile sports programs and united by an overriding interest in the outcomes of the sports events. In these places, athletes, coaches, cheerleaders, and others involved in the success of the programs are among the most admired persons on campus. The sports culture and the campus culture become, for all practical purposes, one and the same.

In a very large number of K–12 settings, then, if school officials desire to change the campus culture, they must inevitably address the sports culture as well. This culture continues to present a very difficult set of circumstances for LGBTs, because it has proven particularly resistant to change.[3]

Consistent with the inquiry in chapters 6 and 7 and building on the research set forth in those pages, this chapter seeks to ascertain why many sports programs have been unwelcoming to LGBT persons, examining the cultural and institutional norms that persist at all levels. Acknowledging the challenging nature of these realities, which are exemplified by the stories of gay and lesbian athletes who have wrestled with their identities in settings where only a tiny percentage dare to be out—even after their sports careers have ended—it concludes by identifying possible approaches that might be employed to help change the status quo.

Organized Sports and LGBT Communities: An Unwelcoming Climate at Every Level

The reaction of key members of the National Basketball Association's "elite" to former player John Amaechi's coming out, in 2007, highlighted for many the challenges that remain for gay, lesbian, and gender-nonconforming persons in organized sports. Amaechi was the sixth former athlete from the major professional men's team sports to go public with his gay identity, but he was the first former NBA player to do so. The reactions of the professional basketball community were in many ways a more significant story than the coming-out event itself. Arguably, none of these reactions was more revealing than that of former NBA superstar Tim Hardaway.

Hardaway had enjoyed a distinguished thirteen-year career as an inspirational team leader, primarily with the Golden State Warriors and the Miami Heat. A five-time NBA All-Star as a point guard who was among the league leaders in assists, he was also a reliable scorer, averaging more than twenty points per game during his peak years. Many saw him as the consummate unselfish player, always placing the interests of the team above his own. When he retired, he became a prominent spokesperson for the NBA, traveling around the country and speaking to young people on behalf of professional basketball.

After Amaechi came out, Hardaway was interviewed by a Miami radio station and asked how he would interact with a gay teammate. "First of all," he stated, "I wouldn't want him on my team. And second of all, if he was on my team, I would, you know, really distance myself from him because . . . I don't think that is right. I don't think he should be in the locker room while we are in the locker room." When talk show host Dan Le Batard responded by telling the former star that his comments were "flatly homophobic" and amounted to "bigotry," Hardaway added even more inflammatory remarks: "You know, I hate gay people, so I let it be known. I don't like gay people and I don't like to be around gay people. I'm homophobic. I don't like it. It shouldn't be in the world or in the United States." Hardaway also said that if he found out that a teammate were gay, he would ask for the player to be removed from the team. "Something has to give," he said. "If you have 12 other ballplayers in your locker room that [are] upset and can't concentrate and always worried about him in the locker room or on the court or whatever, it's going to be hard for your teammates to win and accept him as a teammate."[4]

Ten years later, in 2017, former NBA star Amar'e Stoudemire was similarly quoted, declaring that he would "avoid a gay teammate." Stoudemire, then playing in the Israeli Basketball Premier League, also had this to say in an interview with Israel's Walla Sport, ironically just two days after he received the MLK Jr. award for tolerance in Jerusalem: "I'm going to shower across the street, make sure my change of clothes are around the corner. And I'm going to drive, take a different route to the gym."[5]

In response to Stoudemire, former Brooklyn Net Jason Collins—the first and still the only NBA player ever to come out while he was still competing professionally, said, "Very sad and troubling to think that [Amar'e] was just given this award. His homophobic comments have no place in sport or in our society."[6]

The aforementioned and even more outspoken John Amaechi had this to say about Stoudemire's comments:

> These are serious times and we need serious people to lead important conversations, not petulant man-children spouting puerile prejudice. . . .
> In these tumultuous times, these true role models are the men and women whose voices we need to disseminate to every corner.[7]

As a general rule, there is no formal prohibition against the participation of gays and lesbians in organized athletic competition, and transgender people are increasingly able to participate in this area as well, as evidenced by the International Olympic Committee vote in 2004 to include transgender athletes. Still, there is tremendous unstated pressure not to come out, and the major men's team sports continue to present the greatest challenges. At the professional level, as of 2018, not one current member of a men's baseball, football, basketball, or hockey team in this country has come out. Only one, Jason Collins, while still playing in the NBA, has ever come out to the world.[8] And at the college and university level in these same sports, out athletes continue to be very rare.

Some argue that the anti-LGBT climate so widely prevalent in team sports has its roots in Little League baseball, soccer leagues, Pop Warner football, and other organized competition for the youngest participants. Others assert that it stems from the culture and traditions of the most highly visible professional institutions and works its way down to the K–12 level. It is likely that both assertions are true.

Billy Bean, one of the handful of former participants in major men's professional sports who came out after retiring, has written a highly acclaimed book, *Going the Other Way*, about his experiences both during the years he participated in baseball and during the era when he began living as an openly gay man.[9] The book reveals much about Bean's years with the Los Angeles Dodgers, the San Diego Padres, and the Detroit Tigers, but one of the most poignant sections of all is his depiction of how a homophobic and heterosexist culture was already being instilled in organized competition at the fourth-grade level.

Bean tells how he would never forget the first time he heard the word "faggot" on an athletic field. "Don't run like a faggot, boy," he remembers the coach of his Junior All-American Pop Warner football team shouting, after another fourth grader had missed a tackle: "Every kid on the field that day got the message, despite what I suspect was our collective ignorance. What, exactly, was a faggot? How did faggots run? Clearly, it wasn't a good thing. It was probably the worst thing imaginable. It equaled weakness and timidity, everything a budding, insecure jock wanted to avoid." Seeking to contextualize this central event in his young life, Bean notes the generally positive impact that this particular coach, a former marine, had on his development as an athlete. Not only was Coach Thompson a fine teacher of fundamentals but he also "helped instill . . . a drill sergeant's fire for competition." Bean remembers how personable the coach had been and how the man had bonded with Billy's own stepfather, another veteran of military service.

Even as he holds Coach Thompson up as a paradigm of fine teaching, Bean is clearly wrestling with the ambiguities that so many athletes who are coming to terms with their sexual and gender identities feel toward their coaches. "Coach had hardly invented the put-downs that he threw around," Bean writes of the words Thompson used to criticize the athletic performance of young boys on the playing field, words that included "fag," "queer," "girl," and "pussy." Reflecting further on the pervasive use of such words in organized sports, Bean observes, "By the time I reached the majors, I'd heard the terms from almost every coach I'd played for—and many I hadn't." And he notes the importance of recognizing that "as a motivational strategy, it was effective. Coaches invoked the terms again and again. Players responded, almost reflexively raising their intensity level." Finally, Bean highlights the familiar impact that adult role models have on young, impressionable players in this context:

> It wasn't long before kids were berating one another with similar epithets, especially when we did anything out of the jock norm. Copying the coaches, we would go on the attack. "Damn, Bobby, hold onto the fucking ball," we were saying to each other before long. "You're such a sissy."
> Nearly twenty years later, those words still haunted me.[10]

For those LGBT athletes who go on to higher education, it is not too long before they discover that in many places, a less-than-welcoming atmosphere on the part of athletic programs is, even today, firmly ingrained. This is the case, ironically, even on campuses that are more LGBT friendly than any environment the students might have previously encountered.

The *Chronicle of Higher Education* has reported that "at most colleges, the athletic department is the most homophobic place on the campus. The culture of sports tends to be conservative, and most people within it equate male heterosexuality with strength—and homosexuality with weakness." The report adds that "many athletes and coaches alike don't know how to deal with gay teammates." *Chronicle* staff writer Jennifer Jacobson confirms that "the four most highly visible men's sports . . . remain the most unaccepting" and that the climate in other men's sports, "though still far from friendly, is not as hostile." Jacobson also found that lesbians in athletic programs face "a very different, but no less challenging, set of problems."[11]

Susan K. Cahn, a State University of New York professor who has examined gender and sexuality issues in sports, sheds light on some of the differences between men's and women's athletics in this context. On one hand, in male sports, she explains, there is the presumption that all of the athletes are "heterosexually virile and desirable." Thus "for gay men to confront and challenge that [presumption] really cuts into the foundation of the place of men's sports in our culture." Female athletes, on the other hand, often face a very different presumption: that they are all gay or bisexual. Cahn found that, given the association in the eyes of many between athleticism and masculinity, "the perception that lesbianism is tied to masculinity" fuels the stereotype that powerful female athletes are inevitably lesbian. Moreover, straight women in these settings often "go to some lengths to avoid the stereotype," which can establish a major barrier between them and their LGBT teammates.[12]

In some ways, the picture in women's sports is one of conflicting signals and multiple contradictions. There appear to be more out athletes in women's programs than in the respective men's programs, but much depends on the particular sport. Straight women, for example, may be more likely to go into a sport known "for its images of attractive, heterosexual women, like soccer, because it has that kind of 'social approval,' as opposed to softball, which does not." Many who work with LGBTs on college campuses have found that it is easier for women to come out than for men, but coaches in the same settings continue to engage in negative recruiting, whereby they attempt to lure top female athletes away from other schools by trying to portray those schools' teams as dominated by lesbians.

In this regard, a major turning point was reached in late 2005 when

Sheryl Swoopes, the top player in the Women's National Basketball Association, came out publicly on ESPN.[13] Yet in the aftermath of her coming out, many reported that "lesbians in sports" were "still an issue." For example, during the same week that Swoopes made her announcement that she was a lesbian, top female boxer Laila Ali felt the need to make a public announcement that she was *not* a lesbian. "I am not dating, nor will I ever be dating a woman, because I'm not gay," Ali stated for the record. A former player on the Penn State basketball team asserted during the same time period that she had been removed from the team because the coach mistakenly thought she was a lesbian.[14] Swoopes's coming out may have been a turning point, but the stigma remains for many LGBT people in many sports settings.

Given the persistence of this stigma, it is unfortunately not surprising to read about Stanford men's football player Dwight Slater, who was reportedly forced off the team after coming out. It is not surprising to read about the anonymous soccer player at a New England school who—according to a counselor who also requested anonymity—lived with three female friends and kissed them when his male friends were around but declined the opportunity to have sex with them, insisting that he was Roman Catholic and saving himself for marriage. What he did not tell them is that he was gay. The counselor explained that such circumstances are generally the rule rather than the exception: "[College athletes] who identify . . . as bisexual or gay are so deeply closeted that they will only talk about it with a very intimate group of people. They spend most of their time attempting to hide it from their team and others. Even talking about it anonymously . . . in their own closed room would provoke anxiety."[15]

An apparent exception to the rule was Andrew Goldstein, an All-American goalie at Dartmouth University who came out to his teammates during his sophomore year. As reported by ESPN in 2005, "the burden of being a closeted homosexual," for Goldstein, "was suffocating. There were times when his searing secret left him with thoughts of suicide." Yet when he finally did begin coming out, and especially when he fell in love and wanted to tell his lacrosse teammates about it, everything became better. Not only did his teammates and his coaching staff prove to be both accepting and supportive but also, as an out player in a "tough-guy sport" that is often equated with hockey and football, he emerged as one of the finest players in the country.[16]

Goldstein's success as an openly gay college athlete was a major story, in particular because it was such a contrast to the more typical tale of the highly closeted sports star. It is potentially a signpost of movement across our society, pointing perhaps toward a better day, but it remains an exception to the familiar pattern.[17]

At the professional level, a handful of openly LGBT role models who still actively compete do exist, but—with the notable exception of WNBA superstars Sheryl Swoopes in 2005 and Sue Bird in 2017[18]—they tend to be found almost entirely in individual sports rather than team sports. Among the most prominent of these out athletes are tennis great Martina Navratilova and figure-skating champion Rudy Galindo. More typically, athletes—in both individual and team sports—come out only after they have retired from professional competition. Among the biggest names from individual sports in this context are Billie Jean King (tennis), Greg Louganis (swimming and diving), and Caitlyn Jenner (gold-medal-winning decathlete when still known as Bruce Jenner).[19] Their stories are highly complex, reflecting both the tenor of the times and the norms that have persisted. King, for example, acknowledged the existence of a lesbian relationship in 1981, retired in 1983, and formally came out only after all that. By 2006, she was leading an openly LGBT life with her partner and had become a prominent spokesperson for gay rights causes.[20] Louganis, one of the great Olympic divers of all time, achieved great fame in the 1980s. He came out publicly in 1994, and the following year he revealed that he had been HIV positive for some time. A television movie highlighting the many dramatic components of Louganis's life aired nationally in 1997.[21] Jenner came out as transgender in 2015, and her life remains one of the highest-profile stories inside or outside the sports world. In 2017, she published a memoir that was written during her first years as an openly transgender person.[22]

In team sports, the highest-profile comings out thus far have been those of former NFL player Dave Kopay (1977), Billy Bean (1999), NFL star Esera Tuaolo (2002), and John Amaechi (2007). All have since written books about their experiences and have continued to speak freely and openly about their lives.[23] In so doing, they have shed great light on the institutional norms facing K–12 educators, given the extent to which the culture of interscholastic athletics continues to mirror that of higher-level programs. And these authors confirm that, in idolizing standout athletes, many young gays and lesbians adopt role models who often act as if LGBTs do not exist and would not be welcome.

The Dynamic of Closeted Gay Men in Major Professional Sports

Hall of Fame legend Sandy Koufax was one of the most spectacular play-ers in the history of Major League Baseball. Before retiring in 1966 at the age of thirty, he set numerous pitching records, spearheaded the rise of the Los Angeles Dodgers to the top of the baseball world, and attained a level of greatness very few professional athletes before him or after him had ever achieved.

After his retirement, Koufax remained with the Dodger organization in various capacities for more than thirty years, serving most prominently as a spring training coach and role model for the younger players. Yet he left baseball in a sudden and highly public way, in 2003, severing ties with the Dodgers because of a gossip-column item that ran in the *New York Post,* a newspaper owned by the team's parent company at the time.[24]

The *Post* piece stated that a "Hall of Fame baseball hero" had "coop-erated with a best-selling biography only because the author promised to keep it secret that he is gay. The author kept her word, but big mouths at the publishing house can't keep from flapping." Koufax was not men-tioned by name, but it was apparently clear within the publishing world that it was referring to him. Jane Leavy's biography, *Sandy Koufax: A Lefty's Legacy,* had been published a few months earlier.

A handsome man who always dressed well and carried himself with understated style and great poise, Koufax had led a highly private life outside of sports, thus fueling speculation from time to time that he might have been gay. But whether he was gay or straight or somewhere in between, the sad message of this story is that he appeared to view such an allegation as so demeaning and so personally damaging that, because of a highly attenuated corporate connection between the newspaper column and the team, he left an organization he had been with for almost fifty years of his life.[25]

Koufax's decision to make a highly public statement of extreme anger in this matter is further evidence that even an allegation that one *might* be gay is still viewed by many in the highest ranks of professional sports as denigrating, defamatory, and perhaps the worst possible name one could be called. One hopes that things are different today, in the aftermath of the 2003 *Lawrence v. Texas* decision and the 2015 *Obergefell v. Hodges* de-cision, and some fifteen years after Koufax's angry departure.[26] But given that, at the present time, there are still absolutely no active out athletes in the major men's professional sports, it appears that these institutional norms still persist.

In their respective ways, former Dodger Billy Bean and former Atlanta Falcon Super Bowl star Esera Tuaolo have probably shed more light on these issues than anyone else. Bean and Tuaolo both came out to themselves while still active players and then wrestled with decisions regarding whether and to what extent to come out to others. In revealing so much about their own experiences as gay men in athletic programs, documenting in their respective books the turmoil and the anguish that were at times all consuming, they have done much to help others understand the barriers to change at every level of organized sports, from the professional ranks down to K–12 settings.

Bean reveals how, while married to a woman, he began to come to terms with his gay identity. He tells of how the marriage disintegrated in steps, particularly as he met and fell in love with his first boyfriend. In one of the most difficult episodes to read, Bean describes his anguish at the death of the boyfriend from AIDS, which was greatly exacerbated when he found that, because he was closeted from the team and the public, he could not even take a personal day off but had to report to the baseball park, suit up, and play on that very day.

Focusing primarily on the Dodgers, Bean highlights the dimensions of the homophobic and heterosexist team environment that kept him from even thinking that he could come out and still be part of the organization. While he was coming out to himself—at times exhilarated (such as when he secretly went to the Castro District when the team was in San Francisco) and at times "wracked with shame" (for doing nothing more than going to a bookstore and seeking out the gay section)—he was playing for manager Tom Lasorda. A loud, gregarious, and highly successful team leader who could be both inspiring and overbearing, Lasorda was apparently adept at making comments that cut to the very heart of what Bean was wrestling with. From calling Bean "the boy of every girl's dream" to jokes about "cocksuckers," Lasorda's regular stream of remarks led Bean to feel increasingly more outside and apart. He writes that "his private reaction couldn't have been . . . more different" from the outward reactions of his teammates and that the jokes were "a stake through the heart" of his "denial."

Although Lasorda's locker room style was very much in the mainstream, reflecting the norm rather than the exception, and certainly no apparent malice toward anyone in particular, his public statements after his own son's death left no doubt in Bean's mind as to where he stood on LGBT issues. Lasorda's son Spunky was an apparently openly gay person who had become gravely ill with HIV/AIDS, and the young man had passed away while Bean was still with the Dodger organization. Yet, when asked about it afterward, Lasorda not only refused to confirm the cause of death but expressly denied that his son had been gay. "Having spent most of his adult life in the world of gladiators," Bean writes, "Tommy must have found it difficult to deal with the truth about his son. It must have been equally hard for Spunky, having spent his youth in this same world, to accept himself."

Reflecting back on his experiences in organized sports from his earliest K–12 days "on the playing fields of Southern California," it is clear to Bean that both his coaches and his teammates "equated homosexuality with weakness and failure. From [the] Pop Warner football coach's warning not to 'run like a faggot' to Tommy Lasorda's 'cocksucker' jokes, the drumbeat of homophobia was as relentless as the roar of a capacity crowd urging on the home team." "It never occurred to me [at the time]," Bean declares, "that there might be something wrong with these crude and dehumanizing comments." In retrospect, he says, "I spent far too much time wondering whether I measured up to the guys around me, whether I could match their toughness, ferocious competitiveness, and even their masculinity." It was only after coming out and finding such great acceptance among both gay and straight communities that he realized the fallacious nature of the entire mind-set. He also, finally, realized that he was not alone.[27]

Esera Tuaolo's anguish was as deep-seated and as difficult to overcome as Billy Bean's. And his documented experiences as a closeted gay man in the National Football League provides important background perspective on the efforts of Michael Sam to become the first openly gay player in professional football. Sam, a consensus All-American for the highly successful Missouri Tigers football team in 2013, came out as gay in 2014, three weeks before the NFL draft. While some cautioned that he was small by NFL standards and might not be rated highly by the scouts, he was also very fast, very savvy, and very popular with his teammates. There was no reason to believe that he would not be drafted and would not at least be given an opportunity to play.

However, he was not drafted until the last round, and when—on live national TV—he hugged and kissed his boyfriend, as so many of those who were picked hugged and kissed their respective lovers, spouses, and so on—commentators cast negative aspersions on Sam's judgment and wondered if he would have "the character" to succeed in the NFL. Indeed, he did not succeed. He never made the final cut with the St. Louis Rams or the Dallas Cowboys, played for a time in the Canadian Football League, and eventually left the game. Many wondered whether things would have been different had he not been so openly gay at the time that he was drafted, given the reputation of the NFL as described in Esera Tuaolo's book and subsequent interviews.[28]

Tuaolo, born in Hawai'i of Samoan descent, emerged from a low socioeconomic background to become a highly successful football player in both college and the pros. As he explained when he came out via ESPN, in late 2002, he was a 280-pound nose tackle who could run forty yards in 4.8 seconds. He was voted the best defensive lineman in the Pac-10 in 1989, at Oregon State, and he made the NFL All-Rookie team two years later, with Green Bay. He played in the Super Bowl, sang the national anthem at the Pro Bowl, and earned the respect of the top players in the league. Yet while achieving great success on the playing field, he was experiencing such a disconnect between the homophobic environment of professional football and his own struggle to come to terms with his gay identity that he came close to committing suicide on more than one occasion.

In his coming-out piece for ESPN, for example, he described an anxiety attack after one of his best games, in which he imagined that someone who knew he was gay and had seen televised highlights of his exploits might "call the coach, the owner, or the papers" and out him. "By Monday night," he recalled of this and similar episodes, "the panic would change to numb depression. That's when I'd start to drink . . . into the next day . . . hoping to get so drunk that after I finished crying alone . . . I'd pass out and never wake up . . . or maybe I'd go out and get loaded . . . and drive home drunk and wonder if I should just turn the wheel and end it all that way": "The one thing I could never do was talk about it. Never. No one in the NFL wanted to hear it, and if anyone did hear it, that would be the end for me. I'd wind up cut or injured. I was sure that if a GM didn't get rid of me for the sake of team chemistry, another player would intentionally hurt me, to keep up the image. Because the NFL is a supermacho culture. It's a place for gladiators. And gladiators aren't supposed to be gay."[29]

Tuaolo, a person of faith who has apparently become even more devoted to Christianity since he came out, highlighted in his book *Alone in the Trenches* that religion can play a central but not always positive role in shaping an environment for those involved in organized sports. He describes how the Jacksonville Jaguars in the 1990s were perhaps the "most Christian" team in professional football, with about half of the players involved in an organization called Champions for Christ and exerting ongoing peer pressure on the others to join in. In an ironic parallel, although Billy Bean does not address this aspect in his book, the Dodgers during the Lasorda era were known as one of the most Christian teams in Major League Baseball.

Tuaolo tells how he agreed to attend a Bible study group, particularly because it was led by former college athlete Darryl Flowers, whom Tuaolo had known at Oregon State. In an unexpected turn of events, Flowers began quoting from Leviticus and saying that homosexuality was an abomination. Going even further, Flowers declared that "if Hitler in his last breath asked God for forgiveness, he would be forgiven," but that homosexuality could not be forgiven. When attendees broke into small discussion groups, Tuaolo found himself in the same group as Flowers. He decided to reveal that he had a gay brother who had died of AIDS. "You're telling me that . . . Hitler would be forgiven . . . but my brother [who helped so many people] would not be?" Tuaolo asked. "Yes," Flowers responded. "Murder is different from an abomination. Murder is a sin that can be forgiven. Homosexuality can't be forgiven." The discussion became very heated, with Flowers holding his ground and Tuaolo saying that he could not accept that and walking out.[30]

The exchange apparently so upset Tuaolo's equilibrium that not only did he contemplate suicide again but he almost broke up with the man who had by this point become his partner. He was angry with himself for not disclosing his sexual identity, angry with Flowers, and outraged at the whole dynamic. At the same time, he was trying to hold on to his own deeply felt beliefs about God and religion. "Back in my drab room," he wrote, "I started to drink tequila. The more I thought about what had happened and the more I drank, the more upset I became": "I had spoken up about [my brother], but I hadn't had the guts to tell the other guys about me. Once again, I was a coward. Why must I always deny who I was? How long would I have to feel ashamed of myself? All of my confusion and conflict came out in rage. I drove my fist through the wall. I wanted to kill myself. I felt the despair and defeat that I had known so many times. . . . Once again, I was alone and confused and wanted to die. If I had had a gun that night, I would have used it."[31]

That a man of such great physical and emotional strength was driven to such despair because of the anti-gay environment he continued to experience in organized sports says much about the culture and the challenges that remain. And that he was able to overcome the experiences and ultimately live an open and healthy life as an out gay person and a person of faith says much about the power of the coming-out experience.

Barriers to Change: Parallels between Organized Sports and the Military

In addition to the perspectives that can be gleaned from the documented experiences and coming-out stories of LGBT athletes, it is possible to gain additional insights into both the underlying reasons for the cultural norms and the possibilities for changing these norms by examining the close institutional connections between American sports communities and the U.S. military. A key similarity, of course, is that both institutions have placed severe limits on the ability of LGBTs to be out. In sports, the restrictions are implicit and cultural: gays and lesbians have a legal right to be out, but they are subject to extreme pressures to remain closeted. In the military, gays and lesbians had no legal right to be out and were subject to immediate and dishonorable discharge until the policy known as "Don't Ask, Don't Tell" was repealed.[32] A similar ban was in existence for transgender persons, although in their case they were simply disqualified from serving.[33] That ban was lifted in 2016, but President Trump has announced that it would be reinstated.[34]

Other parallels between the sports and the U.S. military are readily apparent. An educative function, for example, is at the very heart of the respective missions of both institutions. In organized sports, the teaching and training of athletes by coaches is the predominant ongoing activity, while in the military, the education of soldiers takes place at every stage of the process. In addition, the education that occurs in both can be characterized as mostly *public* in nature; a large percentage of it takes place in the publicly funded military and the athletic programs of public schools, colleges, and universities. Moreover, both can be characterized as public in a different way. Athletic competition, for example—even if privately funded—is often very public in that many of the events take place in public arenas, are broadcast live to millions of people, and can directly impact the economic well-being of the public sector.

Given the educative and highly public nature of the respective institutions, one would expect both the military and organized sports to have an influence on the lives of our young people. But the word *influence* is a significant understatement. Not only is the percentage of American youth participating in organized sports larger than ever, but the military remains, by far, the single largest employer of young adults in the country.

By examining the parallels and intersection points between organized sports and the military, it may be possible to begin shedding light on the reasons why such an ostensibly anti-LGBT dynamic persists. First, it should be noted that many people participate in both institutions at different points in their lives. A substantial percentage of those who choose to enlist, for example, have also represented their high schools and perhaps even their colleges in organized sports. Also, of course, many coaches may be veterans of military service. Thus cultural norms in one institution necessarily influence the course of events in the other, and formal limitations that may have been implemented in one setting can have an unavoidable impact on the other.

It must also be recognized that both the military and organized sports are built on intense competition. In the military, the competition can be a fight to the death for national or international dominance. In sports, the competitive events can have a real and palpable impact on the careers and life chances of those involved. And even for those who do not participate actively, the large financial gains that may be at stake for individuals, corporations, and communities can make the results of sporting events at least as important as, if not more important than, just about anything else.

In addition, both institutions continue to be dominated by men. Research has shown that this dominance has fueled the ongoing perception not only that a certain kind of strength is required to succeed in these highly competitive endeavors but also that women, gays, and gender-nonconforming persons dissipate this strength or personify a lack of strength. Such a perception excludes or marginalizes anyone who does not appear to fit the proverbial mold and also helps perpetuate the aforementioned myths and misconceptions about LGBTs.[35]

All of these realities combine to generate ongoing fear of LGBTs—within the military and organized sports and throughout U.S. society as a whole. Many participants in these institutions have come to view gays and lesbians as people who are not to be trusted, people who will weaken the effort, and people who will prey on others if given the chance. This fear, to some, justifies extreme violence against LGBTs by validating the use of the "gay panic" and "trans panic" defenses. In the same manner, this fear justifies the conclusion that gays and transgender people are security risks in the military and weak, untrustworthy teammates in organized sports. The predator myth, in particular, is still invoked by those who argue that it would be disastrous to allow openly LGBT persons to dress and shower in the same communal environment as their straight counterparts.[36]

The Weakness and "Security Risk" Myths

As a result of the paranoia that gripped the country in the early days of the Cold War, gays in the 1940s and 1950s were ranked right along with Communists as the number one threat to national security. But although Senator McCarthy and President Eisenhower played key roles in fostering such an atmosphere of fear and persecution, the demonization of gays and lesbians had its roots in policies adopted by the military during World War II.[37]

As documented by Allan Bérubé in his 1990 book *Coming Out under Fire,* and Arthur Dong in follow-up interviews conducted for the 1994 film of the same name, gays and lesbians became targets of newly created "antihomosexual" policies. Concerned that World War II would bring a repeat of the many psychological problems that had developed among American soldiers during World War I, the military adopted policies designed to ferret out the "mentally ill" before they could become a problem in the armed forces. Gays were still seen as mentally ill by the leading associations of psychologists and psychiatrists during that era, and the military establishment embraced this view with a passion. Indeed, a documentary film shown to soldiers during the 1940s included "homosexuals" on a list of undesirables that also featured "grotesque pathological liars," vagrants, kleptomaniacs, and pyromaniacs.[38]

The new World War II–era policies classified gays as unfit to serve and mandated that all recruits be interrogated in the most personal manner regarding their sexual orientation. Those who were out to themselves at the time had to lie, which many did, or, if they told the truth, they were officially labeled sex perverts. Once they were in the military, soldiers discovered to be gay could be subject to involuntary psychiatric treatments, incarceration in "queer stockades," and a dishonorable discharge that included the loss of all veteran's benefits and the official branding of "sex pervert" for life.

In 1950, a special congressional subcommittee recommended that these military policies be used as a model for banning all gays from government service. Pursuant to this recommendation, in 1953, President Eisenhower issued his infamous executive order banning "homosexuals" from all federal jobs.[39] And the institutional memory that includes the perception of gays as a "security risk" still persists.

In a like manner, particularly in light of the evidence presented by Billy Bean, Esera Tuaolo, and so many others, the weakness myth in organized sports is still widely prevalent. Gayness and gender nonconformity are consistently equated with weakness, and LGBTs are seen both as personifying a lack of strength and as dissipating strength. Exposing this inaccuracy is thus a central step that must be taken before things can get better. LGBTs, in fact, are often among the *strongest* people in our society as a result of all the challenges they have had to overcome. And this is true not just in reference to emotional strength. Athleticism and physical prowess are highly valued within gay and lesbian communities, and—while no data appear available to document this—many observers have found that a large percentage of openly LGBT persons are more athletic and in better physical condition than their straight counterparts. This may seem surprising to those who have little or no contact with gay and transgender persons, but it is viewed as patently obvious by many gays and lesbians themselves, as well as by straights who live in gay neighborhoods or interact extensively with gays.

The late Mark Bingham, a national hero on 9/11, is a paragon in this regard. Bingham was a physically powerful and highly athletic openly gay man who achieved great success as a rugby player, as a public relations executive, and as a leader and role model within the San Francisco LGBT community. In 1991 and 1993, he helped his UC Berkeley rugby team win the national championship, and he continued his involvement in the sport with the San Francisco Fog. In fact, he was looked up to by his neighbors and friends for a whole host of reasons, including his wrestling a gun from the hands of a mugger on a San Francisco street one evening.[40]

Bingham became a national hero when he played a key role in taking on the terrorist hijackers and almost preventing United Airlines Flight 93 from going down in a Shanksville, Pennsylvania, field. In addition, Bingham and other passengers and crew succeeded in stopping what could have been an even greater tragedy and an even greater loss of life. He has been honored posthumously in many ways since that tragic day.[41]

The Perennial Shower Question

In addition to the weakness/security risk myth, those who have sought to limit an LGBT presence in the military invariably have attempted to justify their position by bringing up the question of what would happen in the showers. To hear those who raise the specter of potential anarchy in the locker room, one would think that gay men have never showered at the same time and in the same place as straight men, and that lesbians have never showered at the same time and in the same place as straight women. In fact, gays and straights have showered "together" from time immemorial, and not just in the military and in other educational institutions. Public swimming pools, YWCAs, public beaches, public and private gyms, fitness centers, and similar entities and environments have facilities where people of the same or similar gender use showers at the same time. It is always the case that some of the people who use these showers are straight, some are gay, and some are bi. The dynamic is perennial in our society, and we learn to address it over time. Remarkably few disagreements or violent incidents occur in these showers as a result of anyone being out as straight or out as gay.

Many of the strongest allies of the United States, including Israel and the United Kingdom, now allow gays and lesbians to serve openly, and there is no evidence of any problems in regard to the showers.[42] The changes in the United Kingdom are particularly instructive. The country lifted its ban on gays in the military after the European Court of Human Rights ruled unanimously in favor of four LGBT soldiers who had been discharged in the mid-1990s. In ruling against the British government, the court found that the U.K. ban violated the fundamental human right to privacy, as set out in the European Convention on Human Rights.

Soon afterward, in 2000, the United Kingdom joined Canada, France, Germany, and most other NATO countries that already allowed gays and lesbians to serve openly.[43] It also implemented a new code of conduct applicable to all soldiers, gay and straight. The *New York Times* reported a year later that the transition had gone remarkably smoothly. It also discussed the code of conduct in more detail. If the U.S. policy is "Don't Ask, Don't Tell," said Christopher Dandeker, who headed the war studies department at Kings College London, Britain's can be described as "don't fear it, don't flaunt it. The crucial thing for gay personnel is that they have to be service personnel first and gay second. The team comes first. They are not to let their own sexual identity undermine the service identity."[44]

In 2005, the *New York Times* reported that "five years after Britain lifted its ban on gays in the military, the Royal Navy has begun actively encouraging them to enlist and has pledged to make life easier for them when they do."[45] During the same year, the *Economist* called the U.S. ban "a piece of discrimination of no practical benefit" and urged Americans to follow the lead of its powerful ally.

Yet to hear some people talk about these matters, the most horrific scenarios can be conjured up. In the area of organized sports, for example, when it comes to the showers, gays are often presented not as weak at all but as powerful, hypersexualized predators who cannot be trusted and must be feared. In the aftermath of John Amaechi's coming out, subsequent statements by Philadelphia 76ers Shavlik Randolph and Steven Hunter reflected the same perceptions as Tim Hardaway's and Amar'e Stoudemire's and helped perpetuate the same nefarious myths. Randolph, a former standout at Duke University, immediately invoked the specter of the gay man as a threat: "As long as you don't bring your gayness on me I'm fine," Randolph said. "As far as business-wise, I'm sure I could play with him. But I think it would create a little awkwardness in the locker room." Hunter, even as he tried to appear supportive, invoked both the predator myth and the perception that gays are "not men" and not good people: "As long as he [doesn't] make any advances toward me I'm fine with it," Hunter said. "As long as he came to play basketball like a man and conducted himself like a good person, I'd be fine with it."[46]

These perceptions have no more basis in reality than does the weakness myth. Billy Bean has made particularly pointed observations in this context. Describing in his book the comments made by a number of Major League Baseball players after he came out—comments that referenced the showers and mirrored those of Randolph and Hunter—Bean says he believed the words would have been much less pointed had the two actually known a gay teammate. It "infuriated" him, Bean continues, "to think that players would actually believe that a gay teammate would be any less serious about his job." He also notes just how much hard work it takes to get to the major leagues and wonders if they "really believe a player would sacrifice his career for a cheap thrill." Bean then takes on the shower myth directly: "Being gay doesn't mean you lack self-control. On the contrary, gays and lesbians have had to suppress their natural desires far more often than heterosexuals. Restraint comes with the territory."[47]

Charting a Road Map for Transformative Change

The research-based principles identified in chapters 6 and 7 are directly applicable to school sports, physical education classes, and related activities on K–12 campuses. A broad general focus on school climate plus additional support for LGBT students through programs such as gay–straight alliances, safe zones, and wellness centers will undoubtedly have an impact on sports programs and those who participate in them. Incremental professional development and additional modifications to curriculum and pedagogy at the individual classroom level that are implemented by willing faculty can contribute even more to further understanding and the identification of common values, which can then have a salutary effect on the working relationships between and among sports team members of different sexual orientations and gender identities.

Enlisting the Help of the Campus Sports Community

Without the active involvement of persons from within the campus sports community, change may be very slow in coming. Coaches, athletic directors, team captains, and fans and supporters in the larger community can together form a very insular group, and even in a school that is developing an inclusive and gay-friendly environment overall, many of those involved in sports may decline to participate in such initiatives. Thus, if at all possible, it is highly recommended that school leaders coordinating LGBT-related initiatives gain the active assistance of key personnel involved in campus athletic programs. Ideally, this would include coaches and team leaders as well as school-site administrators who are former coaches or former athletes. Such persons would have the standing to help create additional change by working together with everyone else for the common good. And, in a best-case scenario, some of the same people would be out LGBTs themselves. The potential impact of an out coach, athlete, administrator, or former athlete as a role model in this area cannot be overstated.

Openly LGBT persons from within the campus sports community, working together with other committed faculty and staff, could exemplify the ideal of a positive, welcoming, and collaborative school climate. Such persons might help facilitate the participation of current athletes in existing gay–straight alliances or even the formation of a gay–straight alliance specifically for athletes. They could take the lead in helping to plan changes in curriculum and pedagogy, which might entail a discussion of out sports figures in classroom lessons that focus on such topics as sports history or sports-related current events. Finally, with regard to pedagogy, coaches and PE instructors who are knowledgeable regarding the obligation to respect the right to be out and who commit to treating all students with equal dignity can have a substantial impact by voluntarily making it clear, in a truly genuine manner, that anti-gay slurs and other forms of gay bashing are completely unacceptable on the field, in the gym, in the locker room, and in any other athletic setting under their supervision.[48]

Initiatives of this nature can go a long way toward changing the mindsets of young people as they go forward. But the prospective long-term impact of these initiatives may be significantly limited by the persistently homophobic culture that exists in so many sports-related environments outside of education settings. Indeed, more so than for any other issue addressed in this book, school officials cannot go at it alone here. Educators seeking to effect positive change in school sports have benefited greatly from the LGBT-related work of many within the larger community, and in a like manner, they need the help of people at the institutional level within organized sports nationwide. In addition, they can benefit greatly from the assistance of persons in related institutions, such as the military, who can do much to help transform damaging cultural norms.

Challenges That Remain

Beyond players and coaches, sports fans and the media add an additional wrinkle to the dynamic explored here, an effect with no parallels to any other area covered in these pages. In many cases, the fans may be worse than the teammates, the coaches, or the management. Several reporters covering Amaechi's coming-out story speculated on the extent of the "nightmare" that might ensue if an active NBA player decided to come out. "Homophobic fans," Greg Hernandez wrote, "especially those for opposing teams, would most certainly rear their ugly heads at games." *Salt Lake Tribune* NBA writer Phil Miller stated that it would definitely be "an issue with fans; a lot of bigots are out there. It would be a challenge to the player to live with the taunts. People can be pretty ugly."[49]

Moreover, although religion certainly has a presence in much of public education generally, it can in certain instances have an even greater presence in organized sports. As Esera Tuaolo referenced, many teams have traditions of organized prayer and even Bible study in the locker room. Certain coaches and even the management of certain teams may be highly religious, and they may be determined to make their religion a central part of the team experience.[50] And the brand of religion that one often sees in a sports locker room does not typically reflect that of the many branches and denominations that are welcoming to LGBTs. This can contribute further to a harsh and confrontational atmosphere, as Tuaolo makes abundantly clear in his description of the Jacksonville Jaguars Bible discussion group.

Finally, those participating in men's team sports face circumstances that are even more complicated than those in the military because of what has been called the "homo-camaraderie" that is often the rule rather than the exception. The term refers to the sexual undertones in physical aspects of men's sports experience that have been documented and analyzed at great length, including hugging, patting on backsides, tackling, and very close physical contact in particular competitions, such as wrestling.[51]

"The pro locker room," John Amaechi writes in *The Man in the Middle*, "was the most flamboyant place I'd ever been this side of a swanky club full of martini-drinking gay men." Describing the dynamic in detail, he tells how his teammates "flaunted their perfect bodies," "checked out" each other's private parts, and "primped in front of the mirror." He writes about one teammate who "painted his toenails with seasonal colors" and describes how others "stood shoulder-to-shoulder, naked," looking over a glossy lifestyle magazine for the affluent.[52] He reflects on the entire picture: "Watching this thoroughly decent group of guys helped me understand why the presence of openly gay men . . . was so threatening. Coming out threatens to expose the homoerotic components of what they prefer to think of as simply male-bonding. . . . There's a tremendous fear that the behavior might be labeled as [homosexual]. Or, as I heard the anti-gay epithets pour forth, that gay men in the locker room would somehow violate this sacred space by sexualizing it."[53]

The combination in a sports environment of a more anarchic locker room dynamic, greater acceptance of homophobic and heterosexist comments in the privacy of a team setting, a frequent religious presence that is often rigid and even fundamentalist in nature, and the homo-camaraderie that guards against anything and anyone that might truly be gay is an explosive one and can exacerbate the negative impact on LGBTs at the K–12 level to a deeper extent than any of the other environments discussed in this book. Add in the ongoing deference, at the institutional level, to false perceptions and nefarious myths, and the result is an environment that continues to be incredibly resistant to change.

Reasons for Optimism

Changing the institutional norms of school sports is perhaps the single most difficult problem identified in this book. Not that the picture is entirely pessimistic, by any stretch of the imagination. Circumstances inevitably vary from sport to sport, from gender to gender, and from team sports to individual competition. In addition, the increasingly visible interest and involvement of LGBTs in sports, as spectators and as participants, cannot be ignored. As more gays and lesbians and transgender persons come out, it will become even more obvious to everyone just how much athleticism and physical conditioning are valued in LGBT communities. Such a revelation will inevitably serve to further break down barriers in this area. And, from a legal and public policy perspective, the right to be out in sports at every level has never been more firmly in place and is bound to have a positive effect.

One of the many ironies in this context is that if Sandy Koufax were in fact gay, and if instead of exiting the Los Angeles Dodgers in outrage, he had decided to come out, he would have found—as many who come out a bit later in life learn—that the institutional mind-set that keeps them in denial and locks them deep in the closet does not reflect the reality of the larger world around them. Many LGBT persons who come out as established adults find—often much to their surprise, given how they are typically led to believe otherwise—that their coming out elicits tremendous support, admiration, and community backing from both gay and straight populations. In particular, John Amaechi, Billy Bean, Billie Jean King, Martina Navratilova, Sheryl Swoopes, and Esera Tuaolo, among others, have achieved great success since they came out. They are prominent national figures who have become role models for many and have brought about tremendous ongoing empathy and acclaim in the national and international media. Bean references this dynamic in his book, particularly when he documents his interaction with Diane Sawyer on ABC. "It was a revelation to me," he wrote, "after so many years of fearing media exposure, that so many journalists were sympathetic to my struggle and eager to share it with the country. What I'd feared would be a shameful revelation had become a source of great pride."

Indeed, there are a good number of other positive indicators that could point the way toward a brighter day in organized sports. The reaction to Amaechi's coming out in 2007, which quickly morphed into a reaction to Hardaway's stunningly hateful comments about gay people, was, in the aggregate, a clear step in the right direction. While many sportswriters and bloggers—and more than just a few current and former players—fell back on the anachronistic claim that they had no choice but to be "OK with Amaechi's coming out" because otherwise they would be viewed as politically incorrect, many others demonstrated a more enlightened and inclusive perspective.[54] In marked contrast to the comments of Hardaway, Randolph, and Hunter, other current and former NBA standouts were much more supportive of Amaechi. Former college and professional player Grant Hill said that "the fact that John has done this, maybe it will give others the comfort or confidence to come out as well, whether they are playing or retired." Veteran player and coach Doc Rivers stated, "It was brought up to me and you look and say: 'So what? Can he rebound? Can he shoot? Can he defend?'" Sixteen-year NBA veteran Charles Barkley said that in his view, "it shouldn't be a big deal to anybody. I know I've played with gay players and against gay players and it just shouldn't surprise anybody or be any issue." And NBA commissioner David Stern himself acted swiftly and unequivocally in not only prohibiting Hardaway from participating in the upcoming All-Star Game but also removing him from a position as a spokesperson for the league.

Moreover, the reaction of both the NBA leadership and the NBA Players Association in 2013 when Jason Collins became the first and only NBA player to come out could not have been more supportive. NBA commissioner David Stern commended Collins with the following statement:

> As [then Deputy Commissioner] Adam Silver and I said to Jason, we have known the Collins family since Jason and Jarron joined the NBA in 2001 and they have been exemplary members of the NBA family. Jason has been a widely respected player and teammate throughout his career and we are proud he has assumed the leadership mantle on this very important issue.

The NBA Players Association released the following statement:

> As Jason wrote, pro basketball is a family, and he has and always will be our brother. The NBPA is dedicated to fighting for the best interests of and uniting all players regardless of race, creed, color, age, national origin, or sexual orientation. Today is another example that we are intent on con-

tinuing that work. We congratulate Jason for having the courage to "raise his hand," as he wrote in his story, and start the conversation.

Moreover, Kobe Bryant, then one of the top scorers in the game and one of the NBA's all-time greatest players, tweeted his support with the following statement: "Proud of @jasoncollins34," the tweet read. "Don't suffocate who u r because of the ignorance of others #courage #support #mambaarmystandup #BYOU."[55]

Reflecting what appears to be continued movement in this area, a growing number of stories documenting the achievements of out athletes have appeared in the news over the past decade, including information about a Rutgers swimmer, a UC Santa Barbara tennis player, a Columbia University triathlete, and a UC Santa Cruz volleyball player.[56] Another story tells of Lea Robinson, an African American woman who identifies openly as lesbian and is a former athlete and coach. Robinson enrolled in a graduate program in education at Suffolk University, and she received a fellowship to fund her work in the school's Office of Diversity Services, working with LGBT students and students of color. One of her major goals is to develop a leadership program helping LGBT students of color make the transition from high school to college. Her stated mission "is to bring young gay athletes of color out of the closet and into what she hopes will be a better, more comfortable place for everyone."[57]

Finally, a report out of Brown University documents the growing leadership role that water polo standout Hank Weintraub chose to take on. As the school's only out male varsity athlete playing in a team sport, he worked with the university's queer alliance to form what is perhaps the first known campus organization for LGBT athletes in the nation. He also signed on as a blogger for the NCAA, covering developments in water polo nationwide, and he included in his blog a discussion of his own sexuality. One of his express goals is to conduct research on issues confronted by gay athletes.[58]

Indeed, it should be noted that the National Collegiate Athletic Association (NCAA)—a member-led organization that includes 1,117 colleges and universities, 100 athletic conferences, and 40 affiliated sports organizations[59]—is in a unique position to build on the efforts of people such as those who have been highlighted in this chapter for their efforts to help change the homophobic and transphobic culture that is still all too prominent in organized sports. As referenced above in chapter 2 of this book, the NCAA has stepped up during the past decade and is committed to setting a more inclusive tone on the LGBT front. In 2013, for example, the NCAA released an 82-page guide "intended to help its constituents—administrators, coaches and students—navigate the broadening world of gay, lesbian and transgender athletes amid its myriad sports":

> The guide, titled "Champions of Respect," was co-authored by Pat Griffin, professor emeritus of social justice education at Massachusetts-Amherst, and Hudson Taylor, founder of Athlete Ally, an organization with a mission of ending homophobia in sports.
>
> It includes everything from terminology to guidelines for creating an inclusive environment, according to Taylor, a former all-American wrestler at Maryland. It provides instructions for a variety of scenarios, including how a coach should react when an athlete comes out.[60]

By 2018, when this edition of The Right to Be Out was published, the NCAA had added LGBT issues and resources to its "Inclusion Initiative," and to that end, it maintains a web page filled with valuable and supportive information regarding this territory.[61]

As discussed throughout this book, the more people who are out and the more others come in contact with LGBTs who are out, the less of a problem LGBT issues tend to become. This is particularly the case in a school sports setting. As straight people interact with openly gay and lesbian athletes on a regular basis, they soon recognize (if they did not know already) that LGBTs are not weak, are not security risks who cannot be trusted, and are not predators who are to be avoided in the showers like the plague. Such a scenario is playing out over and over again, especially at the higher education level, but increasingly at the K–12 level as well. Of course, transformative change will not happen automatically when sports figures come out, and especially within men's team sports, there is still a very long way to go. But if out athletes are able to play prominent leadership roles in the range of multiple strategies identified in these pages, they can be the keys to a very different and much more welcoming reality at some point in the not-too-distant future.

9

CONFRONTING THE CHALLENGES FACED BY TRANSGENDER YOUTH

For members of the education community who seek to address transgender issues, perhaps the key point to recognize at the outset is that this is an area filled with misconceptions. Contrary to popular perception, for example, while many transgender persons choose to have at least some type of gender affirmation surgery, many others do not.[1] The most common transgender health care is hormone therapy, and a good number not only take estrogen or testosterone on a regular basis but plan to continue doing so indefinitely; others use these hormones occasionally or not at all. For some, it is extremely important to be out and open as trans, while for others, it is important to be seen only as members of their identified gender. There are easily as many different ways to be transgender as there are ways to be gay, and the nature of one's identity can change over time.

Transgender persons typically confront issues relating to both their sexual orientation and their gender identity. With regard to the former, transgender persons may identify as gay or lesbian, but sometimes, or in addition, they may identify as heterosexual, bisexual, or queer. With regard to the latter, they may see their gender identity as conforming to the traditional binary model of male or female, or they may identify as perhaps more male than female or more female than male, but not exclusively one or the other.[2]

In this regard, it is important to note that not every gay person and not every trans person is comfortable being grouped under the abbreviation "LGBT." In a noteworthy essay, Shannon Minter identifies the arguments for and against this typical grouping, ultimately concluding that there is a natural and discernible interrelationship between the two identities. Minter contends that "homophobia and transphobia are tightly intertwined" and that anti-gay bias "so often takes the form of violence and discrimination against those who are seen as transgressing gender norms." He also highlights the little-known fact that many of the people historians now tend to view as gay may in fact have been transgender as that word is currently defined.[3]

Not surprisingly, then, the right to be out for transgender persons can prove to be quite different—both in its conception and in its application—from the right to be out on the basis of sexual orientation. Many gender-expansive people, for example, may want to be out only as male or female. This is who they are, and this is how they want to be seen. Transgender, for at least some of these folks, is not necessarily the equivalent of an identity at all but may be the description of a process that they went through and have now completed. For others, transgender may be seen as primarily or perhaps even entirely as the equivalent of a medical condition.[4] Still others, of course, view transgender as central to their very persona, and it is highly important for these persons to be able to identify openly.[5]

Under the basic First and Fourteenth Amendment principles described in Part I of this book, all persons have the right to decide what fundamental aspects of their identity and personhood they do or do not wish to disclose. Yet the right to be out as transgender has not yet gained a similar level of recognition as the right to be out for members of other recognized groups. Still, things are changing in this area as well. Particularly in the public sector and especially in education settings, the venerable right to equal educational opportunity has been bolstered implicitly and explicitly to include increased protection for trans persons. The protection encompasses a right to be open about one's gender identity and to be treated equally as a result of this openness.[6]

The right to be out also includes a concurrent right not to be out. This aspect of the right is rooted not only in the First Amendment right not to speak but also in privacy rights granted to everyone under the Fourth Amendment, the Fourteenth Amendment, common-law tort doctrine, and other relevant federal and state statutes and constitutional provisions. Privacy concerns are among the most significant challenges faced by transgender persons, because many people still do not believe that someone who is identifying as a different gender from the one assigned at birth should be entitled to keep that to himself or herself. Those who adopt such a position see this not as a privacy issue but as a deception issue; they view transgender persons as engaged in a deceit that can have negative consequences for all concerned.

The tragic case of transgender teenager Gwen Araujo exemplifies the prevalence of the "deceit" mind-set. Upon learning at a party that Gwen was biologically male, three men who had previously engaged in sexual activity with her attacked her brutally and beat her to death. At their initial trial, the men claimed to have "panicked" at the idea that they might be gay after realizing they had had sex with a biologically male person. The defense team's reliance on this argument outraged many across the country and around the world and was the subject of extensive scrutiny both during and after the murder trials.[7]

In recent years, there has been growing criticism of the deception argument, and a significant body of scholarly literature and personal narrative is now available to document the fallacies inherent in such a way of thinking.[8] Indeed, both legally and as a matter of policy, there is no justification—other than fear or misunderstanding—for requiring members of this particular group to disclose what may be highly personal aspects of such things as their past, their medical condition, or their anatomy. Such a level of total disclosure on a day-to-day level is not required or expected of any other group.

Things are changing, however, in this area as well. Legal developments, including but not limited to litigation victories by transgender persons and the discrediting of the gay and transgender "panic" defenses, have been bolstered by a growing acceptance of gender-expansive people in our society.[9]

This chapter addresses what can be done within the education community to give effect to the emerging rights of transgender persons to be out, not to be out, or to be out to some but not to others. After exploring definitions, it focuses on viewing these issues from the perspective of transgender and gender-nonconforming youth. It then examines strategies for confronting and ameliorating the range of challenges that these young people are facing today, including the legal battles that have received so much attention in recent years.

What It Is Like to Be a Transgender Youth, and What It Means

Although the word *transgender* continues to be employed by many as an umbrella term for those who see their gender identity as different from the gender they were assigned at birth, a growing number of people have started to see *gender expansive* as a wider and more flexible umbrella term that includes transgender along with other gender-variant persons.[10] The range of people encompassed by these umbrella terms may include trans women, trans men, transsexuals, drag queens, drag kings, cross-dressers, androgynous persons, and those who identify as multi-gender or genderqueer. The definitions for these terms can vary, with different people defining them in different ways, sometimes without any apparent consensus.

Generally uncontested definitions include *trans woman* (an individual assigned male at birth who identifies as female), *trans man* (an individual assigned female at birth who identifies as male), and *cross-dresser* (a person who, regardless of motivation, wears clothes and accessories that are considered appropriate for another gender but not that person's own). Other definitions may vary depending on context or community.

Among the more contested definitions are those for the words *transsexual* and *genderqueer.* For example, *transsexual* is often used to describe a transgender person who has had at least one surgical intervention that may be classified as gender affirmation surgery, although some people define the term more broadly. *Genderqueer* is typically employed to characterize someone who, at least at certain times, identifies as not entirely male and not entirely female but somewhere in between or apart from those binaries. But some people view the term as contextually different from that characterization.[11]

Indeed, there is sometimes a significant difference of opinion even among those who identify as belonging to a particular category, with regard to both the identifying term itself and whether the group should be viewed as belonging under the transgender umbrella. Some within trans communities question even the efficacy of using an umbrella term at all.

Categories of Gender-Nonconforming Youth

It may be appropriate in this context to differentiate between separate but interrelated categories of gender-nonconforming youth. One category may include those who now identify as a gender other than the one they were assigned at birth. Another category may include those who may view themselves and/or may be viewed by others as not conforming to the so-called traditional or accepted gender norms. Some in this latter group may one day come out as transgender or genderqueer or both, but they do not currently identify under the trans umbrella. Others may never be transgender or genderqueer but may still be subject to a great deal of ongoing mistreatment and abuse—especially in a K–12 environment—because of how much their gender expression differs from perceived norms.

Unless stated otherwise, the analysis in this chapter should be viewed as encompassing all the preceding categories of gender-nonconforming youth, because all are very much at risk in an education setting. Feminine boys who do not identify as transgender, for example, may be no less at risk than those who might see themselves as transitioning from male to female. And given that research has shown that a significant percentage of all gay bashing is actually gender related, the realities many gays and lesbians face are encompassed by and relevant to this discussion.

Coming Out as Transgender in a K–12 Setting

For purposes of addressing the needs of transgender youth at the K–12 level, it is important to recognize that it is not typically possible to pursue a gender transition without coming out as transgender.[12] Gays and lesbians may take years to come out to everyone and in every setting that matters to them, but transgender persons cannot come out gradually unless they change environments. Once they begin presenting differently, they are immediately and abruptly out to those who knew them previously. Many cannot or will not do this and instead transfer to a different school. Some even leave home.[13]

Thus the typical transgender student who is transitioning and/or coming out has either recently changed schools or is making a statement at the current school that flies in the face of traditionally accepted gender norms and often leads to dramatic changes in day-to-day interaction. In either case, the experience is invariably unsettling to the student, even with the unconditional support of family, friends, and/or the school community.

Realities Faced by Transgender Youth and Their Allies

More often than not, transgender persons who come out in a K–12 setting today are presenting primarily as one gender but have the physical and biological characteristics of the other. Not only are those who desire gender affirmation surgery of any kind not generally able to afford it at this stage of their lives, but doctors do not typically perform such surgeries on people that young. This reality is central and cannot be ignored.

A second key aspect of this territory is that many gender-expansive youth desire to obtain hormones, although medical doctors may refrain from prescribing them to persons that young. Hormones taken in a controlled environment can prove very beneficial even for younger trans persons, yet experts have warned of the possible damage that high doses of estrogen or testosterone can cause for those who are still going through puberty.[14] Still, many trans youth work very hard to obtain such hormones, often illegally. Not only are they at risk during the process of obtaining these items, given that attempts to find the hormones and pay for them can sometimes lead to dangerous circumstances, but they may subsequently be at risk medically—particularly if they are making ad hoc determinations as to the quantity and strength of the hormones they are taking.[15]

Over the past ten to fifteen years, there has been an apparent medical breakthrough in this area: the identification and dissemination of hormone blockers that can delay the onset of puberty as well as enable persons who later decide to transition to obtain enhanced benefits from subsequent treatments and interventions. Supportive parents and their allies in the medical community have increasingly chosen to opt for hormone blockers when young people, at a relatively early age, begin to come out as transgender. Highly acclaimed reporter Zak Szymanski described in 2006 how some doctors have begun to advise parents that "their best options, assuming their children consistently express a desire for physical transition, is to allow some natural development but administer hormone blockers to delay puberty. Such a process leaves fewer undesired gender traits to overcome later in life without causing permanent effects, and for trans boys, allows that often-desired extra height since testosterone can be administered at an older age but before the bones are closed."[16]

In addition, Szymanski reported that "parents' decisions to allow or delay physical transitions would not, in the long run, matter as much to a child as parents who handle the process in a loving and accepting manner." A counselor who worked closely with transgender youth said, "The most critical thing is less about hormones and surgery and more about compassion and love. There is more than one cause to an effect when it comes to identity and . . . the mind, body, soul, and spirit cannot be disconnected in such a discussion."[17]

Still, a large percentage of gender-expansive youth face tremendous opposition from the adults in their lives, and great contempt from their peers, when they reveal that they are transgender. Support is rarely forthcoming across the board from family, friends, and the community in general. It can be argued, in fact, that transgender persons are among the most misunderstood of any identifiable group in existence today. Even many gays and lesbians are not only unfamiliar with the area of gender identity but actually quite uncomfortable with trans issues in general. The discomfort can be intensified by the fact that typical assumptions within gay and lesbian communities can be turned on their proverbial heads when transgender realities are included in the mix. For example, once we recognize that more than two genders can exist for many transgender persons, the terms *homosexual, heterosexual,* and *bisexual* may "no longer make sense."[18]

Given the misunderstanding, the lack of support, and the discomfort that many have with people who do not adhere to conventional gender norms, it is not surprising that gender-expansive youth face additional challenges above and beyond those faced by other members of traditionally disenfranchised groups. But the actual numbers in this area go far beyond what most people might contemplate. For example, one recent study revealed that 30 percent of transgender youth report a history of at least one suicide attempt; nearly 42 percent report a history of self-injury, such as cutting; 58 percent had at least one additional psychiatric diagnosis in addition to gender dysphoria; 63 percent indicated a history of bullying; and 23 percent reported a history of school suspension or expulsion.[19] In addition, the percentages of transgender youth involved in substance abuse, runaway and homeless situations, and prostitution are significantly higher than those of their peers. Moreover, transgender persons are faced with pandemic employment discrimination at all levels of society, and they are much more likely than other recognizable groups to be victims of violent assaults, including rape and murder. Although anti-trans violence accounts for only about 2 to 4 percent of all reported hate-violence incidents, those incidents account for approximately 20 percent of all anti-LGBT murders and approximately 40 percent of police-initiated violence.[20]

The Context of Transgender Issues:
From Westminster, California, to Largo, Florida

Two noteworthy controversies provide an important national context for addressing transgender issues. In the first, a school board in Orange County, California, was willing to risk the loss of millions of dollars in state money rather than adopt a new policy protecting gender-expansive youth. In the second, the City Commission of Largo, Florida, sought to fire the longtime city manager after learning that she was transgender.

The school board controversy took place in the city of Westminster, California, in 2004. State legislators had adopted an expanded definition of "gender," leading for the first time to explicit antidiscrimination protection for gender-nonconforming youth in the state's public schools. Under relevant state Board of Education regulations, every school district was now required to have a policy against discrimination that applied to transgender students as well.[21] Although many districts had questions about the new requirements and it was generally agreed that formulating such policies would present difficult questions, the mandate set forth in a California Department of Education legal advisory appeared to sum up the prevailing view:

> Changing perceptions of gender-appropriate "identity, appearance, and behavior" are a challenge that must be faced by school officials, parents, and students throughout the State of California. That challenge can and must be met without violating the nondiscrimination laws passed by the Legislature and the regulations promulgated by the State Board of Education.[22]

The Westminster District, however, did not agree, and it chose to risk the loss of up to $40 million in state money for its refusal to comply with state law. It was the only district in the state that refused to comply. And its decision was the result of a 3–2 vote by a school board majority that garnered local and national headlines for its outspoken comments on the issue. It is instructive to review these comments, which are very direct.

Board member Judy Ahrens, for example, set the tone for all that followed when she told the *Los Angeles Times* that "I might take a lot of heat for [the decision] today, but the rewards are going to be great in heaven."[23] Subsequently interviewed by the *Orange County Register,* Ahrens—along with board members Blossie Marquez-Woodcock and Helena Rutkowski—stated that changing the district's policy would be immoral because it might encourage transsexual behavior in schools. In addition, according to Ahrens and Rutkowski, adopting the new definition of "gender" would further erode family values. "It's time to say enough is enough," Ahrens told the reporters. Rutkowski added that "a person can be anything that they wish to be, but I don't need to accept their behavior."[24]

During the same time period, the *Orange County Weekly* published additional quotes from the three board members as well as other relevant information. According to the paper, for example, Rutkowski—whom they described as a person who once said that school libraries had too many books on Judaism—"saw a horde of transsexuals plotting to 'shove their lifestyle down our throats. . . . I will do everything to protect students from this mindset.' Woodcock was equally defiant: 'I can't, with a clear conscience, vote for this trash. It's amazing how much we've eroded our society.'"[25]

Most defiant of all, according to the *Orange County Weekly*, was Ahrens, "who call[ed] the teachers' union 'communist' . . . and equate[ed] sex education with promiscuity. She noted that it was 'three brave women' who had taken a 'moral stand,' [and] said they were calling the state's 'bluff' in hopes of pleasing God."[26] The Associated Press reported that Ahrens felt "that accepting the policy would promote homosexuality and transsexuality." She also said "the suggestion that the district could lose its funding is 'blackmail' by the state, which she claim[ed] is pushing local officials to accept an agenda of openly tolerating homosexuality." And Ahrens "worrie[d] that changing the district's definition of gender will promote cross-dressing, or that 'mischievous' young boys could decide to declare themselves female in order to get into the girls bathroom."[27]

The Largo, Florida, incident, which received even more publicity, reflects an opposition to transgender persons that is less rooted in religious doctrine but linked instead to arguments invoking deception and untrustworthiness. In early 2007, longtime city manager Steve Stanton announced that he was planning to undergo gender affirmation surgery. As a result of this announcement, and for no other apparent reason, the city commission voted to dismiss the fourteen-year veteran from his position.[28]

It was not long before extensive details regarding these circumstances began appearing in both the local and the national media. The picture of Stanton that emerged in these stories was of someone who had secretly been living as transgender for some time while presenting an entirely different profile to the outside world. Residents of Largo, for example, saw Stanton as a tough city manager who demanded perfection and had built close and productive working relationships with the mayor, the police chief, and the fire chief. Stanton supervised more than one thousand employees, had rappelled with the firefighters, and had trained with the SWAT team. The *St. Petersburg Times* characterized Stanton as "the face of Largo's aggressive annexation policy and its quest to become a real city with 10-story buildings downtown." In addition, Stanton had been married to a woman for more than fifteen years, a marriage that had produced a biological son.[29]

One of the many reasons that this story captivated the country was that Stanton appeared to everyone around her to be the diametric opposite of someone who would be coming out as a trans woman. Most Americans, unfamiliar as they are with the diversity of transgender communities, could not even begin to imagine that a person so outwardly masculine had been wrestling with her gender identity since the age of six, was traveling to other cities on weekends so that she could present as a woman, and was about to have gender affirmation surgery.

The emotions generated by this story were wide ranging. Many were sympathetic, but many others expressed intense outrage and contempt. The negative comments in the local and national media are characteristic of reactions to the coming out of transgender persons in other settings over time. Michelle Keller, for example, a resident of Largo, wrote that any support that Stanton received was undeserved and that she was on "an extended ego trip." James Anderson, a resident of nearby Palm Harbor, went much further. "Stanton," Anderson wrote,

> can do whatever he wishes on his own time—even negatively affect the lives of his family with his "urges." It happens all the time—people who "decide" they want to drink too much and abuse their family, people who "decide" that negative sexual behavior is "their right," and the list goes on. He does not have the right, as the non-elected manager of a city with other employees, to manipulate the personnel rules to benefit his "transition" and to protect his job from his negative behavior. If it wasn't generally considered deviant and negative, he wouldn't be in therapy for it. Even in our totally liberated, do your own thing world, this is over the top. . . . We can feel sorry for his maladjustment, but don't allow this to creep into human resources decisions for thousands of other workers and torture them with his oddness.[30]

Coverage across the nation led to extensive commentary in other cities as well. At UCLA, for example, much of the reaction was supportive of Stanton, but second-year law student David Montoya wrote the following in the *Daily Bruin*: "Stanton's decision to undergo a sex-change operation marks a huge shift in his values. He is clearly not who the people of Largo voted into office. The other representatives of Largo have a duty as representatives of their constituents to remove any office holder who has deceived his own people about who he is."[31]

Taken together, the public comments by those in Westminster who were opposed to any policy that would address the needs of gender-expansive youth and those in Largo and across the country who endorsed the firing of the Largo city manager because she had come out as transgender are very revealing. Not only do the language, the tone, and the implicit assumptions in these comments reflect what people are thinking when they condemn transgender persons but the intensity of emotion demonstrates the parameters of the challenges that gender-expansive youth face today.

The issues raised in these statements also reveal the many dimensions of the transphobia that still exists. It is clear, for example, that at least some of the opposition to anything transgender is based on the teachings and interpretations of certain conservative religious leaders. And just as some highly religious people continue to assert that there is no such thing as a gay or lesbian identity, many of them insist that there is no such thing as a transgender identity. For this segment of the religious population, gays and transgender persons are deviants who could be cured if only they would admit to the error of their ways.

It is apparent, as well, that from a secular perspective, the same aversion to gender nonconformity that fuels much of the opposition to gays and lesbians is at play in a transgender context. But there are also aspects of this aversion that are unique. While a majority of Americans on at least some level have come to accept the existence of a gay identity and recognize that there always have been and always will be gays and lesbians, many do not typically have the same view of transgender persons. Even a significant percentage of those who are incredibly supportive of gays—and in fact many gays themselves—still see transgender not only as odd, strange, and deviant but as embodying an unacceptable form of deceit.

Thus people still feel confident about saying in public that it is acceptable to fire those who come out as transgender because they are "not the person people thought they were" or because they have "lost credibility."[32] A growing number of Americans find such comments unacceptable, but many others continue to see transgender persons themselves as unacceptable. The Westminster and Largo controversies are indicative of how far we still have to go.[33]

Providing Support for Transgender Youth in K–12 Public Schools

The great majority of Americans have never interacted knowingly with a transgender person, and even fewer have developed any sort of close personal relationship with one. Thus educators seeking to move forward in this area would do well to identify memoirs, films, novels, poetry, and other works of art that document the experiences of those who identify under the transgender umbrella. Although such representative stories will not have the same impact as actual friendships, they can go a long way toward contextualizing these topics on a very different scale. Especially if such material can be further enhanced by bringing in guest speakers who are gender-expansive, the aggregate impact of the input might lead members of the school community to stop viewing transgender persons as "the other," as some sort of aberration, or as an act in a circus or freak show.

Was Lawrence King Transgender?

There is much we do not know, and may never know, regarding the brief and tragic life of Lawrence King, who was first mentioned in the introduction to this book. Solely on the basis of reports in the mainstream media, we know that he was an LGBT person of color and a resident of Southern California who chose to present in his final days as gender nonconforming and perhaps even as gender transgressive. He came out as gay, but middle school students who come out as gay do not typically show up at school wearing lipstick, high-heeled boots, and women's jewelry. He also reportedly told people during the last two weeks of his life to call him "Leticia." It appears that he was still sorting everything out when he was brutally murdered, in 2008, by a fellow classmate who was a member of the Young Marines.

In 2010, when the first edition of this book was published, we did know more from the media reports. We knew that King was short for his age, very strong spirited, and adopted. We were not privy, however, to information regarding the circumstances that led to his adoption or the reason he was subsequently removed from his adoptive parents and placed in Casa Pacifica, a home for foster-care youth. The news stories indicated that this was a group home for abused and neglected teenagers. But it was unclear if we would ever know whether and to what extent King's coming out, a process that likely began some time before his killing, led to his removal and subsequent placement.[34]

Over the past five years, however, three very important works have shed valuable light on all these questions: the 2013 documentary *Valentine Road: A Path to Teen Tragedy* directed by Marta Cunningham; the 2016 book *A Murder over a Girl: Justice, Gender, Junior High* by Ken Corbett; and the 2018 book *The Life and Death of Latisha King: A Critical Phenomenology of Transphobia* by Gayle Salamon. Chapter 2 of *A Murder over a Girl* provides the most direct responses to these questions, supplemented to a great extent by the thoughtful *Valentine Road* and by Salamon's detailed exploration in her book of the gender dynamics at the heart of these events. Taken together, the three works suggest that King may very well have been transgender, and that his attempts to sort all this out were at the very center of the volatility that led to the whole series of terribly tragic events.[35]

The following key facts can be gleaned from these three works.

Lawrence was born in Ventura County to an apparently single mother who was fifteen years old at the time and addicted to crack cocaine and alcohol. She was seventeen when the state took custody of Lawrence and his newborn brother Rocky, and she died not long before her son was killed. Lawrence was adopted by the Kings, a white couple, when Dawn was forty and Greg was thirty. In interviews with Corbett, they claimed that Lawrence's "erratic behavior never seemed to subside" and that they "collected diagnoses" from seven therapists in ten years. The Kings tried to raise Lawrence with what Corbett described as "nineteenth century child-rearing practices" but were apparently unsuccessful.

Grandmother Sharon Townsend said that "Larry was always femme." Dawn taught him to crochet, and he enjoyed it. The two made scarves for the soldiers in Iraq. The Kings had faced a lot of criticism, often public, about their parenting. Corbett wrote that they did not believe Lawrence was transgender, and that they were vocal and adamant about not wanting him to cross-dress or speak of himself as trans. Lawrence "wanted out" of the King house. He spoke out and claimed abuse. In *Valentine Road,* a case manager for Casa Pacifica said that the county had been working to get him out of the King home and that twenty-two complaints about abuse all went unfounded. She also said that county health workers had long been aware of the family's "issues" with Lawrence's "gender variance."

Lawrence apparently called Dawn from Casa Pacifica and said he was going to get "a sex change." Corbett described Casa Pacifica as a place where there were people to talk to, who wanted to listen. There were other gay and trans kids there, "room for fantasy, and room to try on the name Leticia." In concluding his analysis of this era, Corbett wrote that "Leticia got to live only for a few weeks and in the face of tremendous anxiety about gender." In the end, "her transgender identity was not granted. Leticia is perhaps best understood as a question or the act of questioning."[36]

In the group home, according to news reports, the staff appear to have been very supportive of King's coming-out process. Yet it also appeared that King did not have the benefit of engaged adult advice regarding the dangerous circumstances he was facing at his middle school as a result of his increasingly open presentation as a gay and gender-nonconforming person of color. Limited staff and budgetary constraints clearly contributed to this dearth of support.

It is evident from the news stories that King was comfortable presenting as gender nonconforming or perhaps even as genderqueer at school. He appeared happy and almost defiant to be wearing high-heeled boots, lipstick, makeup, and women's jewelry. In addition, the school officials appear to have been aware of what had been going on. They seemed to act deferentially toward King with regard to his gender presentation, yet his former teacher indicated that she had sometimes sent mixed signals to him. She had given him a dress, but at another point she suggested that he tone his presentation down. In general, school officials appear not to have been willing to take on the confrontational nature of the interaction between King and his bullies, and particularly between King and his murderer, Brandon McInerney, a white student from an apparently white supremacist family who had a copy of *Mein Kampf* in his backpack along with his gun the day he shot Lawrence.[37]

Of course, we will never know, but it may very well be that if King was transgender and if the school had engaged in professional development and even changes in curriculum and pedagogy relating to gender-transgressive and gender-nonconforming youth, the tragic murder might never have taken place. Certainly much could have been done that was not done in Lawrence's middle school in late 2007 and early 2008.

School Climate Strategies, Professional-Development Content, and Related Curricular Reforms

The types of strategies described in part II of this book can do much to help prevent the highly disproportionate victimization and marginalization of gender-nonconforming youth. Indeed, the principles that support a broad focus on school climate, proactive and incremental professional development, and LGBT-inclusive curriculum and pedagogy are equally applicable to the transgender area. At the faculty and staff level, very few K–12 educators know much about what it means to be transgender, and most have never been privy to information regarding the unique challenges that gender-expansive youth face. At the classroom level, fellow students can benefit greatly from the same information, which can help generate an appreciation of differences and foster the type of collaboration that can maximize campus safety.

Transgender-related subject matter is rich with possibilities for substantial, age-appropriate coverage within public school classrooms. Transgender issues are a part of history, and the contributions of many people over time have been informed by their gender-nonconforming status. Developments in this area are often major news stories, with important implications for society as a whole. Indeed, the push for transgender rights is viewed by some as perhaps the last frontier in the battle for gender equity.[38]

Just as there have always been gays and lesbians in society, so have there also been transgender persons. One of the most famous female figures in history, for example, Joan of Arc, was condemned not only for being a pagan but also for cross-dressing. There is also evidence that she went even further with her gender expression and that this defiance, combined with other, more well-known aspects of her life, led to her death at the stake.[39] Other historical figures, from the Welsh transgender guerrilla Rebecca, who led her "daughters" into battle in the early nineteenth century, to the cross-dressing activist Luisa Capetillo are noteworthy for their intimate involvement with social movements around the world.[40]

It is often forgotten that the New York City bar that was the site of the rioting that launched the modern LGBT rights movement, the Stonewall Inn, was an establishment popular with many genderqueer patrons of color. According to one account of the events, a transgender woman named Sylvia Rivera set much of the protest in motion by throwing a bottle at a police officer after being prodded with his nightstick.[41] Rivera subsequently worked to ensure that the transgender community would be included in any fight for gay and lesbian rights and also to establish homeless shelters for queer youth. Later in her life, she was recognized by the City of New York when a street corner near the Stonewall Inn was named in her honor. Her story would fit perfectly into classroom discussions on issues relating to disenfranchised persons in our society, as would the story of Marsha P. Johnson, who is generally believed to have led the Stonewall uprising along with Sylvia Rivera.[42]

Memoirs and fiction written by trans people are perhaps the most available resources in this area and often the most accessible for both students and teachers. The novel *Stone Butch Blues,* for example, traces the story of Jess Goldberg from childhood through adulthood and includes passages exemplifying the experiences of those who have to put up with questions such as "Is it a he or a she?" *Exile and Pride,* by Eli Clare, is the autobiographical tale of a gender-nonconforming poet with cerebral palsy contemplating her disability, her sexual identity, and her gender identity on a journey up a mountain. *Gender Outlaw,* by Kate Bornstein, is part coming-of-age story, part manifesto, and part description of her work in alternative theater.[43] Among other things, the book can be used to introduce a discussion regarding the changing nature of gender roles in the United States today.

Beyond books such as these, a wealth of resources are available for students and teachers looking to explore this topic. On the legal front, activist attorneys have written numerous pieces documenting their experiences. Dean Spade, for example, was instrumental in founding the Sylvia Rivera Law Project.[44] Among other experiences, he was arrested in 2003 for using a men's bathroom in New York's Grand Central Station, ultimately serving twenty-three hours in jail along with three friends. His experience is now included in Amnesty International's training on behalf of the LGBT community, and it is readily accessible by students.[45]

Art and music classes can also incorporate discussions of contributions by transgender individuals. There is a variety of traditional artistic representations of transgender figures, and both Chinese and Japanese theater have a long history of males playing female roles, and vice versa. Billy Tipton, a noted jazz pianist and saxophonist who achieved popular success in the 1950s, lived as a woman for decades, and his transgender identity was discovered by his wives (both current and former) and children only upon his death in 1989.[46] Many rock stars, including Boy George, David Bowie, Annie Lennox, and Freddie Mercury, have had notably ambiguous gender identities during portions of their careers.

A number of well-known depictions of transgender realities have been presented on film.[47] *Boys Don't Cry*, for example, tells the tragic story of Brandon Teena, a young Nebraska transgender man who was brutally raped and murdered by his peers after they learned of his gender-nonconforming identity. Teena is played by Hilary Swank, who won an Academy Award for her performance. Teena's life is also remembered in *The Brandon Teena Story*, a 1998 documentary that inspired the production of *Boys Don't Cry*.[48]

More recently, *Transamerica*, starring Felicity Huffman, tells the story of Bree Osbourne, a trans woman at the beginning of her transition. Just weeks before a major surgery, Bree learns that she had once fathered a child, then finds her son and travels with him across the country. Huffman was nominated for an Academy Award for Best Actress, and the movie was one of the surprise hits of 2005.[49]

Other movies that address transgender themes in great detail include *Ma vie en rose*, a 1997 Belgian film about a young boy struggling with his gender identity, and *Beautiful Boxer*, a Thai movie based on the true story of Nong Thoom, a trans woman Muay Thai fighter.[50] *Ma vie en rose* resonates especially well with students who have been bullied by their peers or who have experienced a lack of acceptance within the larger community. *Beautiful Boxer* can serve as the centerpiece of classroom discussions focusing on multiculturalism and gender issues, and it also approaches those topics from a sports perspective.

Adopting Legal and Public Policy Mandates to Address Day-to-Day Transgender Issues

Informed by content such as that contained in the resources described in these pages, educators can more appropriately address day-to-day transgender issues that often prove challenging. However, while positive change in this difficult area continues to happen in many places without invoking the legal system, sometimes it is only via legislation, litigation, regulatory and nonregulatory guidance from government agencies, and mandatory policy changes at the state and local levels that effective change can happen on a massive and widespread scale. Especially since the transgender rights movement has arguably emerged only since the 1990s, the coming decade is an appropriate time to set in place a legal regime that will provide a strong foundation for reform in this area. But this is also a time when anti-LGBT organizations and anti-LGBT politicians have been zeroing in on transgender issues, working to roll back the progress that has already been made and block any further movement toward equal rights for gender-expansive youth. Thus all the more reason to focus on what can be done now, at this point in time.

The following pages summarize the legal terrain that existed at the time this second edition went to press.

Noteworthy Legislation

STATES PROHIBITING GENDER IDENTITY DISCRIMINATION

As of 2018, twenty states and the District of Columbia prohibit gender identity employment discrimination. These states include California, Colorado, Connecticut, Delaware, Hawaii, Illinois, Iowa, Maine, Maryland, Massachusetts, Minnesota, Nevada, New Jersey, New Mexico, New York, Oregon, Rhode Island, Utah, Vermont, and Washington. The jurisdictions also prohibit sexual orientation employment discrimination.[51]

These same states, with the exception of Utah, also prohibit gender identity discrimination in public accommodations. According to the LGBT Movement Advancement Project (MAP), "public accommodation non-discrimination laws protect LGBT people from being unfairly refused service or entry to, or from facing discrimination in, places accessible to the public, . . . including retail stores, restaurants, parks, hotels, doctors' offices, and banks."[52]

Seven additional states prohibit gender identity employment discrimination, but only for state employees: Indiana, Kentucky, Michigan, Montana, Ohio, Pennsylvania, and Virginia.[53]

With regard to discrimination in the schools, as discussed in chapter 3, thirteen states plus the District of Columbia protect students from discrimination in schools based on both sexual orientation and gender identity and nineteen states plus Washington, D.C., prohibit bullying in schools on the basis of both sexual orientation and gender identity.[54]

FEDERAL HATE CRIMES LAW EXPANDED TO INCLUDE
GENDER IDENTITY

In 2009, as referenced in chapter 2, the Mathew Shepard and James Byrd, Jr., Hate Crimes Prevention Act broadened the definition of federal hate crimes by doubling the number of categories implicated. Federal hate crimes law originally covered attacks motivated by race, color, religion, or national origin, and the 2009 legislation added actual or perceived gender, sexual orientation, gender identity, and disability.

CALIFORNIA BECOMES FIRST STATE TO MANDATE
TRANSGENDER-POSITIVE CONTENT IN ITS CURRICULUM

In what many hope will be a model for other states in the future, the California State Legislature adopted the FAIR Education Act, which took effect in 2012. In so doing, California became the first state in the country not only to require the inclusion of lesbian, gay, bisexual, *and transgender* content in its K–12 public school social studies curriculum but also to ban any content that cast negative aspersions on lesbian, gay, bisexual, and transgender persons in general. The legislation added lesbian, gay, bisexual, *and transgender* persons and people with disabilities to an existing law that already included the same mandate and the same ban for other identity groups. This legislation is discussed in detail in chapter 7.

NONREGULATORY GUIDANCE ISSUED BY THE OFFICE FOR
CIVIL RIGHTS (OCR) OF THE U.S. DEPARTMENT OF EDUCATION

Sources of education law also include nonregulatory guidance: nonbinding policies or guidance issued by executive branch agencies that are nevertheless often widely heeded and given deference by the courts. In 2016, nonregulatory guidance pertaining to transgender persons was issued by the Office for Civil Rights (OCR) of the U.S. Department of Education. While this guidance was abrogated by President Trump pursuant to an executive order in early 2017, it does not mean that educational institutions cannot follow selected aspects of the guidance, or even go further than the guidance suggests, should they wish to do so.[55]

OCR GUIDANCE (THAT CAN BE FOLLOWED, ABSENT ADDITIONAL FACTS,
EVEN IF NO LONGER "ON THE BOOKS")

The following is an overview of guidance regarding transgender students, issued by the U.S. Departments of Education and Justice in May

2016. Although they are no longer on the books, many of these recommendations have already been adopted by educational institutions, and other educational institutions are not precluded from adopting selected aspects of this guidance, or even going further, absent additional facts:[56]

1. A school must not treat a transgender student differently from the way it treats other students of the same gender identity.
2. There is no medical diagnosis or treatment requirement that students must meet as a prerequisite to being treated consistent with their gender identity.
3. Harassment that targets a student based on gender identity, transgender status, or gender transition is harassment based on sex and therefore should be prohibited.
4. School staff and contractors should use pronouns and names consistent with a transgender student's gender identity.
5. When a school provides sex-segregated activities and facilities, transgender students should be allowed to participate in such activities and access such facilities consistent with their gender identity. A school may, however, make individual-user options available to all students who voluntarily seek additional privacy.
6. A school should not discipline students or exclude them from participating in activities for appearing or behaving in a manner that is consistent with their gender identity or that does not conform to stereotypical notions of masculinity or femininity (e.g., in yearbook photographs, at school dances, or at graduation ceremonies).
7. A school should respond to a request to amend information related to a student's transgender status consistent with its general practices for amending other students' records.[57]

U.S. MILITARY REGULATIONS AND POLICIES

As referenced in chapter 8, transgender persons were disqualified from serving in the armed forces during the era of "Don't Ask, Don't Tell." The U.S. military considered transgender to be a disqualifying psychiatric condition, both for those wishing to enlist and for those already serving who wished to transition. The ban was lifted in 2016, but President Trump issued a memorandum in March 2018 announcing that it would be reinstated, pursuant to a report released by the Secretary of Defense.[58] In his memorandum, the president stated the following:

Among other things, the policies set forth by the Secretary of Defense state that transgender persons with a history or diagnosis of gender dysphoria—individuals who the policies state may require substantial medical treatment, including medications and surgery—are disqualified from military service except under certain limited circumstances.[59]

As referenced in chapter 8, the new ban is being contested in federal court.

Litigation, Past and Present

DOE V. YUNITS (2000)

In education settings, school officials often seek to restrict students to clothing that is consistent with the gender they were assigned at birth. Challenging this practice, perhaps for the first time, a transgender student in Massachusetts in the late 1990s argued that her First Amendment freedom of expression rights had been violated when she was told by school officials that she could not wear girls' clothing to school. In the legal complaint, she explained that every single day, first thing in the morning, she had been required to go to the principal's office, where the principal would look at her and decide if she was dressed enough like a boy. At a certain point, the student stopped attending school and was required to repeat the eighth grade the following year. Soon afterward, a lawsuit was filed.[60]

The court determined that the plaintiff was "likely to establish that, by dressing in clothing and accessories traditionally associated with the female gender, she is expressing her identification with that gender. In addition, plaintiff's ability to express herself and her gender identity through dress is important to her health and well-being, as attested to by her treating therapist. Therefore, plaintiff's expression is not merely a personal preference but a necessary symbol of her very identity."

The court went on to find that, under the *Tinker* rule, the student's expression did not constitute material and substantial disruption of schoolwork, discipline, or the rights of others. Pursuant to an agreement reached between the Brockton, Massachusetts, School Department and the attorneys for "Pat Doe," the student was allowed "to wear girls clothing to the Champion Charter School" the following fall.[61]

MARRIAGE EQUALITY FOR TRANSGENDER PERSONS
AFTER *OBERGEFELL* (2015)

It is generally accepted that pursuant to *Obergefell v. Hodges,* transgender couples have also won marriage equality in every state. As the reasoning goes, after *Obergefell* (even though the word *transgender* does not appear in the decision), "states may no longer restrict marriage based on gender. This means that whatever your gender, and regardless of whether state officials recognized your gender, this should not affect your ability to marry."[62]

However, as attorney Kylar Broadus explains in a 2017 article for the American Bar Association, although *Obergefell* "removed the question of whether someone is 'biologically' a man or a woman, . . . still unresolved . . . is how the marriages of those who are genderqueer or gender nonconforming fit into the post-*Obergefell* framework. Many people in the transgender community identify this way and don't necessarily identify as male or female."[63]

EQUALITY UTAH V. UTAH STATE BOARD OF EDUCATION (2017)

As recently as early 2017, Utah was one of eight states that had laws that limited how teachers could talk about LGBT issues with students or that forbid it altogether. In 2017, however, a lawsuit that sought to overturn Utah's discriminatory prohibition was successful, resulting in the repeal of this law and eventually leading to a broader settlement, *Equality Utah v. Utah State Board of Education.*

According to the National Center for Lesbian Rights, which was among the legal organizations representing Equality Utah and three students, the lawsuit—the first of its kind in the country to challenge such state laws—successfully alleged that the laws violated the U.S. Constitution and federal education law by discriminating against LGBT people and restricting the First Amendment rights of students and teachers. The lawsuit also successfully challenged a school district's failure to protect a kindergarten student who was brutally harassed because of his gender nonconformity.[64]

NICOLE SHAH BRAR V. HERITAGE OAK PRIVATE EDUCATION (2017)

In summer 2017, Nicole Brar, an eight-year-old transgender student, filed a lawsuit against her former Orange County, California, private school, Heritage Oak, in state court. The lawsuit alleges that the private school in

Yorba Linda would not let her dress as she chose, use the restroom of her choice, and go by female pronouns.[65]

According to the *Los Angeles Times*, "the complaint contends that the school violated the Unruh Civil Rights Act, a California law that outlaws a broad range of discrimination, including by sex or sexual orientation, and that it fraudulently advertised itself as nondiscriminatory and focused on the 'whole child.'"[66]

"This is the first [transgender rights] case to use a state anti-discrimination law as one of the grounds for relief," said Mark Rosenbaum, who directs the pro bono Public Counsel Opportunity under Law, which has taken on the lawsuit, along with several law school professors. Proceedings are pending.[67]

Lawsuits Focusing Primarily on Restroom Issues

On a day-to-day level, restrooms are one of the most important and pressing concerns for transgender persons. Indeed, a transgender focus group conducted by the Gay Straight Alliance Network found that among participants, the lack of safe bathrooms was the biggest problem that gender-nonconforming students faced.[68] Joel Baum, director of education and training at Gender Spectrum—which provides programs and resources to help communities address gender identity issues—cannot emphasize strongly enough how fundamentally important this issue is on a day-to-day level. "Rather than go to the facility of their assigned gender," Baum explains, "transgender and gender variant youth frequently simply do not go the bathroom [at all]. For younger children, this [can mean] humiliating accidents. For older students, various health risks [may arise], as well as distractedness and [a greater likelihood of dropping out]."[69]

During the past two decades, a significant number of people in both the legal and the education communities have wrestled with this topic, and a growing percentage have concluded that statutes prohibiting discrimination in this context encompass a right to safe and appropriate restroom facilities for all students, which includes the right to use a restroom that corresponds to the student's gender identity. Such a conclusion is based on the reasoning that these statutes advance the state's compelling interest in protecting the safety, equality, and privacy of *all* students. As quoted earlier, arguments counter to this position allege that mischievous schoolboys will take advantage of such laws to obtain entry to girls' restrooms, but the reality is clearly otherwise—with virtually no reported instances of anything such as this ever happening in this way.

CALIFORNIA EDUCATION COMMITTEE V. O'CONNELL (2009)

In *California Education Committee v. O'Connell,* a state court considered a challenge to Senate Bill 777, a 2008 statutory scheme that strengthened the nondiscrimination provisions of the Education Code pertaining to LGBT persons. Focusing on what they perceived to be a threat to gender-segregated facilities in public schools, and implicitly characterizing transgender students as dangerous trespassers and potential assailants, the plaintiffs alleged that the legislation violated nontransgender students' rights to privacy and safety under Article 1, section 1 of the California Constitution.[70]

In response to the alleged safety concerns, a key assertion set forth in defense of SB 777 was that transgender students are at a much greater risk of danger than nontransgender students in these settings if they are forced to use the restroom corresponding to the gender they were designated at birth. For example, a transgender girl who consistently identifies and presents herself as a female might find herself in much greater danger in facilities designated for boys only, while the safety of nontransgender persons in settings where a transgender peer might be using a stall in the same restroom is highly unlikely to be compromised.[71]

In response to the alleged privacy concerns, a noteworthy friend-of-the-court brief in *California Education Committee* provided extensive support for the proposition that "no legally protected privacy interest is implicated [under federal or state law] when schools permit transgender students to use gender-segregated facilities consistent with their gender identity." The brief also emphasized the fact that transgender students have privacy concerns as well and that those concerns are "at far greater risk of infringement than the privacy interests alleged by the Plaintiffs." Finally, the brief highlighted the potential for compromise in circumstances where disputes might arise, declaring that "a reasonable accommodation of the interests of all students in privacy and equal treatment, determined for individual students on a case-by-case basis, can easily avert any conceivable conflicts between those interests."[72]

In June 2009, California Superior Court judge Shelleyanne W. L. Chang issued a ruling on behalf of the defendants, finding, among other things, no credence in the plaintiffs' safety and privacy claims.[73] Looking back on the decision, it is clear that the arguments generated by the *California Education Committee* litigation have helped clarify a number of key points that can inform the thinking of school-site personnel in this area. First, a central fallacy in the SB 777 challenge was the implicit assumption that transgender students are "the other" and that "normal" students must be protected from them. Such assumptions are no longer acceptable, either under the law or as a matter of policy. All students are equal under the law, the safety of all students must be protected, and a growing number of jurisdictions have adopted explicit nondiscrimination statutes that reinforce these principles.

In addition, a compelling argument on behalf of the defendants that undoubtedly played a key role in the court's decision is that if there are concerns regarding safety and privacy in this area, the proven dangers are much greater for transgender youth than for nontransgender youth. Moreover, as a matter of logistical reality, trans youth using the restroom will inevitably be doing so in private stalls, and any nontrans student who has privacy issues can also use stalls. Although some students may be uncomfortable with the thought that a transgender student might be using the same restroom at the same time, such subjective discomfort, absent additional facts, provides no legal justification for banning the transgender student. Indeed, courts and legislatures have found a limited right of privacy with regard to who else might be in a public restroom outside of a stall.[74]

WHITAKER V. KENOSHA UNIFIED SCHOOL DISTRICT NO. 1 BOARD OF EDUCATION (2017)

The Seventh Circuit holding in the *Whitaker* case is perhaps the most noteworthy federal court decision on transgender rights to date. The appellate panel upheld the lower court's decision in favor of Ash Whitaker, a transgender high school boy, and in so doing, they broke new ground in finding that the school district discriminated against Ash under both Title IX of the Education Amendments of 1972 to the Civil Rights Act of 1964 and the Equal Protection Clause of the Fourteenth Amendment.[75] A key excerpt from the decision follows:

> The School District did not permit Ash to enter the boys' restroom because, it believed, that his mere presence would invade the privacy rights of his male classmates. Ash brought suit, alleging that the School District's unwritten bathroom policy violates Title IX of the Education

Amendments Act of 1972 and the Fourteenth Amendment's Equal Protection Clause.

In addition to filing suit, Ash, beginning his senior year, moved for preliminary injunctive relief, seeking an order granting him access to the boys' restrooms. He asserted that the denial of access to the boys' bathroom was causing him harm, as his attempts to avoid using the bathroom exacerbated his vasovagal syncope, a condition that renders Ash susceptible to fainting and/or seizures if dehydrated. He also contended that the denial caused him educational and emotional harm, including suicidal ideations. The School District vigorously objected and moved to dismiss Ash's claims, arguing that Ash could neither state a claim under Title IX nor the Equal Protection Clause. The district court denied the motion to dismiss and granted Ash's preliminary injunction motion. * * *

The School District has failed to provide any evidence of how the preliminary injunction will harm it, or any of its students or parents. The harms identified by the School District are all speculative and based upon conjecture, whereas the harms to Ash are well-documented and supported by the record. As a consequence, we affirm the grant of preliminary injunctive relief.[76]

Model Policies

Pursuant to the statutory changes in California that required all school districts to adopt guidelines protecting transgender youth, several public interest agencies developed recommendations that informed the development of policies in major California cities. Areas highlighted in these policies include the most volatile and controversial issues that may arise in K–12 settings: pronouns, restrooms, locker rooms, sports and gym classes, and dress codes. By approaching these areas in a sensitive and informed manner, school officials will be better able to take into account the needs of all persons.[77]

NAMES AND PRONOUNS

Everyone who has worked with gender-nonconforming youth agrees that if gender identity is to be a protected category under the law and as a matter of policy, people should have the right to be addressed by a name and a pronoun fittingly corresponding to that identity. Professionals in the field have emphasized that it is very important for trans persons to have their gender recognized and validated.

Policies adopted in San Francisco and Los Angeles include the caveat that one's gender identity must be "exclusively and consistently asserted at school." Students are not required to obtain a court-ordered name and/or gender change or to change their official records as a prerequisite to being addressed by the name and pronoun that corresponds to their gender identity.

RESTROOMS

Although, as discussed at length in these pages, the default recommended policy should allow for equal access, compromise can be made available by school officials through reasonable accommodations on a case-by-case basis, including optional single-stall, gender-neutral facilities. However, Joel Baum emphasizes the importance of updating relevant policies to include the principle that "while single-stall bathrooms should be a privacy option available to all students, the use of these facilities should be required for no one. Such an approach addresses . . . discomfort in the bathroom in a way that does not single out the transgender student."[78]

LOCKER ROOM ACCESSIBILITY

Locker rooms present many of the same issues as restrooms. On some level, the issues may be more challenging, because typical locker rooms rarely have the type of private or even semiprivate stalls that many restrooms have, but on another level, the territory is simpler, because the basic act of changing clothes requires less in the way of additional fixtures or plumbing.

Gender-expansive students are too often subject to harassment and physical assault no matter what locker room they use. It would certainly not be a solution to require transgender students to use the locker room corresponding to their originally assigned gender. Fortunately, a range of accommodations have been identified that can address the challenge of locker rooms. These may include, but are not limited to, the use of a private area within the public area (such as a bathroom stall with a door, an area separated by a curtain, or a PE instructor's office in the locker room), a separate changing schedule in the private area (utilizing the locker room before or after the other students), use of a nearby private area (a nearby restroom or a nurse's office, for example), or satisfaction of PE requirements through "independent study" outside of gym class (either before or after school or at a local recreational facility).[79]

SPORTS AND PHYSICAL EDUCATION PROGRAMS

Too often, transgender youth are restricted to sports teams that do not correspond to their gender identities. Gender-expansive students cannot help but see this as yet one more way in which they are not taken seriously and are told that their identities are not valid.

In general, it is recommended that, as much as possible, students should be permitted to participate in gender-segregated sports and gym class activities in accordance with the gender they have identified with. The International Olympic Committee's decision in early 2004 to allow both trans men and trans women to participate in the Olympic competitions that corresponded to their gender identities provides an important road map for this territory.[80] In some situations at the high school level, legitimate questions regarding fairness in athletic competitions may need to be resolved on a case-by-case basis. But no such questions need be raised with regard to gym class, where the activity is recreational and not formally competitive.

DRESS CODES AND GENERAL CLOTHING ISSUES

In light of the aforementioned *Yunits* case and the relevant legal principles, it is recommended that a balanced policy be adopted that not only enables students to dress according to their gender identity but also allows school districts to "enforce reasonable student dress codes for the purposes of maintaining a safe and orderly school environment, and ensuring that the school can fulfill its educational mission."[81]

Finally, it is important to note the extent to which race, class, gender, and sexuality intersect for transgender youth. Issues relating to LGBT persons of color have been addressed throughout this book, but it must be emphasized that trans persons of color often face the most difficult challenges of all. Transgender people are disproportionately low income across the board, and too often the combination of their socioeconomic status, ethnicity, and gender nonconformity leads to a level of mistreatment in our society, both by their peers and by public officials, that is truly unconscionable.

Transgender law professor, attorney, and activist Dean Spade has written that the clients who come to the Sylvia Rivera Law Project in New York City typically face the "serious consequences of failing to fit within a rigid binary structure" in the institutions that are designed to deliver essential services. Indeed, he notes that low-income and homeless people in particular are faced with a much greater emphasis on gender-segregated facilities than those who are employed and live in stable housing:

> All the essential services . . . (jails, homeless shelters, group homes, drug treatment facilities, foster care facilities, domestic violence shelters, juvenile justice facilities, housing for the mentally ill) that increasingly dominate the lives of poor people and disproportionately people of color use gender segregation. . . . For the most part, these institutions recognize only birth gender, or rely on identity documents such as birth certificates to determine gender. In every state . . . that allows people to change their gender markers on their birth certificates, evidence of sex reassignment surgery is required.[82]

This dynamic can have a devastating impact on transgender persons in these settings who are already faced with so many other day-to-day challenges. The combination of disproportionate poverty, the overincarceration of the poor, the literal inaccessibility of services because of rigid gender-segregation requirements, and the general refusal of the legal authorities to defer to a person's gender identification without proof of medical evidence can be "especially deadly" on many levels. Spade emphasizes that not only are non-LGBT social and legal services generally ill equipped to provide advocacy for transgender persons in this regard but LGBT organizations themselves rarely provide such services. These are the realities that many transgender youth are facing as they come of age and leave the world of K–12 education.[83]

The issues for transgender youth may be incredibly complex, but they are not intractable. There are wonderful opportunities for people in education communities to be creative here, and an instinctive reliance on sensitivity, awareness, and genuine humanity may be the most important starting point.

CONCLUSION

With the emergence of a right to be out, openly LGBT persons should be able to aspire to any position of leadership, influence, or authority that may exist in our society. Yet many still view societal realities through the anachronistic lens of an earlier era, and in so doing, they take the position that gay and transgender persons who seek to lead organizations, corporations, universities, states, or even entire nations had best keep their LGBT status to themselves. More people conceptualize the world in this manner even today than might readily be apparent, holding to the view that coming out at the highest levels of leadership is a career-ending act.

Such a mind-set is reflected in stories like Alan Drury's *Advise and Consent,* a highly influential 1959 Pulitzer Prize–winning novel, subsequently produced as a Broadway play and eventually made into an Otto Preminger film. It tells of a fictional senator who is destroyed by revelations of past "homosexual" activity, and it is instructive to examine both the story itself and the misconceptions that it perpetuates.[1]

In the novel, an ailing president puts his reputation on the line by attempting to appoint a controversial figure as the new secretary of state. Among those standing in the president's way is Utah senator Brigham Anderson, chair of the subcommittee considering the nomination. The complex plot turns on the revelation that Anderson, while serving in the armed forces during World War II, had a month-long affair with another male soldier. Anderson is a devout Mormon, married to a woman and the father of a child, but the book suggests that he has indeed been wrestling with his sexuality and that he is probably gay. In the end, faced with the knowledge that details of his gay affair will become public, the senator tragically commits suicide by shooting himself in his Capitol office. (In the film, Senator Brigham Anderson cuts his own throat.)

Although this work has been praised for taking on the topic of homosexuality and for presenting a gay protagonist in a relatively sympathetic light,[2] it does not question and in fact helps perpetuate several unstated premises that were prevalent at the time it was written: that there is a terrible stigma attached to being gay, that one cannot even mention the word "gay" or "homosexual" in proper society, and that there is a terrible price to pay for gay relations.[3] Anderson may be a victim of blackmail by unethical fellow politicians, but the reader cannot avoid seeing him as someone who has brought it on himself by making a terrible mistake of judgment that ultimately disgraces his family, his party, and his religion. In Anderson's mind, the only honorable thing he can do is commit suicide.

The film was arguably even more egregious than the book in its treatment of these issues. Especially notorious in the eyes of many was the depiction of Anderson's visit to a gay bar to seek out his former lover. After a difficult encounter in which he pays for information as to the bar's location, he finds the establishment in a dark, secluded, and clearly run-down area of New York City. Entering the bar, he is immediately filled with loathing and disgust. Secretive men, drinking silently and shiftlessly to the sound of Frank Sinatra singing about "lonely losers,"[4] appear no less melancholy and no less desperate than Anderson himself. The senator quickly rushes out of the bar to get away from the former lover and immediately afterward pushes the man into a filthy Manhattan gutter.

Vito Russo, in his classic book on the treatment of gays and gender-nonconforming persons in film, characterizes the final shot of this scene as well as the ending of the film as yet two more examples of the then-unstated rule that gay characters either had to die or at least come to some unhappy ending. Thus Anderson's former lover ends up facedown in the gutter, and Anderson himself commits suicide. The message that nothing good can come from same-sex love is reinforced for the entire world to see.[5]

Many versions of this story continue to play out in American public life. In 2004, for example, New Jersey governor James E. McGreevey became the highest-ranking and most powerful U.S. political leader ever to come out as a gay person. McGreevey had a right to be out, and he could very well have chosen to stay in office and confront the complex set of challenges he was facing in his administration and in his personal life. But instead he announced his resignation.[6] By doing so, he sent a message to the world—intended or not—that coming out was still a career-ending act. Indeed, the *Washington Post,* in its front-page story, communicated the same unfortunate message. "The New Jersey governor," the *Post* reporters wrote, "is the latest in a series of public figures whose careers have been seriously damaged or destroyed by revelations of their homosexual activities."[7]

In 2006, Florida congressman Mark Foley became another high-profile LGBT politician to leave office because of circumstances relating to his sexual orientation. Foley, a closeted gay man who, unlike McGreevey, had never married, was publicly outed and resigned in disgrace after it was revealed that he took advantage of a great power differential to make advances toward young congressional pages.

Yet at the same time that people such as Foley and McGreevey are still playing out stories from another era, stuck in a mind-set of fear on the part of LGBTs and fear *of* LGBTs, many others have been moving forward to a different place and time. Although an *Advise and Consent* atmosphere still exists in many locations, with some people continuing to perpetuate myths and misconceptions that can lead to dire consequences, others have broken through beyond the fear and have pointed the way past marginalization. One of the first to do so was Harvey Milk, the openly LGBT California politician whose message of optimism and hope stands in direct contrast to the messages of those who, like Foley and McGreevey, came out publicly and simultaneously resigned.

Milk, whose stature continues to grow with the passage of time, has been honored posthumously by an Academy Award–winning documentary in 1984, a widely acclaimed biopic in 2008, the Presidential Medal of Freedom in 2009, and California's decision to create a state day of recognition for him on his birthday. Personable, charismatic, and unabashedly out, he emerged as a popular leader within the San Francisco gay and lesbian community in the 1970s, only a few years after he had moved there. At the same time, he became known as an effective coalition builder who reached out not only to unions (in a union town) but also to people of color, senior citizens, and persons with disabilities.[8]

By the time he was elected to the San Francisco Board of Supervisors in 1977, Milk had already achieved a great deal, both for the city as a whole and for LGBTs. Admitting that he "wore two hats," he not only proved to be a key figure in a new and influential San Francisco Bay Area coalition but also emerged as an unquestioned leader of the gay and lesbian community. In this manner, Milk's success reflected a model that has worked so well for many politicians who are also members of traditionally disenfranchised groups. Prominent politicians of color, for example, have often been able to establish themselves as both effective public servants for the larger community and important advocates for their own racial or ethnic groups.

Milk's groundbreaking prominence as an openly gay man led to increased stature for all LGBT people, and his highly visible work on behalf of gays and lesbians was a source of great hope and strength for many who were wrestling with decisions regarding the extent to which they should be seeking to come out and lead complete lives. Perhaps more than anything else, in fact, Harvey Milk is known for his relentlessly successful efforts to convince gay people that coming out and being out would have not only great personal value for them but great political value as well. Indeed, Milk's contributions both before and during his term in office proved to have lasting impact for many people across the nation, including folks who were not even alive at the time. His story remains a signpost that points to how it is possible to move past the brutal marginalization of the past and transcend the corrosive fear that still rears its ugly head in many places today.[9]

Openly LGBT persons have increasingly followed in Milk's footsteps by looking forward and seeking positions of leadership, not just in politics but in all walks of life. By contrast, the McGreeveys and the Foleys still try to stay in the closet, causing, at a minimum, tremendous consternation to themselves and the people around them and risking worst-case scenarios that can blow up in their faces. McGreevey and Foley might very well have been unelectable in their respective jurisdictions had they run as openly gay men at the time. But other out politicians during the same era did win election to similarly prestigious offices, or came out while in office and won reelection, in both parties and in all parts of the country. In the U.S. Congress alone, they have included Gerry Studds (D-Massachusetts), Barney Frank (D-Massachusetts), Steve Gunderson (R-Wisconsin), Jim Kolbe (R-Arizona), Tammy Baldwin (D-Wisconsin), Jared Polis (D-Colorado), David Cicilline (D-Rhode Island), Kyrsten Sinema (D-Arizona), Mark Takano (D-California), Sean Patrick Maloney (D-New York), and Mark Pocan (D-Wisconsin).

Time and again, it has been shown in this context that with increasing openness comes increasing visibility, and with increased visibility comes increased strength, on both a personal and a professional level. By resisting this openness and fighting against the visibility even after recognizing their identities in private, McGreevey and Foley became paradigmatic examples of what gays and lesbians should *not* be doing at the present time. Indeed it can be argued that what got them into trouble more than anything else was the closet itself and their efforts to keep their identities private in such a public age. Conservative gay commentator Andrew Sullivan sought to tackle this dynamic in a widely debated September 2006 *Atlantic* column: "I don't know Foley, although, like any other gay man in D.C., I was told he was gay, closeted, [and] afraid. . . . What the closet does to people—the hypocrisies it fosters, the pathologies it breeds—is brutal. . . . The closet corrupts. The lies it requires and the compartmentalization it demands can lead people to places they never truly wanted to go, and for which they have to take ultimate responsibility. From what I've read, Foley is another example of this destructive and self-destructive pattern for which the only cure is courage and honesty."[10]

It has become increasingly clear that at this point, an openly LGBT politician is in a stronger position than a closeted one. Two of the most notable examples are Tammy Baldwin, U.S. senator from Wisconsin, and longtime California legislator Sheila Kuehl, elected Los Angeles County supervisor for the Third District in 2014, a district that encompasses 431 square miles and nearly two million residents. Both, in their own respective ways, have followed the Harvey Milk model, running for office as openly LGBT but wearing the proverbial two hats: serving their larger communities with great distinction and also serving as LGBT activists at the highest levels of federal and state government.[11]

Other out politicians are also following in the footsteps of Harvey Milk, viewing the *Advise and Consent* mind-set as increasingly anachronistic. Examining the political terrain as of 2018, one is struck by the growing number of success stories for openly gay, lesbian, and transgender persons in the United States and across the globe. Not only has there been an increase in the number of highly influential politicians generally but openly LGBT candidates are also being elected as mayors of major cities for the first time. These include Glen Murray (elected mayor of Winnipeg, Manitoba, in 1998), Kenneth Reeves (elected mayor of Cambridge, Massachusetts, in 1999), Klaus Wowereit (elected mayor of Berlin, Germany, in 2001), Bertrand Delanoe (elected mayor of Paris, France, in 2001), Toni Atkins (appointed mayor of San Diego, California, in 2005), Sam Adams (elected mayor of Portland, Oregon, in 2008), Corine Mauch (elected mayor of Zurich, Switzerland, in 2009), Mark Kleinschmidt (elected mayor of Chapel Hill, North Carolina, in 2009), and Annise Parker (elected mayor of Houston, Texas, in 2010).[12] And Kate Brown, who identifies as bisexual, is the first openly LGBT person to be elected governor in the United States (in Oregon, 2016).

In addition, openly gay and lesbian persons are being elected and appointed to prestigious political positions throughout Europe and in countries as diverse as Brazil, Israel, and Mexico. Five LGBTs have now been heads of government: Johanna Sigurdardottir (prime minister of Iceland), Elio Di Rupo (prime minister of Belgium), Xavier Bettel (prime minister of Luxembourg), Leo Varadkar (taoiseach [prime minister] of Ireland), and Ana Brnabic (prime minister of Serbia). In Australia, openly lesbian Virginia Bell was appointed justice of the High Court in 2009, joining a growing number of out politicians in that country. And recent years have also seen the election of several openly transgender candidates to prominent positions, including but not limited to Vladimir Luxuria (deputy in Italy), Jenny Bailey (mayor of Cambridge, England), Georgina Beyer (mayor and MP in New Zealand), Aya Kamikawa (city councillor in Japan), Nikki Sinclaire (member of European Parliament), Zuliana Araya (councilmember in Chile), Michelle Suarez Bertora (legislator in Uruguay), and Madhu Bai Kinnar (mayor of Raigarh, India).[13]

Finally, a Zogby International poll found that as many as 72 percent of Americans regard a candidate's sexual orientation as unimportant and that they would vote for a gay man or a lesbian as long as the candidate had a record of "getting things done for everyone" in the community.[14] These numbers are further bolstered by consistently documented and publicized findings regarding the growing recognition that openly LGBT persons are an integral part of mainstream society.

The increasing prevalence of out LGBTs in highly visible positions of leadership is mirrored by the growing number of openly gay and gender-nonconforming persons who are serving as leaders in the education community. Indeed one of the recurring scenarios in this book is the picture of openly LGBT students and educators willing to participate in highly public legal battles and, in so doing, lead the way for a multitude of others.

Another recurring scenario in these pages, one that is likely to be even more important now that attention is shifting in many places from the courtroom to the classroom, is the reliance on lesbian, gay, bisexual, and transgender persons as resources. As referenced throughout Part II, programs and initiatives that seek to improve school climate and to provide an equal level of support for all students can benefit greatly from the active participation of LGBTs on individual campuses. Across the country, there has been a growing shift in perspective: school officials no longer see out students and out educators as problems that have to be dealt with but instead regard them as valuable resources who can play important leadership roles at local school sites. As demonstrated in the preceding chapters, such an approach can be particularly beneficial in areas that are often the most challenging, such as curriculum reform, school sports, and issues relating to transgender youth. The value of having people on campus who understand the issues because they have lived them, have the standing within the community to step forward, and can work collaboratively to help create a positive and welcoming environment for everyone cannot be underestimated.

In this context, perhaps the most important of all the themes that reappear throughout this book is the value of working toward a reasonable middle ground. Influential people of every political persuasion are increasingly identifying principles, guidelines, and compromise positions that can help address the needs of all persons without hurting anyone.

More than forty years ago, embattled students who sought to establish a Gay Student Organization (GSO) at the University of New Hampshire set forth a statement of purpose that contemplated a heartfelt common ground. "The GSO was created," the court in *Gay Students Organization of the University of New Hampshire v. Bonner* explained, "as its Statement of Purpose attests, to promote the free exchange of ideas among homosexuals and between homosexuals and heterosexuals, and to educate the public about bisexuality and homosexuality. GSO claims that social events in which discussion and exchange of ideas can take place in an informal atmosphere can play an important part in this communication. . . . And beyond the specific communications at such events is the basic 'message' GSO seeks to convey—that homosexuals exist, that they feel repressed by existing laws and attitudes, that they wish to emerge from their isolation, and that public understanding of their attitudes and problems is desirable for society."[15]

Similarly, when K–12 students began forming gay–straight alliances in the mid- to late 1990s, an analogous mind-set was put forth in mission statements like the one documented in *Colin v. Orange Unified School District*. Written by a twelfth grader, the statement emphasized that "public schools have an obligation to provide an equal opportunity for all students to receive an education in a safe, nonhostile, nondiscriminatory environment" and that the alliance's goal was "to raise public awareness and promote tolerance."[16]

In a like manner, conservative Seventh Circuit judge Richard A. Posner sought to highlight the parameters of a reasonable middle ground in this area, lauding an Illinois school district for adopting a policy that would address the needs of all students. "The policy," Judge Posner stated, prohibits derogatory comments "on unalterable or otherwise deeply rooted personal characteristics about which most people, including—perhaps especially including—adolescent schoolchildren, are highly sensitive. People are easily upset by comments about their race, sex, [and] sexual orientation, because for most people these are major components of their personal identity. . . . Such comments can strike a person at the core of his being."[17]

Finally, Judge Donovan W. Frank, who decided in favor of the student with the "Straight Pride" shirt in Minnesota, captured in a highly cogent manner the nature and extent of the spirit that would appropriately guide everyone's efforts in this area down the road. "All students benefit," Judge Frank wrote, "from the respectful and thoughtful exchange of ideas and sharing of beliefs and practices. Schools, in particular, are vital environments that can provide an education of both the substance of diversity and the responsible manner with which such diversity is approached and expressed."[18]

Almost two decades later, such sentiments can still inform the work of all of us as we go forward from here.

NOTES

Introduction

1. This book uses the abbreviation most typically employed by those addressing gay and transgender issues at this time: LGBT (referring to lesbian, gay, bisexual, and transgender). As discussed throughout the text, other acronyms and a range of terms are also in use, and definitions can vary considerably. To avoid repetition but maintain stylistic consistency, this book often uses *LGBT, gay, bi, and trans,* and *gay and gender-expansive* interchangeably, as synonyms for the same groups of people.

Depending on context, the word *queer* may also be employed. Once used primarily as a pejorative or even as an anti-gay slur, this word is now used within many LGBT communities as a positive descriptive term. For many, *queer* is defined simply as "not straight" or "other than straight." For others, to be queer means to have embraced an identity or to have become part of a community that is not only different from straight but also different from lesbian, gay, or bisexual. In light of the growing popularity of the word *queer* as a positive descriptive term, many now add the letter *Q* to the LGBT acronym, resulting in the expanded acronym *LGBTQ*. Others who add the letter *Q* do so because they intend it to mean "questioning," while a growing number of people prefer the acronym *LGBTQ+,* used to signify lesbian, gay, bisexual, trans, queer, questioning, and others.

The book adopts mainstream definitions for the relevant terms under the LGBT "umbrella," recognizing that there is ongoing disagreement in the literature and within the respective communities regarding labels, umbrella terms, identity formation, and in fact whether identity categories should be adopted at all. It also adopts as a premise the mainstream view that every person has a sexual orientation and that every person has a gender identity.

Trans persons are distinguished by their gender identities, which are typically different from the ones they were assigned at birth and which may or may not span the spectrum between the traditional binaries of male and female. See, e.g., Joel Baum et al., "Supporting and Caring for Our Gender-Expansive Youth," http://www.hrc.org/youth-report/.

2. It must be noted, of course, that just as there is a concurrent right, under the First Amendment free speech clause, not to speak, there is a concurrent right in this context not to be out. Indeed, the right not to be out is an important component of the right to privacy.

3. These hurdles and the stigma that accompanied them are reflected not only in the federal and state statutory schemes of the times but also in the writings of federal judges in the highest courts of the land. See, e.g., Jack M. Balkin, "The Constitution of Status," *Yale Law Journal* 106 (1997): 2313, 2316–20, which seeks to provide both a historical and a cultural context for the various opinions in Romer v. Evans, 517 U.S. 620 (1996); Robert G. Bagnall, "Burdens on Gay Litigants and Bias in the Court System: Homosexual Panic, Child Custody, and Anonymous Parties," *Harvard Civil Rights–Civil Liberties Law Review* 19 (1984): 497, 515–46, which addresses the challenges faced by gay and lesbian parents who wished to maintain custody of their children during the decades following World War II; and Barbara Ponse, *Identities in the Lesbian World: The Social Construction of Self* (Westport, Conn.: Greenwood Press, 1978), which analyzes the extent to which a lesbian identity during this era could be seen as shaped by the widely prevalent stigma that so many women faced. See, generally, Stuart Biegel, Robert Kim, and Kevin Welner, "Conceptualizing the Parameters of the Right to Be Out," in *Education and the Law,* 4th ed., 153–65 (St. Paul, Minn.: West Academic Press, 2016).

An opinion written by Chief Justice Warren Burger, while serving on the U.S. Court of Appeals for the D.C. Circuit in 1965, exemplifies the legal and public policy terrain of the era. Rejecting the argument of a gay plaintiff that his sexual identity should not disqualify him for employment, Burger dismissed "homosexuals" as "sex deviates" who suffer from infirmities analogous to those of chronic alcoholics and former felons. Scott v. Macy, 349 F.2d 182, 190 (D.C. Cir. 1965) (Burger, J., dissenting). Burger went on to serve as the chief justice of the U.S. Supreme Court from 1969 to 1986.

4. See William N. Eskridge Jr., *Gaylaw: Challenging the Apartheid of the Closet* (Cambridge, Mass.: Harvard University Press, 1999), 98.

5. See, e.g., Devon W. Carbado, ed., *Black Like Us: A Century of Lesbian, Gay, and Bisexual African American Fiction* (San Francisco: Cleis, 2002), and Sharon Lim-Hing, ed., *The Very Inside: An Anthology of Writings by Asian and Pacific Islander Lesbians and Bisexual Women* (Toronto: Sister Vision, 1994). See also, generally, Margaret Rosario, Eric W. Schrimshaw, and Joyce Hunter, "Ethnic/Racial Differences in the Coming-Out Process of Lesbian, Gay, and Bisexual Youths: A Comparison of Sexual Identity Development over Time," *Cultural Diversity and Ethnic Minority Psychology* 10 (2004): 215–28.

6. A large body of literature has documented the remarkable changes that have led to the "life of the closet" becoming a discredited and anachronistic relic of another era for so many LGBTs. See John D'Emilio, *Sexual Politics, Sexual Communities: The Making of a Homosexual Minority in the United States, 1940–1970* (Chicago: University of Chicago Press, 1983), and Marcia M. Gallo, *Different Daughters: A History of the Daughters of Bilitis and the Rise of the Lesbian Rights Movement* (New York: Carroll and Graff, 2006). See also, generally, Steven Seidman, *Beyond the Closet: The Transformation of Gay and Lesbian Life* (New York: Routledge, 2002). It must be recognized, however, that circumstances are significantly different from place to place in this regard. Although major urban areas in the United States and Western Europe, for example, increasingly provide comfortable and supportive environments for LGBTs, rural areas in these same countries often remain very unwelcoming. And even within the urban areas, many challenges still remain.

7. American Psychological Association, "Sexual Orientation and Homosexuality," http://www.apa.org/; Bruce Bawer, *A Place at the Table: The Gay Individual in American Society* (New York: Simon and Schuster, 1993); Edward Stein, "Queers Anonymous: Lesbians, Gay Men, Free Speech, and Cyberspace," *Harvard Civil Rights–Civil Liberties Law Review* 38 (2003): 159, 205–8; Chris Glaser, *Coming Out as Sacrament* (Louisville, Ky.: Westminster John Knox, 1998). See also Christian de la Huerta, *Coming Out Spiritually: The Next Step* (New York: Tarcher, 1999).

8. Despite the readily apparent differences between and among LGBT people, recurring stereotypes and misconceptions persist. Indeed, one of the most persistent misconceptions is that LGBT issues are primarily, if not exclusively, wealthy white male issues. Yet not only is the poverty rate among LGBT populations disproportionately high but gay and gender-expansive people are also prominently represented among nonwhite populations. For example, a study released by UCLA's Williams Institute in 2013 revealed that same-sex couples raising children are both more racially and ethnically diverse and also less affluent than their different-sex counterparts. See Gary J. Gates, "LGBT Parenting in the United States," February 2013, 4–5, http://williamsinstitute.law.ucla.edu/wp-content/uploads/LGBT-Parenting.pdf. In addition, the study found that "among same-sex couples with children under age 18 in the home," 61 percent are female couples.

9. In a 2006 public debate at the UCLA School of Law jointly sponsored by the Williams Institute and Brigham Young University, legal scholar Tobias Barrington Wolff posed this question from the audience to two panelists who were arguing against marriage equality: what were LGBTs supposed to do if they were not allowed to live full and complete lives with the persons they loved? Both panelists declined to respond to this question. In an interview with me, Professor Wolff added that he had participated in many debates on the marriage issue and

that he had asked this question at every one of those debates. No opponent of marriage equality was ever willing to answer the question. Interview with Tobias Barrington Wolff, University of Pennsylvania Law School, July 24, 2007.

10. Numerous polls in recent years have documented the growing support among all segments of U.S. society for the legal recognition of same-sex couples. A tipping point may have been reached in 2007, when a New York Times/CBS Poll reported that Americans in every age category favored such legal recognition, with the younger generations continuing to do so by the largest margin. About 68 percent of Americans aged eighteen through twenty-nine supported some form of legal recognition for same-sex couples, while only 25 percent opposed it. But even those over age sixty-five favored such recognition (49 percent to 45 percent). See Janet Elder, "Those Young People, They're So Unpredictable," *New York Times*, April 22, 2007.

In April 2009, pollster Anna Greenberg reported that, "depending on how the question is asked, . . . 65 to 75 percent of people in this country now [supported] some kind of legal recognition of same-sex unions." Salon Roundtable (hosted by Tom Schaller), April 20, 2009, http://www.salon.com/. And an ABC News–Washington Post poll found that, for the first time in the six years they had been polling on this issue, support for same-sex marriage nationwide outweighed the opposition, 49 percent to 46 percent. See Gary Langer, "49 Percent Support Gay Marriage: New High," *Washington Post*, April 30, 2009.

11. Many do not realize just how large a percentage of gays have entered into marriages with persons of a different gender at some point in their lives. Studies using 1990 U.S. census and survey data, for example, suggested that anywhere from 20 to 30 percent of gay men and 30 to 46 percent of lesbians had been married to opposite-sex partners. Dan Black et al., "Demographics of the Gay and Lesbian Population in the United States: Evidence from Available Systematic Data Sources," *Demography* 37, no. 2 (2000): 139–54.

12. Many scholars have set forth examples of the harm that the closet can perpetrate and the benefits that can flow to all members of society if LGBTs are empowered to come out. William Eskridge, for example, asserts that "the social costs of suppressing identity speech in this context" include "perversion of identity, empowerment of the vicious, and social anger." By contrast, he argues, there is great value in identity speech, both for LGBTs and for society as a whole. William N. Eskridge Jr., "A Jurisprudence of 'Coming Out': Religion, Homosexuality, and Collisions of Liberty and Equality in American Public Law," *Yale Law Journal* 106 (1997): 2411.

13. For a detailed and multifaceted analysis of both the progress that has been made and the challenges that remain, see Kenji Yoshino, *Covering: The Hidden Assault on Our Civil Rights* (New York: Random House, 2006). See also Ellen Ann Andersen, *Out of the Closets and into the Courts: Legal Opportunity Structure and Gay Rights Litigation* (Ann Arbor: University of Michigan Press, 2006).

14. See, e.g., Randal Donelson and Theresa Rogers, "Negotiating a Research Protocol for Studying School-Based Gay and Lesbian Issues," *Theory into Practice* 43, no. 2 (2004): 128–35.

15. See, e.g., Catherine Saillant and Amanda Covarrubias, "Oxnard Shooting Called a Hate Crime," *Los Angeles Times,* February 15, 2008. Although we can never be certain, it may be the case that King was actually transgender. See chapter 9 of this book. See also Gayle Salamon, *The Life and Death of Latisha King: A Critical Phenomenology of Transphobia* (New York: NYU Press, 2018).

16. See Charles Blow, "Two Little Boys," *New York Times,* April 24, 2009.

17. In an appearance on the program *Anderson Cooper 360 Degrees,* Carl Walker-Hoover's mother, Sirdeaner Walker, said of her son, "Some people may say he was flamboyant. He was very dramatic." Randi Kaye, the CNN correspondent, added, "Sirdeaner Walker says she never asked her son if he was gay, but she says students called him gay and feminine and told him, You act gay." *Anderson Cooper 360 Degrees,* CNN, April 17, 2009, transcript 2009 WLNR 7231137.

18. National Mental Health Association, "Bullying in Schools: Harassment Puts Gay Youth at Risk," http://www.nmha.org/, quoting Jonathan W. Vare and Terry L. Norton, "Understanding Gay and Lesbian Youth: Sticks, Stones, and Silence," *Clearing House* 71, no. 6 (1998).

19. See, e.g., Robert Tomsho, "Schools' Efforts to Protect Gays Face Opposition," *Wall Street Journal,* February 20, 2003.

20. Karen Franklin, "Psychosocial Motivations of Hate Crime Perpetrators: Implications for Educational Intervention," paper presented at the annual convention of the American Psychological Association, August 1998, http://files.eric.ed.gov/fulltext/ED423939.pdf.

21. See C. J. Pascoe, *Dude, You're a Fag: Masculinity and Sexuality in High School* (Berkeley: University of California Press, 2007).

22. Franklin, "Psychosocial Motivations." Because many gays and lesbians now view the word *homosexual* as an anachronistic, inappropriate, or even pejorative term when it is used as a noun, this work includes it as a noun only when it appears within a quotation. Such use is consistent with the style manuals of both the *New York Times* and the *Washington Post.* See, e.g., Sean Lund, "The 'H' Word," *Huffington Post,* July 25, 2007, http://www.huffingtonpost.com/, which discusses the "deeply problematic connotation" of the word because of its association with the now-discredited diagnosis of a "psychological disturbance" and its preferred use in an anti-gay context by those who see an LGBT identity as only about sex.

23. On some level, all four of Franklin's motivations can be implicated in the actions of principals, teachers, and even parents who have harassed, mistreated, and complained about LGBT students and educators. These adults may very well have been engaged in a process of contemplating self-defense for themselves and their children, enforcement of gender norms, and an escalation of actions based on what peers were doing.

1. The Legal Foundations of the Right to Be Out

1. See Ronald Dworkin, *Freedom's Law: The Moral Reading of the American Constitution* (Cambridge, Mass.: Harvard University Press, 1996), 1–14.

2. Kenneth L. Karst, "Myths of Identity: Individual and Group Portraits of Race and Sexual Orientation," *UCLA Law Review* 43 (1995): 263, 360.

3. Indeed, one of the primary arguments that LGBT plaintiffs have relied on in school-related equal protection lawsuits is that too many educators have treated them as if their gay identity makes them "less worthy" of protection than their straight counterparts are.

4. See Karst, "Myths of Identity," 361.

5. In particular, scholars have highlighted a built-in tension in the area of sexual harassment law between the "value of democratic autonomy" reflected in the Free Speech Clause and the "antidiscrimination norm" reflected in the hostile environment of the sexual harassment framework. See Robert C. Post, "Sexual Harassment and the First Amendment," in *Directions in Sexual Harassment Law,* ed. Catharine A. MacKinnon and Reva B. Siegel, 382–98 (New Haven, Conn.: Yale University Press, 2003).

Hate speech controversies that have arisen within the context of campus speech codes, online "acceptable use" policies, speaker bans, and related matters have also led some to blame the intractable nature of these problems on a built-in tension between the First Amendment (designed to further the "marketplace of ideas") and the Fourteenth Amendment (designed to protect traditionally disadvantaged persons and groups against discriminatory activity of any kind).

6. Public forums are those generally open to all communication that is protected under the First Amendment, but these forums can be restricted as to the time, place, and manner of speech. See Grayned v. City of Rockford, 408 U.S. 104 (1972). Schools may create "limited public forums" and define their scope through "policy and practice" in light of the special characteristics of the K–12 environment. Hazelwood School Dist. v. Kuhlmeier, 484 U.S. 260 (1988). In this context, see also Doni Gewirtzman, "'Make Your Own Kind of Music': Queer Student Groups and the First Amendment," *California Law Review* 86 (1998): 1131.

7. Niemotko v. Maryland, 340 U.S. 268, 272 (1951). See also Fowler v. Rhode Island, 345 U.S. 67 (1953), where Jehovah's Witnesses successfully contested the refusal of the governmental agency to allow them to conduct religious services in a park, although other religious groups had been permitted to do so.

8. Police Department of the City of Chicago v. Mosley, 408 U.S. 92 (1972). Six justices joined in the opinion as written. Justice Blackmun and then Justice Rehnquist concurred in the result, without comment. Chief Justice Burger, in a one-paragraph concurring opinion, wrote separately to express his view that "the First Amendment does not literally mean that we 'are guaranteed the right to express any thought, free from government censorship.'" But as to the interplay

between the First and Fourteenth Amendments, and how in this context they operated harmoniously to strengthen the rights of the plaintiffs, there was no disagreement.

9. *Mosley,* at 96. In the years following the *Mosley* decision, Kenneth Karst highlighted the importance of the intersection between the First and Fourteenth Amendments for those working on behalf of civil rights: "It is no accident that strains on the system of freedom of expression typically come from the disadvantaged. The boisterous assertiveness of much of the civil rights movement, for example, is traceable not only to a need to use the streets and parks as a 'public forum,' but more fundamentally to a need for self-assertion simply as a way of staking a claim to equal citizenship. Equality of expression is indispensable to a society committed to the dignity of the individual." Kenneth Karst, "Equality and the First Amendment," *University of Chicago Law Review* 43 (1975): 20, 26.

10. San Antonio v. Rodriguez, 411 U.S. 1, 35 (1973). In this context, Justice Powell wrote, "Education ... is essential to the effective exercise of First Amendment freedoms and to intelligent utilization of the right to vote. In asserting a nexus between speech and education, appellees urge that the right to speak is meaningless unless the speaker is capable of articulating his thoughts intelligently and persuasively. The 'marketplace of ideas' is an empty forum for those lacking basic communicative tools. Likewise, they argue that the corollary right to receive information becomes little more than a hollow privilege when the recipient has not been taught to read, assimilate, and utilize available knowledge."

11. *Rodriguez,* at 62 (Brennan, J., dissenting).

12. Plyler v. Doe, 457 U.S. 202, 221 (1982) (citations omitted). Justice Brennan went on to conclude that the Court "cannot ignore the significant social costs borne by our Nation when select groups are denied the means to absorb the values and skills upon which our social order rests."

13. See Serrano v. Priest, 5 Cal. 3d 584, 608, n. 25 (1971): "The sensitive interplay between education and the cherished First Amendment right of free speech has also received recognition by the United States Supreme Court.... [The Court has declared that] the vigilant protection of constitutional freedoms is nowhere more vital than in the community of American schools." Similarly, the Court observed that "the classroom is peculiarly the market place of ideas. The Nation's future depends upon leaders trained through wide exposure to [a] robust exchange of ideas."

14. Rose v. Council for Better Educ., 790 S.W.2d 186 (Ky. 1989).

15. See Anuj Desai, "Attacking Brandenburg with History: Does the Long-Term Harm of Biased Speech Justify a Criminal Statute Suppressing It?," review of *Destructive Messages: How Hate Speech Paves the Way for Harmful Social Movements,* by Alexander Tsesis, *Federal Communications Law Journal* 55 (2003): 353, 394: "There is ... a huge volume of literature on the relationship between

the principles of equality and freedom of expression generally and between the Fourteenth Amendment's Equal Protection Clause and the First Amendment's Free Speech Clause more specifically." Topics, doctrines, and areas of the law that have been examined in this context include, but are not limited to, prior restraint law, the public forum doctrine, the viewpoint discrimination doctrine, fundamental rights analysis, the right to vote, the right to an education, public finance law, hostile environment harassment law, and academic freedom.

16. See Dudley Clendinen and Adam Nagourney, *Out for Good: The Struggle to Build a Gay Rights Movement in America* (New York: Simon and Schuster, 1999). See also David M. Cruz, "'Just Don't Call It Marriage': The First Amendment and Marriage as an Expressive Resource," *Southern California Law Review* 74 (2001): 925, which examines the continuing vitality of the First Amendment for LGBT rights in the twenty-first century.

17. For a historical perspective on the police harassment of gay and gender-nonconforming persons during the years leading up to the Stonewall uprising, see generally Jon J. Gallo et al., "The Consenting Adult Homosexual and the Law: An Empirical Study of Enforcement and Administration in Los Angeles County," *UCLA Law Review* 13 (1966): 43, the first known law review article regarding LGBT rights ever published.

18. See Richard D. Lyons, "Psychiatrists, in a Shift, Declare Homosexuality No Mental Illness," *New York Times,* December 16, 1973, which documents the American Psychiatric Association trustees' 13–0 decision, and Harold M. Schmeck Jr., "Psychiatrists Approve Change on Homosexuals," *New York Times,* April 9, 1974, 12, reporting on the referendum vote by the entire membership, with 58 percent voting to approve the decision.

19. The venerable right to equal educational opportunity has appeared in many different guises, typically in the form of judicially recognized rights or state statutory entitlements. In its various forms, and in a growing number of states, it has been deemed applicable to persons who have been marginalized or disenfranchised on the basis of their race, ethnicity, gender, religion, national origin, language status, sexual orientation, gender identity, and/or disability.

20. Romer v. Evans, 517 U.S. 620 (1996). Amendment 2, the broad and sweeping provision at issue in this case, was added to the Colorado Constitution by the voters in 1992. Justice Kennedy, writing for the majority in *Romer,* explained that the "impetus" for the statewide ballot initiative "came in large part from ordinances that had been passed in various Colorado municipalities," such as Aspen, Boulder, and Denver, that banned discrimination on the basis of sexual orientation. Kennedy confirmed that not only did Amendment 2, "in explicit terms," repeal or rescind these provisions but it also prohibited "all legislative, executive or judicial action at any level of state or local government . . . whereby homosexual, lesbian or bisexual orientation, conduct, practices or relationships shall

constitute or otherwise be the basis of or entitle any person or class of persons to have or claim any minority status, quota preferences, protected status or claim of discrimination" (623–24).

21. Wide-ranging gains for same-sex couples in this context include medical coverage and retirement benefits in both public and private sector workplaces as well as legal recognition for same-sex relationships in a growing number of states.

22. See Eskridge, *Gaylaw*, 123.

23. See Nan D. Hunter, "Expressive Identity: Recuperating Dissent for Equality," *Harvard Civil Rights–Civil Liberties Law Review* 35 (2000): 1, 39–43.

24. Gay Students Organization of the University of New Hampshire v. Bonner, 509 F.2d 652 (1st Cir. 1974).

25. *Gay Students Organization*, at 661. The First Circuit noted that even dancing itself might, in this context, be considered expressive conduct protected by the Free Speech Clause. In the end, the panel not only affirmed the lower court's ruling in favor of the student group under "right of association" principles but went even further than the trial court by determining that the Free Speech Clause applied. See 660.

26. *Gay Students Organization*, at 662. In language that reflects a convergence of free speech and equality-based principles in this regard, Chief Judge Coffin emphasized that the court's "First Amendment analysis" relied "heavily upon the conclusions which must be drawn from the fact that *only the GSO* among campus groups has been forbidden to hold social events" (662n6).

27. Gay Alliance of Students v. Matthews, 544 F.2d 162 (4th Cir. 1976); Gay Lib v. Univ. of Missouri, 558 F.2d 848 (8th Cir. 1977); Gay Rights Coalition of Georgetown University Law Center v. Georgetown University, 536 A.2d 1 (D.C.D.C. 1987) (en banc).

28. Hunter, "Expressive Identity."

29. Nabozny v. Podlesny, 92 F.3d 446 (7th Cir. 1996).

30. *Nabozny*. See also Nabozny v. Podlesny, Appellant's Brief (December 18, 1995), and Appellant's Reply Brief (February 2, 1996).

31. See Mark Walsh, "Can Schools Do More to Protect Gays?," *Teacher*, August 1, 1996.

32. See Lu-in Wang, "The Complexities of Hate," *Ohio State Law Journal* 60 (1999): 799. Clearly, had Nabozny done any of the same things to his straight classmates, he would have been punished. See also Joanna P. L. Magnum, "Wrightson v. Pizza Hut of America, Inc.: The Fourth Circuit's 'Simple Logic' of Same-Sex Sexual Harassment under Title VII," *North Carolina Law Review* 76 (1997): 306.

33. *Nabozny*, at 454–58. Because the school district punished male-on-female battery and harassment but not male-on-male, the school district's treatment of Nabozny violated equal protection based on gender. For the sexual orientation claim, the Seventh Circuit avoided the question of whether homosexuals were

a suspect class and instead ruled that there was no rational basis to justify the school district's allowing other students to assault another based on sexual orientation. As the plaintiff stated in the brief submitted to the court of appeals, "based on defendants' stated policies, it is simply inconceivable that a serious investigation and strong punishment would not follow if *a girl* of Jamie's age were pinned down and subjected to a mock sexual assault in a classroom, or urinated on or beaten to the point of missing several days of school and requiring hospitalization." See Plaintiff's Appellate Brief, 453–54.

34. Had the school district chosen to settle at the outset, the price would have been much lower, and there still would have been no recorded federal cases addressing the Fourteenth Amendment's equal protection clause as it pertains to gay or lesbian students in public schools.

35. See, e.g., Courtney Joslin and Eric Manke, "Fifteen Expensive Reasons Why Safe Schools Legislation Is in Your State's Best Interest," National Center for Lesbian Rights and Gay, Lesbian, and Straight Education Network, http://www .trans-parenting.com.

36. Lawrence v. Texas, 539 U.S. 558 (2003).

37. Petitioners Lawrence and Garner appealed after being convicted of engaging in "deviate sexual intercourse" in violation of the Texas Penal Code. Section 21.06(a) of the code stated at the time that "a person commits an offense if he engages in deviate sexual intercourse with another individual of the same sex." The statute defined "deviate sexual intercourse" as follows: "(A) any contact between any part of the genitals of one person and the mouth or anus of another person; or (B) the penetration of the genitals or the anus of another person with an object" (§ 21.01[1]).

38. Paul Smith, already a veteran of eight Supreme Court arguments on the morning that the *Lawrence* case was heard, was the managing partner in Jenner and Block's D.C. office at the time. The fact that Smith was openly gay was highlighted in commentary regarding the case, and it is especially noteworthy within the context of an examination of the right to be out. See Tony Mauro, "Gay Rights Movement Gets Its Day in the Supreme Court," *Legal Times,* March 31, 2003, 12. Perhaps the most significant aspect of Smith's openly gay status was the fact that he had once clerked for Supreme Court Justice Lewis Powell, a Virginian who had apparently cast the deciding vote against the gay plaintiff in the 1986 *Bowers v. Hardwick* case, which upheld a Georgia statute criminalizing sodomy and which was overruled by the *Lawrence* Court seventeen years later. Powell reportedly had said to a law clerk at the time, "I don't believe I've ever met a homosexual," apparently unaware not only that the clerk to whom he was speaking was a gay person but also that several of his previous clerks—including Smith—were gay as well. There has been much speculation as to how different things might have been in 1986 had Smith and other Powell clerks not remained

closeted during that era. Smith noted that after Powell left the Court, in 1987, he said he regretted his vote in *Bowers*: "Obviously it was very troubling to him, and he came to believe he had made a mistake," said Smith. "Justice Powell was very much on my mind as I argued [*Lawrence*]." See Mauro.

39. David G. Savage, "Justices Engage in Debate over Equal Rights for Gays," *Los Angeles Times*, March 27, 2003. In his dissent, Justice Scalia followed up on these comments with a strong condemnation of the Court's decision. He called the opinion "the product of a Court . . . [and] . . . a law-profession culture that has largely signed on to the so-called homosexual agenda." And he defended those who had supported the Texas statute by asserting that "they view this as protecting themselves and their families from a lifestyle that they believe to be immoral and destructive." *Lawrence*, at 602 (Scalia, J., dissenting).

40. The fact that Justice Kennedy and Justice O'Connor—both conservative Republicans appointed by President Reagan—took the lead on this case and wrote the key opinions was, for many, a highly compelling aspect of the decision, lending both additional credence and additional weight to the holding.

41. *Lawrence*, at 575.

42. *Lawrence*, at 560, 571–78, 582. See also Stuart Biegel, Robert Kim, and Kevin Welner, "Employment Discrimination on the Basis of LGBT Status," in *Education and the Law*, 4th ed. (St. Paul, Minn.: West Academic Press, 2016), 1052–55.

43. For example, there was an ongoing debate regarding the prospective impact of the language in the respective opinions of Kennedy and O'Connor rejecting the so-called moral justification argument of the State of Texas. Justice Scalia contended in his *Lawrence* dissent that the majority opinion's rejection of a morality justification "effectively decree[d] the end of all morals legislation" and would open the door to the invalidation of "state laws against bigamy, . . . adult incest, prostitution, . . . bestiality, and obscenity" (590, 599). Indeed, he predicted "a massive disruption of the current social order" (591). Others insist that the justices are not saying that moral principles that may be identified in a given fact situation can never be used as a justification for a decision. Rather, they assert that, under *Lawrence*, a court must carefully assess the basis for the moral justification, the nature of the underlying activity being targeted for prohibition, and the other justifications proffered by the state. See, generally, Suzanne B. Goldberg, "Constitutional Tipping Points: Civil Rights, Social Change, and Fact-Based Adjudication," *Columbia Law Review* 106, no. 8 (2006): 1955.

It should be noted that in the years since the 2003 decision came down, Scalia's warnings did not come to pass. Numerous cases upheld sex-related laws over the petitioner's reliance on *Lawrence*. See, e.g., State v. McKenzie-Adams, 915 A.2d 822 (Conn. 2007), regarding consensual sex with students by a teacher; People v. McPhee, 2007 WL 912116 (Mich. Ct. App. 2007), regarding incest;

and United States v. Thompson, 458 F. Supp. 2d 730 (N.D. Ind. 2006), regarding prostitution. The circuit split regarding the constitutionality of statutes prohibiting the commercial distribution of sex toys can be viewed as reflecting these trends and is not inconsistent with their implications. In Williams v. Morgan, 478 F.3d 1316 (11th Cir. 2007), the Court upheld the constitutionality of the Alabama "sex toy" statute, whereas in Reliable Consultants v. Earle, 517 F.3d 738 (5th Cir. 2008), the Court found a similar Texas statute violative of the Fourteenth Amendment. The Alabama decision demonstrated that not every sex-related law will be deemed automatically unconstitutional after *Lawrence*. The Texas case, however, arguably demonstrated that government efforts to prohibit devices that are being employed by persons simply to enhance their lovemaking are inconsistent with both the letter and the spirit of *Lawrence*. In this regard, see, generally, Dale Carpenter, "Is Lawrence Libertarian?," *Minnesota Law Review* 88 (2004): 1140.

44. See Obergefell v. Hodges, 135 S.Ct. 2071 (2015). See generally chapter 2 of this book.

45. In Bowers v. Hardwick, 457 U.S. 186 (1986), the Court considered a Fourteenth Amendment challenge to a Georgia antisodomy statute but found the statute constitutional. Seventeen years later, the Court not only invalidated all remaining antisodomy statutes but expressly overruled *Bowers* (*Lawrence*, at 576–78).

46. Even if, under a narrow interpretation of *Lawrence*, the sweeping and deferential language in the opinions of Justices Kennedy and O'Connor is viewed as "dicta"—the functional equivalent of an aside and not an integral part of the Court's holding—a bare-bones interpretation of the ruling will in and of itself inevitably carry considerable weight in future cases.

47. *Gender-expansive* is an increasingly popular umbrella term that "conveys a wider, more flexible range of gender identity and/or expression than typically associated with the binary gender system." See, e.g., Baum et al., "Supporting and Caring for Our Gender-Expansive Youth." For a growing number of people, *gender-expansive* appears to have replaced terms such as *gender-nonconforming* and *gender-variant*. See generally chapter 9 of this book.

48. Indeed, certain segments of organized religion are a primary driving force behind the opposition to equal treatment for gays and lesbians and transgender persons in the public square. It is increasingly rare to find anyone openly and aggressively committed to an anti-gay position in courtrooms, legislatures, or the media who is not affiliated with organized religion, has not adopted a more fundamentalist interpretation of the doctrine, and does not view this doctrine as a justification for such a position. See, e.g., the web sites of the Traditional Values Coalition (http://www.traditionalvalues.org/), Focus on the Family (http://www.family.org/), and the Alliance Defending Freedom (formerly the Alliance De-

fense Fund; http://www.adflegal.org/), which are among the most prominent national organizations actively working to oppose equal rights for LGBT persons.

49. A July 2006 Pew Forum study, for example, indicated that sizable majorities of white mainline Protestants and Catholics supported civil unions (but not marriage) for same-sex couples. Pew Forum on Religion and Public Life, "Pragmatic Americans Liberal and Conservative on Social Issues," 2006, http://www.pewforum.org/.

50. In this regard, religious liberty has been an important component of the debates regarding marriage equality. Proponents of same-sex marriage argued that deference to religious doctrine as interpreted by the more conservative and fundamentalist branches enables some religious leaders to dictate religious practices for everyone, in violation of the Religion Clauses of the Constitution. At the same time, opponents of same-sex marriage expressed concerns about being forced to perform marriage-related tasks in their line of work that might violate their own personal religious beliefs. See, e.g., Douglas Laycock Jr., Anthony Picarello, and Robin Fretwell Wilson, *Same-Sex Marriage and Religious Liberty: Emerging Conflicts* (Lanham, Md.: Rowman and Littlefield, 2008).

Seeking to address these concerns, some of the first states to legalize gay marriage included "religious conscience protections" in their legislation. Connecticut, for example, added such protections in April 2009. See, generally, Connecticut Substitute Senate Bill no. 899 (Public Act no. 09-13). In New Hampshire, Governor John Lynch, originally opposed to gay marriage, ultimately signed a bill to legalize it after the legislature agreed to include similar protections. See, generally, New Hampshire House Bill no. 73, June 2009, which not only exempts members of the clergy from having to perform same-sex weddings but also states that "each religious organization, association, or society has exclusive control over its own religious doctrine, policy, teachings and beliefs regarding who may marry within their faith."

51. See, e.g., Andrew Harvey, ed., *The Essential Gay Mystics* (Cleveland, Ohio: Pilgrim, 1997), a rich collection of spiritual writings from the earliest days of civilization through the current era, written by authors who have acknowledged their gay identities as well as by those who are believed to have been LGBT.

52. See, e.g., Janet Jakobsen and Ann Pelegrini, *Love the Sin: Sexual Regulation and the Limits of Religious Tolerance* (New York: New York University Press, 2003).

53. See, e.g., Epperson v. Arkansas, 393 U.S. 97, 104 (1968): "Government in our democracy, *state and national,* must be neutral in matters of religious theory, doctrine, and practice" (emphasis added). Other early cases extending the First Amendment Religion Clauses to state actions include Everson v. Board of Education, 330 U.S. 1 (1947), and McCollum v. Board of Education, 333 U.S. 203 (1948).

54. Under *Lemon v. Kurtzman,* the Court in 1971 set forth a three-part test for

determining whether a policy or practice would be violative of the Establishment Clause, focusing on purpose, effects, and entanglement. Over time, many came to believe that this approach was inappropriately "hostile to religion," and the *Lemon* test itself was ultimately modified. Moreover, additional establishment clause frameworks focusing on endorsement, coercion, and perhaps even neutrality alone were developed, with the justices struggling to identify guidelines that would help determine which principles and frameworks to apply in what types of situations.

55. Recognizable patterns in Establishment Clause cases are beginning to emerge. In a school setting, for example, endorsement is typically found to be an appropriate test for displays and programs, a coercion test is applied within the context of school prayer, and neutrality is a central principle underlying the inquiry into public funding for private religious education. As a general rule, public education is expected to be secular in nature, with parents having the right to send their children to private sectarian schools or to homeschool them if they wish to provide them with an education that is religious in nature. But cases and statutes recognize numerous instances where religion-related expression and activities can in fact take place in a public educational setting. There is indeed an ongoing battle over boundaries in this regard.

56. McCreary County v. ACLU, 125 S. Ct. 2722, 2746–47 (2005) (O'Connor, J., concurring).

57. Commentators have explored such points of intersection for some time, identifying parallels, consistencies, inconsistencies, and nuances. See, e.g., Alan E. Brownstein, "Harmonizing the Heavenly and Earthly Spheres: The Fragmentation and Synthesis of Religion, Equality, and Speech in the Constitution," *Ohio State Law Journal* 51 (1990): 89, which sorts out the interrelationship between and among the respective clauses, and Ira C. Lupu, "Keeping the Faith: Religion, Equality, and Speech in the U.S. Constitution," *Connecticut Law Review* 18 (1986): 739, which explores points of comparison across principles and doctrines. See, generally, Christopher L. Eisgruber and Lawrence G. Sager, *Religious Freedom and the Constitution* (Cambridge, Mass.: Harvard University Press, 2007).

58. See, e.g., Eugene Volokh, "A Common Law Model for Religious Exemptions," *UCLA Law Review* 46 (1999): 1465, which identifies parallels, analogies, and an ongoing interplay between the Free Speech Clause and the Free Exercise Clause over time. The cases have recognized a broad "freedom of conscience" in this area as well, which encompasses both a religious component and a freedom-of-expression component. As Justice Stevens explained on behalf of the Court's majority in *Wallace v. Jaffree*, "just as the right to speak and the right to refrain from speaking are complementary components of a broader concept of individual freedom of mind, so also the individual's freedom to choose his own creed is the counterpart of his right to refrain from accepting the creed established by the

majority. . . . The Court has unambiguously concluded that the individual *freedom of conscience* protected by the First Amendment embraces the right to select any religious faith or none at all." Wallace v. Jaffree, 472 U.S. 38, 52–54 (1985) (emphasis added).

59. As was the case with the public forum and right-to-an-education disputes, some decisions may build explicitly on the Equal Protection Clause, whereas others may implicitly adopt antidiscrimination values. It is interesting to note that the Jehovah's Witness cases of *Niemotko* and *Fowler,* decided under the public forum doctrine, not only reflected the intersection between the Free Speech Clause and the Equal Protection Clause but also expressly referenced religion. Indeed, religion was a central aspect of these disputes.

60. See Board of Educ. of Kiryas Joel Village School Dist. v. Grumet, 512 U.S. 687 (1994), where the Court considered the constitutionality of a New York State statute that carved out a separate school district for a religious enclave of Hasidic Jews. Writing for the majority, Justice Souter set forth an establishment clause analysis that was linked to the question of whether there had been "equal treatment." "The fact that this school district was created by a special and unusual Act of the legislature," Souter wrote, "gives reason for concern whether the benefit received by the [Hasidic] community is one that the legislature will provide *equally* to other religious (and nonreligious) groups. . . . Because the religious community of Kiryas Joel did not receive its new governmental authority simply as one of many communities eligible for *equal treatment* under a general law, we have no assurance that the next similarly situated group seeking a school district of its own will receive one" (702–3; emphasis added).

In her separate opinion, Justice O'Connor was even more explicit, stating that, in her view, "the Religion Clauses . . . and the Equal Protection Clause as applied to religion . . . all speak with one voice on this point" (715; O'Connor, J., concurring in part and concurring in the judgment). Justice Kennedy, in an additional concurrence, directly reinforced the efficacy of deciding the case by identifying a point of intersection between the Establishment Clause and the Equal Protection Clause: "The Establishment Clause forbids the government to use religion as a line-drawing criterion. In this respect, the Establishment Clause mirrors the Equal Protection Clause. Just as the government may not segregate people on account of their race, so too it may not segregate on the basis of religion. The danger of stigma and stirred animosities is no less acute for religious line-drawing than for racial" (728; Kennedy, J., concurring).

61. See Pierce v. the Society of Sisters of the Holy Names of Jesus and Mary, 268 U.S. 510 (1925); West Virginia State Bd. of Educ. v. Barnette, 319 U.S. 624 (1943); and Wisconsin v. Yoder, 406 U.S. 205 (1971).

2. Marriage Equality and Its Aftermath

1. For noteworthy perspectives on the marriage equality movement generally, see, e.g., Carlos Ball, *After Marriage Equality: The Future of LGBT Rights* (New York: New York University Press, 2016), a collection of essays by scholars in this area. See also *The Freedom to Marry* (2017), a documentary video starring Evan Wolfson, Mary Bonauto, and April DeBoer (three prominent pioneers in this area).

2. The Mexico Supreme Court ruled in 2015 that a ban on same-sex marriage is unconstitutional. Legally, the question is settled. However, fewer than half of its states, plus Mexico City, currently allow such weddings. See Matthew Bell, "Gay Marriage Is Legal in Mexico, but Mexicans Are Still Fighting Over Whether It Should Be Allowed," *PRI's the World,* September 13, 2016.

3. With regard to Taiwan, see Johnson Lai and Christopher Bodeen, "Taiwan Becomes First in Asia to Recognize Same-Sex Marriage," *San Francisco Chronicle,* May 24, 2017. In its majority opinion, Taiwan's Constitutional Court "said a provision in the current civil code barring same-sex marriages violated two articles of the constitution safeguarding human dignity and equality under the law. Authorities must now either enact or amend relevant laws within two years, failing which same-sex couples could have their marriages recognized by submitting a written document."

4. Countries permitting some form of civil union as of July 2018 include Andorra, Chile, Croatia, Cyprus, Czech Republic, Ecuador, Estonia, Greece, Hungary, Italy, Japan (in some states/regions), Liechtenstein, Malta, Slovenia, Switzerland, and Venezuela. See, e.g., "Freedom of Marriage World Map," http://marriage.hiddush.org/about/same-sex-marriage-and-civil-unions.

On the other hand, it should be noted that "homosexuality is still a crime in 73 of the world's 193 countries, according to the International Lesbian, Gay, Bisexual, Trans and Intersex Association; in 13, the death penalty can be applied." See Somini Sengupta, "After Orlando, Gay Rights Moves Off Diplomatic Back Burner," *New York Times,* June 14, 2016.

5. Romer v. Evans, 517 U.S. 620 (1996).

6. Nabozny v. Podlesny, 92 F.3d 446 (7th Cir. 1996). See generally the discussion of *Nabozny* in chapter 1 of this book.

7. Lawrence v. Texas, 539 U.S. 558 (2003). See generally the overview of the *Lawrence* case and its impact in chapter 1 and the following discussion in this chapter.

8. The Matthew Shepard and James Byrd, Jr., Hate Crimes Prevention Act of 2009 broadened the definition of federal hate crimes by doubling the number of categories implicated. Federal hate crimes law originally covered attacks motivated by race, color, religion, or national origin, and the 2009 legislation added actual or perceived gender, sexual orientation, gender identity, or disability. It

also empowered the Department of Justice to become involved in monitoring and prosecuting crimes in the four additional areas. See generally Meredith Boram, "The Matthew Shepard and James Byrd, Jr., Hate Crimes Prevention Act: A Criminal Law Perspective," *University of Baltimore Law Review* 45 (2016): 343.

9. See chapter 8 of this book.

10. The *Perry* case began as Perry v. Schwarzenegger, 704 F.Supp.2d 941 (2010), in which two same-sex couples successfully challenged the constitutionality of California Proposition 8 under the Equal Protection Clause of the Fourteenth Amendment. The decision was upheld on appeal, in Perry v. Brown, 671 F.3d 1052 (9th Cir. 2012), but the U.S. Supreme Court, per Chief Justice John Roberts, vacated the appellate decision because it found that defendants lacked standing under federal law, and it remanded the case to the Ninth Circuit. Hollingsworth v. Perry, 133 S.Ct. 2652 (2013). On remand, and in accordance with the Supreme Court's opinion, the Ninth Circuit, per Judge Stephen Reinhardt, dismissed the appeal for lack of jurisdiction, and the clerk was directed to issue the mandate that would enable same-sex marriages to begin again in California, Perry v. Brown, 725 F.3d 1140 (9th Cir. 2013). All these developments effectively left the original 2010 opinion by Chief Judge Vaughn Walker, Northern District of California, as the final statement of the decision in the case. This opinion is discussed further later in this chapter.

11. U.S. v. Windsor, 133 S.Ct. 2675 (2013).

12. Obergefell v. Hodges, 135 S.Ct. 2584 (2015).

13. See generally *Obergefell*.

14. It should be noted that strict scrutiny is also applied by the federal courts in cases where a fundamental right has allegedly been infringed. See generally Stuart Biegel, "Reassessing the Applicability of Fundamental Rights Analysis: The Fourteenth Amendment and the Shaping of Educational Policy after Kadrmas v. Dickinson Public Schools," *Cornell Law Review* 74 (1989): 1078.

15. It should also be noted, however, that sometimes the term *heightened scrutiny* or *heightened level of judicial review* may refer to any level of review that is more strict than rational basis. See, e.g., Biegel, "Reassessing the Applicability of Fundamental Rights Analysis," 1087–95.

16. See U.S. v. Virginia, 518 U.S. 515, 524, 533 (1996), per Justice Ginsburg, on behalf of the Court: "A party seeking to uphold government action based on sex must establish an 'exceedingly persuasive justification' for the classification. . . . The burden of justification is demanding and it rests entirely on the State. . . . The justification must be genuine, not hypothesized or invented *post hoc*. And it must not rely on overbroad generalizations about the different talents, capacities, or preferences of males and females."

17. See Plyler v. Doe, 457 U.S. 202 (1982). See also Biegel, "Reassessing the Applicability of Fundamental Rights Analysis," 1096: "The heightened scrutiny

employed by the *Plyler* Court [balances] a recognized student interest against the interests of the school district and the state. . . . Under this emerging framework, intermediate judicial review is applied to protect burdened classes that have been denied these important interests. A favorable decision in a school setting typically requires the identification of at least (1) the important interest in education, (2) the right to equal opportunity, and (3) an arguably burdened class of injured plaintiffs."

18. Lawrence v. Texas, 539 U.S. 558, 575 (2003). For an overview of the *Lawrence* case and its groundbreaking holding that state laws prohibiting homosexual relations between consenting adults violate the Fourteenth Amendment, see chapter 1 of this book.

19. *Lawrence,* at 579–80 (O'Connor, J., concurring).

20. In Witt v. Dept. of Air Force, 527 F.3d 806 (9th Cir. 2008), for example, the Ninth Circuit determined not only that the *Lawrence* ruling was applicable to a former air force major's challenge to "Don't Ask, Don't Tell" but also that *"Lawrence* requires something more than traditional rational basis review" (819). See also Nan D. Hunter, "Twenty-First Century Equal Protection: Making Law in an Interregnum," *Georgetown Journal of Gender and Law* 7 (2006): 141 (identifying a heightened rational basis in *Lawrence* that could benefit LGBT plaintiffs in future discrimination cases).

See, generally, the briefs of the respondent Edith Windsor and the United States in *U.S. v. Windsor,* the 2013 case that found portions of the Defense of Marriage Act (DOMA) unconstitutional. Both briefs argued that the Court should, consistent with the appellate panel, apply heightened scrutiny to the alleged violations of the Equal Protection Clause. Brief on the Merits for Respondent Edith Schlain Windsor, U.S. v. Windsor, 2013 WL 701228, February 26, 2013 (arguing in part I that because DOMA discriminates on the basis of sexual orientation, it triggers, and fails, heightened scrutiny, and arguing in Part II that DOMA [also] fails rational basis); Brief for the United States on the Merits Question, U.S. v. Windsor, 2013 WL 683048, February 22, 2013 (first noting that the appellate panel in *Windsor* applied heightened scrutiny, then arguing that "classifications based on sexual orientation should be subject to heightened scrutiny" [and if not, then they should be subject to a heightened rational basis per Justice O'Connor in *Lawrence*]. The Court majority, however, while deciding in favor of Windsor, declined to follow these recommendations at that time).

21. Perry v. Schwarzenegger, 704 F.Supp.2d 941 (2010).

22. *Schwarzenegger,* at 997.

23. See Perry v. Brown, 725 F.3d 968 (9th Cir. 2013) (dissolving the stay); Perry v. Brown, 725 F.3d 1140 (9th Cir. 2013) (dismissing the appeal).

24. For personal perspectives on the Proposition 8 litigation in federal court, see, e.g., Theodore Olson and David Boies, *Redeeming the Dream: The Case for*

Marriage Equality (New York: Viking Press, 2014) (written by the lead attorneys for the plaintiffs in the case). See generally Kenji Yoshino, *Speak Now: Marriage Equality on Trial* (London: Crown, 2015) (focusing on the twelve-day trial and providing important legal and public policy context).

25. See In Re Marriage Cases, 43 Cal.4th 757, 840–41; 76 Cal.Rptr.3d 683, 751 (2008). It should be noted that the Hawaii Supreme Court, in the 1993 case of Baehr v. Lewin, 74 Haw. 530, 852 P.2d 44 (1993), did hold that its state's ban on same-sex marriage was a "sex-based classification" subject to strict scrutiny, but—unlike the California Supreme Court in 2008—it explicitly did not hold that "homosexuals" were a suspect class.

26. Strauss v. Horton, 46 Cal.4th 364, 411–12; 93 Cal.Rptr.3d 591, 627 (2009). The portion of Chief Judge Ronald George's opinion that provided a limited exception for the word *marriage* was subsequently overruled, implicitly, by *Obergefell v. Hodges*.

27. Kerrigan v. Comm'r of Pub. Health, 289 Conn. 135, 957 A.2d 407, 423–24 and n19 (2008).

28. See Varnum v. Brien, 763 N.W.2d 862, 889–96 (2009).

29. Obergefell v. Hodges, 135 S.Ct. at 2595, 2599, 2602–5.

30. With this language, Justice Kennedy recalls the words of President Abraham Lincoln in his Gettysburg Address (1863), which describe this nation as being founded on the dual precepts of liberty and equality: "Four score and seven years ago, our fathers brought forth on this continent a new nation, *conceived in liberty, and dedicated to the proposition that all men are created equal*" (emphasis added).

31. See *Obergefell*.

32. For examples of commentators who discerned, for various reasons, the applicability of a heightened level of judicial review in the *Obergefell* case, see, e.g., Craig Green, "Turning the Kaleidoscope: Toward a Theory of Interpreting Precedents," *North Carolina Law Review* 94 (2016): 379, 471 ("Perhaps the case should apply to many forms of LGBT rights, thereby highlighting the Court's references to sexual orientation as 'immutable.' Under that scenario, every state-imposed effort to 'demean,' 'stigmatize,' 'harm,' or otherwise discriminate based on sexual orientation might be presumptively unconstitutional. This could be called a 'heightened scrutiny' interpretation of *Obergefell*, although the Court did not use that technical term"); Autumn L. Bernhardt, "The Profound and Intimate Power of the *Obergefell* Decision: Equal Dignity as a Suspect Class," *Tulane Journal of Law and Sexuality* 25 (2016): 1, 11 ("The *Obergefell* opinion did not use the magic words of "heightened scrutiny," but it is clear from the language and disposition of the case that the Supreme Court gave same-sex couples exactly the ruling and the underlying reasoning they asked for in their briefs. . . . *Obergefell* applied heightened scrutiny review in practice by allocating the burden to the

States seeking to uphold the marriage bans, identifying marriage as a fundamental right, and discussing the four elements of the Suspect Class Doctrine under equal protection analysis"); Tobias Barrington Wolff, "The Three Voices of *Obergefell*," *L.A. Lawyer* 38 (2015): 28 ("It is too soon to know how much has changed following" *Obergefell*, "but it is apparent that it is a new day. . . . *Obergefell* did not expressly hold that antigay laws provoke heightened judicial scrutiny. . . . But the components of a core equal protection holding are scattered throughout the majority opinion"); Jack B. Harrison, "At Long Last Marriage," *American University Journal of Gender, Social Policy, and the Law* 24 (2015): 1, 15, 53 ("In *Obergefell*, Justice Kennedy employed some form of heightened scrutiny, but one not rooted in the traditional concerns about suspect groups or classifications").

For additional perspectives on the case, see generally Neo Khuu, "*Obergefell v. Hodges*: Kinship Formation, Interest Convergence, and the Future of LGBTQ Rights," *UCLA Law Review* 64 (2017): 184.

33. Richard Socarides, "The Year of Marriage Equality," *The New Yorker*, January 18, 2015, http://www.newyorker.com/news/news-desk/year-marriage -equality.

34. It should be noted that California and Maine had also legalized same-sex marriage during this time, only to have the decisions reversed by the voters (California Proposition 8 in 2008 and Maine Question 1 in 2009). In 2012, the Maine voters reversed their decision and approved same-sex marriage, and as discussed earlier in this chapter, Proposition 8 was invalidated by the federal courts beginning with a trial court decision in 2010, and marriages began again in that state three years later.

35. In 2001, less than 40 percent had favored same-sex marriage, and almost 60 percent opposed it. By 2016, 55 percent favored it. See Pew Research Center Public Opinion on Same-Sex Marriage, May 12, 2016, http://www.pewforum .org/2016/05/12/changing-attitudes-on-gay-marriage/.

36. "The one-year anniversary of marriage equality in the U.S.," the author wrote, "comes at a watershed moment for LGBT organizers, who are launching new initiatives and forging fresh alliances amid a conservative backlash." See Peter Montgomery, "One Year after Marriage Equality, Progress and Peril for LGBT Americans," *The American Prospect*, June 30, 2016.

37. See, e.g., Stuart Biegel, "Unfinished Business," *NYU Journal of Legislation and Public Policy* 14 (2011): 357, 365–66 (documenting the resistance to anti-bullying programs in 2010 and 2011): "Anti-bullying initiatives—critical in an era in which bullying in schools is often rampant and out of control—have been derided as covert attempts to advance a 'homosexual agenda.' Although anti-bullying campaigns strive to improve the school environment for all students, the disproportionate victimization of gay and gender non-conforming students in public schools—coupled with the increased reporting of teen suicides linked

to anti-gay bullying—has led to efforts to curtail homophobia in K–12 settings. Yet . . . in the fall of 2010, for example, both the mainstream media and the online blogs were filled with charges that 'liberals and gay rights groups are using the antibullying banner' to pursue their 'hidden' agenda, as is evident in the following excerpt: 'In tense community hearings, some parents made familiar arguments that innocent youngsters were not ready for explicit language. [Others] . . . saw a darker purpose. . . . Barely heard was the plea of Harlan Reidmohr, 18, who graduated last spring and said he was relentlessly tormented and slammed against lockers after coming out during his freshman year. Through his years in the Helena schools, he said at [a] school board meeting, sexual orientation was never once discussed in the classroom, and "I believe this led to a lot of the . . . harassment I faced"' (Erik Eckholm, "In Schools' Efforts to End Bullying, Some See Agenda," *N.Y. Times,* Nov. 6, 2010). Thus the right of gay and transgender persons to live their lives openly is highly contested today in America's public schools. The opposition to anything gay-positive in education settings reflects discomfort with and prejudice against LGBTs. Evidence shows that discomfort and prejudice are especially acute among those who may have had little or no contact with openly LGBT persons throughout their lives."

38. Franklin, "Psychosocial Motivations of Hate Crime Perpetrators."

39. See FBI/UCR, Hate Crime Statistics, 2011, https://ucr.fbi.gov/hate-crime/2011/hate-crime. Although *bullying* is defined differently in different contexts and by different researchers, policy makers, and law enforcement officials, most experts would agree that "anti-gay hate crimes" are a form of bullying. It should be noted that efforts to combat bullying in the early years of the marriage equality backlash did have a positive impact by 2013–15. See, e.g., a U.S. Department of Education report citing 2013 data from the National Center for Education Statistics showing lower percentages of students reporting being bullied, https://www.ed.gov/news/press-releases/new-data-show-decline-school-based-bullying; see also a GLSEN report citing 2015 data from its National School Climate Survey showing that "LGBTQ students experience pervasive harassment and discrimination, but school-based supports can make a big difference," https://www.glsen.org/article/lgbtq-secondary-students-still-face-hostility-school-consider-able-improvements-show-progress. However, in the aftermath of the 2016 elections, numerous reports documented a new rise in hate-related crimes generally, which included a noticeable uptick in anti-LGBT activity. See, e.g., Anna North, "A Wave of Harassment after Trump's Victory," *New York Times,* November 18, 2016; Sarah Maslin Nir, "Finding Hate Crimes on the Rise, Leaders Condemn Vicious Acts," *New York Times,* December 5, 2016; Andrew Solomon, "Fear and Loathing in Trump's America," *The New Yorker,* February 3, 2017.

40. See Erin Fuchs, "Expert: 'Desperate Anger' Is Driving the Rise in Anti-gay Hatred," *Business Insider,* May 21, 2013.

41. See Frank Bruni, "Do Gays Unsettle You?," *New York Times,* February 7, 2015.

42. Matt Baum, "Marriage Equality Backlash Has Only Just Begun," *The Advocate,* January 21, 2015.

43. See "New Study Sheds Light on Problems Facing LGBTQ Youth Experiencing Homelessness," Williams Institute, June 10, 2015, http://williamsinstitute .law.ucla.edu/press/press-releases/new-study-sheds-light-on-problems-facing -lgbtq-youth-experiencing-homelessness/. "Cisgender" persons have gender identities consistent with the sex they were assigned at birth.

44. See "New Study Sheds Light."

45. See Reina Gattuso, "Why Are There So Many LGBT Youth in Prison?," July 17, 2015, http://www.attn.com/. See also chapter 3 of this book for additional perspectives on the mistreatment of LGBT youth—by faculty, staff, and fellow students—and the inevitable consequences of such mistreatment.

46. Katie Rogers, "Seventeen Transgender Killings Contrast with Growing Visibility," *New York Times,* August 20, 2015.

47. Frank Bruni, "Gay and Marked for Death," *New York Times,* August 21, 2015.

48. Richard Socarides, "North Carolina and the Gay Rights Backlash," *The New Yorker,* March 28, 2016.

49. See Socarides.

50. Amber Phillips, "2016 Could Be a Very Difficult Year for LGBT Activists," *Washington Post,* February 11, 2016.

51. Richard Wolf, "Gay Marriage Victory at the Supreme Court Triggering Backlash," *USA Today,* May 29, 2016.

52. Kareem Abdul-Jabbar, "Every GOP Candidate Is Wrong about Political Correctness," *Washington Post,* February 22, 2016. Abdul-Jabbar, the all-time leading scorer in the National Basketball Association, has become a noted commentator on national affairs. He is the author or coauthor of several best-selling books.

53. See Abdul-Jabbar: "'Political correctness is killing our country,' Donald Trump warned on the 'Today' show last month. Ben Carson told Bill O'Reilly last summer, when he was the leading Republican presidential candidate, that political correctness was 'destroying our nation.' Ted Cruz criticized President Obama's ISIS strategy by claiming 'political correctness is killing people.' Carly Fiorina said, 'Political correctness is now choking candid conversation.' Marco Rubio complained that he doesn't discuss his faith in public because 'I had been conditioned by political correctness.' Jeb Bush agreed: 'The political correctness of our country needs to be shattered.'"

54. Abdul-Jabbar.

55. See Ralph Ellis, Ashley Fantz, Faith Karimi, and Eliott C. McLaughlin,

"Orlando Shooting," CNN, June 13, 2016, https://www.cnn.com/2016/06/12/us/orlando-nightclub-shooting/index.html. See also Jim Downs, "Before Orlando, There Was New Orleans," *New York Times,* June 13, 2016.

56. See Pete Williams, Tracy Connor, Erik Ortiz, and Stephanie Gosk, "Gunman Omar Mateen Described as Belligerent, Racist, and Toxic," June 13, 2016, http://www.nbcnews.com/.

57. See Jeremy Diamond, "Donald Trump to LGBT Community: I'm a 'Real Friend,'" CNN, June 13, 2016, https://edition.cnn.com/2016/06/13/politics/donald-trump-lgbt-community/index.html. Reacting to Trump's comments in a positive manner, Gregory Angelo, the president of the Log Cabin Republicans, which represents LGBT Republicans, praised Trump's comments as "historic" and said his outreach showed true leadership: "'Donald Trump here is showing leadership on LGBT issues and we haven't seen that from Republican presidential nominees in decades. Certainly we've never seen a nominee so directly engage with and seek the support from LGBT voters,' Angelo said in an interview. . . . 'Given his statements . . . and his actions, there is every indication to believe that Mr. Trump would do no harm on LGBT equality and might actually advance LGBT equality under his presidency.'"

58. See Helena Andrews-Dyer, "Donald Trump Says Caitlyn Jenner Can Use Whatever Bathroom She Wants at Trump Tower," *Washington Post,* April 21, 2016.

59. See Gabby Morrongiello, "Trump Praises GOP for Applauding His Vow to Protect LGBT Americans," *Washington Examiner,* July 21, 2016.

60. With regard to Vice President Mike Pence, see, e.g., Andrew Solomon, "Fear and Loathing in Trump's America," *The New Yorker,* February 3, 2017: "During his tenure in Congress, Mike Pence, as head of the Republican Study Committee, supported a constitutional amendment against gay marriage, opposed the repeal of the military ban on openly gay soldiers, and averred that 'societal collapse was always brought about following an advent of the deterioration of marriage and family,' suggesting that gay families would operationalize such a disruption of the social order. . . . He later proposed cutting funding for AIDS research and diverting the money to 'ex-gay' therapy programs."

With regard to Attorney General Jeff Sessions, see, e.g., Jennifer Bendery, "Pick Any LGBTQ Rights Issue. Jeff Sessions Has Voted against It," *Huffington Post,* February 10, 2017: "Donald Trump . . . tapped one of the most anti-gay politicians in Washington to be the nation's next top lawyer. . . . Jeff Sessions . . . has consistently opposed pro-LGBTQ legislation throughout his 20 years in Congress. He voted in support of a constitutional ban on same-sex marriage, against taking up a bill providing workplace discrimination protections for LGBTQ people, against repealing the military's 'don't ask, don't tell' policy, and—two times—against expanding the definition of hate crimes to include attacks on people because of their sexual orientation and gender identity. In 2014, a year after the Supreme Court struck down part of the now-defunct Defense of Marriage Act, Sessions co-sponsored a bill that would allow the state definition of marriage to supersede the federal definition."

61. Michael D. Shear and Charlie Savage, "In One Day, Trump Administration Lands 3 Punches against Gay Rights," *New York Times,* July 27, 2017.

62. Linda Greenhouse, "The Supreme Court and the Politics of Fear," *New York Times,* July 5, 2015.

63. See Greenhouse.

64. See Barbara Bradley Hagerty, "Religious Undercurrent Ripples in Anti-gay Bullying," *NPR,* October 26, 2010.

65. See, generally, Dennis Romboy, "LDS Church, LGBT Advocates Back Anti-discrimination Religious Rights Bill," *Deseret News,* March 5, 2015. "We have to find a way to live together," law professor Robin Fretwell Wilson stated. "We just can't endlessly be litigating against each other."

66. See Laurie Goodstein, "Evangelicals Open Door to Debate on Gay Rights," *New York Times,* June 8, 2015: "Youth ministers and chaplains are studying how to respond to students struggling with their sexual identities. Governing boards are re-examining their policies on allowing openly gay people in Bible studies. And pastors are preaching and writing about, rather than ignoring, the recent books arguing that the Bible can be read to support same-sex marriage.

"Few are dropping their opposition. But aware that they are seen by many as bigots, some evangelical leaders are trying to figure out how to stand firm without alienating the rising share of Americans—especially younger ones—who know gay people and support gay rights, or who may themselves come out as gay."

67. Samuel G. Freedman, "On Religion: Push within Religions for Gay Marriage Gets Little Attention," *New York Times,* July 24, 2015.

68. Freedman.

69. "Closely held corporations" are those where the stock is not publicly traded on a stock exchange.

70. Burwell v. Hobby Lobby Stores, Inc., 134 S.Ct. 2751, 2766 (2014).

71. *Hobby Lobby,* at 2763–64. It should be noted that religious employers, such as churches, and religious nonprofit organizations with religious objections to providing such coverage were already effectively exempt from this mandate.

72. *Hobby Lobby,* at 2785. In light of this holding, the majority declined to address the free exercise clause issue under the First Amendment.

73. Kevin Russell, "*Hobby Lobby* and Claims for Religious Exemptions from Anti-discrimination Laws," *SCOTUSblog,* June 30, 2014, http://www.scotus blog.com/2014/06/analysis-hobby-lobby-and-claims-for-religious-exemptions -from-anti-discrimination-laws/.

74. Douglas Nejaime and Reva B. Siegel, "Conscience Wars: Complicity-

Based Conscience Claims in Religion and Politics," *Yale Law Journal* 124 (2015): 2516.

75. Masterpiece Cakeshop LTD v. Colorado Civil Rights Commission, 138 S.Ct. 1719 (2018). By a vote of 7–2, the Court found that because some members of the state's civil rights commission had made statements hostile to religion, the baker's Free Exercise Clause rights had been violated. Justice Kennedy emphasized that this was a narrow ruling and suggested that another case with similar facts but lacking the hostile statements might be decided differently.

76. Nejaime and Siegel, "Conscience Wars," 2518–19.

77. Nejaime and Siegel, 2532–33.

78. Nejaime and Siegel, 2564–65.

79. Michael Barbaro and Erik Ekholm, "Indiana Law Denounced as Invitation to Discriminate against Gays," *New York Times,* March 27, 2015.

80. See Bob Egelko, "Meaning of 'Religious Freedom' Very Different Than in '93," *San Francisco Chronicle,* March 31, 2015.

81. See Sandhya Somashekhar, "Christian Activists: Indiana Law Tried to Shield Companies against Gay Marriage," *Washington Post,* April 3, 2015.

82. See generally Somashekhar: "Critics of the laws say Conkle is splitting hairs. Refusing any type of service amounts to discrimination, they say, and should not be permitted.

"During legislative debate, the Indiana lawmakers who sponsored the measure did not raise the plight of Christian wedding vendors. Instead, they cited last year's Supreme Court decision in the *Hobby Lobby* case, which gave businesses the right to refuse to provide certain contraceptives to their workers through company health plans. That case, they said, demonstrated the need to strengthen protections for religious liberties generally."

83. Obergefell v. Hodges, 135 S.Ct. 2584, 2639 (2015), Thomas, J., dissenting. It should be noted that each of the four dissenting justices wrote his own dissenting opinion. Roberts filed a dissenting opinion, in which Scalia and Thomas joined. Scalia filed a dissenting opinion, in which Thomas joined. Thomas filed a dissenting opinion, in which Scalia joined. Alito filed a dissenting opinion, in which Scalia and Thomas joined.

84. Richard A. Posner, "The Chief Justice's Dissent Is Heartless," *Slate,* June 27, 2015.

85. See Amber Phillips, "Mississippi's New Law Allowing Refusal of Service to LGBT People Is the Most Sweeping Yet," *Washington Post,* April 5, 2016.

86. See Mark Tran, "UK Warns LGBT Tourists of North Carolina and Mississippi Travel," *Guardian,* April 25, 2016.

87. See Barber v. Bryant, 860 F.3d 345 (5th Cir. 2017). In January 2018, the U.S. Supreme Court denied certiorari, letting the Fifth Circuit's decision stand. See Kathryn Rubino, "Supreme Court Refuses to Act in the Face of Extreme Anti-

LGBTQ Law," *Above the Law,* January 8, 2018, https://abovethelaw.com/2018/01/supreme-court-refuses-to-act-in-the-face-of-extreme-anti-lgbtq-law/.

88. Everdeen Mason, Aaron Williams, and Kennedy Elliott, "The Dramatic Rise in State Efforts to Limit LGBT Rights," *Washington Post,* June 11, 2016, https://www.washingtonpost.com/graphics/national/lgbt-legislation/?hpid=hp_no-name_graphic-story-a%3Ahomepage%2Fstory.

89. Douglas Laycock and Thomas C. Berg, "Protecting Same-Sex Marriage and Religious Liberty," *Virginia Law Review in Brief* 99 (2013): 1. See also Thomas C. Berg, "Religious Exemptions and Third-Party Harms," *Federalist Society Review* 17 (2016): 50.

90. Douglas Nejaime and Reva B. Siegel, "Conscience Wars: Complicity-Based Conscience Claims in Religion and Politics," *Yale Law Journal* 124 (2015): 2516, 2586–89.

91. See, generally, Marie Killmond, "Why Is Vaccination Different? A Comparative Analysis of Religious Exemptions," *Columbia Law Review* 117 (2017): 913.

92. These "rights" movements include, but are not limited to, the African American civil rights movement, the Chicano–Latino rights movement, the movement for greater equality for Asians and Pacific Islanders, the women's rights movement, the veterans rights movement, and the disability rights movement. Along with the LGBT rights movements, they all have their similarities, and they all have their differences. But at the same time, they all borrow from each other, and they all have learned from each other. In addition, it must be noted that many people have participated in multiple rights movements. Many veterans, for example, are also women, also lesbians, also people of color, and also people with disabilities.

93. See chapters 5 and 7 of this book for additional details regarding the FAIR Education Act.

94. Four states plus the District of Columbia had banned conversion therapy for minors by 2015: California (2012), D.C. (2014), Oregon (2015), New Jersey (2015), and Illinois (2015). The number has continued to increase in recent years, with Vermont (2016), New Mexico (2017), Nevada (2017), Connecticut (2017), Rhode Island (2017), and Washington (2018) joining a growing list. See LGBT Movement Advancement Project (MAP), Conversion Therapy Laws, data current as of March 29, 2018, http://www.lgbtmap.org/equality-maps/conversion_therapy. In addition, although New York does not have an outright ban, the state "effectively prohibits conversion therapy through administrative regulations." See Amy B. Wang, "Supreme Court Upholds California's Ban on Gay 'Conversion Therapy,'" *Washington Post,* May 2, 2017.

95. Also see chapter 8 for further discussion and analysis of the NCAA's groundbreaking work in this area over the past five to ten years.

96. See Hively v. Ivy Tech Community College of Indiana, 853 F.3d 339 (7th Cir. 2017).

97. Whitaker v. Kenosha School District, 858 F.3d 1034 (7th Cir. 2017). See chapter 9 of this book for additional information regarding the *Whitaker* case and related litigation and legislation.

98. Christian Legal Society Chapter of the University of California, Hastings College of the Law v. Martinez, 561 U.S. 661 (2010).

99. *Christian Legal Society,* at 672 (emphasis added). Any Hastings student could attend the meetings, but only those who complied with the bylaws could be voting members and run for office.

100. See *Christian Legal Society,* at 698–99, Stevens, J., concurring.

101. The viewpoint discrimination doctrine may be raised in First Amendment freedom of expression cases by students who believe that their expression has been limited in some fashion because school officials disagree with the students' viewpoints and are discriminating against them as a result. Its clearest articulation in a higher education setting can be found in Rosenberger v. Rector & Visitors of the University of Virginia, 515 U.S. 819 (1995). As stated by Justice Kennedy for the majority of the Court, "in the realm of private speech or expression, government regulation may not favor one speaker over another. Discrimination against speech because of its message is presumed to be unconstitutional. These rules informed our determination that the government offends the First Amendment when it imposes financial burdens on certain speakers based on the content of their expression. When the government targets not subject matter, but particular views taken by speakers on a subject, the violation of the First Amendment is all the more blatant. Viewpoint discrimination is thus an egregious form of content discrimination. The government must abstain from regulating speech when the specific motivating ideology or the opinion or perspective of the speaker is the rationale for the restriction." *Rosenberger,* at 828–29.

At the K–12 level, the doctrine is somewhat unsettled, although recent cases have found that if the *Tinker* rule applies (e.g., if material and substantial disruption is a likely result of the student expression), then the expression may be banned, even if the ban constitutes viewpoint discrimination. See, e.g., Dariano v. Morgan Hill USD, 767 F.3d 764, 780 (9th Cir. 2014); Harper v. Poway USD, 445 F.3d 1166, 1184–85 (9th Cir. 2006).

102. *Christian Legal Society,* at 668–69.

103. Keeton v. Anderson-Wiley, 664 F.3d 865 (11th Cir. 2011).

104. *Keeton,* at 874–75.

In Ward v. Polite, 667 F.3d 727 (6th Cir. 2012), the Sixth Circuit considered a higher education counseling case with facts that were very similar to those in *Keeton.* Julea Ward was also a student in a counseling program at a state university (Eastern Michigan), and she was also disciplined because of issues that she had raised—based on her religious beliefs—with the counseling of a gay client. However, the appellate panel ruled in favor of Ward, distinguishing *Keeton.* The key difference was that Ward had only requested that the gay client be referred to another counselor. Unlike Keeton, she did not seek to "convert" the client. See Ward at 740–41.

105. See David Jackson, "Obama Backs Efforts to End 'Conversion Therapy,'" *USA Today*, April 9, 2015.

106. King v. N.J., 767 F.3d 216 (3d Cir. 2014). Cert. denied, 2015.

107. See Pastors Protecting Youth v. Madigan, 237 F.Supp.3d 746 (N.D. Ill., Eastern Division 2017).

108. Welch v. Brown, 834 F.3d 1041 (9th Cir. 2016). Cert. denied, 2017 WL 58598 (May 2017).

109. Martha Nussbaum, for example, has argued that the "gay panic" and "trans panic" defenses are reminiscent of earlier defenses that were commonly used to justify attacks against Jews, blacks, and other minority groups. See Nussbaum, *Hiding from Humanity: Disgust, Shame, and the Law* (Princeton, N.J.: Princeton University Press, 2004).

110. See, e.g., David Alan Perkiss, "A New Strategy for Neutralizing the Gay Panic Defense at Trial: Lessons from the Lawrence King Case," *UCLA Law Review* 60 (2013): 778, 780.

111. See Pete Kane, "California's Ban on 'Gay Panic' and 'Transgender Panic' Is a Model for Other States," *San Francisco Weekly*, September 30, 2014.

112. See Mark Joseph Stern, "'Gay Panic' Is No Longer a Legitimate Reason to Murder Someone in Illinois," *Slate*, June 1, 2017.

113. See Boy Scouts of America et al v. Dale, 530 U.S. 640 (2000). The five justices who voted for the Boy Scouts and upheld the ban were Chief Justice Rehnquist and Justices Kennedy, O'Connor, Scalia, and Thomas.

114. See Elizabeth Weise, "Boy Scouts Vote to Allow Gay Members," *USA Today*, May 23, 2013.

115. Todd Leopold, "Boy Scouts Change Policy on Gay Leaders," CNN, July 28, 2015, https://www.cnn.com/2015/07/27/us/boy-scouts-gay-leaders-feat/index.html.

116. Scott Taylor and Ben Lockhart, "Boy Scouts of America Announces That It Will Allow Transgender Youth in Boys-Only Program," *Deseret News*, January 30, 2017.

117. See Hively v. Ivy Tech Community College of Indiana, 853 F.3d 339 (7th Cir. 2017).

118. See Biegel, "Unfinished Business," 358–60: "In June of 1994, during the early years of the Clinton administration, Senator Edward M. Kennedy introduced the Employment Non-Discrimination Act (ENDA), which sought to ban employment discrimination on the basis of sexual orientation. Despite the failure of Congress to pass the act, even as poll data over the next fifteen years began to show that a clear majority of Americans endorsed its goals, Senator Kennedy remained a staunch supporter of this legislation for the rest of his life. Indeed, in

August 2009—less than a month before his death—he joined three other senators in introducing a 'transgender-inclusive' version of the bill, which would prohibit discrimination on the basis of both sexual orientation and gender identity.

"By late 2010, despite the stated commitment of President Barack Obama and the Democratic Party leaders in the House of Representatives, efforts to pass ENDA had stalled again. Although some prominent Republicans became involved in efforts to establish full equality for lesbian, gay, bisexual, and transgender (LGBT) persons throughout the country, congressional Republicans appeared to be united in their opposition to the legislation, and not all Democrats could be counted on to support it. ENDA remained, on every level, unfinished business."

119. See Stuart Biegel, Robert Kim, and Kevin Welner, *Education and the Law*, 4th ed. (St. Paul, Minn.: West Academic, 2016), 1055: "Seeking to address [the] challenges that remain, lawmakers in the House and the Senate [recently] introduced the Equality Act, a bill that would broaden legal protections by amending the Civil Rights Act of 1964, the Fair Housing Act and the Equal Credit Opportunity Act to explicitly cover sexual orientation and gender identity."

120. See Mark Joseph Stern, "A Thunderbolt from the Seventh Circuit," Slate, April 5, 2017. Indeed, in February 2018, the U.S. Court of Appeals for the Second Circuit followed suit, deciding by a 10–3 margin in Zarda v. Altitude Express, Inc. that discrimination on the basis of sexual orientation is a form of sex discrimination barred by Title VII of the Civil Rights Act of 1964. Although it was not an education-related case, the fact that a second U.S. court of appeals came to the same conclusion with regard to the applicability of Title VII to sexual orientation discrimination has the potential to further strengthen the rights of gays and lesbians in the workplace under federal law. See Zarda v. Altitude Express, Inc., 883 F.3d 100 (2d Cir. 2018).

3. Emerging Rights of LGBT Students

1. Although the discussions in this chapter also impact transgender students to the extent that controversies may arise regarding their sexual identities, the unique nature of the challenges faced by trans persons in the public schools lend themselves to a completely separate chapter. Thus issues regarding gender identity, gender-expansive behavior, and controversies impacting persons who identify within one or more of the categories that are typically viewed as composing the "transgender" umbrella are examined at length in chapter 9.

2. See Tinker v. Des Moines Indep. Commun. Sch. Dist., 393 U.S. 503 (1969): "First Amendment rights, applied in light of the special characteristics of the school environment, are available to teachers and students. It can hardly be argued that either students or teachers shed their constitutional rights to

freedom of speech or expression at the schoolhouse gate. This has been the un-mistakable holding of this Court for almost 50 years."

3. See *Tinker.*

4. See, e.g., Chandler v. McMinnville Sch. Dist., 978 F.2d 524, 529 (9th Cir. 1992), and Karp v. Becken, 477 F.2d 171, 175 (9th Cir. 1973).

5. See Lavine v. Blaine School District, 257 F.3d 981 (9th Cir. 2001). In synthesizing these principles, the Ninth Circuit also looked to its 1992 decision Chandler v. McMinnville Sch. Dist., 978 F.2d 524 (9th Cir. 1992), where middle school students had been disciplined for wearing provocative political buttons that supported striking teachers and criticized "scabs" during a bitter school strike.

6. See *Lavine,* at 989: "In applying *Tinker,* we look to the totality of the rel-evant facts. We look not only to James' [Lavine's] actions, but to all of the cir-cumstances confronting the school officials that might reasonably portend dis-ruption." Thus, in *Lavine,* the Ninth Circuit found that the school district did not violate plaintiff's rights when it expelled James Lavine on an emergency basis for events arising out of his writing of a poem that read, in part, "As I approched, the classroom door, I drew my gun and, threw open the door, Bang, Bang, Bang-Bang. / When it all was over, 28 were, dead, and all I remember, was not felling, any remorce, for I felt, I was, clensing my soul."

7. Saxe v. State College Area Sch. Dist., 240 F.3d 200, 211 (3d Cir. 2001).

8. Bethel Sch. Dist. No. 403 v. Fraser, 478 U.S. 675 (1986); Hazelwood v. Kuhlmeier, 484 U.S. 260 (1988); Morse v. Frederick, 551 U.S. 393 (2007).

9. See, e.g., Anthony B. Schutz, "Public School Restrictions on 'Offensive' Student Speech in Boroff v. Van Wert City Bd. Of Educ.: Has Fraser's 'Exception' Swallowed Tinker's Rule?," *Nebraska Law Review* 81 (2002): 443, 446, arguing that the Sixth Circuit's application of the *Fraser* rule to the facts of the *Boroff* case "swallows the generally applicable rules," and Lawrence A. Jegen III, *"Tin-ker* and Student Free Speech Rights: A Functionalist Alternative," *Indiana Law Review* 41 (2008): 105, 131, making the case, in light of recent developments, for either a "dramatic redefinition" of "the scope of disruption or rights-violation" or "a more candid and explicit modification of *Tinker."*

10. Judge Alito, for example, writing on behalf of a unanimous Third Cir-cuit panel in 2001, characterized the two cases as illustrative of the point that "since *Tinker,* the Supreme Court has carved out a number of narrow categories of speech that a school may restrict even without the threat of substantial disrup-tion." *Saxe,* at 212–14.

11. See Morse v. Frederick, 551 U.S. 422 (Alito, J., concurring). In *Morse,* stu-dents displayed a banner with the words "Bong Hits for Jesus" outside of school grounds as the Olympic torch relay passed in front of their school on its way through Juneau, Alaska. (Students had been given permission to leave school to

watch the relay pass by.) When the principal saw the sign, she insisted that it be taken down immediately, but one student refused to comply, was subsequently disciplined, and brought a lawsuit alleging a violation of his First Amendment rights. Chief Justice Roberts, writing for the majority, stated, consistent with principles set forth in *Tinker, Fraser,* and *Hazelwood,* "We hold that schools may take steps to safeguard those entrusted to their care from speech that can reasonably be regarded as encouraging illegal drug use. We conclude that the school officials in this case did not violate the First Amendment by confiscating the pro-drug banner and suspending the student responsible for it" (397). However, Justice Alito and Justice Kennedy, two of the five justices who joined the opinion in its entirety, wrote separately to emphasize their determination that the decision was a narrow one and highly fact specific (422).

12. See, e.g., DePinto v. Bayonne Board of Education, no. 06-5765, 2007 WL 2726534, *4 (D.N.J., Sept. 14, 2007): "*Morse* adds a third exception to *Tinker,* allowing a school to censor student speech that is 'reasonably viewed as promoting illegal drug use'" (citing Morse v. Frederick, 127 S.Ct., 2625).

It must be noted, however, that—in the decade since *Morse* was decided—the case has begun to emerge as a broader exception than it originally appeared to be. For example, some courts are applying *Morse* to uphold restrictions of student speech that may have nothing to do with drug use but may have the effect of endangering students in other ways. See, e.g., Judge Richard Posner's opinion in Nuxoll v. Indian Prairie School District, 523 F.3d 668 (7th Cir. 2008), construing *Morse* as potentially enabling educators to restrict speech that may have negative "psychological effects." Posner wrote that "if there is reason to think that a particular type of students' speech will lead to a decline in students test scores, an upsurge in truancy, or other [similar] symptoms of substantial disruption[,] the school can forbid the speech." *Nuxoll,* at 674. See also Harper v. Poway, No. 04CV1103 JAH(POR), Order Denying Plaintiff's Motion for Reconsideration, February 11, 2008, 6–10, interpreting *Morse* to enable school officials to "insulate vulnerable students from harmful speech."

13. Fricke v. Lynch, 491 F.Supp. 381 (D. R.I. 1980).

14. See Julie Scelfo, "Out at the Prom," *Newsweek,* June 9, 2003. The growth in the number of out students at high school proms can be linked, at least in part, to the fact that LGBT students appear to be coming out, on average, at a younger age. See Scelfo. See also John Cloud, "The Battle over Gay Teens," *Newsweek,* October 10, 2005, 43, which surveys the phenomenon of more gay teens coming out at younger ages and the attendant religious, familial, and educational issues.

15. See, e.g., Paul Chandler, "High School Diary: I Learned the Truth at Seventeen," *Advocate,* April 9, 2003, http://www.advocate.com/.

16. *Fricke,* at 383–84. It is important to note that the discipline issues and the mistreatment of Guilbert took place after the denial of his request and the

accompanying publicity regarding the principal's fear of violence and disruption. A different response by the principal, setting a positive tone and fostering a collaborative environment within the school community, may very well have led to a completely different outcome. Indeed, the warning of impending "violence" conceivably became a self-fulfilling prophecy, giving certain students the idea that they were *expected* to react in that way toward Guilbert. In fact, the court states that "perhaps one cannot be at all sure a totally different approach by Lynch might have kept the matter from reaching its present proportions." *Fricke,* at 384.

17. According to the court, "it was not until this April . . . [that] he had . . . 'come out of the closet' by publicly acknowledging his sexual orientation." *Fricke,* at 383.

18. *Fricke,* at 384.

19. *Fricke,* at 387.

20. In spring 2009, for example, Sergio Garcia, an openly gay senior at Fairfax High School in Los Angeles, not only was able to take a same-sex date to the prom but also was allowed to run for prom queen, an election that he won. See Ari B. Bloomkatz, "Fairfax High's Prom Queen Is a Guy," *Los Angeles Times,* May 28, 2009.

See also McMillen v. Itawamba County School Dist., 2010 WL 1172429 (N.D. Miss. 2010), where the U.S. District Court considered the case of Constance McMillen, an openly lesbian high school student in rural Mississippi who was prohibited from taking a same-sex date to the prom and also prohibited from wearing a tuxedo to the event. Relying in particular on *Fricke* and *Gay Students Organization of New Hampshire v. Bonner,* and also referencing *Romer v. Evans,* the court found "that Constance's First Amendment rights [were indeed] violated."

21. *Fricke,* at 388.

22. This pattern worked in the opposite direction at the higher education level, with religious student groups building on the victories of LGBT student groups to win victories against universities engaging in viewpoint discrimination. See Rosenberger v. Rector and Visitors of the University of Virginia, 515 U.S. 819 (1995). See also Alice Riener, "Pride and Prejudice: The First Amendment, the Equal Access Act, and the Legal Fight for Gay Student Groups in High Schools," *American University Journal of Gender, Social Policy, and Law* 14 (2006): 613, comparing the gay–straight alliance cases with the religious student group cases.

23. Colin v. Orange USD, 83 F. Supp. 2d 1135 (C.D. Cal. 2000).

24. *Colin,* at 1135 (emphasis added).

25. *Colin,* at 1142. Indeed, at the beginning of its analysis, the court in the *Colin* case referenced Justice Kennedy's description of the act in a 1990 U.S. Supreme Court ruling: "One of the consequences of the statute, as we now interpret it, is that clubs of a most controversial character might have access to the student life of high schools that in the past have given official recognition only to clubs of a more conventional kind."

See Bd. of Educ. v. Mergens, 496 U.S. 226 (1990), where the U.S. Supreme Court agreed with the plaintiff that the Equal Access Act, 20 U.S.C. §§ 4071–74 (2000), prohibits a high school "from denying a student religious group permission to meet on school premises during noninstructional time" and that the act, so construed, does not violate the Establishment Clause of the First Amendment. In so doing, the Court set forth guidelines for schools to follow pursuant to the act.

26. A central feature of the Equal Access Act and the U.S. Supreme Court cases construing it is that if the only student clubs on campus are those that are "curriculum related" (i.e., math clubs, science clubs), the school need not allow noncurriculum-related clubs to be formed. But once it allows even one noncurriculum-related club, it cannot prohibit other such clubs from being formed, absent additional facts, such as safety concerns or failure to comply with appropriate procedures.

27. *Colin*, at 1142, 1144–46.

28. Boyd County High School Gay Straight Alliance v. Bd. of Ed., 258 F. Supp. 2d 667 (E.D. Ky. 2003).

29. *Boyd*, at 670–71.

30. *Boyd*, at 688, citing 20 U.S.C. § 4071(c)(4) and 20 U.S.C. § 4071(f).

31. *Boyd*, at 690 (emphasis added). Plaintiffs challenging their school district's decisions to ban gay–straight alliances tend to prevail under the Equal Access Act. In addition to *Colin* and *Boyd*, see, e.g., East High Gay/Straight Alliance v. Board of Education of Salt Lake City Sch. Dist., 81 F. Supp. 2d 1166 (D. Utah 1999); East High School Prism Club v. Seidel, 95 F. Supp. 2d 1239 (D. Utah 2000); Gay–Straight Alliance Network v. Visalia Unified School District, 262 F.Supp.2d 1088 (E.D. Cal. 2001); Franklin Cent. Gay/Straight Alliance v. Franklin Township Community School Corporation, 2002 WL 32097530 (S.D. Ind. 2002); Gonzalez v. School Board of Okeechobee County, 571 F. Supp. 2d 1257 (S.D. Fla. 2008); and Gay–Straight Alliance of Yulee High School v. School Board of Nassau County, 602 F. Supp. 2d 1233 (M.D. Fla. 2009). But see also Caudillo v. Lubbock Independent School District, 311 F. Supp. 2d 550 (N.D. Tex. 2004), which ruled on behalf of the school district, finding prior lower court decisions to be distinguishable, in part, because the court was "unable to find that any of the cases involved a school [such as the one in Lubbock] that maintained an abstinence-only policy and banned any discussion of sexual activity on its campuses" (559).

In a gay–straight alliance case out of suburban Minneapolis–St. Paul that reached the appellate level in 2006, the Eighth Circuit Court of Appeals held in favor of the student group under the Equal Access Act, consistent with the broad general trend. The panel affirmed the decision of the lower court to grant "the same access for meetings, avenues of communication, and other miscellaneous rights afforded to groups referred to as 'curricular.'" Straights and Gays for Equality v. Osseo Area Schools—District No. 279, 471 F.3d 908, 909–10 (8th Cir. 2006).

32. See Henkle v. Gregory, 150 F. Supp. 2d 1067 (D. Nev. 2001).

33. *Henkle,* at 1069–71.

34. *Henkle,* at 1076.

35. Nguon v. Wolf, 517 F.Supp.2d 1177 (C.D. Cal. 2007).

36. *Nguon, at* 1188.

37. See *Nguon,* at 1182–91.

38. See Order, Nguon v. Wolf, D.C. no. CV-05–00868-JVS-MLG (C.D. Cal. March 5, 2008).

39. *Nguon,* at 1191–97.

40. Holning Lau, "Pluralism: A Principle for Children's Rights," *Harvard Civil Rights–Civil Liberties Law Review* 42 (2007): 317, 369–71.

41. Gillman v. Sch. Bd. for Holmes County, Fla., 567 F. Supp. 2d 1359 (N.D. Fla. 2008).

42. *Gillman,* at 1362.

43. *Gillman,* at 1363.

44. *Gillman,* at 1365–70.

45. In Nabozny's case, the court was "unable to garner any rational basis for permitting one student to assault another based on the victim's sexual orientation, and the defendants do not offer . . . one." Nabozny v. Podlesny, 92 F.3d 446 (7th Cir. 1996).

46. See Courtney Joslin and Eric Manke, "Fifteen Expensive Reasons Why Safe Schools Legislation Is in Your State's Best Interest," National Center for Lesbian Rights (NCLR) and Gay, Lesbian, and Straight Education Network (GLSEN), http://www.trans-parenting.com/. In all fifteen of the cases documented, the student either prevailed after trial or achieved a settlement; school districts paid anywhere from $40,000 to more than $1.1 million in settlements or judgments; the dollar figures do not include the districts' attorney's fees, which, in many cases, were far greater than the amount of the settlements themselves; and many of the lawsuits were brought and successfully won or settled in states that do not have state statutes prohibiting discrimination on the basis of sexual orientation, including Kentucky, Missouri, and Nevada.

47. Flores v. Morgan Hill USD, 324 F.3d 1130 (9th Cir. 2003).

48. See, generally, *Flores.* See also "Case Background: Flores v. Morgan Hill USD," American Civil Liberties Union, January 6, 2004, http://www.aclu.org/.

49. "Case Background."

50. See, generally, "Case Background." See also *Flores,* at 1138.

51. Adam Tanner, "California Students Get $1.1 Mln in Gay Taunting Case," Reuters, http://ww.reuters.com/.

52. See generally Ramirez v. LAUSD, Complaint (2004), available at http://ncflr.convio.net/site/DocServer/ramirez_v_lausd_complaint.pdf?docID=1521.

53. Catherine Lhamon, quoted in "ACLU of Southern California Stands Up for Gay and Lesbian High School Students Harassed by School Officials on Basis

of Sexual Orientation," press release, ACLU of Southern California, October, 28, 2004, http://www.aclusocal.org/.

54. *Ramirez,* Complaint, at 1–2.

55. *Ramirez,* at 12–13.

56. Other claims were based on Title IX, and additional claims were set forth based on antidiscrimination provisions in both the California Constitution and the California Education Code.

57. See *Ramirez,* Complaint, at 17–18.

58. See KSA 2004 Supp. 21-3522.

59. State v. Limon, 280 Kan. 275; 122 P.3d 22 (Kan. 2005).

60. See State v. Limon, 280 Kan., 286, 291, 293–94; 122 P.3d, 29, 32–34.

61. These cases are generally brought under state law negligence principles and might vary from state to state because of immunity doctrines and differing statutory schemes. The extent to which a school owes its students duties for injuries that students inflict on other students is subject to litigation. See, e.g., Seiwert v. Spencer-Owen Community School Corp., 497 F. Supp. 2d 942 (S.D. Ind. 2007) (where the federal court ruled that plaintiff, after experiencing two years of alleged bullying on the basis of his perceived sexual orientation, could state a claim for the alleged negligent supervision of a school bus driver under Indiana law). See also A.E. v. Harrisburg School Dist. No. 7, 2012 WL 4794314 (D. Or. 2012) (where the Oregon court ruled that plaintiff student could state a claim for negligence on the part of school officials for failing to intervene to stop the apparent bullying on the basis of perceived sexual orientation). Although neither plaintiff identified as gay at the time of the litigation, extensive evidence was put forth in both cases to show that others perceived the respective students to be gay.

62. See, e.g., N.Y. Educ. Law § 3214(3)(a), allowing the suspension of a pupil who "endangers the safety, morals, health or welfare of others," and Tex. Educ. Code § 37.006(d)(2), allowing removal from the classroom and placement in a disciplinary program if a student's continued presence threatens the safety of others.

63. See, e.g., Cal. Penal Code § 422, regarding punishment for threatening statements meant as threats of death or great bodily harm, regardless of intent to carry the threat out, and Mass. Gen. Law ch. 275 § 2, allowing courts to examine the complaints of threat victims.

64. See Davis v. Monroe County Bd. of Educ., 526 U.S. 629 (1999), which holds that Title IX may apply if peer-to-peer sexual harassment is so severe as to exclude the victim from an educational opportunity on the basis of sex.

65. See L. W. v. Toms River Reg'l Sch. Bd. of Educ., 189 N.J. 381, 915 A.2d 535 (N.J. 2007), extending New Jersey's Law against Discrimination to recognize a cause of action against the school for sexual orientation discrimination by one student toward another student.

66. The unsettled status of Title IX with regard to transgender rights is addressed in chapter 9.

67. See OCR–DOJ Letter to Richard L. Swanson, Superintendent, Tehachapi Unified School District, June 29, 2011, U.S. Dep't of Educ., Office for Civil Rights, OCR Case No. 09-11-1031, DOJ Case No. DJ 169-11E-38 (hereinafter referred to as Swanson Letter). In addition to violating Title IX, sexual harassment may also violate Title IV of the Civil Rights Act of 1964, which prohibits public schools and colleges from discriminating against students on the basis of sex.

68. See Swanson Letter: "Although [use of anti-gay slurs and other homophobic language] is not, by itself, sufficient to establish prohibited harassment under Title IX or Title IV, the evidence in this case indicated that the use of such language stemmed, to a substantial degree, from gender-based animus related to the Student's nonconformity with gender stereotypes. Specifically, students at the School routinely use homophobic epithets and related insinuations to ridicule those who do not conform to common gender expectations; incident reports show that male students in particular are called anti-gay slurs for conduct such as styling their hair a certain way, wearing makeup, and crying in public. . . . This evidence establishes that the use of homophobic epithets in many instances stemmed from commonly held attitudes and perceptions about gender and masculinity from which also flowed the sexual and other gender-based conduct described above. To the extent that it did, such adverse conduct is within the scope of Title IX and Title IV.

". . . Based on the above facts and analysis, the United States concludes that the Student was subject to persistent, pervasive, and often severe sex-based harassment that resulted in a hostile educational environment of which the District had notice, and that the District failed to take steps to sufficient to stop the harassment, to prevent its recurrence, or to eliminate the hostile environment."

The letter also noted that, "although such conduct is not covered by Title IX or Title IV, California state law specifically prohibits discrimination and harassment based on both gender and sexual orientation, as well as other categories. *See* Cal. Ed. Code §§ 200–234.3." Although federal agencies do not generally enforce state laws, the district is obligated to comply with both federal and state laws.

See, generally, Kevin Welner, Robert Kim, and Stuart Biegel, "Investigation of Tehachapi Unified School District Re: Sex-Based Harassment," in *Legal Issues in Education: Rights and Responsibilities in U.S. Public Schools Today,* 95–96 (Saint Paul, Minn.: West Academic, 2017).

69. See Lisa Leff, "Feds: CA School District Failed to Help Gay Teen," Associated Press, July 2, 2011.

70. See Brown v. Ogletree, 2012 WL 591190 (S.D. Tex. 2012).

71. See Jennifer Radcliffe, "Bullying Lawsuit in Cy-Fair Student's Death Dropped," *Houston Chronicle,* March 29, 2013.

72. See "Safe School Laws," Movement Advancement Project Equality Maps,

data current as of March 29, 2018, http://www.lgbtmap.org/equality-maps/safe
_school_laws. See also Mudasar Khan et al., "Challenges Facing LGBTQ Youth,"
Georgetown Journal of Gender and the Law 18 (2017): 475, 489: "As in the federal
context, six states exempt educational institutions controlled by religious organizations from the application of antidiscrimination laws that would not be consistent with the religious tenets of that organization."

73. Khan et al., 489–90. While public accommodations laws were traditionally limited to hotels, motels, restaurants, theaters, and similar places open to the
public, the definition of the term has been expanded over the years to include
everything from public parks to commercial retailers. California, for example, de-
notes "all business establishments" as public accommodations (see Cal. Civ. Code
Section 51 (b)), and New Jersey defines public accommodations to include "any
retail shop, store, establishment, or concession dealing with goods or services
of any kind" (see N.J. Stat. Section 10:5–5). Some public accommodations laws
explicitly cover sexual orientation. See, generally, Holning Lau, "Transcending
the Individualist Paradigm in Sexual Orientation Antidiscrimination Law," *California Law Review* 94 (2006): 1277–78.

74. California Penal Code § 422.6 (a) does not just protect against particular
hateful actions directed against persons on the basis of their real or perceived
sexual orientation; it also includes explicit protection for those victimized on the
basis of real or perceived race, color, religion, ancestry, national origin, disability,
or gender. Yet although this statute has come to be viewed as groundbreaking in
a number of important ways, it must be noted that "no person shall be convicted
of violating subdivision (a) based upon speech alone, except upon a showing that
the speech itself threatened violence against a specific person or group of persons
and that the defendant had the apparent ability to carry out the threat." California Penal Code § 422.6 (c). California also provides that school officials may suspend or expel students in grade 4 or higher who harass or mistreat their peers on
the basis of real or perceived sexual orientation. See Cal. Educ. Code § 48900.3.

75. It should be emphasized that because school personnel may not be aware
of just how different the laws are today, and also because too many persons have
contributed to the unequal treatment of LGBT students through acts or omissions of their own, many of the court decisions and settlement agreements in
this area have mandated professional development for faculty and staff. Such activities, addressed in Part II of this book, have the potential to play a key role in
changing the realities at individual school sites over time.

4. Challenges for LGBT Educators

1. See, e.g., E. Edmund Reutter Jr., *The Law of Public Education* (New York:
Foundation Press, 1994), 657. See also Acanfora v. Bd. of Educ. of Montgomery County, 491 F. 2d 498 (4th Cir. 1974); Gish v. Bd. of Educ., 145 N.J. Super.

96 (1976); and Gaylord v. Tacoma School Dist. No. 10, 88 Wash.2d 286, 559 P.2d 1340 (en banc) (1977). All are examples of cases where courts upheld the removal of openly gay teachers from public school teaching positions. See also generally Karen M. Harbeck, *Gay and Lesbian Educators: Personal Freedoms, Public Constraints* (Malden, Mass.: Amethyst, 1997).

2. The Briggs initiative, though favored overwhelmingly in early polls, was defeated by the voters 59 percent to 41 percent. Many credit the unequivocal opposition of Governor Jerry Brown, President Jimmy Carter, and then former governor Ronald Reagan for the defeat of this initiative. See, e.g., *The Times of Harvey Milk,* directed by Rob Epstein (1984; New York: New Yorker Films, 2004), DVD, the Academy Award–winning documentary film that addresses these and related issues.

3. David Alan Sklansky, "Privacy, Policing Homosexuality, and Enforcing Social Norms—'One Train May Hide Another': Katz, Stonewall, and the Secret Subtext of Criminal Procedure," *UC Davis Law Review* 41 (2008): 875, 906–7. In this context, Sklansky added that "the terror and cruelty of a charge of homosexuality, the way such a charge could destroy, in a blow, a man's reputation and livelihood, his family life and his place in the community—all of this was well known to Americans regardless of their own sexual practices, and witnessed repeatedly, often close at hand" (911).

4. Sklansky, 913, quoting from "The Homosexual in America," *Time,* January 21, 1966. See also Hendrik Hertzberg, "Stonewall Plus Forty," *The New Yorker,* July 6 and 13, 2009.

5. See Elizabeth Mehren, "The Times Poll: Acceptance of Gays Rises among New Generation," *Los Angeles Times,* April 11, 2004. See also Gregory Lewis and Howard E. Taylor, "Public Opinion toward Gay and Lesbian Teachers: Insights for All Public Employees," *Review of Public Personnel Administration* 21 (2001): 133–51.

6. See Shawn Neidorf and Rich Morin, "Four-in-Ten Americans Have Close Friends or Relatives Who Are Gay," Pew Research Center for the People and the Press, May 23, 2007, http://pewresearch.org/pubs/485/friends-who-are-gay.

7. Neidorf and Morin.

8. GSS: General Social Survey, 2008, http://www.norc.org/GSS+Website. Data from the GSS reveal similar differences regarding geography when the focus turns to higher education. Although the number of Americans who believe that gays and lesbians should not be allowed to teach at colleges and universities is noticeably lower than at the K–12 level, the percentages of those who would bar LGBTs from academic positions at postsecondary institutions still range from a low of 14.6 percent, in the Pacific region, to a high of 26.9 percent, in the "West South Central" portion of the country.

9. See Parker v. Hurley, 514 F.3d 87, 105–7 (1st Cir. 2008). In *Hurley,* the court

addressed claims that the reading aloud of *King and King,* a gay-positive book, by a teacher in an elementary school classroom constituted indoctrination in violation of the Free Exercise Clause. Determining that the U.S. Supreme Court "has never utilized an indoctrination test under the Free Exercise Clause, much less in the public school context," the First Circuit did not address "whether or not an indoctrination theory under the Free Exercise Clause is sound." It did find an "intent to influence" the students' point of view. But "even assuming there is a continuum along which an intent to influence could become an attempt to indoctrinate," Judge Lynch wrote, "this case is firmly on the influence-toward-tolerance end. There is no evidence of systemic indoctrination. There is no allegation that Joey [a second grader] was asked to affirm gay marriage. Requiring a student to read a particular book is generally not coercive of free exercise rights."

10. See, e.g., Title VII of the Civil Rights Act of 1964 and also the Americans with Disabilities Act of 1990 (ADA). See further the Age Discrimination in Employment Act (ADEA) of 1967.

11. Glover v. Williamsburg Local School District, 20 F. Supp. 2d 1160 (S.D. Ohio 1998).

12. *Glover,* at 1165.

13. *Glover,* at 1169, 1174–75. The court quoted here from *Romer v. Evans:* "If the constitutional conception of 'equal protection of the laws' means anything, it must at the very least mean that a bare . . . desire to harm a politically unpopular group cannot constitute a legitimate governmental interest."

14. See *Glover,* at 1174: "Perhaps the Board feared that a gay teacher would act inappropriately or somehow be a trouble-maker. Or perhaps the Board was responding to perceived disapproval in the community of having a gay teacher at Williamsburg. Regardless of the Board's reasoning, Glover had established that he was an above average first-year teacher who was more qualified than the woman chosen by the Board to replace him. [Additional] evidence introduced at trial supports a finding that the Board's decision was motivated by animus towards him as a homosexual."

15. Weaver v. Nebo School District, 29 F. Supp. 2d 1279, 1280–81 (D. Utah 1998).

16. *Weaver,* at 1285, 1287.

17. *Weaver,* at 1287–89. The court added the following: "The record now before the court contains no job-related justification for not assigning Ms. Weaver as volleyball coach. Nor have the defendants demonstrated how Ms. Weaver's sexual orientation bears any rational relationship to her competency as teacher or coach, or her job performance as coach—a position she has held for many years with distinction."

18. In fact, a later state suit on the Weaver matter brought by a citizens group

was dismissed by the Supreme Court of Utah, with Ms. Weaver winning all court costs. Miller v. Weaver, UT 12, 66 P.3d 592 (2003).

19. See Evelyn Nieves, "After Sex Change, Teacher Is Barred from School," *New York Times,* September 27, 1999.

20. See Nieves. See also Marvin Dunson III, "Sex, Gender, and Transgender: The Present and Future of Employment Discrimination Law," *Berkeley Journal of Employment and Labor Law* 22 (2001): 465.

21. "One parent stood up at a board meeting and said that her daughter was traumatized," Bender said. "But right after that, her daughter stood up and told the board that her mother was wrong." Quoted in Nieves, "After Sex Change."

22. Nieves.

23. See Nieves.

24. See Cynthia Hubert, "Being Herself: Dana Rivers Has a New Home, a New Campus—and a New Life as a Woman," *Sacramento Bee,* November 14, 2001. See also Helen Y. Chang, "My Father Is a Woman, Oh No! The Failure of the Courts to Uphold Individual Substantive Due Process Rights for Transgender Parents under the Guise of the Best Interests of the Child," *Santa Clara Law Review* 43 (2003): 649.

25. Morrison v. State Bd. of Educ., 1 Cal. 3d 214 (1969).

26. *Morrison,* at 218–19.

27. "Neither sodomy (Pen. Code § 286), oral copulation (Pen. Code § 288a), public solicitation of lewd acts (Pen. Code § 647, subd. [a]), loitering near public toilets (Pen. Code § 647, subd. [d]), nor exhibitionism (Pen. Code § 314) [was] involved. Conviction of such offenses would have resulted in the mandatory revocation of all diplomas and life certificates issued by the State Board of Education." *Morrison,* at 218, n4.

28. After the affair had been disclosed, Morrison resigned his position with the school district. The record does not indicate what transpired between him and his employers, but at the time, a common practice involving acts appearing to fall under the category of "immoral or unprofessional" was that employees would be suspended without pay pending the results of an investigation, and if the allegations were true, they would ultimately be presented with the choice of either resigning or being dismissed.

29. It is important to note that these events happened before the Stonewall riots and long before specific statutory protections for LGBT individuals were in place, even in California. Admitting one's homosexuality would have been a radical step in the early 1960s, especially for a person seeking to retain a public position such as teaching.

30. In a particularly poignant footnote, Justice Tobriner stated, "The problem of ascertaining the appropriate standard of 'morality' was aptly put in Robert N. Harris, Jr., *Private Consensual Adult Behavior: The Requirement of Harm to*

Others in the Enforcement of Morality, 14 UCLA L. Rev. 581, 582 and n.4. '[I]n a secular society—America today—there may be a plurality of moralities. Whose morals shall be enforced? . . . There is a tendency to say that public morals should be enforced. But that just begs the question. Whose morals are the public morals?'" *Morrison,* at 227n19.

31. The court concluded that the terms themselves are capable of multiple interpretations even within the same community and noted that "in the opinion of many people laziness, gluttony, vanity, selfishness, avarice, and cowardice constitute immoral conduct." *Morrison,* at 225–26.

32. The court explained that in determining whether particular conduct indicated unfitness to teach, a board may consider such matters as "the likelihood that the conduct may have adversely affected students or fellow teachers," the degree of such adverse effect, the "remoteness in time" of the conduct, any extenuating or aggravating circumstances, the praiseworthiness or blameworthiness of the teacher's motives, and the likelihood of the conduct's recurrence. Examining the circumstances surrounding Morrison's brief affair under this framework, the court found "no evidence" whatsoever that his conduct "indicated his unfitness to teach." *Morrison,* at 229, 236.

33. For example, in 1976, the Colorado Supreme Court explicitly cited the language in *Morrison* when discussing the definition of "immorality" in that state's teaching regulations. The court held that any immorality that would force a teacher from his or her position must be directly related to his or her unfitness to teach. Weissman v. Board of Education, 190 Colo. 414, 420–21 (1976).

34. Exec. Order No. 10,450, Sec. 8, 18 *Fed. Reg.* 2489 (1953).

35. See, e.g., David K. Johnson, *The Lavender Scare: The Cold War Persecution of Gays and Lesbians in the Federal Government* (Chicago: University of Chicago Press, 2004).

36. The Employment Non-discrimination Act (ENDA) was first introduced in Congress in 1994 as an important step toward addressing the issue of LGBT employment discrimination, but the legislation never received sufficient support to pass. See, e.g., Arthur S. Leonard, "Sexual Minority Rights in the Workplace," *Brandeis Law Journal* 43 (2004–5): 145.

In July 2015, U.S. House and Senate Democrats introduced the Equality Act, "the most expansive LGBTQ civil rights bill ever," and President Obama announced that he would support it: "The Equality Act would effectively expand the Civil Rights Act [of 1964], to protect people from discrimination based on sexual orientation and gender identity in the workplace, housing, public accommodations (hotels, stores, and similar public places), education, and various other settings." See German Lopez, "The Equality Act, the Most Comprehensive LGBTQ Rights Bill Ever, Explained," November 10, 2015, http://www.vox.com/.

To date, the Equality Act has not moved forward in Congress, even as recent data show that 72 percent of the American public supports laws protecting lesbians and gay men from job discrimination, and 75 percent for transgender people. See, e.g., Andrew R. Flores, "National Trends in Public Opinion on LGBT Rights in the United States," Williams Institute, last updated November 2014, https://williamsinstitute.law.ucla.edu/research/census-lgbt-demographics-studies/natl-trends-nov-2014/.

37. See Movement Advancement Project Equality Maps, data current as of March 29, 2018, http://www.lgbtmap.org/equality-maps/non_discrimination_laws.

38. See, generally, Kitty Krupat and Patrick McCreery, eds., *Out at Work: Building a Gay–Labor Alliance* (Minneapolis: University of Minnesota Press, 2000).

39. See Tinker v. Des Moines Indep. Commun. Sch. Dist., 393 U.S. 503, 506 (1969): "First Amendment rights, applied in light of the special characteristics of the school environment, are available to teachers and students. It can hardly be argued that either students or teachers shed their constitutional rights to freedom of speech or expression at the schoolhouse gate. This has been the unmistakable holding of this Court for almost 50 years."

40. Pickering v. Bd. of Educ., 391 U.S. 563 (1968). The school board sought to justify its decision by insisting that the publication of the letter was "detrimental to the efficient operation and administration of the schools" and that, under relevant Illinois law, the "interests of the schools" required his dismissal.

41. *Pickering*, at 572.

42. Connick v. Myers, 461 U.S. 138 (1983).

43. See, e.g., Karen C. Daly, "Balancing Act: Teachers' Classroom Speech and the First Amendment," *Journal of Law and Education* 30 (2001): 1. See, generally, R. Weston Donehower, "Boring Lessons: Defining the Limits of a Teacher's First Amendment Right to Speak through the Curriculum," *Michigan Law Review* 102 (2003): 517, and Ailsa W. Chang, "Resuscitating the Constitutional 'Theory' of Academic Freedom: A Search for a Standard beyond Pickering and Connick," *Stanford Law Review* 53 (2001): 915.

44. See, e.g., Alexander Wohl, "Oiling the Schoolhouse Gate: After Forty Years of Tinkering with Teachers' First Amendment Rights, Time for a New Beginning," *American University Law Review* 58 (2009): 1285, and Richard T. Geisel and Brenda R. Kallio, "Employee Speech in K–12 Settings: The Impact of *Garcetti* on First Amendment Retaliation Claims," *Education Law Reporter* 251 (2010): 19. See, generally, Michael D. Simpson, "Defending Academic Freedom: Advice for Teachers," *NCSS Magazine*, 2010.

45. Garcetti v. Ceballos, 547 U.S. 410 (2006).

46. *Garcetti*, at 421.

47. See *Garcetti* generally.

48. Mayer v. Monroe County Community School Corp., 474 F.3d 477 (7th Cir. 2007).

49. *Mayer,* at 480.

50. See generally "Frequently Asked Questions: Senate Bill 48 [The Fair Education Act]," California Department of Education, http://www.cde.ca.gov/ci/cr/cf/senatebill48faq.asp.

51. Downs v. Los Angeles Unified Sch. Dist., 228 F.3d 1003, 1005–6 (9th Cir. 2000). The memo goes on to state that the school district's multicultural and human relations education policy includes the expectations that "each student has equal access to a quality education and an opportunity to participate fully in the academic and social activities of the school" and that "school policies and practices act to foster a climate that reduces fears related to difference and deters name-calling and acts of violence or threats motivated by hate and bigotry."

52. *Downs,* at 1006. "In recognition that some of the materials can be controversial in nature," the memo further states that "the representations on the posters" were reviewed by, among other groups, the Parent Community Services Branch. The memo also "recognizes that schools are part of a community and must respect the sentiments held by the local community."

53. See, generally, Amanda Covarrubias, "Not So Happily Ever After," *Los Angeles Times,* March 24, 2004.

54. Covarrubias.

55. See Covarrubias.

56. The current definition of "age-appropriate" from the California Education Code reads as follows: "'Age appropriate' refers to topics, messages, and teaching methods suitable to particular ages or age groups of children and adolescents, based on developing cognitive, emotional, and behavorial capacity typical for the age or age group." Cal. Ed. Code § 51931 (2018).

57. See, generally, Obergefell v. Hodges, 135 S.Ct. 2584 (2015). It should be noted in this context that the First Circuit Court of Appeals confirmed that Puerto Rico's ban on same-sex marriage was also overturned by *Obergefell.* See In Re Conde Vidal, 818 F.3d 765 (1st Cir. 2016).

58. See http://www.youtube.com/watch?v=0PgjcgqFYP4. See chapter 5 of this book for a detailed analysis of *Parker v. Hurley* and its implications. It must be emphasized that, contrary to the assertion in the Yes on 8 ad, the First Circuit Court of Appeals never ruled that the parent plaintiffs had no legal right to object. Not only is this language nowhere to be found in the decision but in fact the court made it clear that parents are not powerless, that they can object by bringing their case to the school board, and that they can vote out of office any official whose job performance is found to be lacking. The appellate panel even identified the parameters of an "indoctrination" analysis that might be employed by

future litigants. However, the panel concluded that, under the facts of this case, no constitutional violation occurred. See *Hurley,* at 100–107.

59. For a detailed examination of K–12 curriculum and pedagogy issues within the context of conflicting values in the aftermath of Proposition 8, see, generally, Douglas NeJaime, "Inclusion, Accommodation, and Recognition: Accounting for Differences Based on Religion and Sexual Orientation," *Harvard Journal of Law and Gender* 32 (2009): 303.

60. Allegations of the existence of a so-called homosexual agenda include the aforementioned statements of Justice Scalia in his *Lawrence v. Texas* dissent. See also Alan Sears and Craig Osten, *The Homosexual Agenda: Exposing the Principal Threat to Religious Freedom Today,* rev. ed. (Nashville, Tenn.: B and H, 2003), a book cowritten by the heads of the Alliance Defense Fund and featured on the website of Focus on the Family. Goals that are allegedly embodied in this conspiratorial agenda include talking about "gays and gayness" as loudly and as often as possible; portraying gays as victims, not as aggressive challengers; giving "homosexual protectors" a just cause; making gays look good; making victimizers look bad; and getting funds from corporate America.

61. Schroeder v. Hamilton School District, 282 F.3d 946 (7th Cir. 2002).

62. *Schroeder,* at 948–49. In another incident, the superintendent herself failed to intervene when, during a meeting with Schroeder, a student directed an anti-gay slur at him in her presence.

63. See *Schroeder.*

64. *Schroeder,* at 952, 954–55.

65. *Schroeder,* at 961 (Wood, J., dissenting).

66. California Education Code, § 44807, for example, states that "every teacher in the public schools shall hold pupils to a strict account for their conduct on the way to and from school." In the federal courts, recent cases have found that school officials have increasingly broad power to hold students accountable for their expression outside of the school setting, online or offline, that may have an impact on day-to-day affairs within a school community. See, e.g., Wisniewski v. Bd. of Educ. of the Weedsport Cent. Sch. Dist., 494 F.3d 34 (2nd Cir. 2007).

67. The assistant principal herself conceded to Schroeder that she would have handled allegations of sexual harassment by a female teacher differently than she had handled his complaints.

68. *Schroeder,* at 961. Not only did the panel majority understate the case by refusing to acknowledge either the existence or the impact of the outright hostility toward gays in this setting but at times it appeared to be justifying the very hostility that it would not acknowledge. Judge Manion, for example, suggested that religious views could justify such hostility.

69. Twenty-five of our fifty states (but not Wisconsin) had antisodomy laws at the time Schroeder began teaching, in 1990. In 2002, when the court decided

against Schroeder, such activity was ostensibly legal in the Seventh Circuit states of Wisconsin and Illinois but still illegal right next door in Michigan, Missouri, and the nearby states of Kansas, Oklahoma, and Texas, as well as in eight other states across the land. See American Civil Liberties Union, "Getting Rid of Sodomy Laws: History and Strategy That Led to the Lawrence Decision," June 26, 2003, http://www.aclu.org/.

70. See, e.g., Milligan-Hitt v. Board of Trustees of Sheridan County School Dist. No. 2, 523 F.3d 1219 (10th Cir. 2008), upholding a rural Wyoming school district's ostensible demotion in 2002–3 of two principals who were living together as a lesbian couple, even in light of acknowledged anti-gay animus presented into evidence, but at the same time expressly situating the facts implicating the qualified immunity analysis in the pre-*Lawrence* era: "Although the district court found that there were genuine issues of material fact as to whether Superintendent Dougherty's actions had been unconstitutional, it held that the law governing discrimination on the basis of sexual orientation had not been clearly established in 2002 and early 2003, before the Supreme Court's decision in *Lawrence v. Texas,* which arguably clarified the issue" (*3).

71. See, generally, Nan D. Hunter, "Living with *Lawrence,*" *Minnesota Law Review* 88 (2004): 1103; Pamela S. Karlan, "Loving *Lawrence,*" *Michigan Law Review* 102 (2004): 1447; and Laurence H. Tribe, "Lawrence v. Texas: The 'Fundamental Right' That Dare Not Speak Its Name," *Harvard Law Review* 117 (2004): 1893.

72. See, e.g., Witt v. Dept. of Air Force, 527 F.3d 806 (9th Cir. 2008), where the Ninth Circuit determined that *Lawrence* was applicable to a former air force major's challenge to "Don't Ask, Don't Tell" and also found that "*Lawrence* requires something more than traditional rational basis review" (819). See generally chapter 2 of this book.

73. Varnum v. Brien, 763 N.W.2d 862 (2009).

74. *Varnum,* at 889–96.

75. *Varnum,* at 893.

5. Curriculum, Religion, Morality, and Values

1. See, generally, Steve Hogan and Lee Hudson, *Completely Queer: The Gay and Lesbian Encyclopedia* (New York: Holt, 1998), a history of gays and lesbians from time immemorial, focusing in particular on the twentieth century. The book is organized in an encyclopedia format but also contains a seventy-page chronology dating back to 12,000 B.C.

2. The cognitive domain is one of the three learning domains posited by Benjamin Bloom in his highly influential taxonomy. The others are the affective and the psychomotor domains. See, generally, Lorin W. Anderson and Lauren A.

Sosniak, eds., *Bloom's Taxonomy: A Forty-Year Retrospective* (Chicago: University of Chicago Press, 1994).

The Every Student Succeeds Act (ESSA) is a wide-ranging, bipartisan statutory framework with requirements that extend across a broad spectrum. Although many of its provisions are controversial, none have generated more emotion than those relating to accountability. See, e.g., the ESSA Statement of Purpose, 20 U.S. Code § 6301.

3. With regard to the role that LGBT-related content can play in helping both LGBTs and straight persons who are sorting out these issues, see, e.g., Nancy G. Guerra and Emilie Phillips Smith, eds., *Preventing Youth Violence in a Multicultural Society* (Washington, D.C.: APA Books, 2005), and Jeff Perrotti and Kim Westheimer, *When the Drama Club Is Not Enough* (Boston: Beacon Press, 2001).

4. See Reno v. ACLU, 521 U.S. 844, 867, 885 (1997); Mainstream Loudoun v. Bd. of Trustees of the Loudoun County Library, 2 F.Supp.2d 783 (E.D. Va. 1998), affirming the relevance of *Pico* to disputes regarding mandatory internet filtering in public libraries; and U.S. v. American Library Association, 539 U.S. 194, 216 (2003) (Breyer, J., concurring), citing *Pico* in support of a warning that the Children's Internet Protection Act "directly restricts the public's receipt of information."

5. Gonazalez v. Douglas, 269 F.Supp.3d 948 (D. Ariz. 2017), A. Wallace Tashima, U.S. Circuit Judge, Sitting by Designation.

6. Mozert v. Hawkins County Board of Education, 827 F.2d 1058 (6th Cir. 1987).

7. *Mozert,* at 1062–64.

8. While standing in front of a picture of a boy dressed in a skirt and speaking of the protections California has in place for transgender students, Robert H. Knight of the Culture and Family Institute claimed in 2002 that "if most parents understood the depth of the homosexual agenda in the schools, there would be a revolution." Kelley Beaucar Vlahos, "Critics Slam 'Gay Agenda' in Public Schools," *Fox News,* May 7, 2002, http://www.foxnews.com/. See, generally, William N. Eskridge Jr., "No Promo Homo: The Sedimentation of Antigay Discourse and the Channeling Effect of Judicial Review," *New York University Law Review* 75 (2000): 1327, 1329–30.

9. *Mozert,* at 1063 (emphases added).

10. These states include Alabama and Texas (which expressly require sex ed programs to portray homosexuality in a negative light), Arizona (which expressly prohibits the programs from portraying homosexuality in a positive light), Mississippi and South Carolina (which vaguely prohibit LGBT-positive content), Oklahoma (which vaguely mandates a negative portrayal of homosexuality), and Louisiana (which vaguely prohibits the presentation of any LGBT content).

In addition, it has been noted by researchers at the Gay, Lesbian, and Straight

Education Network (GLSEN) that "while these laws generally are written to apply only to sexual health education, they are often vague and can be misapplied by schools to limit other parts of the curriculum, school events and programs, and even extracurricular activities." See "'No Promo Homo' Laws: How Are These Laws Applied?," http://www.glsen.org/learn/policy/issues/nopromohomo. Moreover, some school districts have also voluntarily adopted "No Promo Homo" policies in the absence of state law.

However, it should be noted that Utah, which had expressly prohibited supportive speech about LGBT people in public school classrooms and student clubs, repealed this law in 2017 as a result of the lawsuit *Equality Utah v. Utah State Board of Education,* discussed in chapter 9 of this book.

11. See generally ALA. CODE § 16-40A-2 (West, Westlaw through Act 2017-130 of the 2017 Regular Session); TEX. HEALTH & SAFETY CODE ANN. § 163.002 (V.T.C.A. through end of 2015 Reg. Sess. of 84th Leg.); Ariz. Rev. Stat. Ann. § 15-716 (West, Westlaw through legislation effective April 4, 2017 of the First Regular Session of the Fifty-Third Legislature (2017)); MISS. CODE ANN. § 37-13-171 (West, Westlaw current with laws from the 2017 Regular Session effective upon passage as approved through March 29, 2017); S.C. CODE ANN. § 59-32-30 (West, Westlaw through the 2016 session, subject to technical revisions by the Code Commissioner as authorized by law before official publication); OKLA. STAT. ANN. tit. 70, § 11-103.3 (West, Westlaw, Current with emergency effective provisions through Chapter 12 of the First Regular Session of the 56th Legislature (2017)); LA. REV. STAT. ANN. § 17:281 (West, Westlaw through the 2017 First Extraordinary session).

12. See, generally, "'No Promo Homo' Laws: What Is the Current State of These Laws?," http://www.glsen.org/learn/policy/issues/nopromohomo.

13. At Evanston High School in Evanston, Illinois, for example, teachers began a Safety Zone Project, where they volunteer to designate their room or office as a place where students can be out and not have to worry about harassment. See Becky Raisman, "Gay/Straight Alliances in Chicagoland High Schools," *Windy City Times,* September 17, 2003, http://www.windycitymediagroup.com/.

14. See Downs v. LAUSD, 228 F.3d 1003, 1005–6 (9th Cir. 2000).

15. While it is generally accepted that there is no word in ancient Hebrew—and thus no term in the Old Testament—that can be viewed as a synonym for "homosexuality," many have construed the reference in Leviticus 18 as applying to this area. There, a man "lying with another man in the lyings of a woman" is included in a section of acts that Moses characterizes as abominations. The other acts include seeing family members unclothed, shaving one's beard, trimming one's hair a certain way, mixing certain fabrics together, cursing one's parents, and sorcery. Later on, penalties such as being cut off from the community or even stoned to death are suggested as applicable in this context, although there is no

evidence that such penalties were ever implemented by the ancient Israelites. Over time, religious leaders and scholars have set forth a variety of interpretations for this material, and it remains controversial even today. See, generally, Leviticus 18 and 20.

16. *Downs,* at 1013. The court also noted that Robert Downs had many other opportunities to share his opinion on the morality of homosexuality and his displeasure with his employer's policy: "Subject to any applicable forum analysis, he may do so on the sidewalks, in the parks, through the chat-rooms, at his dinner table and in countless other locations. He may not do so, however, when he is speaking as the government, unless the government allows him to be its voice" (1016).

17. *Downs,* at 1014 (emphasis added).

18. Morrison v. Board of Education of Boyd County, Kentucky, 419 F.Supp.2d 937 (E.D. Ky. 2006). In the previous lawsuit, Boyd County High School Gay Straight Alliance, et al. v. Board of Education of Boyd County, et al., 258 F. Supp. 2d 667 (E.D. Ky. 2003), a group of Boyd County High School students successfully enjoined the defendants from denying their organization, the Boyd County High School Gay Straight Alliance, club status. Following the issuance of a preliminary injunction, the parties in that case entered into a consent decree, which required, among other things, "that the school put into effect written anti-harassment policies and conduct mandatory staff and student diversity training, a significant portion of which would be devoted to issues of sexual orientation and gender harassment." *Morrison,* at 939.

19. See *Morrison,* at 940, 946.

20. The court found that the curriculum at issue was "consistent with Tinker and its progeny" and thus was protected (*Morrison,* at 942). Likewise, because the students were given comment cards and an opportunity to respond to the training, there were no prohibitions on free speech and thus no infringement of the First Amendment (943). The court further concluded that there was no unconstitutional burden on the free exercise of religion, nor did parents have the right to choose the curriculum of their children while they were in public schools (943, 946).

21. The *Morrison* court distinguished the facts of the Kentucky case from an unpublished decision in Maryland a year earlier that held for the plaintiffs in a similar challenge to mandatory training sessions on LGBT issues, Citizens for a Responsible Curriculum v. Montgomery County Public Schools, 2005 WL 1075634 (D. Md. 2005) (not reported).

22. Brown v. Hot, Sexy, and Safer Productions, Inc., 68 F.3d 525 (1st Cir. 1995).

23. Leebaert v. Harrington, 332 F.3d 134 (2d Cir. 2003).

24. Fields v. Palmdale Sch. Dist., 427 F.3d 1197 (9th Cir. 2005).

25. Parker v. Hurley, 514 F.3d 87 (1st Cir. 2008).

26. See the California Fair, Accurate, Inclusive, and Respectful (FAIR) Act, CA Senate Bill 48, which was signed by Governor Jerry Brown in 2011 and took effect in January 2012. See, generally, chapter 7 of this book.

27. See CA SB 1172, signed by Governor Jerry Brown in 2012.

28. Chambers v. Babbitt, 145 F.Supp.2d 1068, 1073 (D. Minn. 2001): "Those students who identify themselves as gay, lesbian, bisexual, or transgender . . . struggle with the added pressures of potential alienation from friends, family, and community, and the potential for ridicule or even violence. Indeed, studies show that more than ninety percent of high school students hear negative comments regarding homosexuality during the school day. It is no wonder that there are significantly higher reports of depression and suicide amongst our GLBT youth, a problem that cannot be ignored."

29. *Chambers*, at 1072–73.

30. Hansen v. Ann Arbor Public Schools, 293 F.Supp.2d 780, 782–83 (E.D. Mich. 2003).

31. Once a court has determined that an activity is school sponsored, the school's power to regulate student speech for reasons relating to legitimate pedagogical concerns is afforded great deference. See, generally, Hazelwood v. Kuhlmeier, 484 U.S. 260 (1988).

32. See, e.g., Muller v. Jefferson Lighthouse Sch., 98 F.3d 1530, 1536–37 (7th Cir. 1996), which comments on court deference to schools as exemplified by both the *Hazelwood* decision and Bethel Sch. Dist. No. 403 v. Fraser, 478 U.S. 675 (1986).

33. Rosenberger v. Rector and Visitors of Univ. of Va., 515 U.S. 819, 829 (1995).

34. Principal Caudle went on to testify that "Pioneer High School is very diverse, and that's a good thing. And we are just trying to help students to understand that they should feel fortunate to be in such an environment where they can learn from others who are different[;] we look different, we think differently, and we're just trying to set a comfortable environment for that to take place." *Hansen,* at 801 (citing defendant's brief).

35. Indeed, many have criticized the way the term *politically correct* has been used as a pejorative to deride the opinions or perspectives of others. Wayne Besen, for example, argues that "dismissing something as politically correct" has increasingly become an easy way for people to demonstrate a lack of mutual respect. Wayne Besen, "A Race to the Bottom," *San Francisco Bay Times,* September 28, 2006, http://www.sfbaytimes.com/index.php?sec=article&article_id=5517.

36. The front of Harper's T-shirt was slightly different on each of the two days. On the first day, its slogan read "I will not accept what God has condemned"; on the second day, it was changed to read "Be ashamed, the school has accepted what God has condemned." The slogan on the back, stating "Homosexuality Is

Shameful" and citing Romans 1:27, was the same on both days. See Harper v. Poway Unified Sch. Dist., 345 F.Supp.2d 1096 (S.D. Cal. 2004).

Romans was only referenced, not quoted. It should be noted in this context, however, that Romans 1:27 (NIV) reads as follows: "In the same way the men also abandoned natural relations with women and were inflamed with lust for one another. Men committed indecent acts with other men, and received in themselves the due penalty for their perversion."

37. *Harper* (2004) was the first lower-court decision, which held that Harper was not likely to prevail on the substantive issues.

38. For example, in what some have characterized as the Seventh Circuit version of the *Harper v. Poway* case (*Nuxoll v. Indian Prairie Sch. Dist.*, discussed in detail later in this chapter), the ACLU, a consistent supporter of equal rights for LGBTs over the years, actually filed an amicus brief on behalf of the conservative religious students. See "Neuqua Valley High School Student Can Wear Anti-Gay T-shirt to School, Appeals Court Rules," *Chicago Tribune*, April 24, 2008.

39. Harper v. Poway Unified Sch. Dist., 445 F.3d 1166 (9th Cir. 2006).

40. *Harper,* at 1178.

41. *Harper,* at 1183. In his concurring opinion denying a rehearing for the case before the Ninth Circuit judges sitting en banc, Judge Reinhardt reemphasized the harm that could be done to minority students through such verbal attacks (1052, 1053). However, in an amendment to the original Ninth Circuit decision, he explicitly left open the possibility that the case's reasoning could be applied to protect a nonminority student as well. Harper v. Poway Unified Sch. Dist., 2006 U.S. App. LEXIS 13402 at *1 (9th Cir. May 31, 2006) (order amending opinion).

42. *Harper* (2006), at 1188.

43. *Harper* (2006), at 1197 (Kozinski, J., dissenting). Judge Kozinski mischaracterizes the focus of the Day of Silence when he states, "By participating in the Day of Silence activities, homosexual students perforce acknowledge that their status is not universally admired or accepted; the whole point of the Day of Silence, as I understand it, is to dispute views like those characterized by Harper's t-shirt" (1200). In fact, the stated purpose of the Day of Silence is to highlight ongoing issues of name-calling, bullying, and harassment. The entire focus is on campus safety.

44. The Ninth Circuit majority explained that "the Court in *Tinker* held that a school may prohibit student speech, even if the consequence is viewpoint discrimination, if the speech violates the rights of other students or is materially disruptive." *Harper* (2006), at 1184–86. See also Tinker v. Des Moines Independent Community School District., 393 U.S. at 511, 89 S.Ct. 733, which states that a school cannot prohibit "expression of one particular opinion" unless it makes a specific showing of constitutionally valid reasons.

45. Judge Kozinski wrote that "the only support [the majority provides for

the assertion that the demeaning of gays is detrimental to their 'psychological health and well being . . . and their educational development'] are a few law review articles, a couple of press releases by advocacy groups and some pop psychology." *Harper* (2006), at 1198–99. The majority opinion, in fact, cites eight different sources, including six scholarly articles, a study by the Human Rights Watch, and a study by the National Mental Health Association (see 1178–79).

Ongoing concerns have been set forth in many venues regarding the applicability of psychological research, and many continue to see psychological injury as less significant than physical injury. Yet, given the fact that psychological evidence carried the day in Brown v. Bd. of Educ., 347 U.S. 483 (1954), Lee v. Weisman, 505 U.S. 577 (1992), and *Harper* (2006), the law appears to have moved beyond the outmoded view that people with psychological issues simply need to toughen up. Such a trend is reflected in the state of disability rights law in the aftermath of the passage of major federal legislation over time. See, generally, Peter Blanck, Eve Hill, Charles Siegal, and Michael Waterstone, *Disability Civil Rights Law and Policy*, Hornbook Series (St. Paul, Minn.: West, 2004).

46. Judge Kozinski, for example, argued that "supporters of the Day of Silence may prefer to see views such as Harper's channeled into public discourse rather than officially suppressed but whispered behind backs or scribbled on bathroom walls. Confronting—and refuting—such views in a public forum may well empower homosexual students, contributing to their sense of self-esteem." *Harper* (2006), at 1200.

47. See, e.g., Dale Carpenter, "Right Result under a Bad Precedent," *Volokh Conspiracy* (blog), April 21, 2006, http://www.volokh.com/archives/archive_2006_04_16–2006_04_22.shtml, where the University of Minnesota law professor agrees with the result in the *Harper* case but disagrees with Judge Reinhardt's reasoning: "Of course, a single T-shirt bearing the words 'Homosexuality is shameful' isn't that sort of direct face-to-face harassment and doesn't, by itself, create a pervasively hostile environment. No single derogatory statement, taken by itself, creates a pervasively hostile environment. The problem is that it's expressed in a context that is already a living hell for gay kids in many public schools, as it probably was in this one, making it difficult for them to concentrate on getting an education. When you're a closeted gay kid sitting in math class behind that guy wearing that T-shirt staring you in the face the whole time, and you know you have nobody to talk to about how it demeans your most intimate feelings, your whole world starts to look pretty desolate."

48. Several noteworthy law review articles acknowledged the validity of both the school climate issues raised by Judge Reinhardt's 2006 opinion and his statements during the previous year's oral argument, even as they came to different conclusions regarding the efficacy of the panel's First Amendment analysis. See, e.g., "Ninth Circuit Upholds Public School's Prohibition of Anti-Gay T-Shirts,"

Harvard Law Review 120 (2007): 1691, 1698; Brian J. Bilford, "Harper's Bazaar: The Marketplace of Ideas and Hate Speech in Schools," *Stanford Journal of Civil Rights and Civil Liberties* 4 (2008): 447, 471; and Martha McCarthy, "Student Expression That Collides with the Rights of Others: Should the Second Prong of *Tinker* Stand Alone?," *Education Law Reporter* 240 (2009): 1, 11–12.

49. See Harper v. Poway Unified Sch. Dist., 549 U.S. 1262, 127 S.Ct. 1484 (2007).

50. See, e.g., DHX, Inc. v. Allianz AGF MAT, Ltd., 425 F.3d 1169, 1176 (9th Cir. 2005): "At minimum, a vacated opinion still carries informational and perhaps even persuasive or precedential value." See also U.S. v. Joelson, 7 F.3d 174, 178 n. 1 (9th Cir.1993), which states that a certain vacated court of appeals opinion "has no precedential effect" but cites the vacated opinion for its informational and persuasive value; Gould v. Bowyer, 11 F.3d 82, 84 (7th Cir. 1993), which notes that a vacated district court opinion carries informational value "even if the reviewing court intoned in its most solemn voice that the district court's decision would have no precedential effect"; and County of Los Angeles v. Davis, 440 U.S. 625, 646 n. 10, 99 S.Ct. 1379, 59 L.Ed.2d 642 (1979) (Powell, J., dissenting), which asserts that the opinion of the court of appeals, though vacated, "will continue to have precedential weight and, until contrary authority is decided, [is] likely to be viewed as persuasive authority if not the governing law of the . . . Circuit" (Beezer, J., concurring).

51. Harper v. Poway, Order Denying Plaintiff's Motion for Reconsideration, 545 F.Supp.2d 1072, 1095–1103 (S.D. Cal. 2008). This time, however, the judge based his analysis on two decisions that had come down since the case was first heard: the vacated Ninth Circuit opinion and the U.S. Supreme Court's holding in *Morse v. Frederick*. Addressing Kelsie Harper's motion requesting that the court reconsider the case, Judge Houston proceeded to determine the likelihood of her success in putting forth convincing First Amendment arguments. Revisiting his earlier free speech analysis under the *Tinker* rule, he quoted key passages from Judge Reinhardt's opinion and noted with approval the Ninth Circuit panel's reasoning in the 2006 decision against Harper's brother. He then stated that he "[did] not agree with plaintiff's contention that [Reinhardt's] decision was in error."

52. Unpublished opinions are typically issued when courts determine that no new ground has been broken with regard to the development of the law.

53. Harper v. Poway USD, 318 Fed. Appx. 540, 541–42, 2009 WL 605819 at **1 (9th Cir. 2009). The 2008 opinion was vacated in part and affirmed in part. "The only issue remaining" in March 2009, the panel wrote, was the plaintiff's claim "for nominal damages against the defendants in their individual capacities." The panel proceeded to affirm the lower court's decision with regard to the claim, deciding that the plaintiff was not entitled to any financial remuneration because

the law was unclear at the time the controversy arose (and thus the defendants should be granted "qualified immunity").

54. See, e.g., Eve Sedgwick, "Queer and Now," in *Tendencies,* ed. Eve Kosofsky Sedgwick and Michèle Aina Barale (Durham, N.C.: Duke University Press, 1993), 1; also 3 ("I hate that I grew up thinking I was the only queer in the world, and I hate even more that most queer kids still grow up the same way"). See also Teemu Ruskola, "Minor Disregard: The Legal Construction of the Fantasy That Gay and Lesbian Youth Do Not Exist," *Yale Journal of Law and Feminism* 8 (1996): 269, 270, which argues that the invisibility and neglect of a segment of the youth population has significant negative effects on individual children who might have no safe space in their school lives.

55. For a prominent example of the literature exploring alternative interpretations of the passages that allegedly address homosexuality in the Old and New Testaments, see Daniel A. Helminiak, *What the Bible Really Says about Homosexuality* (San Francisco: Alamo Square, 2000).

56. In 2008, Day of Silence demonstrations were held across the nation for the twelfth consecutive year, with the express purpose of "bring[ing] attention to anti-LGBT name-calling, bullying and harassment in schools." See, e.g., Gay, Lesbian, and Straight Education Network (GLSEN), "Day of Silence—April 25, 2008," http://www.dayofsilence.org/. See also Phillip Zonkel, "Speaking Out through Silence," *Long Beach Press-Telegram,* April 25, 2008: "Day of Silence is not about changing beliefs or values, but changing the behavior that causes bullying and causes students to feel alienated and that schools don't care about them."

57. The Alliance Defense Fund, "one of the largest legal organizations in the United States championing Christian rights," changed its name in 2012 to the Alliance Defending Freedom. Stoyan Zaimov, "Alliance Defense Fund Changes Name to Alliance Defending Freedom," *Christian Post,* July 11, 2012, http://www .christianpost.com/.

58. See, e.g., "How Can Lies Be Truth?," a YouTube video narrated and filmed by ex-ex-gay Daniel Gonzalez, discussing the Alliance Defense Fund's Day of Truth campaign in the K–12 public schools and documenting strong connections between Focus on the Family, the Alliance Defense Fund, and the "ex-gay" movement, http://www.youtube.com/watch?v=HI4-eDG3Bb0.

59. See *Zamecnik* (2007), at *5. The school apparently had no problem with the slogan on the front of Zamecnik's shirt. Indeed, officials would have allowed it again in 2007.

60. Nuxoll v. Indian Prairie Sch. Dist. No. 204 Bd. of Educ., 523 F.3d 668 (7th Cir. 2008).

61. Indeed, the school district invoked the very same alternative slogans in its defense: "School officials indicate that a positively-worded phrase such as 'Be Happy, Be Straight' would be acceptable. They liken the phrase 'Be Happy, Not

Gay' to expressions such as 'Be Happy, Not Christian,' 'Be Happy, Not Jewish,' or 'Be Happy, Not Muslim,' which they say would be an offensive interference with the rights of other students and pose a risk of disruption in a secondary school setting where they are responsible for young students." *Zamecnik* (2007), at *1.

Analogous questions were asked of ADF attorney Kevin Theriot by both Judge Reinhardt and Judge Kozinski in the *Harper v. Poway* (2006) oral argument. Both judges wondered, for example, about T-shirts that might say "Christianity Is Shameful" instead of "Homosexuality Is Shameful." The judges also raised similar questions regarding slogans that would substitute instead the names of racial or ethnic minorities.

62. *Zamecnik* (2007), at *1, *6. See also Holning Lau, "Pluralism: A Principle for Children's Rights," *Harvard Civil Rights–Civil Liberties Law Review* 42 (2007): 317, 319–20: "Children are harmed when they are pressured to suppress traits of minority social groups in order to fit into the mainstream."

63. Consistent with the earlier references to the precedential value of an opinion vacated on procedural grounds, Judge Hart stated, "*Harper* was vacated by the Supreme Court when the case was dismissed as moot in the district court. *Harper*, though, may still be considered for its persuasive authority. See *Christianson v. Colt Industries Operating Corp.*, 870 F.2d 1292, 1298–99 (7th Cir.), *cert. denied*, 493 U.S. 822, 110 S.Ct. 81, 107 L.Ed.2d 47 (1989); and *Pfizer Inc. v. Novopharm Ltd.*, 2001 WL 477163 *3 (N.D.Ill. May 3, 2001). Decisions of other circuits are to be given respectful consideration and followed where possible." *Zamecnik* (2007), at *6. See also Colby v. J.C. Penny Co., 811 F.2d 1119, 1123 (7th Cir.1987).

64. *Zamecnik*, at *11.

65. *Nuxoll*, at 669–74.

66. *Nuxoll*, at 674.

67. *Nuxoll*, at 675–76.

68. *Nuxoll*, at 676. In 2011, Judge Posner issued a final opinion in the Zamecnik–Nuxoll litigation, consistent with the one he had issued in 2008. Addressing remaining procedural matters, he emphasized the extent to which the First Amendment does not prohibit the regulation of K–12 student expression that constitutes "severe harassment" and "crosses the line between hurt feelings and substantial disruption of the educational mission." See Zamecnik v. Indian Prairie Sch. Dist. No. 204 Bd. of Educ., 636 F.3d 874, 877–78 (7th Cir. 2011).

6. Addressing School Climate

1. Depending on the needs of the particular community, there are a number of different ways such a combination of general school climate initiatives and LGBT-specific programs might be implemented. Ideally, the implementation of one or more LGBT-related programs at individual sites would happen not only

within a broader focus on school climate but also as one of a series of concurrent initiatives designed to provide additional support for marginalized and disenfranchised groups of students. LGBTs would be one category, but a number of others might be identified as well, depending on community realities.

2. See, e.g., Stuart Biegel, Robert Kim, and Kevin Welner, "The T-Shirt Cases: Addressing Inflammatory Slogans and Images on School Clothing," in *Education and the Law,* 4th ed., 139–53 (Saint Paul, Minn.: West Academic, 2016); see, generally, Stephen Kotok, Sakiko Ikoma, and Katerina Bodovski, "School Climate and Dropping Out of School in the Era of Accountability," *American Journal of Education* 122 (2016): 569–99.

3. To the extent that there is tension in an education setting between individuals or groups, policies and practices geared toward identifying areas of common ground represent the best of what public education and American values are supposed to be about. Research-based approaches that have been employed in this area to build and maintain an exemplary school climate apply not only to LGBT issues but to those of all students and to every possible level of interaction. Indeed, everyone benefits from a nurturing school environment where all students are provided with the same level of understanding and support. See, e.g., George G. Bear, Chunyan Yang, Lindsey S. Mantz, and Angela B. Harris, "School-Wide Practices Associated with School Climate in Elementary, Middle, and High Schools," *Teaching and Teacher Education* 63 (April 2017): 372–83; see, generally, Megan L. Marshall, "Examining School Climate: Defining Factors and Educational Influences" (white paper, Center for Research on School Safety, School Climate, and Classroom Management, Georgia State University), http://education.gsu.edu/.

4. Interview with Hoover Liddell, June 26, 2006. Liddell, an African American educator who worked for decades primarily with underserved and low-income students of color in the San Francisco Bay Area, has been a classroom teacher, a principal, an assistant superintendent, and a member of the school-desegregation Consent Decree Advisory Committee for the U.S. District Court, Northern District of California.

5. See CASEL: Educating Hearts, Inspiring Minds, http://www.casel.org/.

6. See "The Whole Child Approach," Association for Supervision and Curriculum Development, http://www.ascd.org/.

7. "Whole Child Approach."

8. See Kathleen Megan, "Beyond the Three R's: More Schools Taking Note of Emotional Intelligence," *Hartford Courant,* November 12, 2006. Such a broad-based approach to education is also consistent with conclusions that other researchers have reached in recent decades. In *Social Intelligence: The New Science of Human Relationships,* for example, Dr. Daniel Goleman synthesizes the latest findings in biology and brain science, revealing that we are designed for

sociability and are constantly engaged in a "neural ballet" that connects us brain to brain with those around us. The book confirms what successful educators have known instinctively from time immemorial: that emotions are contagious and can have a significant impact on human growth and development within the education process. See Goleman, *Social Intelligence: The New Science of Human Relationships* (New York: Bantam, 2006).

9. See Daniel Goleman, interview by Neal Conan, *Talk of the Nation,* NPR, aired October 23, 2006, available at 2006 WLNR 22956888.

10. See Susan Black, "Respecting Differences: Diverse Learners Can Blossom in Culturally Responsive Classrooms," *American School Board Journal,* January 2006, http://www.asbj.com/, which documents the importance for educators of learning the cultural and social characteristics of their students, and Cynthia Johnson, "Unmasking the Truth: Teaching Diverse Student Populations," National Association for Elementary School Principals, February 2006, http://www.naesp.org/, which explains why we must confront low expectations and personal assumptions that inhibit learning for diverse students.

11. See, e.g., Linda M. Raffaele Mendez and Howard Knopf, "Who Gets Suspended from School and Why: A Demographic Analysis of Schools and Disciplinary Infractions in a Large School District," *Education and Treatment of Children* 26, no. 1 (2003): 30–51, and Norma L. Day-Vines and Beth O. Day-Hairston, "Culturally Congruent Strategies for Addressing the Behavioral Needs of Urban, African American Male Adolescents," *Professional School Counseling* 8, no. 3 (2005): 236–43.

12. Brenda Townsend, "Disproportionate Discipline of African American Children and Youth: Culturally-Responsive Strategies for Reducing School Suspensions and Expulsions," *Exceptional Children* 66 (2000): 381–91, which focuses on African American youth but sets forth principles also applicable to others experiencing cultural discontinuity, including LGBT youth, and particularly LGBT students of color.

13. Russell J. Skiba et al., "The Color of Discipline: Sources of Racial and Gender Disproportionality," *Urban Review* 34, no. 4 (2002): 317–42.

14. Nabozny v. Podlesny, 92 F.3d at 452 (7th Cir. 1996). It is not clear from the Seventh Circuit decision what justification for placing Nabozny in special education had been expressed. No additional facts are put forth in the briefs on behalf of the appellant. However, the briefs do allege that the special education placement was part of a larger pattern: "[The placement] was part of a pattern that highlighted the school's message to students that abuse of a boy because he is gay would be accommodated at his expense, not the perpetrators' expense. The pattern included placing Jamie in different classes, placing him in a separate part of the bus, placing him in the special education class and forcing him to use a separate bathroom. Such affirmative acts by the school emphasized the message that Jamie was unworthy of respect and worthy of further abuse." Nabozny v. Podle-

sny, Appellant's Brief, filed with the Seventh Circuit Court of Appeals, December 18, 1995, http://www.lambdalegal.org/.

15. See Henkle v. Gregory, 150 F. Supp. 2d 1067 (D. Nev. 2001).

16. In today's special education system, a range of options and organizational structures exist. But reports documenting special education practices nationwide have found that, too often, apparently in violation of express provisions of the Individuals with Disabilities Education Act (IDEA)—which requires that students with disabilities be segregated "only when the nature or severity of the disability of a child is such that education in regular classes with the use of supplementary aids and services cannot be achieved satisfactorily"—many students are separated out into "special day classes" (SDCs) for the entire day and often for their entire public school careers. Nationwide, researchers and practitioners continue to report that students of color are disproportionately represented in special education and are much more likely than their white counterparts to end up in the SDCs. This is especially true for African American and Latino students in urban educational environments. See, e.g., Alfredo J. Artiles, Nancy Harris-Murri, and Dalia Rostenberg, "Inclusion as Social Justice: Critical Notes on Discourses, Assumptions, and the Road Ahead," *Theory into Practice* 45, no. 3 (2006): 260–68, and Russell J. Skiba et al., "The Context of Minority Disproportionality: Practitioner Perspectives on Special Education Referral," *Teachers College Record* 108, no. 7 (2006): 1424–59.

17. See, e.g., Eric Buhs, Gary Ladd, and Sarah Herald, "Peer Exclusion and Victimization: Processes That Mediate the Relation between Peer Group Rejection and Children's Classroom Engagement and Achievement," *Journal of Educational Psychology* 98, no. 1 (2006): 1–13, which identifies the effect of peer exclusion on school achievement.

18. See, e.g., Skiba et al., "Context of Minority Disproportionality."

19. See, e.g., Jonathan Cohen, "Social, Emotional, Ethical, and Academic Education: Creating a Climate for Learning, Participation in Democracy, and Well-Being," *Harvard Educational Review* 76, no. 2 (2006): 201.

20. See Howard Gardner, *Frames of Mind: The Theory of Multiple Intelligences* (New York: Basic Books, 1983). Gardner's research is often cited by opponents of "excessive" reliance on standardized tests. The argument typically asserted is that current test programs fail to measure this range of intelligences and thus present distorted pictures of human capability and achievement.

21. Gardner. See also Elaine Woo, "Teaching That Goes beyond IQ," *Los Angeles Times,* January 20, 1995.

22. Information about PATHS can be found on its national web page, http://www.channing-bete.com/prevention-programs/paths/paths.html; Project ACHIEVE is described at http://www.projectachieve.info/; and details on the Tribes Learning Community are found at http://tribes.com/.

23. A noteworthy California Department of Education publication, for

example, discusses model antibullying programs and recommended approaches. It also includes a chapter titled "Preventing School Bullying and Other Hateful Behaviors," addressing the role of peers, the role of adults, and concrete preventive steps that school officials can take in this regard. See "Bullying at School," http://www.cde.ca.gov/ls/ss/se/documents/bullyingatschool.pdf.

In response to such efforts, certain persons and groups have mounted campaigns to oppose any implementation of antibullying policies. Some of the opposition is based on arguments that antibullying programs are unnecessary and misguided, because bullying will always be with us and because traditional discipline offers the best opportunity for keeping things under control. Some even argue that antibullying programs are a subterfuge on the part of gay rights advocates seeking to "promote a homosexual agenda." See, e.g., David J. Hoff, "Texas Quits Group amid Debate over Gays," *Education Week,* December 14, 2005, which describes the decision of the Texas State Board of Education to quit the National Association of State Boards of Education because of disagreements regarding approaches to bullying.

24. See Robert Kim et al., "A Report on the Status of Gay, Lesbian, Bisexual, and Transgender People in Education: Stepping Out of the Closet, into the Light," National Education Association, http://www.nea.org/assets/docs/HE/glbtstatus09.pdf.

25. See Robert Tomsho, "Schools' Efforts to Protect Gays Face Opposition," *Wall Street Journal,* February 20, 2003. See also, generally, James T. Sears, *Homophobic Bullying* (Philadelphia: Haworth, 2007).

26. Gloria Moskowitz-Sweet, "Taking Bullying Seriously," *Bay Area Reporter,* June 19, 2009. Moskowitz-Sweet is a longtime counselor and clinical social worker who has worked with young people and their families in relation to this topic.

27. See "Public Comment of Stuart Biegel," UCLA Graduate School of Education and Information Studies and School of Law, May 18, 2011, cited in "Peer to Peer Violence and Bullying: Examining the Federal Response," U.S. Commission on Civil Rights, September 2011, http://www.usccr.gov/pubs/2011statutory.pdf.

28. See, e.g., Catherine Saillant, "Oxnard Teacher Is Still Haunted by Student's Slaying," *Los Angeles Times,* July 19, 2009.

29. See, generally, Charles Blow, "Two Little Boys," *New York Times,* April 24, 2009. Refer to the introduction to this book for details of the incidents involving King, Walker-Hoover, and Herrera.

30. See Ryan Lee, "'Boy Code' a Factor in Fatal School Shootings: Experts Say Masculinity Standards Overlooked in Search for Answers," *Washington Blade,* April 15, 2005.

31. See Lee.

32. Kim et al., "Report on the Status."

33. See California Department of Education, "Bullying and Hate-Motivated Behavior Prevention," http://www.cde.ca.gov/ls/ss/se/bullyprev.asp.

34. See Stuart Biegel and Sheila James Kuehl, "Safe at School: Addressing the School Environment and LGBT Safety through Policy and Legislation," a Collaboration of the National Education Policy Center and the Williams Institute, funded in part by the Great Lakes Center for Education Research and Practice, http://nepc.colorado.edu/publication/safe-at-school.

35. Biegel and Kuehl.

36. Capstone Institute/Howard University, "About Us," https://www.ideal ist.org/en/nonprofit/1fd2f583049249eb8442907ee2b9c0ea-capstone-institute -howard-university-washington.

37. Capstone Institute/Howard University.

38. See Johns Hopkins Center for Social Organization of Schools, CRESPAR, http://www.jhucsos.com/crespar/.

39. See, e.g., Robert E. Slavin and Nancy A. Madden, eds., *Success for All: Research and Reform in Elementary Education* (Abingdon on Thames: Routledge, 2001).

40. See, e.g., Nettie E. Legters (ed.), Robert Balfanz, W. J. Jordan, and James M. McPartland, *Comprehensive Reform for Urban High Schools: A Talent Development Approach* (New York: Teachers College Press, 2002).

41. Upward Bound is a federally funded education program with a very broad scope. See, generally, https://www2.ed.gov/programs/trioupbound/index.html.

42. See, e.g., Ritch C. Savin-Williams, *The New Gay Teenager* (Cambridge, Mass.: Harvard University Press, 2005), which presents stories of contemporary gay teenagers who can characterize their adolescent years in a positive light through factors that may include institutional and family support, a greater comfort level with fluidity in sexual relations within their social settings, and a level of resilience that has enabled them to transcend the homophobia that still exists.

43. Susan Talburt, a professor of education policy, warns against classifying all LGBT youth as either at risk or secure, noting that such normative constructions can exclude youth and ignore their creativity. Indeed, it is important to emphasize that many students fall between these polar opposites. Susan Talburt, "Constructions of LGBT Youth: Opening Up Subject Positions," *Theory into Practice* 43, no. 2 (2004): 116–21.

In August 2009, the *Journal of Youth and Adolescence* devoted its entire issue to new research on LGBT youth. In the introduction, the authors note that investigations of gay and gender-nonconforming youth still focus primarily on "deficits such as the role of victimization on mental and physical health, academic achievement, and identity." However, they also acknowledge that over the past decade, a growing number of scholars and practitioners have urged that a greater focus be placed on the tremendous strength and resilience of LGBT youth. The authors conclude that "it is necessary to continue examining the risks and challenges," yet it is also important to "incorporate additional perspectives of LGBT youths' lives and to view these youth as resilient and thriving rather than simply 'at-risk.'" They propose a new paradigm that moves beyond classifying the entire universe of LGBT youth as either at risk or resilient, one that instead examines the ways in which the social contexts that shape all their lives "influence the persistent inequalities in health risk behavior, mental health, and long-term psychosocial adjustment." See Stacey S. Horn, Joseph G. Kosciw, and Stephen T. Russell, "New Research on Lesbian, Gay, Bisexual, and Transgender Youth: Studying Lives in Context" (special issue introduction), *Journal of Youth and Adolescence* 38, no. 7 (2009): 863–66.

44. See Caitlin C. Ryan and Donna Futterman, *Lesbian and Gay Youth: Care and Counseling* (New York: Columbia University Press, 1998). This book has won several awards, including a 1999 Distinguished Book Award from the American Psychological Association.

45. See "The Family Acceptance Project: Building Healthy Futures for LGBT Children and Youth through Research, Education and Training, Family-Oriented Services, and Informed Public Policy," https://familyproject.sfsu.edu/.

46. See James T. Sears, "Peering into the Well of Loneliness: The Responsibility of Educators to Gay and Lesbian Youth," in *Social Issues in Education: Challenge and Responsibility,* ed. Alex Molnar, 79–100 (Alexandria, Va.: Association for Supervision and Curriculum Development, 1987); James T. Sears, "Helping Students Understand and Accept Sexual Diversity," *Educational Leadership* 49, no. 1 (1991): 54–56; James T. Sears, ed., *Curriculum, Religion, and Public Education: Conversations for an Enlarging Public Square* (New York: Teachers College Press, 1998); and James T. Sears, ed., *Gay, Lesbian, and Transgender Issues in Education: Programs, Policies, and Practices* (Binghamton, N.Y.: Haworth, 2005).

47. See Kimberlé Crenshaw, "In Theory: Why Intersectionality Can't Wait," *Washington Post,* September 24, 2015. Professor Crenshaw's noteworthy scholarship includes *Critical Race Theory: The Key Writings That Formed the Movement,* coedited by Neil Gotanda, Gary Peller, and Kendall Thomas (New York: New Press, 1996); *Black Girls Matter: Pushed Out, Overpoliced, and Underprotected,* a report coauthored by Priscilla Ocen and Jyoti Nanda (New York: African American Policy Forum, Center for Intersectionality and Social Policy Studies, 2016), https://www.atlanticphilanthropies.org/app/uploads/2015/09/BlackGirlsMatter_Report.pdf; and *On Intersectionality: Essential Writings* (New York: New Press, forthcoming 2019).

48. See Kevin K. Kumashiro, "Queer Students of Color and Antiracist, Antiheterosexist Education: Paradoxes of Identity and Activism," in *Troubling Intersections of Race and Sexuality,* ed. Kevin K. Kumashiro, 1–25 (Lanham, Md.: Rowman and Littlefield, 2001).

49. See Molly O'Shaughnessy et al., *Safe Place to Learn: Consequences of Harassment Based on Actual or Perceived Sexual Orientation and Gender Nonconformity and Steps for Making Schools Safer* (report of the California Safe Schools Coalition and the 4-H Center for Youth Development, University of California, Davis, January 2004), http://www.casafeschools.org/SafePlacetoLearn Low.pdf. For additional examples of Russell's work, see, e.g., Stephen T. Russell and T. B. Consolacion, "Adolescent Romance and Emotional Health in the U.S.: Beyond Binaries," *Journal of Clinical Child and Adolescent Psychology* 32 (2003): 499–508; and Stephen T. Russell, "Sexual Minority Youth and Suicide Risk," *American Behavioral Scientist* 46 (2003): 1241–57.

50. Eric Rofes, "Opening Up the Classroom Closet: Responding to the Educational Needs of Gay and Lesbian Youth," *Harvard Educational Review* 59, no. 4 (1989): 444–53.

51. See Eric Rofes, *A Radical Rethinking of Sexuality and Schooling: Status Quo or Status Queer?* (Lanham, Md.: Rowman and Littlefield, 2005). For an overview of Rofes's many achievements, see, generally, Douglas Martin, "Eric Rofes, Commentator on Gay Issues, Dies at 51," *New York Times,* June 29, 2006.

52. See Anthony R. D'Augelli and Charlotte J. Patterson, *Lesbian, Gay, and Bisexual Identities and Youth: Psychological Perspectives* (Oxford: Oxford University Press, 2001); Nila Marrone, "Advice to Latino Parents of LGBT Children," *SIECUS Report* 29, no. 4 (2001): 32–36; and Corrine Munoz-Plaza, Sandra Crouse Quinn, and Kathleen A. Rounds, "Lesbian, Gay, Bisexual, and Transgender Students: Perceived Social Support in the High School Environment," *High School Journal* 85, no. 4 (2002): 52–63.

53. See, e.g., V. Paul Poteat, Dorothy L. Espelage, and Brian W. Koenig, "Willingness to Remain Friends and Attend School with Lesbian and Gay Peers: Relational Expressions of Prejudice among Heterosexual Youth," *Journal of Youth and Adolescence* 38 (2009): 952–62. See also, generally, Kim et al., "Report on the Status." It is important to note that the documented findings of researchers in the NEA report mirrored, in many ways, the findings of Ryan, Sears, and Rofes over the previous decade.

54. A Google search of the words "blaming the gays" revealed on June 19, 2009, that LGBTs have been deemed the cause of everything from Hurricane Katrina, the failure of the war effort in Iraq, the reelection of George W. Bush, an epidemic of gun-related murders in the United States, and the destruction of heterosexual marriage. Country singer Tammy Flowers has written a parody about this dynamic, entitled "Blame the Gays," which became a very popular feature of her live performances.

55. During this era, the scapegoating of gays in public life is generally found at the margins. Yet religious leaders in Israel blamed the summer 2006 Hezbollah attacks from across the Lebanese border on the gays who were planning a world

gay pride event in Jerusalem. See Etgar Lefkovits, "Rabbi Links Hizbullah Violence to Planned Jerusalem Gay Parade," *Jerusalem Post,* July 20, 2006. And the late Reverend Jerry Falwell famously put some of the blame for the September 11 tragedies on gays and lesbians in an appearance on the *700 Club* shortly after the tragedy (Christian Broadcasting Network, September 13, 2001); transcript available on the web page of the Common Dreams Progressive NewsWire, http://www.commondreams.org/news2001/0917-03.htm: "I really believe that . . . the gays and the lesbians who are actively trying to make that an alternative lifestyle . . . all of them who have tried to secularize America. I point the finger in their face and say 'you helped this happen.'" In addition, ruthless treatment of gays and lesbians who dare to come out in public continues in many parts of the world. See, e.g., Megan K. Stack, "Russia Police Break Up a Gay Protest," *Los Angeles Times,* May 17, 2009.

56. See, e.g., William B. Rubenstein, "My Harvard Law School," *Harvard Civil Rights–Civil Liberties Law Review* 39 (2004): 318, a highly poignant piece by the law professor and longtime gay rights advocate. In the article, Rubenstein explains how lonely a person with an emergent sexuality can be and how frightening coming to terms with it can be, even in elite academia. He then documents at some length his efforts to bring LGBT resources and an LGBT curriculum to major American law schools. Rubenstein also tells of the extent to which the AIDS epidemic had already been raging when he entered law school, in the early 1980s, and how, although many people were already ill and dying, even an HIV test would not be available until 1986. Indeed, it was because he assumed he was as likely to die from the disease as all those around him that Rubenstein decided to focus his legal work on AIDS issues in what he perceived to be the short time remaining to him (322).

57. See, e.g., Rebecca Bethard, "New York's Harvey Milk School: A Viable Alternative," *Journal of Law and Education* 33 (2004): 417–23, which documents the efforts at this school to address the social imbalances that exist for many LGBTs in the nation's K–12 schools.

58. In this context, gays, lesbians, and transgender persons are often accused of "flaunting their sexuality" whenever they hold hands or embrace in public, or in fact when they even mention their sexual identities. Kenji Yoshino has argued that the current frontier of gay civil rights for those LGBT people who live "beyond the closet" includes the decision whether to "flaunt" their sexuality or "cover" their identity to more easily assimilate into a largely straight culture. Kenji Yoshino, *Covering: The Hidden Assault on Our Civil Rights* (New York: Random House, 2006), 76. Even in areas of the country that are considered especially gay friendly—Chelsea in Manhattan, for example—public displays of affection between same-sex individuals can be risky actions. LGBTs continue to disagree among themselves about how safe it is to embrace in public as any straight couple would. See Guy Trebay, "A Kiss Too Far?," *New York Times,* February 18, 2007.

59. Gays and lesbians invariably remember that at some point in their childhood, they realized that they were different. See, e.g., Lisa C. Moore, ed., *Does Your Mama Know? An Anthology of Black Lesbian Coming Out Stories* (Washington, D.C.: Redbone, 1997); Russell Leong, *Asian American Sexualities: Dimensions of the Gay and Lesbian Experience* (New York: Routledge, 1995); and Edmund White, *A Boy's Own Story* (New York: Modern Library, 1982).

60. Munoz-Plaza et al., "Lesbian, Gay, Bisexual, and Transgender Students," 54, 57, 60.

61. See, generally, Stephen T. Russell and Stacey S. Horn, *Sexual Orientation, Gender Identity, and Schooling: The Nexus of Research, Practice, and Policy* (Oxford: Oxford University Press, 2016). The essays in this book, which address interrelated issues that have emerged across the globe, are divided into five categories, with two of the categories, "Section I—Victimization, Bullying, and Harassment in Schools" and "Section II—Cutting Edge Issues on Sexual Orientation and Gender Identity in Schools," especially applicable to the themes set forth in this chapter.

62. See Russell and Horn, 5–6.

63. Kim et al., "Report on the Status." See also Caitlyn Ryan et al., "Family Rejection as a Predictor of Negative Health Outcomes in White and Latino Lesbian, Gay, and Bisexual Adults," *Pediatrics* 123 (2009): 346–52.

64. See, e.g., Kevin Kumashiro, *Restored Selves: Autobiographies of Queer Asian-Pacific American Activists* (New York: Routledge, 2003).

65. See Jason Cianciotto and Sean Cahill, *Education Policy: Issues Affecting Lesbian, Gay, Bisexual, and Transgender Youth* (New York: National Gay and Lesbian Task Force Policy Institute, 2003), http://www.thetaskforce.org/down loads/reports/reports/EducationPolicy.pdf. See also Nova Gutierrez, "Resisting Fragmentation, Living Whole: Four Female Transgender Students of Color Speak about School," *Journal of Gay and Lesbian Social Services* 16 (2004): 69.

66. A 2001 study, for example, found that many LGBT students of color appear to have much more pleasant school experiences than their white counterparts, and many also experience greater support from their biological families. See Stephen T. Russell, Hinda Seif, and Nhan L. Truong, "School Outcomes of Sexual Minority Youth in the United States: Evidence from a National Study," *Journal of Adolescence* 24 (2001): 111. In another study, Asian American, African American, and Latino youth were less likely than white youth to disclose their sexual identity to family members, whereas white youth were more likely to hide their sexual identity in school, citing fears of harassment and violence. Neil W. Pilkington and Anthony R. D'Augelli, "Victimization of Lesbian, Gay, and Bisexual Youth in Community Settings," *Journal of Community Psychology* 23, no. 1 (1995): 34–56. But see, generally, Lance T. McCready, "Understanding the Marginalization of Gay and Gender Non-conforming Black Male Students," *Theory into Practice* 43, no. 2 (2004): 136–43.

67. For information and resources regarding safe zones, see, e.g., "GLSEN Safe Space Kit: Be an Ally to LGBTQ Youth," https://www.glsen.org/safespace.

68. See Stephen T. Russell et al., "Youth Empowerment and High School Gay–Straight Alliances," *Journal of Youth and Adolescence* 38 (2009): 891–903.

69. See Billie Gastic and Dominique Johnson, "Teacher-Mentors and the Educational Resilience of Sexual Minority Youth," *Journal of Gay and Lesbian Social Services* 21, no. 2–3 (2009): 219–31.

70. See, generally, the GLSEN website, https://www.glsen.org/.

71. A particularly noteworthy example of this work is *Take It Back: A Manual for Fighting Slurs on Campus* (San Francisco: Tides Center/Gay–Straight Alliance Network, 2003). See http://gsanetwork.org/files/getinvolved/TakeItBack -Manual.pdf.

72. Research on disproportionality in suicide rates and the nature and extent of the suicide problem within LGBT communities date back to the pioneering work of Martin and Hetrick in the 1980s. See A. Damien Martin and Emery S. Hetrick, "The Stigmatization of the Gay and Lesbian Adolescent," *Journal of Homosexuality* 15, no. 1–2 (1988): 163–83. For a more recent analysis of issues in this area, focusing in particular on the risks faced by transgender youth, see Arnold H. Grossman and Anthony R. D'Augelli, "Transgender Youth and Life-Threatening Behavior," *Suicide and Life-Threatening Behavior* 37, no. 5 (2007): 527–37.

73. The *Washington Post,* in its June 2006 series "Being a Black Man," reported that "the suicide rate among young black men has doubled since 1980." In related, highly relevant data, the *Post* also reported that "one in four black men have not worked for at least a year, twice the proportion of male non-Hispanic whites or Latinos. And trends suggest a third of black males born today will spend time in prison." Steven A. Holmes and Richard Morin, "Poll Reveals a Contradictory Portrait Shaded with Promise and Doubt," *Washington Post,* June 4, 2006.

With regard to young Hispanic women, in late July 2006, the *New York Times* reported the results of a federal study that found that "a startling one in six young Hispanic women had attempted suicide, a rate roughly one and a half times as high as that among non-Hispanic black and white teenage girls. . . . A five-year study now in its second year in New York is being led by Dr. Luis Zayas, a professor of social work and psychiatry at Washington University in St. Louis, who says the self-destructive behavior seems to affect Latinas of every origin and every region of the country." "Young Latinas and a Cry for Help," editorial, *New York Times,* July 21, 2006.

74. The Trevor Helpline is at (866) 488-7386 ([866] 4-U-TREVOR). For more information, see http://www.thetrevorproject.org/helpline.aspx. The Trevor Facebook page is at http://www.facebook.com/TheTrevorProject. The LGBT National Help Center is at http://www.glnh.org/; its National Hotline is at (888) 843-4564, and its National Youth Talkline is at (800) 246-7743 ([800] 246-PRIDE). The organization also offers an online Peer Support Chat.

75. See HIV-Related Services: Prevention Programs, LA LGBT Center, https://lalgbtcenter.org/health-services/hiv-related-services/prevention-programs.

76. Welcome to API Wellness, http://apiwellness.org/site/.

77. See, generally, "Respect for All Project" Films, http://groundspark.org/respect-for-all/rfap-films.

78. *Gay Youth*, directed by Pam Walton (1992; United States: New Day Films), DVD.

7. Creating Change in the Classroom

1. See later in this chapter for an overview of California's FAIR Education Act (2011), which requires age-appropriate and LGBT-positive content in the public school social studies curriculum.

2. Morrison v. Bd. of Ed. of Boyd County, 419 F.Supp.2d 937 (E.D. Ky. 2006).

3. Citizens for a Responsible Curriculum v. Montgomery County Public Schools, 2005 WL 1075634 (D. Md. 2005) (not reported).

4. *Morrison*, at 944.

5. *Morrison*, at 944–45.

6. *Morrison*, at 943–44.

7. The term *professional development* has gradually taken the place of the more traditional term *staff development*, reflecting ongoing efforts on many fronts to enhance the stature and indeed the self-image of K–12 classroom teachers. The terms are generally viewed as synonymous and are often used interchangeably.

8. See Willis Hawley and Linda Valli, "The Essentials of Effective Professional Development," in *Teaching as the Learning Profession: Handbook of Policy and Practice*, ed. Linda Darling-Hammond and Gary Sykes, 127–50 (San Francisco: Jossey-Bass, 1999), and Luz Maldonado, "Effective Professional Development: Findings from Research," College Entrance Examination Board, 2002, https://secure-media.collegeboard.org/apc/ap05_profdev_effectiv_41935.pdf. Learning Forward, a professional learning association devoted to the synthesis and dissemination of best practices in this area, emphasizes that learning communities are perhaps the most central of all the principles for effective professional development. See https://learningforward.org/standards/learning-communities.

9. See Eric Rofes, *A Radical Rethinking of Sexuality and Schooling: Status Quo or Status Queer?* (Lanham, Md.: Rowman and Littlefield, 2005). See also Report 22 of the San Francisco Consent Decree Monitoring Team, submitted to the U.S. District Court, Northern District of California, July 31, 2005, appendix 1, 17–18 (on file with the author), lauding the approach taken by the Harvey Milk Civil Rights Academy, which "has a deep commitment to maintaining a diverse student body and educating the neediest of students": "At every level of the school's operations and day-to-day activities, this is an environment that recognizes LGBT persons and their needs, naturally and with great support. . . .

Perhaps more than any other school in the City [San Francisco], Harvey Milk reaches out to the surrounding neighborhood, and has established close ties to local businesses and community groups."

10. See, generally, James T. Sears, "Thinking Critically/Intervening Effectively about Heterosexism and Homophobia: A Twenty-Five Year Research Retrospective," in James T. Sears and Walter L. Williams, eds., *Overcoming Heterosexism and Homophobia: Strategies That Work*, 13–48 (New York: Columbia University Press, 1997).

11. See Samuel Marc Davidson, "Exploring Sociocultural Borderlands: Journeying, Navigating, and Embodying a Queer Identity," *Journal of Men's Studies* 14, No. 1 (2006): 13–26, which documents a study that examined the recent experiences of a young gender-nonconforming Latino male: "Heteronormativity is like the air we breathe. It is with us from the day of our birth . . . the belief that 'normal' sexuality is heterosexual. Making transparent its pervasiveness is the first step in addressing the threat to well-being . . . of young men and women in general who feel constrained by the limited range of representations of masculinity made available to them throughout their schooling."

12. Michael Nava, "Coming Out and Born Again," in *Wrestling with the Angel: Faith and Religion in the Lives of Gay Men*, ed. Brian Bouldrey (New York: Riverhead, 1995), 178.

13. Mychal Copeland and D'vorah Rose, eds., *Struggling in Good Faith: LGBTQI Inclusion from 13 American Religious Perspectives* (Nashville, Tenn.: Skylight Paths, 2015).

Rabbi Mychal Coleman, currently the spiritual leader at Congregation Sha'ar Zahav in San Francisco, "speaks and writes about the inclusion of LGBTQI people and interfaith families in religious life." D'vorah Rose, "a multifaith chaplain, rabbi, and palliative care and hospice nurse, consults with and advises healthcare institutions . . . on the intersections of religious and cultural diversity . . . with a specific focus on historically underserved communities." See "About the Author[s]," https://www.amazon.com/Struggling-Good-Faith-Inclusion-Perspectives/dp/1594736022.

14. Copeland and Rose.

15. See Rev. Chris Glaser, "Pride and Passion: Claiming Our Faith," April 6, 2008, http://www.chrisglaser.com/writings/PrideandPassion.htm.

16. See Rabbi Steven Greenberg, *Wrestling with God and Men: Homosexuality in the Jewish Tradition* (Madison: University of Wisconsin Press, 2004).

17. See Carrie Sturrock, "Meeting for Gays Focuses on God," *San Francisco Chronicle*, November 14, 2005.

18. See http://www.irenemonroe.com/ for a profile of the Reverend Irene Monroe.

19. See Dalton Walker, "Going Far from Home to Feel at Home," New York

Times, July 17, 2007. See also Melissa Hoskins and Harlan Pruden, "Hello from NE2SS," *Two-Spirit Times,* Spring 2007, http://ne2ss.typepad.com/northeast_twospirit_socie/files/2spirit_times_spring_07.pdf.

20. Soulforce gained much attention in 2006 with its widely publicized Equality Ride. Inspired by the Freedom Rides of the 1960s, thirty-three young adults traveled to nineteen colleges and universities throughout the United States to publicize and confront policies that typically mandated expulsion of openly gay students and even prohibited those enrolled from advocating pro-LGBT views. In some locations, the Soulforce members were arrested, but in other places, they were welcomed in and allowed to dialogue with members of the college community. See, generally, http://www.soulforce.org/.

21. See the federal school accountability requirements in the Every Student Succeeds Act (ESSA) and its statutory predecessor, the No Child Left Behind Act (NCLB). See, generally, Welner et al., *Legal Issues in Education,* 267–98.

22. See, generally, David Rigsby, "Sex Education in Schools," *Georgetown Journal of Gender and Law* 7 (2006): 895, 898–900.

23. See "Politically Correct History," editorial, *Los Angeles Times,* May 9, 2006, and "California History: What's Sexual Preference Got to Do with It?," editorial, *Sacramento Bee,* May 8, 2006. At the same time, the bill-analysis report prepared for the California Senate on SB 1437 referenced a GLSEN study finding that 76.2 percent of youth reported that LGBT issues were never addressed or discussed in class and that in many classrooms where issues *were* addressed, LGBTs were portrayed negatively or in relationship to pathology. See Dee Brennick, "SB 1437 Senate Bill Analysis," June 14, 2006.

24. Deborah Howell, "Public Death, Private Life," *Washington Post,* March 30, 2008. Kevin Naff, editor of the *Washington Blade,* added, "It's a double standard to report basic facts about straight subjects like marital status, while actively suppressing similar information about gay subjects. It was clear that Maj. Rogers led as openly gay a life as was possible, given his military service. He worked for a gay rights organization, had gay friends and patronized D.C.-area gay clubs. It's unfortunate *The Post* . . . chose not to present a full picture of this brave man's life."

25. Howell. For additional details regarding these disputes, including whether and to what extent Rogers should be identified as a gay man in his obituaries, memorial services, and related documents, see, e.g., Ben McGrath, "A Soldier's Legacy," *The New Yorker,* August 4, 2008.

26. John D'Emilio, "The Universities and the Gay Experience," in *Making Trouble: Essays on Gay History, Politics, and the University,* 117–27 (New York: Routledge, 1992).

27. "GAU's purpose reflected both personal and professional concerns: combating discrimination, mutual support in coming out, encouraging unbiased scholarship, and the teaching of gay studies." John D'Emilio, "The Issue of

Sexual Preference on College Campuses: Retrospect and Prospect," in *Making Trouble*, 126.

28. John D'Emilio, "Gay History: A New Field of Study," in *Making Trouble*, 96–113.

29. John D'Emilio, "Gay and Lesbian Studies: New Kid on the Block?," in *Making Trouble*, 160–75.

30. See California Education Code Section 51204.5.

31. See "State Board Approves Instructional Materials That Give K–8 Students a Deeper, Broader Understanding of History and Social Sciences," news release, California Department of Education, November 9, 2017, https://www.cde.ca.gov/nr/ne/yr17/yr17rel82.asp.

32. See Scott Hirschfeld, "Stonewall Jackson and the Stonewall Riots Together," Gay, Lesbian, and Straight Education Network, July 1, 2003. A representative collection of curricular resources for K–12 educators can be found on the website of the Washington Safe Schools Coalition, http://www.safeschoolscoalition.org/blackboard-teachers.html. Through the efforts of community leader Beth Reis and other longtime educators and activists, the coalition has developed materials and compiled links to sample LGBT-related lesson plans and curricula created by educators across the nation.

33. See, e.g., Bayard Rustin, *Time on Two Crosses: The Collected Writings of Bayard Rustin*, ed. Devon W. Carbado and Donald Weise (San Francisco: Cleis, 2003).

34. An additional example of a typical standard is one that mandates describing the Harlem Renaissance, with special attention to writers (e.g., Zora Neale Hurston, Langston Hughes). Literature anthologies typically address basic details of a writer's romantic life, including people they might have fallen in love with, because such details cannot generally be overlooked in assessing the writers' perspectives and the thematic content of their work. If this approach is typical in a literature anthology, it is even more relevant in a history course. Referencing how the work of Hurston might have been informed by her bisexuality and the work of Langston Hughes by his gay identity is consistent with such a mainstream approach to the study of the humanities.

8. The Culture of School Sports

1. In recent decades, the number of young people participating in organized sports appears to be increasing, especially with the growing popularity of soccer leagues among both elementary- and middle school–age children and their parents.

2. See, e.g., Heather Barber and Vikki Krane, "Creating a Positive Climate for Lesbian, Gay, Bisexual, and Transgender Youths," *Journal of PE, Recreation, and Dance* 78, no. 7 (2007): 6–7, 52.

3. See, generally, the overview of the National Center for Lesbian Rights Sports Project, at http://ncflr.convio.net/site/PageServer?pagename=issue_spo rts_overview, "founded in 2001 as the first project of its kind to prioritize, through litigation and policy work, rampant anti-LGBT discrimination and forced invisibility of LGBT athletes, coaches, and sports professionals."

4. Dan Le Batard, "NBA Not Prepared for Amaechi's Revelation," *Pittsburgh Post-Gazette,* February 16, 2007.

5. See Andrew Joseph, "Jason Collins Has Powerful Response to Amar'e Stoudemire's Homophobic Comments," *USA Today,* March 1, 2017. It should be noted that in 2012, Stoudemire was fined $50,000 for tweeting an anti-gay slur while a member of the New York Knicks. This time, in 2017, he did not apologize. Joseph.

6. See Joseph.

7. Joseph.

8. But see Allen Barra, "Actually, Jason Collins Isn't the First Openly Gay Man in a Major Pro Sport," *The Atlantic,* May 2, 2013: "Major league baseball player Glenn Burke was comfortably out to his Dodger teammates and friends in 1976—but back then, it was the press that wasn't ready for a gay male athlete. . . . Burke made no secret of his sexual orientation to the Dodgers front office, his teammates, or friends in either league. He also talked freely with sportswriters, though all of them ended up shaking their heads and telling him they couldn't write *that* in their papers." See, generally, Barra.

9. Billy Bean, *Going the Other Way: Lessons from a Life in and out of Major League Baseball* (New York: Marlowe, 2003).

10. Bean, 107–8.

11. Jennifer Jacobson, "Facing Derision in a Macho Culture," *Chronicle of Higher Education,* November 1, 2002. See also Selena Roberts, "A Player Serves Notice to Homophobic Sports Culture," *New York Times,* February 8, 2007, which describes the settlement in a lawsuit by former Penn State player Jennifer Harris against women's basketball coach Rene Portland.

12. Jacobson, "Facing Derision."

13. See Sheryl Swoopes (as told to L. Z. Granderson), "Outside the Arc," *ESPN Magazine,* October 26, 2005.

14. Tim Dahlberg, "Lesbians in Sports: Still an Issue," Associated Press, November 17, 2005.

15. Quoted in Jacobson, "Facing Derision."

16. See Greg Garber, "Now I Get to Be Like Everybody Else," ESPN, May 27, 2005, http://sports.espn.go.com/ncaa/news/story?id=2069239.

17. In summer 2017, just prior to the start of the 2017 college football season, ESPN reported that two players had come out: Kansas State offensive tackle Scott Frantz and incoming Arizona freshman defensive end My-King Johnson. They apparently were slated to be the only two college football players in the

country at the time who had done so. See, e.g., Tim Bisel, "Scott Frantz, Kansas State Tackle, Tells ESPN He's Gay," *Topeka Capital-Journal,* July 13, 2017.

18. See, e.g., Mechelle Voepel, "Ready to Let You In," July 20, 2017, http://www.espn.com/espnw/feature/20088416/wnba-all-star-sue-bird-ready-let-in (where the WNBA All-Star, Sue Bird, not only comes out but shares the story of her relationship with girlfriend and soccer superstar Megan Rapinoe).

19. See Jacobson, "Facing Derision." See also Martina Navratilova, "Coming Out Was a 'Moment of Truth,'" special to the *Bay Area Reporter,* October 26, 2006; Lauren Effron, Tess Scott, and Christina Ng, "Caitlyn Jenner Reflects on How Her Life Has Changed since Transitioning into a Woman," *ABC News,* April 21, 2017, http://abcnews.go.com/Entertainment/caitlyn-jenner-reflects-life -changed-transitioning-woman/story?id=46861647.

20. See, e.g., Wyatt Buchanan, "Out to Win," *San Francisco Chronicle,* October 8, 2006. In August 2009, King was awarded a Presidential Medal of Freedom by President Obama. In the White House press release, she was described as "an acclaimed professional tennis player . . . [who] helped champion gender equality issues not only in sports, but in all areas of public life. . . . King became one of the first openly lesbian major sports figures in America when she came out." See http://www.whitehouse.gov/the_press_office/President-Obama-Names-Medal -of-Freedom-Recipients.

21. Based on the book of the same name (published by Random House in 1995), the television movie was titled *Breaking the Surface: The Greg Louganis Story,* directed by Steven Hilliard Stern (1997; United States: Ariztical Entertainment, 2003), DVD.

22. See Caitlyn Jenner, *The Secrets of My Life* (New York: Grand Central, 2017).

23. In addition to Bean's *Going the Other Way,* see David Kopay, *The David Kopay Story* (Westminster, Md.: Arbor House, 1977); Esera Tuaolo, *Alone in the Trenches: My Life as a Gay Man in the NFL* (Naperville, Ill.: Sourcebooks, 2006); and John Amaechi, *The Man in the Middle* (New York: ESPN Books, 2007).

24. The *Los Angeles Times* reported that Koufax "would no longer attend spring training at Dodgertown in Florida, visit Dodger Stadium or participate in any activities while they are owned by News Corp." Jason Reid, "Koufax Shuts Dodgers Out," *Los Angeles Times,* February 21, 2003.

25. See "Koufax Cuts Ties after Report Implied He Was Gay," Associated Press, February 21, 2003.

26. Indeed, Koufax has since returned to the Dodger organization. See Dylan Hernandez, "Dodgers and Sandy Koufax Team Up Again after Years Apart," *Los Angeles Times,* January 22, 2013. See also Eric Stephen, "Sandy Koufax 'Still Part of Dodgers Organization and Always Will Be,'" *True Blue LA: A Los Angeles Dodgers Community,* February 28, 2016.

27. Bean, *Going the Other Way*, 112–16, 230. Describing his cathartic experience addressing five hundred thousand people at the Millennium March on Washington for gay and lesbian rights, Bean writes, "I felt more confident now than during my playing days, with no fear of failure, and at last I could speak from my heart. 'When I played baseball, I was all alone,' I said, surveying the crowd. 'Today I'm a member of a big family—one I'm proud to represent.'"

28. See, e.g., Alex Marvez, "Michael Sam Saga Might Keep Other Gay NFL Hopefuls from Coming Out, Former Exec Says," *Sporting News*, May 22, 2017.

29. See Esera Tuaolo, with Luke Cyphers, "Free and Clear," *ESPN: The Magazine*, October 30, 2002, http://espn.go.com/magazine/vol5no23tuaolo.html.

30. Tuaolo, *Alone in the Trenches*, excerpted at the website "Common Ground–Common Sense," http://www.commongroundcommonsense.org/forums/index.php?showtopic=50907.

31. See Tuaolo.

32. Bill Clinton entered the White House in 1993 committed to removing the formal ban on gays and lesbians serving in the military, but he ran into a firestorm of opposition from both the military establishment and many members of Congress on both sides of the aisle. In the end, a compromise was reached: gays and lesbians would be officially allowed to serve in the U.S. military, but only if they kept their identities to themselves. As of 2010, approximately thirteen thousand gays and lesbians had been removed from the military because of this federal mandate, which became known as "Don't Ask, Don't Tell."

In 2011, President Barack Obama made good on his promise and repealed "Don't Ask, Don't Tell." See Elisabeth Bumiller, "Obama Ends 'Don't Ask, Don't Tell' Policy," *New York Times*, July 22, 2011.

33. The military considered transgender to be a disqualifying psychiatric condition, both for those wishing to enlist and for those already serving who wished to transition. See "Survival Guide: Transgender Military Issues," Servicemembers Legal Defense Network, http://www.sldn.org/.

34. See Julie Hirschfeld Davis and Helene Cooper, "Trump Says Transgender People Will Not Be Allowed in the Military," *New York Times*, July 26, 2017. See, generally, Martha Bebinger, "Trump Swaps Complete Ban for 'Qualified Ban' on Transgender Military Service," NPR, March 24, 2018 ("President Trump has revoked a blanket ban on transgender military service he tried to impose last summer. A new detailed ban released late last night has the support of some religious conservatives but has renewed fury among advocates for transgender service members who vow to continue their fight in court.") For additional details, see chapter 9 of this book.

35. Comments by California governor Arnold Schwarzenegger in 2004 typify this line of thinking. Referring to a budget battle among California legislators, which at the time included five gays and lesbians, he said, "If they don't have the

guts, I call them girlie-men. They should get back to the table and they should finish the budget." He later used the same term twice more in reference to the same legislators and did not shirk from the comments when questioned about them. Peter Nicholas, "Schwarzenegger Deems Opponents 'Girlie-Men'—Twice," *Los Angeles Times,* July 18, 2004.

36. Few invoke the predator myth openly at this time, but it is clear that, in private, many still believe it.

As the presidential primary campaigns moved forward in 2007, candidates began staking out positions on the military ban. Both Senator Hillary Clinton (D-N.Y.) and Senator Barack Obama (D-Ill.) issued statements in favor of repealing "Don't Ask, Don't Tell." But Senator John McCain (R-Ariz.) issued a statement in which he said that gay troops pose "an intolerable risk" to national security. Barbara Wilcox, "McCain: Gay Troops Pose 'Intolerable Risk,'" *Advocate,* May 4, 2007, http://www.advocate.com/.

37. See, e.g., Randy Shilts, *Conduct Unbecoming: Gays and Lesbians in the U.S. Military* (New York: St. Martin's, Griffin, 1993), 4: "The military's policies have had a sinister effect on the entire nation: Such policies make it known to every-one . . . that lesbians and gay men are dangerous to the well-being of other Americans; that they are undeserving of even the most basic civil rights. Such policies also create an ambience in which discrimination, harassment, and even violence against lesbians and gays is tolerated and to some degree encouraged."

38. See Allan Bérubé, *Coming Out under Fire: The History of Gay Men and Women in World War II* (New York: Free Press, 1990), and the 1994 documentary of the same name, directed by Arthur Dong (United States: New Video Group, 2005), DVD.

In the Americans with Disabilities Act of 1990, "homosexuals" are included on a list along with pyromaniacs and kleptomaniacs as examples of people whose conditions are not covered by the new law, continuing this association. Adrienne L. Hiegel, "Sexual Exclusions: The Americans with Disabilities Act as a Moral Code," *Columbia Law Review* 94 (1994): 1451, 1474–75.

39. In a sign of the times, the headline in the 1950 *Washington Post* story about the congressional subcommittee recommendation used the word "perverts" to describe gays. As captured in a scene from Dong's film *Coming Out under Fire,* the headline read, "3750 Perverts Hold U.S. Jobs in Capital, Senate Probers Say."

In 2003, transcripts were released from the 161 secret hearings conducted in 1953 and 1954 by Senator McCarthy and his aide Roy Cohn as they probed anti-American activities of those in public service. Among these hearings were many direct interrogations of gay men who had public service positions and were goaded into outing others. Mark Goebel, "Transcripts Confirm McCarthy Gay-Baiting," May 7, 2003, http://www.planetout.com/.

40. See, e.g., the United Airlines tribute to Bingham at http://www.united heroes.com/Mark-Bingham.html.

41. For example, according to Wikipedia, Senators John McCain and Barbara Boxer honored Mark Bingham in a ceremony for San Francisco Bay Area victims on September 17, 2001, presenting a folded American flag to Bingham's former boyfriend, Paul Holm. See http://en.wikipedia.org/wiki/Mark_Bingham. The California Alumni Association of the University of California, Berkeley now annually awards the outstanding achievement of a young alumnus or alumna with the Mark Bingham Award for Excellence in Achievement at its Charter Gala each spring.

42. It should be noted that although Israel does allow openly gay and lesbian persons to serve in the military, this service is restricted to noncombat situations. Interview with Timna Naim, Israeli citizen and UCLA student, winter 2017.

43. According to the International Lesbian and Gay Association, as of November 2006, at least thirty-two countries allowed openly gay, lesbian, and bisexual people to serve in their militaries, and thirteen (including the United States) formally banned them from serving. Daniel Ottosson, "LGBT World Legal Wrap Up Survey," International Lesbian and Gay Association, November 2006, http://www.ilga.org/.

44. Christopher Dandeker, quoted in Sarah Lyall, "Gays in the British Military: Ask, Tell, and Then Move On," *New York Times,* February 10, 2001.

45. Sarah Lyall, "Open Minds on Open Seas: British Royal Navy Woos Gays and Lesbians," *New York Times,* February 22, 2005.

46. See Chris Sheridan, "Amaechi Becomes First NBA Player to Come Out," ESPN, February 9, 2007, http://sports.espn.go.com/nba/news/story?id=2757105.

47. Bean, *Going the Other Way,* 218.

48. As discussed earlier, the importance of voluntariness and genuineness on the part of educators addressing LGBT issues cannot be overstated. K–12 students invariably see right through a lack of genuineness, and they know when their teachers and coaches mean what they say.

49. Greg Hernandez, "Gay in the NBA: The Buzz," *Advocate,* March 13, 2007; Hernandez quotes Phil Miller. See also Richard Roeper, "Many Think Homophobia Is Acceptable: Baseball Fans Reach Dismal Lows at Cubs-Sox Game," *Chicago Sun-Times,* June 30, 2009, describing an apparently popular T-shirt that many wore at the mid-season crosstown rivalry series, which put forth the vacuous proposition that a White Sox "parade" was a World Series victory parade, while a Cubs "parade" was a gay pride parade.

50. In professional sports, among the many high-profile leaders who have been known for their strong religious affiliations are longtime Dallas Cowboys coach Tom Landry, highly acclaimed Indianapolis Colts coach Tony Dungy, and the aforementioned Los Angeles Dodgers manager Tom Lasorda.

51. See, e.g., Alan Dundes, "The American Game of 'Smear the Queer' and the Homosexual Component of Male Competitive Sport and Warfare," *Journal of Psychoanalytic Anthropology* 8, no. 3 (1985): 115–29, and Kenneth B. Muir and

Trina Seitz, "Machismo, Misogyny, and Homophobia in a Male Athletic Subculture: A Participant-Observation Study of Deviant Rituals in Collegiate Rugby," *Deviant Behavior* 25, no. 4 (2004): 303–27.

52. Amaechi, *Man in the Middle,* 140–41. Amaechi adds that "it was an intense kind of camaraderie that to them felt completely natural, but was a little too close for my comfort. . . . As I surveyed the room, I couldn't help chuckling to myself: And I'm the gay one. Hah!"

53. Amaechi, 141. Amaechi adds that from his perspective, nothing could be further from the truth: "There's nothing like spending nine pressure-filled months with a bunch of sweaty, profane, ostensibly hetero guys to de-eroticize any environment."

54. Michael Wilbon, "Sexuality Disclosed, Ignorance Exposed," *Washington Post,* February 9, 2007.

55. See "Jason Collins Says He's Gay," ESPN, April 30, 2013, http://www.espn.com/nba/story/_/id/9223657/jason-collins-first-openly-gay-active-player. In a related matter, it should be noted that Golden State Warriors President and Chief Operating Officer Rick Welts has long been an openly gay man. Among his many achievements, Welts served as former NBA Commissioner David Stern's "right-hand man." See Ann Killion, "Warriors President Rick Welts' Newest Title: Hall of Famer," *San Francisco Chronicle,* March 31, 2018, https://www.sfchronicle.com/warriors/article/Warriors-president-Rick-Welts-newest-title-12796091.php.

56. Information about all these athletes may be found at http://www.outsports.com/.

57. See Dan Woog, "Helping Black Athletes Out of the Closet," *Outsports* (blog), November 27, 2007, http://www.outsports.com/columns/outfield/robinson1127.htm: "Drawing on models like 'It Takes a Team'—the Women's Sports Foundation kit that teaches athletes, coaches, and administrators about diversity . . .—Robinson's leadership program will introduce African-American LGBT students to resource centers, wellness centers, and mentors."

58. See Dan Woog, "Gay Athlete at Brown Diving into Leadership Role," *Outsports* (blog), April 15, 2008, https://www.outsports.com/2008/4/13/3862790/gay-athlete-at-brown-diving-into-leadership-role.

59. See "What Is the NCAA? About Us," http://www.ncaa.org/about/resources/media-center/ncaa-101/what-ncaa.

60. See John Branch, "N.C.A.A. Advises on Sexual Orientation Issues," *New York Times,* March 4, 2013. "Champions of Respect" can be downloaded at http://www.ncaapublications.com/productdownloads/CRLGBTQ.pdf.

61. See "LGBTQ Resources: NCAA Inclusion Initiative Framework," http://www.ncaa.org/about/resources/inclusion/lgbtq-resources.

9. Confronting the Challenges Faced by Transgender Youth

1. As discussed earlier in this book, many terms describing transgender identities and experiences have undergone changes and updates in recent years. For example, what used to be called *gender reassignment surgery* is increasingly referred to as *gender affirmation surgery*. See, generally, "Explore Topics: Medical," https://www.genderspectrum.org/.

2. See, generally, the classic law review article in this area by the cofounder and original codirector of the Transgender Law Center in San Francisco, Dylan Vade, "Expanding Gender and Expanding the Law: Toward a Social and Legal Conceptualization of Gender That Is More Inclusive of Transgender People," *Michigan Journal of Gender and Law* 11 (2005): 253, 255–56, 264–78.

3. Shannon Price Minter, "Do Transsexuals Dream of Gay Rights?," in *Transgender Rights,* ed. Paisley Currah, Richard M. Juang, and Shannon Price Minter (Minneapolis: University of Minnesota Press, 2006), 142, 150–51.

4. The medical term that has been employed to describe transgender identity is *gender dysphoria,* which is included in the American Psychiatric Association's revised 5th edition of its *Diagnostic and Statistical Manual of Mental Disorders* and replaced the term *gender identity disorder.* While some have advocated pursuing equal rights for transgender persons through a "disability civil rights law framework," many others have rejected the notion. For an example of the argument in favor of taking advantage of disability law in this manner, see, e.g., Jennifer L. Levi and Bennett H. Klein, "Pursuing Protection for Transgender People through Disability Laws"; for an articulation of some of the pitfalls of this approach, see, e.g., Judith Butler, "Undiagnosing Gender." Both are pieces in Currah et al., *Transgender Rights.* See also Dean Spade, "Resisting Medicine/Remodeling Gender," *Berkeley Women's Law Journal* 18 (2003): 15, which argues against the use of disability law claims in trans cases.

From a legal perspective, however, it must be emphasized—as Levi and Klein indicated—that although "both the federal Americans with Disabilities Act (ADA) and the federal Rehabilitation Act expressly excluded any protection" for transgender people, "they do not preclude seeking protection under most state disability laws."

But see Blatt v. Cabela's, 2017 WL 2178123 (E.D. Pa. 2017), where the U.S. District Court ruled that a transgender woman's employment discrimination claim under both Title VII of the Civil Rights Act of 1964 *and* the ADA, and perhaps also under the Equal Protection Clause of the Fourteenth Amendment, could proceed. The case has settled, but it is seen as a landmark decision with regard to ADA law. See Kevin Barry and Jennifer Levi, *"Blatt v. Cabela's Retail, Inc.* and a New Path for Transgender Rights," *Yale L.J. Forum* 127 (2017): 373.

5. It is important, of course, not to view transgender issues in either/or or all-or-nothing terms. Indeed, at different points in time, a trans person may see

the word *transgender* as the equivalent of a process, a medical condition, and an identity. For some, it may mean all of these things across different stages of their lives, whereas for others, it may carry one or two of those meanings.

6. See, e.g., the California Student Safety and Violence Protection Act of 2000, a law that extended protections for students to include gender identity.

7. See, e.g., Wyatt Buchanan, "'Gay Panic' Defense Tactic under Scrutiny at Conference," *San Francisco Chronicle,* July 19, 2006, and Kamala Harris, "United against Violence," *Bay Area Reporter,* July 20, 2006. The jury in the first trial remained deadlocked on a first-degree murder conviction, and a mistrial was declared. A second trial was held, at which two defendants were ultimately convicted of second-degree murder and the third of manslaughter. There is still some question as to whether the jury members saw Araujo's actions as amounting to deception. Some transgender activists believe that on some level, the jury must have believed the suspects were at least "surprised," or else they would have convicted them of first-degree murder. See Zak Szymanski, "Araujo's Killers Sentenced," *Bay Area Reporter,* February 2, 2006.

8. See chapter 2 of this book for additional discussion of the gay and trans panic defenses.

9. As discussed in chapter 2, during the past decade, California and Illinois became the first states in the United States to ban the gay and trans panic defenses, and the ABA has called for a nationwide ban.

10. See "Gender-Related Terms and Definitions," in Joel Baum et al., "Supporting and Caring for Our Gender-Expansive Youth," http://www.hrc.org/youth -report/ (documenting the results of a groundbreaking survey by the Human Rights Campaign of more than ten thousand LGBT-identified youth ages thirteen to seventeen, conducted in 2012).

11. See, e.g., Minter, "Do Transsexuals Dream of Gay Rights?" See also, generally, Brett Beemyn, "Transgender Terminology," Gay, Lesbian, Bisexual, and Transgender Student Services, Ohio State University.

In a 2007 report on employment discrimination affecting LGBTs, the Williams Institute defines *transsexual* as "a term for people whose gender identity is different from their assigned sex at birth. Often, but not always, transsexual people alter their bodies through hormones or surgery in order to make it match their gender identity." It defines *genderqueer* simply as "a term used by some individuals who identify as neither entirely male nor entirely female," and it states that genderqueer is "an identity more common among young people." See M. V. Lee Badgett, Holning Lau, Brad Sears, and Deborah Ho, "Bias in the Workplace: Consistent Evidence of Sexual Orientation and Gender Identity Discrimination," Williams Institute, UCLA School of Law, June 2007, http://williamsinstitute.law .ucla.edu/wp-content/uploads/Badgett-Sears-Lau-Ho-Bias-in-the-Workplace -Jun-2007.pdf.

12. The word *transition* is an example of a term that has fallen out of favor among some members of transgender communities, while others continue to find it an appropriate term for the process of coming out as gender expansive. As Dean Spade, professor of law at Seattle University and a prominent transgender scholar, explains, "I think that views on this vary widely among trans people. . . . [An] argument against the term is that it is often used in a universalizing way in various literatures to suggest that *all* trans people go through a medical process called 'transition' and that there is a 'before' and an 'after' (sometimes correlated to a binary identity of male/female). In general, it's useful to not talk about trans experience in ways that overgeneralize—not all people seek medical treatment as part of expressing their gender, not all people understand themselves to be occupying one of two binary gender categories, etc. . . . But the term 'transition' is sometimes used in ways that make those assumptions or have that baggage. In general, I tell my students that good lawyers listen to their clients, use the terms their clients use rather than putting terminology on them that may not match the clients' identities, and expect that in any population there is a great deal of difference about how various people call themselves, like to be called, like their experiences discussed. So using the most non-assumption laden approach possible is key." Interview with Dean Spade, October 8, 2015.

13. See, e.g., Patricia Gagne, Richard Tewksbury, and Deanna McGaughey, "Coming Out and Crossing Over: Identity Formation and Proclamation in a Transgender Community," *Gender and Society* 11, no. 4 (1997): 478–508, which suggests that with more acceptance by parents and teachers, this difficult coming-out process will begin much sooner and be much less painful for trans youth. See also Alan B. Goldberg and Joneil Adriano, "'I'm a Girl': Understanding Transgender Children," ABC News, http://abcnews.go.com/2020/story?id=3088298&page=1. See, generally, the accompanying episode of ABC's spring 2007 news program 20/20, which profiled three families supporting their children's transitions.

14. The World Professional Association for Transgender Health's *Standards of Care for the Health of Transsexual, Transgender, and Gender Nonconforming People, Seventh Edition* (2011), 18–21, takes the position that adolescents can begin reversible hormone therapy intervention as soon as puberty begins but that irreversible genital surgery should take place only after the patient reaches the legal age of majority in a given country and only after the patient has lived continuously for at least 12 months in the gender role that is congruent with their gender identity. With regard to "chest surgery" for "FtM patients" [i.e. trans boys or men], the association takes the position that it could be carried out sooner, "preferably after ample time of living in the desired gender role and after one year of testosterone treatment." See https://www.wpath.org/publications/soc.

15. The availability of hormones on the street and the inability of minors to get hormones legally can be a dangerous combination, as seeing their friends'

progress can fuel a young person's desires to start hormone therapy or even to "catch up" by taking greater doses. Reyhan Harmanci, "They Didn't Wait until Middle Age to Question Their Birth Sex," *San Francisco Chronicle*, September 15, 2005. See also Nona Willis-Aronowitz, "It's a Trans World" (an interview with Chris Beam), *Salon*, http://www.salon.com/. See, generally, Chris Beam, *Transparent: Love, Family, and Living the T with Transgender Teenagers* (San Diego, Calif.: Harcourt, 2007), which documents her work with trans teens in Los Angeles.

16. See Zak Szymanski, "TG Specialists, Parents Ask: When Is Young Too Young?," *Bay Area Reporter*, March 16, 2006. For an example of an institution providing such services for transgender youth and additional details regarding hormone blockers and their effects, see http://www.mazzonicenter.org/, describing the work of the Mazzoni Center in Philadelphia.

17. Szymanski.

18. See Vade, "Expanding Gender and Expanding the Law," 270: "I am someone who identifies as somewhat male, but not completely, as mostly trans, perhaps as trannyfag. So, am I 'homosexual' only if I am attracted to others who have the exact identification that I do? Am I heterosexual if I'm attracted to anyone who does not have my exact identification? The terms 'homo, hetero, and bisexual' presume a world with only two genders."

19. See Claire M. Peterson, Abigail Matthews, Emily Copps-Smith, and Lee Ann Conard, "Suicidality, Self-Harm, and Body Dissatisfaction in Transgender Adolescents and Emerging Adults with Gender Dysphoria," *Suicide and Life-Threatening Behavior* 1–8 (2016).

20. See, generally, Paisley Currah and Shannon Minter, *Transgender Equality: A Handbook for Activists and Policymakers* (Washington, D.C.: National Center for Lesbian Rights and Policy Institute of the National Gay and Lesbian Task Force, 2000), and Jaime M. Grant et al., "Injustice at Every Turn: A Report of the National Transgender Discrimination Survey," National Center for Transgender Equality and National Gay and Lesbian Task Force, 2011, http://www.the taskforce.org/injustice-every-turn-report-national-transgender-discrimination -survey/. See also Gwendolyn Ann Smith, "Transgender Day of Remembrance: Why We Remember," *Huffington Post*, November 20, 2012 (written by the founder and creator of the Transgender Day of Remembrance), and "Violence against the Transgender Community in 2017," Human Rights Campaign, http://www.hrc .org/. It should be noted that in many cases, the victims of anti-transgender violence are not identified as such, owing to the silence of their families, fear of the police among friends of the victims, and the refusal of the police to investigate these murders and/or report them as hate crimes.

A 2007 lawsuit highlighted the particular danger that transgender inmates face in state prisons. According to Valerie Jenness, a University of California, Irvine criminologist who has completed a study on sexual assaults in California prisons, 59 percent of the state's transgender inmates have reported being sexually assaulted, compared to 4 percent of the general prison population. Cited in Lisa Leff, "Transgender Inmate Sues State over California Prison Policy," Associated Press, July 21, 2007.

See also Eli Clare, *Exile and Pride: Disability, Queerness, and Liberation* (Cambridge, Mass.: South End Press, 1999), 138: "In the end, I will sit . . . with [transgender and gender-nonconforming persons] and trade stories long into the night. . . . Sad stories about bodies stolen, bodies no longer here. Enraging stories about false images, devastating lies, untold violence. Bold, brash stories about reclaiming our bodies and changing the world."

21. *Gender* is defined in 5 CCR § 4910(k) as "a person's gender identity and gender related appearance and behavior whether or not stereotypically associated with the person's assigned sex at birth." The California Legislature added an identical definition of *gender* to the California Penal Code in late 2004 (Cal Pen. Code § 422.56[c]). In addition to the equal educational opportunity guarantees explicitly set forth in the California Education Code, sections 201 and 220, the California Code of Regulations provides that "no person shall be excluded from participation in or denied the benefits of any local agency's program or activity on the basis of sex, sexual orientation, gender, ethnic group identification, race, ancestry, national origin, religion, color, or mental or physical disability in any program or activity conducted by an 'educational institution' or any other 'local agency' . . . that receives or benefits from any state financial assistance" (5 CCR § 4900[a]). Since 5 California Code of Regulations, section 4621, requires every school district to "adopt policies and procedures" consistent with these regulations "for the investigation and resolution of complaints," school districts are required to have a policy against discrimination that applies to all the protected categories of students listed in the relevant statutes and a complaint procedure that enforces that policy. See, generally, California Department of Education, *Legal Advisory* L-104, April 30, 2004 (on file with the author).

22. California Department of Education, *Legal Advisory* L-104.

23. Joel Rubin, "Beliefs Imperil Funding," *Los Angeles Times,* March 14, 2004.

24. Fermin Leal, "Board Defying Rules on Gender," *Orange County Register,* March 9, 2004.

25. R. Scott Moxley, "Gays 1, Phobes 0," *Orange County Weekly,* May 10, 2004.

26. The *Orange County Weekly* added that "the same local Christian radio network that claimed homosexuals caused the Sept. 11 terrorist attacks called the Westminster showdown 'glorious' and a 'triumph of God' over 'sodomites' and 'evil.'" See Moxley.

27. Mason Stockstill, "School Trustees in Westminster Won't Recognize Transgender Rule," Associated Press, March 30, 2004.

28. Anthony Caroto, "City Manager Gets Off Fence: Decides to Become Woman," Associated Press, March 5, 2007.

29. Lane Degregory and Lori Helfand, "His Second Self," *St. Petersburg Times,* March 11, 2007.

30. See, generally, letters to the editor, *St. Petersburg Times,* March 20, 2007.

31. David Montoya, letter to the editor, *UCLA Daily Bruin,* March 8, 2007. It should be noted that, contrary to Montoya's assertion, Stanton was hired to be city manager of Largo—it was not an elected position.

32. See, e.g., Jim Stratton, "Sex Change Plans Cost City Manager Job—Again," *Orlando Sentinel,* March 25, 2007.

33. Dean Spade has documented the extent to which transgender persons "are marginalized in employment." Analyzing the circumstances in which gender-transgressive persons find themselves, he concludes that "the high levels of unemployment, homelessness, and poverty in the population [stem] from discrimination and economic marginalization." See Spade, "Documenting Gender," *Hastings Law Journal* 59 (2008): 731, 757. For these reasons, the inclusion of protection on the basis of gender identity in a federal Employment Nondiscrimination Act (ENDA) is essential. See, e.g., Shannon H. Tan, "When Steve Is Fired for Becoming Susan: Why Courts and Legislators Need to Protect Transgender Employees from Discrimination," *Stetson Law Review* 37 (2008): 579.

34. Catherine Saillant and Amanda Covarrubias, "Oxnard Shooting Called a Hate Crime," *Los Angeles Times,* February 15, 2008. The Young Marines is the U.S. Marine Corps version of the army's JROTC. With regard to Lawrence asking to be called Leticia, see, e.g., Robert Kolker, "'A Murder Over a Girl,' by Ken Corbett," book review, *New York Times,* March 21, 2016. See also Janet Mock, "Girlhood Dreams and Fatal Crushes: In Junior High I Was Larry King," *Janet Mock* (blog), September 11, 2011, http://janetmock.com/2011/09/11/larry-king-brandon-mc inerney-trial/. See generally Saillant, "Oxnard Teacher Is Still Haunted by Student's Slaying," Los Angeles Times, July 19, 2009.

35. Valentine Road: A Path to Teen Tragedy, Directed by Marta Cunningham (2013; United States: DOCURAMA, 2014), DVD; Ken Corbett, A Murder over a Girl: Justice, Gender, Junior High (New York: Henry Holt & Company, 2016); Gayle Salamon, The Life and Death of Latisha King: A Critical Phenomenology of Transphobia, (New York: NYU Press, 2018).

36. Cunningham; Corbett; Salamon.

37. See, e.g., Paul Pringle and Catherine Saillant, "A Deadly Clash of Emotions before Oxnard Shooting," *Los Angeles Times,* March 8, 2008. See also Zeke Barlow, Cheri Carlson, and Kathleen Wilson, "Suspected School Shooter's Childhood Marred by Violence," *Ventura County Star,* February 24, 2008, and Rebecca

Cathcart, "Boy's Killing, Labeled a Hate Crime, Stuns Town," *New York Times,* February 23, 2008.

In the volatile trial of Brandon McInerney that took place over three years later, the defense sought to blame the victim, Lawrence King, alleging that he and not Brandon was the bully. They also alleged that Lawrence had sexually harassed Brandon and drove him to commit the murder. The first trial ended in a hung jury, and a settlement was reached before a second trial was set to begin. McInerney, seventeen years old at the time of the trial, pleaded guilty to second-degree murder and was sentenced to twenty-one years in prison. See, e.g., "Calif. Teen Brandon McInerney Sentenced to 21 Years for Point-Blank Murder of Gay Classmate," *CBS News,* December 19, 2011, https://www.cbsnews.com/news/calif-teen-brandon-mcinerney-sentenced-to-21-years-for-point-blank-murder-of-gay-classmate/. See also Jens Erik Gould, "The Lawrence King Case: In Court, Has the Bullied Become the Bully?," *Time,* August 25, 2011 (in which commentators, including the author of this book, took the defense to task for seeking to blame the victim and employing the now discredited "gay panic" defense).

38. Transgender issues fit appropriately within a gender-equity context. Some scholars have argued for a disestablishment of the ties of sex and gender, arguing for effecting equality between genders while incorporating transgender people into the fold. See, e.g., David B. Cruz, "Disestablishing Sex and Gender," *California Law Review* 90 (2002): 997.

39. The testimony from Joan of Arc's trial is telling, especially when she "condemn[s] [her]self in being unwilling to wear the customary clothing of [her] sex." W. S. Scott, trans., *The Trial of Joan of Arc: Being the Verbatim Report of the Proceedings from the Orleans Manuscript* (Westport, Conn.: Associated Booksellers, 1956), 31.

40. See Leslie Feinberg, *Transgender Warriors* (Boston: Beacon, 1996), an extended overview of transgender people throughout history. See also Susan Stryker, *Transgender History* (Berkeley, Calif.: Seal, 2008).

41. Martin Duberman, *Stonewall* (New York: Dutton, 1993).

42. See, e.g., James Withers, "Remembering Sylvia Rivera," *New York Blade,* November 25, 2005. See, generally, Claire Valentine, "Remembering Marsha P. Johnson, the 'Rosa Parks' of the LGBTQ Movement" (unpublished manuscript, July 6, 2017).

In 2017, Netflix acquired worldwide rights to David France's documentary *The Death and Life of Marsha P. Johnson,* which premiered at the Tribeca Film Festival. Dave McNary, "Netflix Buys Documentary 'The Death and Life of Marsha P. Johnson,'" *Variety,* June 2, 2017.

43. Leslie Feinberg, *Stone Butch Blues* (Ann Arbor, Mich.: Firebrand, 1993); Clare, *Exile and Pride*; Kate Bornstein, *Gender Outlaw* (New York: Vintage, 1994).

44. For more on the Sylvia Rivera Law Project (SRLP), see its website, https://srlp.org/.

45. See Amnesty International, *Stonewalled—Still Demanding Respect: Police Abuses against Lesbian, Gay, Bisexual, and Transgender People in the U.S.* (London: Amnesty International, 2006), https://www.amnesty.org/en/documents/AMR51/001/2006/en/. See also Janet Baus and Dan Hunt's documentary *Cruel and Unusual: Transgender Women in Prison* (USA), January 18, 2011, https://www.youtube.com/watch?v=5Yzy8oh5Fw0.

46. Dinita Smith, "One False Note in a Musician's Life," *New York Times,* June 2, 1998.

47. It should be noted that television has seen an increasing focus on transgender issues as well. During the third season of Showtime's hit series *The L Word,* for example, the creators introduced a trans man character, believed to be the first transgender character in the history of television. Producers of *All My Children* followed suit, announcing in 2006 that they would be introducing a trans woman character. Matea Gold, "Zarf Becomes Zoe, and a Soap Evolves," *Los Angeles Times,* December 24, 2006.

More recently, Amazon Studios's original TV production of *Transparent,* focusing on a grandfather coming out as a transgender woman, won great acclaim in its initial seasons.

48. *Boys Don't Cry,* directed by Kimberly Peirce (1999; Los Angeles, Calif.: Twentieth-Century Fox, 2009), DVD; *The Brandon Teena Story,* directed by Susan Muska and Gréta Olafsdóttir (1998; United States: New Video Group, 2000), DVD.

49. *Transamerica,* directed by Duncan Tucker (2005; United States: Weinstein Company/Genius Products, 2006), DVD.

50. *Ma vie en rose,* directed by Alain Berliner (1997; Culver City, Calif.: Columbia Tristar Home Video, 1999), DVD; *Beautiful Boxer,* directed by Ekachai Uekrongtham (2003).

51. See LGBT Movement Advancement Project (MAP), data current as of March 29, 2018, http://www.lgbtmap.org/equality-maps/non_discrimination_laws (hereinafter referred to as "Equality MAPS"). It should be noted that there have been economic consequences for states that mandate LGBT discrimination. For example, in the summer 2017, California banned state-funded travel to Alabama, Kansas, Kentucky, Mississippi, North Carolina, South Dakota, Tennessee, and Texas because of the "discriminatory nature of laws enacted by those states," according to Attorney General Xavier Becerra. See Peter Holley, "California Just Added Four More 'Discriminatory' States to Its Travel Ban," *Washington Post,* June 23, 2017.

52. See "Equality MAPS." Two additional states prohibited sexual orientation discrimination in employment and public accommodations but did not prohibit

gender identity discrimination: New Hampshire and Wisconsin. For an additional discussion of public accommodation laws within the context of discrimination faced by LGBT youth in the schools, see chapter 3 of this book.

53. See "Equality Maps." Kansas had also prohibited gender identity discrimination for its state employees, but in 2015, Governor Sam Brownback removed those protections. See Matt Pearce, "Kansas Governor Removes Protections for LGBT Employees," *Los Angeles Times,* February 10, 2015.

54. Equality MAPS.

55. See, generally, Robert Kim, "Gender Identity Policies in Schools: What Congress, the Courts, and the Trump Administration Should Do," National Education Policy Center, May 2017.

56. "Additional facts," for example, might include explicit prohibitions that may have been enacted in particular jurisdictions. State legislators in Texas, for example, have sought to enact a law that would include restrictions on transgender bathroom use that are similar to those originally enacted in North Carolina. Such restrictions may prohibit school officials from following portions of recommendation 5, unless the restrictions are superseded by subsequent federal legislation and/or litigation. See, e.g., David Montgomery and Manny Fernandez, "Texas Bathroom Bill Dies Again, Raising Republican Acrimony," *New York Times,* August 16, 2017.

57. See, generally, Welner et al., *Legal Issues in Education,* 208–10.

58. See "Memorandum for the President, Military Service by Transgender Individuals, Secretary of Defense, February 22, 2018, https://media.defense.gov/2018/Mar/23/2001894037/-1/-1/0/MILITARY-SERVICE-BY-TRANSGENDER-INDIVIDUALS.PDF. The memorandum provides, in pertinent part, that the Department of Defense should adopt the following policies:

• Transgender persons with a history or diagnosis of gender dysphoria are disqualified from military service, except under the following limited circumstances: (1) if they have been stable for 36 consecutive months in their biological sex prior to accession; (2) Service members diagnosed with gender dysphoria after entering into service may be retained if they do not require a change of gender and remain deployable within applicable retention standards; and (3) currently serving Service members who have been diagnosed with gender dysphoria since the previous administration's policy took effect and prior to the effective date of this new policy, may continue to serve in their preferred gender and receive medically necessary treatment for gender dysphoria.

• Transgender persons who require or have undergone gender transition are disqualified from military service.

• Transgender persons without a history or diagnosis of gender dysphoria, who are otherwise qualified for service, may serve, like all other Service members, in their biological sex.

59. See "Trump Memo: Military Service by Transgender Individuals," March 23, 2018, https://www.voanews.com/a/trump-military-service-transgender-indi viduals/4314251.html.

60. Doe v. Yunits, 2000 WL 33162199 (Mass. Super. Ct. 2000).

61. *Doe.*

62. See, e.g., "Marriage Equality and Transgender People: What the Supreme Court Ruling on the Freedom to Marry Means for Transgender People," National Center for Transgender Equality, June 23, 2015, http://www.transequality.org/issues/resources/marriage-equality-and-transgender-people. See, generally, Kylar W. Broadus, "The Legal Status of Transgender Relationships," 34, no. 1 22, GPSOLO, American Bar Association, January/February 2017.

63. *Broadus.*

64. See "NCLR Eliminates Remnants of LGBT Censorship Rule in Utah Schools," press release, National Center for Lesbian Rights, October 6, 2017, http://www.nclrights.org/press-room/press-release/nclr-eliminates-remnants -of-utah-lgbt-censorship-rule/. For background and reference, see Complaint for Declaratory and Injunctive Relief, *Equality Utah v. Utah State Board of Education,* submitted to the U.S. District Court, District of Utah, Central Division, October 21, 2016, http://www.nclrights.org/wp-content/uploads/2016/10/Equality-Utah-v. -Utah-State-Board-of-Education-Complaint.pdf.

65. See Complaint for Intentional Infliction of Emotional Distress, Negligent Infliction of Emotional Distress, Violation of the Unruh Civil Rights Act, Civil Code Section 51, Violation of Business and Professions Codes Section 17200 et seq. and 17500, and Fraud or Deceit, Nicole Shah Brar v. Heritage Oak Private Education, submitted to the Superior Court of the State of California, County of Orange, August 2, 2017, http://www.publiccounsel.org/tools/assets/files/0910.pdf.

66. See Joy Resmovits, "A Transgender 8-Year-Old Sues a Private School, Saying It Didn't Let Her Be the Girl She Is," *Los Angeles Times,* August 7, 2017.

67. Resmovits.

68. See San Francisco Human Rights Commission, "Gender Neutral Bathroom Survey," Transgender Law Center, Summer 2001, http://www.transgender lawcenter.org/pdf/sbac_survey.pdf.

69. Joel Baum, interview by the author, August 2, 2009. Baum adds that "restrooms are one of the most tangibly gendered spaces in our culture" and that "for the child to use a restroom that does not match affirmed gender is a very concrete rejection of her/his own reality, a betrayal of who one knows oneself to be."

70. California Education Committee v. O'Connell, no. 34-2008-00026507 -CU-CR-GDS (CA Super. Ct. 2009).

71. California public policy, as reflected in its legislation, strongly favors protecting the right of transgender persons to equal treatment. See, e.g., Cal. Penal Code § 422.55 et seq. (prohibiting violence or threats directed at a person based

on gender identity); Cal. Government Code § 12900 et seq. (the Fair Employment and Housing Act, which prohibits discrimination based on gender identity
in employment and housing); Cal. Civil Code § 51 (the Unruh Civil Rights Act,
which prohibits such discrimination in business establishments); Cal. Health and
Safety Code § 1365.5 (prohibiting such discrimination by health plans); and Cal.
Government Code § 11135 (prohibiting such discrimination in state-sponsored
activities).

72. See, generally, Memorandum of Points and Authorities of Amici Curiae in
Support of Defendant's Demurrer, California Education Committee v. O'Connell,
filed November 6, 2008.

73. *California Education Committee.*

74. Both federal and state privacy laws are consistent with regard to the level
of privacy that persons can reasonably expect in restrooms and analogous facilities. For example, the Eighth Circuit has rejected a claim brought by a Minnesota
teacher who objected to sharing the women's restroom with a female transgender coworker. Cruzan v. Special Sch. Dist. No. 1, 294 F.3d 981 (8th Cir. 2002).

In earlier cases focusing on analogous claims, the California Court of Appeal
held, in 1998, that an ordinance requiring restroom attendants in certain business
establishments did not raise any constitutional privacy issues. Tily B. v. City of
Newport Beach, 69 Cal.App.4th 1 (1998). The California Supreme Court found no
privacy violation when a security guard observed a minor's shoplifting activity
through the open space below a dressing room door. The court held that one
who uses a dressing room is entitled only to "the modicum of privacy it appears
to afford." In Re Deborah C., 30 Cal.3d 125, 139 (1981). And in Hill v. National
Collegiate Athletic Association, 7 Cal.4th 1, 41, n. 12; 26 Cal.Rptr.2d 834 (1994),
the court rejected an argument by the plaintiffs that "urine samples of both men
and women . . . generally taken by female nurses or technicians" from behind the
seclusion of closed doors constituted a privacy violation.

75. Whitaker v. Kenosha Unified School District No. 1 Board of Education,
858 F.3d 1034 (7th Cir. 2017). Unlike an earlier Fourth Circuit decision in favor
of a transgender high school boy, G.G. v. Gloucester Board of Education, 822 F.3d
789 (4th Cir. 2016), which relied on nonregulatory guidance that has since been
abrogated by the Trump administration, the *Whitaker* panel relied solely on its
own legal analysis to break new ground under federal law.

76. *Whitaker*, at 1039. Relying on the *Whitaker* decision, the U.S. District
Court for the District of Maryland held in early 2018 that the middle school officials' policy prohibiting a transgender boy (M.A.B.) from using the boy's locker
room to change for P.E. violated both Title IX and the Equal Protection Clause
of the Fourteenth Amendment. The court also determined that the discrimination against the transgender student triggered heightened scrutiny. However, the
court did not grant the plaintiff's motion for a preliminary injunction, because

M.A.B. was not enrolled in P.E. during the 2017–18 academic year. Judge George L. Russell III indicated that should circumstances change, plaintiff could refile his motion. M.A.B. v. Bd. of Educ. of Talbot County, 2018 WL 1257097 (D. Maryland 2018).

77. See, generally, Jody Marksamer and Dylan Vade, "Transgender and Gender Non-conforming Youth Recommendations for Schools," Transgender Law Center, 2002 (on file with the author).

78. Baum, interview. Gender-neutral facilities are an option under current law in a number of places, to accommodate concerns of those who might be uncomfortable in gender-segregated restrooms under these circumstances. Persons desiring such accommodations may include both nontrans students and gender-variant students. Gender-neutral facilities may also serve others on campus with special needs, including the elderly and persons with disabilities.

Baum adds that "separate is not equal. Particularly when the separate facility is in an adult area such as an office, it is stigmatizing and actually draws attention to the child, thereby potentially increasing their risk." See, generally, Stephanie A. Brill and Rachel Pepper, *The Transgender Child: A Handbook for Families and Professionals* (San Francisco, Calif.: Cleis, 2008).

79. Consideration of this range of accommodations was recommended by the Transgender Law Center in 2002. See Marksamer and Vade, "Transgender and Gender Non-conforming Youth Recommendations."

80. The IOC's decision, in May 2004, stated that "individuals undergoing sex reassignment of male to female before puberty should be regarded as girls and women" and trans men should be regarded as boys and men. Trans women and trans men in the process of transitioning should be allowed to compete in "female and male competitions, respectively," under certain enumerated conditions, which included the completion of "surgical anatomical changes," "legal recognition of their assigned sex," and "hormonal therapy administered in a verifiable manner." "IOC Approves Consensus with Regard to Athletes Who Have Changed Sex," International Olympic Committee, May 17, 2004, http://www.olympic.org/uk/includes/common/article_print_uk.asp?ibid=841. See also Rona Marech, "Olympics' Transgender Quandary," *San Francisco Chronicle*, June 14, 2004, for a discussion of the reactions from the American sports community, both positive and negative, to the decision.

81. Marksamer and Vade, "Transgender and Gender Non-conforming Youth Recommendations."

82. Dean Spade, "Compliance Is Gendered: Struggling for Gender Self-Determination in a Hostile Economy," in Currah et al., *Transgender Rights*, 227–28. Spade also asserts that "the reliance on medical evidence in all legal contexts in which transgender and other gender-transgressive people struggle for recognition or rights is highly problematic" (228).

83. See Spade.

Conclusion

1. More than fifty years after it was first published, *Advise and Consent* (Garden City, N.Y.: Doubleday, 1959) remains the "all-time bestseller among Washington political fiction," according to the U.S. Senate's own website, http://www senate.gov/reference/reference_item/advise_and_consent.htm.

2. See Frank Rich, "Just How Gay Is the Right?," *New York Times,* May 15, 2005.

3. Interestingly, neither the word "homosexual" nor the word "gay" ever actually appears in this work—yet another example of "the love that dare not speak its name."

4. The Frank Sinatra song titled "Heart of Mine" was reportedly written expressly for this scene and presented to the public for the first time as the musical background when Anderson first enters the gay bar. It was released as a recording only in 2002, as part of a six-CD comprehensive collection that includes all of Sinatra's movie songs, *Sinatra in Hollywood 1940–1964,* on Rhino Records. See http://www.audiophilia.com/. See also the thread "'Advise and Consent' Theme," Sinatra Family Forum, https://sinatrafamily.com/forum/showthread .php/30353-Advise-and-Consent-Theme (where one contributor confirms that the "rare vocal" appears on *Sinatra in Hollywood 1940–1964* and indicates that it was commonly called "The Losers Song").

5. See Vito Russo, *The Celluloid Closet* (New York: Harper and Row, 1987), 14. See also the 1996 documentary of the same name, written and directed by Rob Epstein and Jeremy Friedman, for a more comprehensive look at the history of homosexuality and the motion picture industry, past and present.

The film *Advise and Consent* did not just shape real life but also reflected it to some extent. In 1954, Senator Lester Hunt, a Democrat from Wyoming, committed suicide rather than run for reelection. The Republicans held the majority in a closely divided Senate, and they apparently pressured Hunt into resigning by threatening to reveal that Hunt's son had been arrested for solicitation of a male police officer. Hunt resigned and then committed suicide nine days later, without leaving a suicide note. It is widely believed that the events surrounding his son's arrest and the use of the event as blackmail by his political opponents contributed to both his resignation and his suicide. Tamara Linse, "A Senator's Suicide," *Casper (Wyo.) Star-Tribune,* November 1, 2004.

6. McGreevey's coming out included the revelation of a gay affair with a man whom he subsequently appointed to a highly paid position in the New Jersey state government. It was also accompanied by allegations of a fund-raising scandal. See, e.g., "The Governor's Secret," *New York Times,* August 13, 2004.

7. Michael Powell and Michelle Garcia, "N.J. Governor Resigns over Gay Affair," *Washington Post,* August 13, 2004. McGreevey has written a book about his story, which details his four decades of life as a closeted gay man and tells of

the practical difficulties of being a political leader in the rough-and-tumble world of New Jersey politics. James E. McGreevey, *The Confession* (New York: Morrow, 2006).

8. See, generally, Randy Shilts, *The Mayor of Castro Street: The Life and Times of Harvey Milk* (New York: St. Martin's, 1988). See also Frances Fitzgerald, "The Castro, Part I," *The New Yorker,* June 21, 1986, and "The Castro, Part II," *The New Yorker,* June 28, 1986.

9. When Milk was posthumously awarded a Presidential Medal of Freedom—America's highest civilian honor—by President Barack Obama in August 2009, the White House press release described him as a man who "encouraged lesbian, gay, bisexual, and transgender (LGBT) citizens to live their lives openly and believed coming out was the only way they could change society and achieve social equality. . . . Milk is revered nationally and globally as a pioneer of the LGBT civil rights movement for his exceptional leadership and dedication to equal rights." See "President Obama Names Medal of Freedom Recipients," White House Office of the Press Secretary, July 30, 2009, https://obamawhitehouse.ar chives.gov/the-press-office/president-obama-names-medal-freedom-recipients.

10. "The Closet," *The Daily Dish* (blog), September 30, 2006, http://andrew sullivan.theatlantic.com/the_daily_dish/2006/09/the_closet.html. Of course, the closet (and those who may be viewed as responsible for its persistence) should certainly not be viewed as an excuse for Foley's actions, which were inexcusable.

11. There is universal agreement with regard to former congressman Foley that his career, and most likely his public life, ended in disgrace. With former governor McGreevey, many see his resignation as the functional equivalent of disgrace—especially given the fact that both his alleged gay lover and his second wife have spoken so negatively of him (the former denying a relationship and accusing him of sexual harassment, the latter lambasting him in a recent book). Many reacted in a similarly negative way to both the publication of his 2006 book and the 2007 announcement that he would be entering an Episcopal seminary. See, e.g., Wayne Parry, "McGreevey's Next Act: Preacher and Teacher," Associated Press, May 11, 2007. Many others admire McGreevey, and the consensus in the national media is that his public life is still a work in progress. Yet few would disagree with the assertion that his resignation and the events surrounding it constituted a debacle—especially because it apparently ended the political career of someone who was being mentioned prominently as a rising young star in the Democratic Party and a possible future presidential candidate. See Josh Benson, "Shocking, but Not Surprising," *New York Times,* August 15, 2004.

For more information about the work of Wisconsin senator Tammy Baldwin, see, e.g., her official senatorial Web page at https://www.baldwin.senate.gov/. For additional details on Los Angeles County supervisor Sheila Kuehl, see, e.g., her Web page at http://supervisorkuehl.com/.

12. Prominent LGBT leaders representing diverse racial and ethnic communities are increasingly being elected in every corner of the United States. These include, but are not limited to, Lupe Valdez, sheriff of Dallas, Texas (elected in 2004); Patricia Todd, state senator, Alabama (elected in 2006); Scott McCoy, state senator, Utah (elected in 2004); Christine Quinn, New York City council member (elected in 1999); Evan Low, Santa Clara, California, city council member (elected in 2006); and Kathy Webb, Arkansas state representative (elected in 2006).

In California, by 2017, the state legislature included eight openly LGBT members, four in the state senate and four in the assembly. See, e.g., Frank Bruni, "The Worst (and Best) Places to Be Gay in America," *New York Times,* August 25, 2017.

13. See the Victory Fund website at https://victoryfund.org/. The fund is a political action committee that raises money for LGBT candidates and is committed to "increasing the number of openly LGBTQ officials at all levels of government." See also "List of the First LGBT Holders of Political Offices," https://en.wikipedia.org/wiki/List_of_the_first_LGBT_holders_of_political_offices.

14. Dyana Bagby, "Poll Shows Coming Out Wouldn't Hurt Most Politicians," *Express Gay News,* April 24, 2006, http://www.expressgaynews.com/. In small cities, 72 percent of voters said they would continue to support a candidate if he or she came out as gay or lesbian, and in rural areas, the proportion was 70 percent. In February 2007, a Gallup poll reported that 55 percent of Americans would vote for a gay man or lesbian as president if he or she were "generally well-qualified." "Poll: 55% of Americans Would Vote for Gay Man or Lesbian for President," *Advocate,* February 23, 2007, http://www.advocate.com/.

15. Gay Students Organization of the University of New Hampshire v. Bonner, 509 F.2d 652, 661 (1st Cir. 1974).

16. Colin v. Orange Unified School District, 83 F. Supp. 2d 1135, 1138 (C.D. Cal. 2000).

17. Nuxoll v. Indian Prairie School District No. 204, 523 F.3d 668, 671 (7th Cir. 2008).

18. Chambers v. Babbitt, 145 F. Supp. 2d 1068, 1072–73 (D. Minn. 2001).

INDEX

Abdul-Jabbar, Kareem, 272n52; on political correctness, 34–35, 272n53
activism, gay Christian, 172–73
activism, LGBT, xvii, 155–56, 228, 246
administrators, school: addressing of LGBT issues, 65–71, 77, 101–4; changing of school sports culture, 207; discrimination by, 65–66, 69–71, 306n14; evaluation of, 144; obligations of, 104
Advise and Consent (film), 243–44, 337n5
A. E. v. Harrisburg School Dist. No. 7 (2012), negligence in, 285n61
Affordable Care Act: access to contraception through, 38–39; employer complicity under, 39
aggression, anti-LGBT, xix–xx; cultural norms supporting, xxi; enforcing gender norms, 16; failure to act on, 65–66, 67; justifications given for, 31; in K–12 education, xxii, 10–13; among male teens, xx; in marriage equality backlash, 31–32; motivations for, xx–xxi, 16, 31, 255n23; persistence of, xxi; by police, xvi, 35, 219, 258n17; secular, 16. *See also* bullying; harassment, murder
Ahrens, Judy, 220, 221
Alabama, sex education program of, 113, 296n10

Ali, Laila: stereotyping of, 193
Alito, Justice Samuel: in *Burwell v. Hobby Lobby Stores, Inc.,* 39; in *Obergefell v. Hodges,* 37, 275n83; on Tinker Rule, 280n10
Alliance Defending Freedom (formerly Alliance Defense Fund): Day of Truth event, 130–31; name change, 303n57; strong connection with Focus on the Family and "conversion therapy," 303n58
All My Children (television serial), transgender character on, 332n47
Amaechi, John: coming out experience, 188–89, 194, 205, 207, 210; on homophobia in sports, 190; *The Man in the Middle,* 208
American Academy of Pediatrics, policy on bullying, 148
American Bar Association, on gay/trans panic defense, 50
American Civil Liberties Union, in *Ramirez v. Los Angeles Unified School District,* 70
American Counseling Association (ACA), Code of Ethics, 48
American Psychiatric Association, *Diagnostic and Statistical Manual of Mental Disorders,* 8, 325n4

Doe v. Yunits (2000), 240; First Amendment in, 233; gender identity in, 233

Dominguez, Tamara: murder of, 33

Dong, Arthur, 163; *Coming Out under Fire*, 202, 322n39

"Don't Ask, Don't Tell," 179, 268n20, 321n32; British equivalent of, 204; *Lawrence v. Texas* and, 295n72; in presidential campaign of 2007, 322n36; repeal of, viii, 178, 200, 321n32; transgender soldiers under, 232. *See also* students LGBT

Dousharm, Jeanette: dropping out, 69; harassment of, 67, 68

Downs, Robert: anti-gay invective of, 114, 298n16

Downs v. LAUSD (2000): First Amendment in, 114; Gay and Lesbian Awareness Month in, 114–15

Drury, Alan: *Advise and Consent*, 243–44, 247, 337n1

Dungy, Tony, 323n50

Dworkin, Ronald, 3, 4; on Equal Protection Clause, 16

Easterbrook, Judge: in *Mayer v. Monroe County Community School Corp.*, 93

education: antibullying, 74; in anti-discrimination laws, 8, 53, 90; equal opportunity in, 258n19; Establishment Clause concerning, 18; in exercise of First Amendment, 256n10, 256n13; multicultural, 155; proactive measures in, xxi; right to, 4, 6–7

education, higher: counseling in, 277n104; LGBT curriculum in, 179–81, 183; sports homophobia in, 191–92

education, K–12: antidiscrimination case law for, 53; anti-LGBT aggression in, xxii, 10–13; civil disagreement in, 130; community relations in, 104, 121, 141, 156; compliance with law, 141; conspiracy theories concerning, 100;

counseling cases in, ix, 48, 277n104; emotional contagion in, 306n8; equal access in, 59, 60, 142, 283n25, 293n51; evidence-based learning policies, 143; exposure to ideas in, 112; expressive activities in, 55–56; fostering of responsibility, 143; gay and lesbian awareness celebrations in, 94, 114–15, 131, 134, 136; gay conversion therapy in, 49–50; gay–straight alliances in, 8, 58–61; genuineness in, 323n48; holistic approach to, 144; inclusiveness in, 142; individuals versus groups in, 305n3; institutional restrictions and, xviii–xxi; LGBT safety in, xx; marriage equality and, 30, 97, 98, 108; negligence law concerning, 73; performance-based, 144; physical education in, 187–88; public forums and, 256n6; religious freedom in, 18; right to be out in, xxii, 53–58, 81, 82–83, 137; strategies for change, 141; transgender policies for, 220–24; transgender youth in, x, 279n1; viewpoint discrimination doctrine and, 125, 277n101; voluntariness in, 323n48. *See also* curriculum, K–12; students, K–12

education, LGBT: antidiscrimination law supporting, 90; obstacles facing, 141; in private schools, xxii; problems in, x, xxi, 16, 51; religious "counter-messages" to, 117–37, 176; research-based principles for, 141, 142, 144–47, 153, 165, 305n3. *See also* curriculum, LGBT; students, LGBT

education, private: LGBT issues in, xxii; religious, 22, 287n72; sectarian, 264n55

educational systems, resistance to change, 141, 163

educators, K–12: assessment of intelligence, 146; awareness of law, 287n75; complicity in peer mistreatment,

law, 74; in *Flores v. Morgan Hill Unified School District*, 67–68; in *Henkle v. Gregory*, 61–62; professional development concerning, 168; schools' targeting of, 147–51; students' responses to, 169–70; in *Ramirez v. Los Angeles Unified School District*, 69

harassment, sexual: of women, 12, 259n33; in workplace, 73

harassment law: development of, 73; states', 76; in student cases, 72–77

Hardaway, Tim, 189; consequences of his homophobia, 210

Harlem Renaissance, in K–12 curriculum, 318n34

Harper, Kelsie, 128, 302n51

Harper, Tyler Chase: appeal to Supreme Court, 128; at Day of Truth event, 130–31; "Homosexuality Is Shameful" shirt, 123–24, 127–28, 129–31, 299n36, 300n43

Harper v. Poway Unified School District (2004): alleged viewpoint discrimination per Judge Alex Kozinski, 124; appeal of, 126–28; authority of, 304n63; commentary on, 126–28; Day of Silence demonstrations in, 123, 124, 130, 300n43; First Amendment rights in, 127, 301n48; harassment in, 126; inflammatory speech in, 129–30, 301n47; LGBT groups in, 126–27; limitations on speech and, 127; *Nuxoll v. Indian Prairie School District* and, 130; post-2006 court activity, 128–29; psychological injury in, 127, 301n45; public forums in, 126; religious "countermessages" in, 123–30; ruling of the panel majority under Tinker per Judge Stephen Reinhardt, 124–25; student safety in, 124; vacating of original Ninth Circuit decision, 302n53, 304n63

Harris, Eric: bullying of, 149

Harris, Jennifer, 319n11

Harris, Robert N., Jr., 290n30

Hart, Judge William T.: in *Zamecnik v. Indian Prairie Sch. Dist.*, 133, 135–36, 304n63

Harvey, Andrew: *The Essential Gay Mystics*, 263n51

Harvey Milk Civil Rights Academy, 315n9

Hasidic Jews, equal protection for, 265n60

Hastings College of the Law (University of California): nondiscrimination policy of, 46. *See also* Christian Legal Society (CLS)

Hastings OUTLaw (LGBT student organization), in *Christian Legal Society* lawsuit, 46–47

hate crimes: Department of Justice and, 267n10; federal law on, 266n8; increase in, 32

hate crimes law: gender identity in, 231

Hate Crimes Prevention Act (New York, 2009), 24

Hawley, Willis, 169

Hazelwood v. Kuhlmeier (1988), 56, 299n34; educators' speech in, 92; relationship to the Tinker Rule, 55

heightened judicial review, 267n15; for discrimination, 106–8; in *Obergefell v. Hodges* (2015), 30, 269n32; in *Plyler v. Doe*, 268n17; in *U.S. v. Windsor* (2013), 268n20

Henkle, Derek: harassment of, 61–62

Henkle v. Gregory (2001): discriminatory discipline in, 145; First Amendment in, 61–62; Fourteenth Amendment in, 61–62; peer mistreatment in, 61–62; Tinker Rule in, 62

Hernandez, Greg, 207

Herrera, Jaheem, xix; suicide of, 149

heteronormativity: effect on LGBT students, 171; in Latino community,

Stuart Biegel is a member of the emeriti faculty at the University of California, Los Angeles, where he continues his teaching and research at the Graduate School of Education and Information Studies and the School of Law. He has served as Director of Teacher Education, Special Counsel for the California Department of Education, and on-site federal court monitor for the San Francisco public schools. He is the author of the casebook *Education and the Law* and *Beyond Our Control? Confronting the Limits of Our Legal System in the Age of Cyberspace.*